WASHINGTON
ROAD & RECREATION ATLAS

Washington Road & Recreation Atlas
Benchmark Maps, Santa Barbara, California 93117
© 2015 by Benchmark Maps
All rights reserved. First edition 2000
Seventh Edition 2015
Printed in Canada

ISBN 10: 0-929591-98-4
ISBN 13: 978-0-929591-98-8

About these maps…

In 1995, principals of three map companies collaborated on a vision they shared for a new series of state road and recreation atlases. The result was Benchmark Maps, a partnership that would apply the unique talents of each company to create atlases with an entirely new kind of look and presentation. These new atlases would combine strikingly beautiful Landscape Maps™ with data collection of unequaled accuracy and detail. To ensure accuracy, teams of field checkers drive throughout each state, collecting road data and gathering important cultural and recreational information. The roads featured in the atlases are classed by type and surface, and recreation opportunities are clearly shown with labels and icons. A complete statewide Recreation Guide is included, with a separate set of maps showing Public Land ownership.

Cover photo: Mount Rainier. Page 85, F8.

Benchmark Maps staff:

Neil Allen, Curtis Carroll, Bridger DeVille, John Glanville, Bill Hunt, Thad Lenker, Ryan Reid, Teri Stavros, and Chaney Swiney.

Benchmark Maps has compiled the information in this atlas with care; it was correct, to the best of our knowledge, at the time of publication. Benchmark Maps does not endorse attractions listed on the maps and recreation guides, and does not imply that sites not shown are unworthy of a visit. We enthusiastically welcome comments and corrections: Benchmark Maps, 120 Cremona Drive Suite H, Santa Barbara, California 93117; (805) 968-4222; fax (805) 968-1145; e-mail atlas@benchmarkmaps.com.

CARTOGRAPHY
of BENCHMARK MAPS

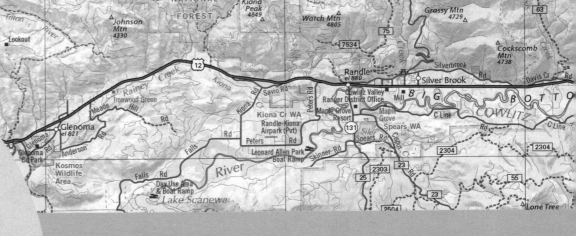

In 1995, three respected mapping firms collaborated on a vision they shared for a new line of state road atlases with unequalled accuracy and an entirely new kind of presentation. The result was Benchmark Maps: a partnership that has produced and sold millions of maps and atlases to discriminating map users from all over the world. First impressions of Washington—The Evergreen State—are those of verdant foliage, huge trees, and luxurious greenness. Its lasting impressions are of proud, snow-capped mountains, frosty-jade rivers, sapphire lakes, and wonderful scenic panoramas. Benchmark's Washington Road & Recreation Atlas, with its comprehensive and field-checked Recreation Guide, is the best resource for exploring every corner of this magnificent state.

How to Read Your Atlas: Front-to-Back

Highways of the Western U.S. and Washington.

Recreation and Public Lands detail.

Landscape Maps™ with the highest detail thanks to our team of expert field-checkers.

Metro Area Maps detailed maps of major cities

Index of counties, cities, parks, mountains, lakes & rivers

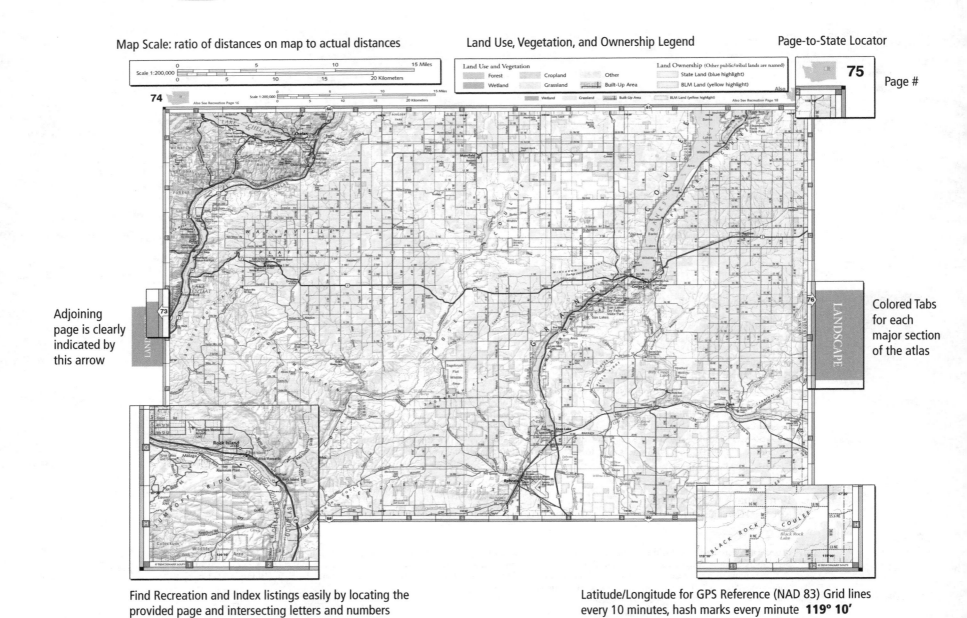

Map Scale: ratio of distances on map to actual distances

Land Use, Vegetation, and Ownership Legend

Page-to-State Locator

Page #

Adjoining page is clearly indicated by this arrow

Colored Tabs for each major section of the atlas

Find Recreation and Index listings easily by locating the provided page and intersecting letters and numbers

Latitude/Longitude for GPS Reference (NAD 83) Grid lines every 10 minutes, hash marks every minute **119° 10'**

Contents

U.S. Highways

Scale 1: 9,600,000

```
0        100      200      300      400 Miles
0    100   200   300   400   500   600 Kilometers
```

Miles to Seattle

Albuquerque, NM 1,450	Indianapolis, Indiana 2,210	Phoenix, Arizona 1,440
Atlanta, Georgia 2,640	Jackson, Mississippi 2,480	Pittsburgh, Pennsylvania 2,490
Baltimore, Maryland 2,720	Jacksonville, Florida 2,970	Portland, Maine 3,020
Billings, Montana................820	Kansas City, Missouri 1,850	Portland, Oregon 170
Bismarck, North Dakota 1,210	Las Vegas, Nevada 1,170	Raleigh, North Carolina 2,820
Boise, Idaho 500	Little Rock, Arkansas 2,240	Rapid City, South Dakota 1,160
Boston, Massachusetts 2,950	Los Angeles, California 1,130	Regina, Saskatchewan 1,090
Calgary, Alberta 660	Louisville, Kentucky 2,320	Reno, Nevada 730
Charleston, S Carolina 2,910	Memphis, Tennessee 2,340	Rochester, New York 2,570
Charleston, West Virginia 2,500	Miami, Florida 3,300	Sacramento, California 750
Charlotte, North Carolina 2,770	Milwaukee, Wisconsin 1,960	Salt Lake City, Utah 830
Cheyenne, Wyoming 1,230	Minneapolis, Minnesota 1,630	San Antonio, Texas 2,190
Chicago, Illinois 2,030	Missoula, Montana 480	San Diego, California 1,260
Cleveland, Ohio 2,370	Montgomery, Alabama 2,660	San Francisco, California 810
Columbus, Ohio 2,360	Montreal, Québec 2,770	Spokane, Washington 280
Dallas, Texas 2,110	New Orleans, Louisiana 2,610	St Louis, Missouri 2,100
Denver, Colorado 1,310	New York, New York 2,810	Tucson, Arizona 1,550
Des Moines, Iowa 1,770	Norfolk, Virginia 2,890	Vancouver, BC 140
Detroit, Michigan 2,280	Oklahoma City, Okla 1,940	Washington, DC 2,730
Hartford, Connecticut 2,870	Omaha, Nebraska 1,670	Wichita, Kansas 1,810
Houston, Texas 2,350	Philadelphia, Penn 2,780	Winnipeg, Manitoba 1,520

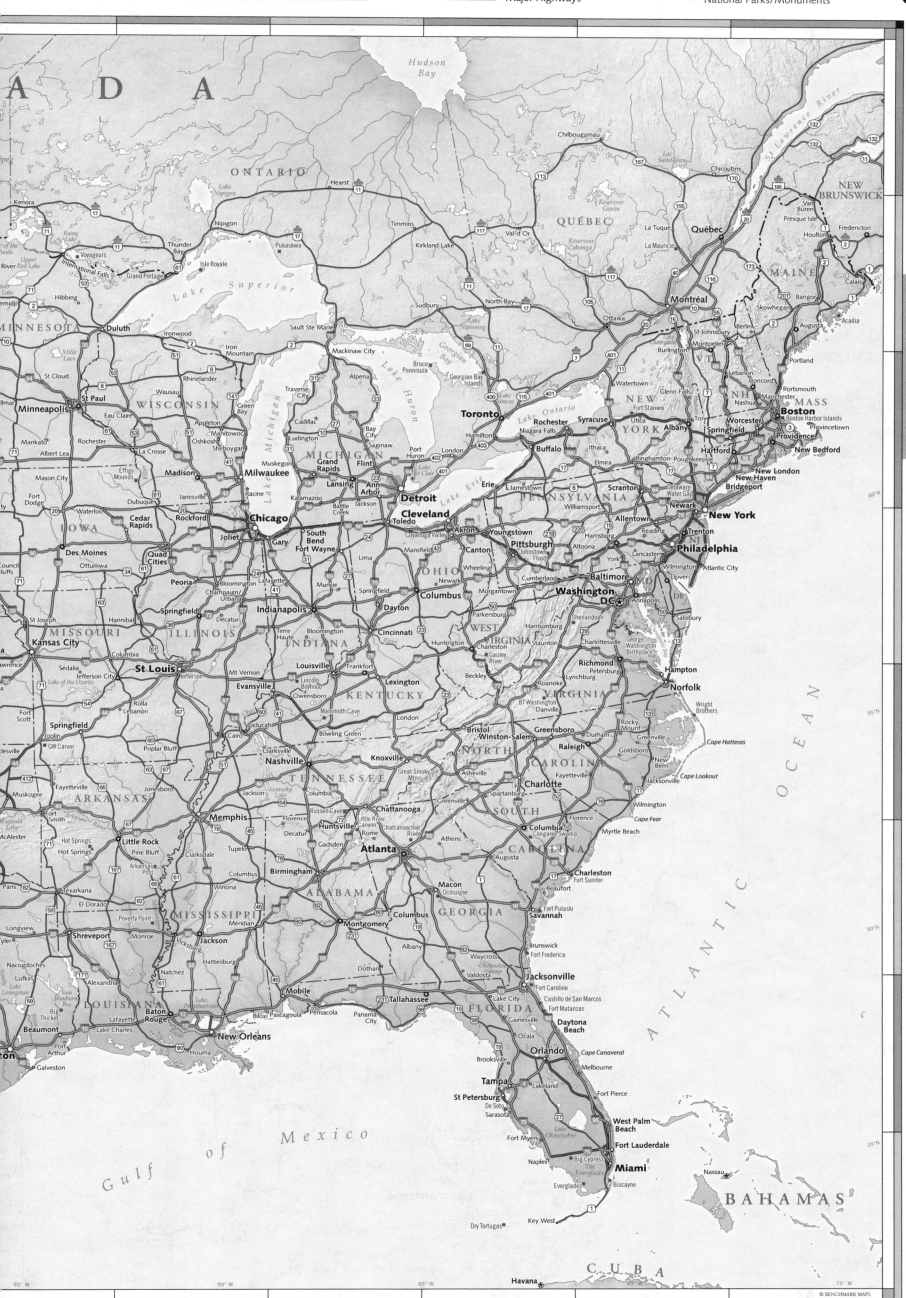

0 feet   2,000   4,000   6,000   8,000   10,000+

Interstate Highways and Freeways
Toll Roads
Major Highways

○ State/Province Capitals
Urban Areas
National Parks/Monuments

© BENCHMARK MAPS

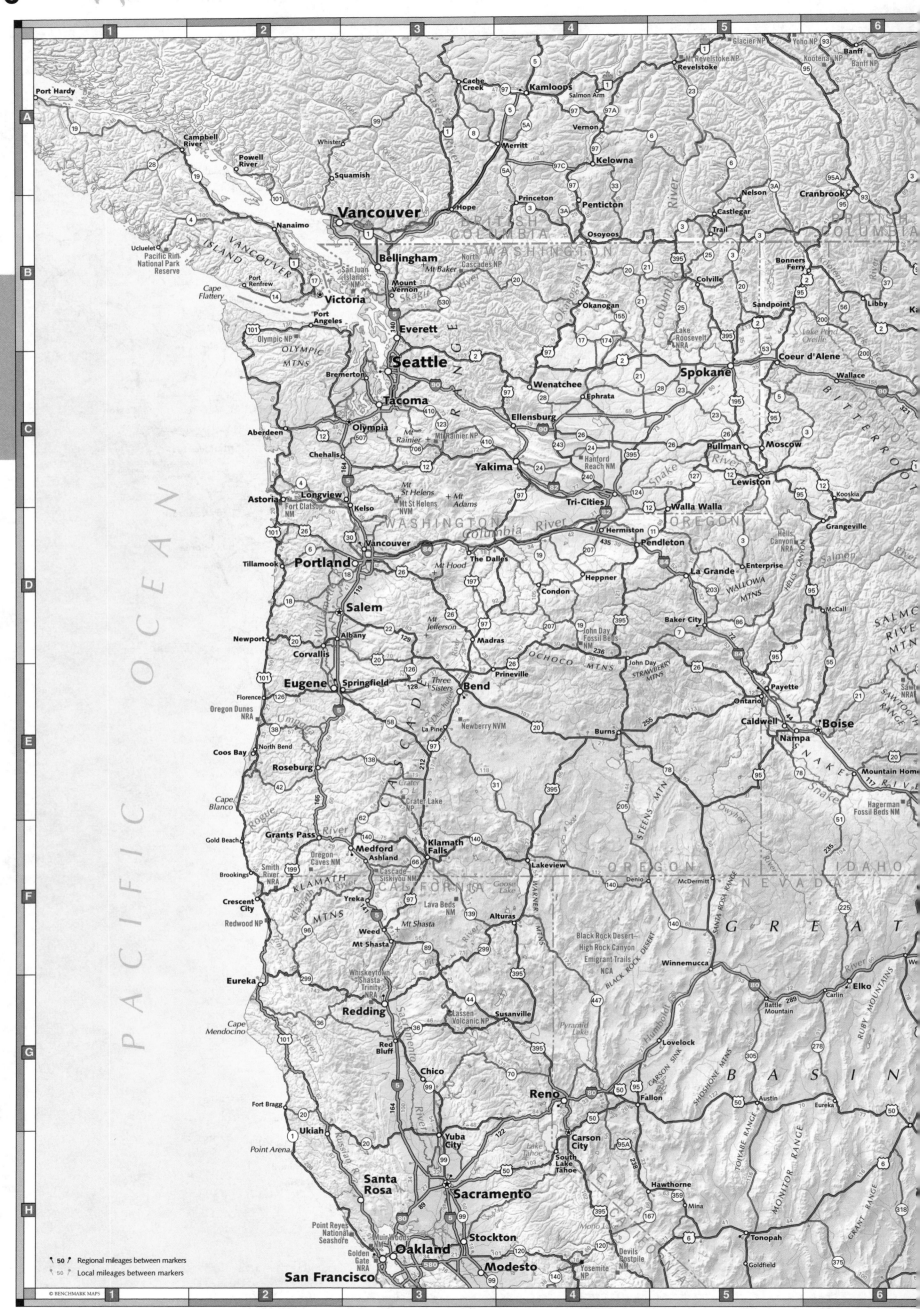

50 Regional mileages between markers
50 Local mileages between markers

© BENCHMARK MAPS

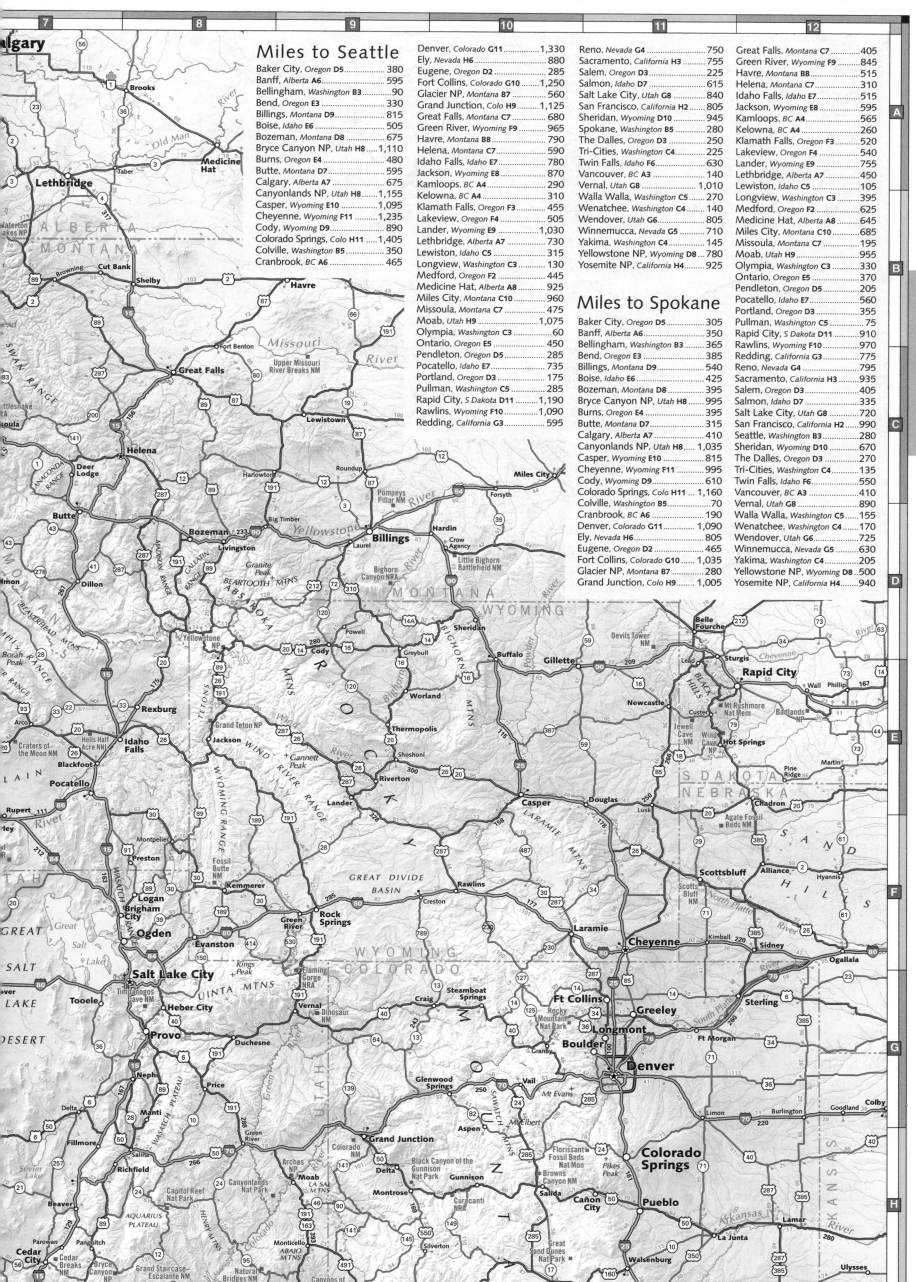

Miles to Seattle

Baker City, *Oregon* D5 380
Banff, *Alberta* A6 595
Bellingham, *Washington* B3 90
Bend, *Oregon* E3 330
Billings, *Montana* D9 815
Boise, *Idaho* E6 505
Bozeman, *Montana* D8 675
Bryce Canyon NP, *Utah* H8 1,110
Burns, *Oregon* E4 480
Butte, *Montana* D7 595
Calgary, *Alberta* A7 675
Canyonlands NP, *Utah* H8 1,155
Casper, *Wyoming* E10 1,095
Cheyenne, *Wyoming* F11 1,235
Cody, *Wyoming* D9 890
Colorado Springs, *Colo* H11 1,405
Colville, *Washington* B5 350
Cranbrook, *BC* A6 465
Denver, *Colorado* G11 1,330
Ely, *Nevada* H6 880
Eugene, *Oregon* D2 285
Fort Collins, *Colorado* G10 1,250
Glacier NP, *Montana* B7 560
Grand Junction, *Colo* H9 1,125
Great Falls, *Montana* C7 680
Green River, *Wyoming* F9 965
Havre, *Montana* B8 790
Helena, *Montana* C7 590
Idaho Falls, *Idaho* E7 780
Jackson, *Wyoming* E8 870
Kamloops, *BC* A4 290
Kelowna, *BC* A4 310
Klamath Falls, *Oregon* F3 455
Lakeview, *Oregon* F4 505
Lander, *Wyoming* E9 1,030
Lethbridge, *Alberta* A7 730
Lewiston, *Idaho* C5 315
Longview, *Washington* C3 130
Medford, *Oregon* F2 445
Medicine Hat, *Alberta* A8 925
Miles City, *Montana* C10 960
Missoula, *Montana* C7 475
Moab, *Utah* H9 1,075
Olympia, *Washington* C3 60
Ontario, *Oregon* E5 450
Pendleton, *Oregon* D5 285
Pocatello, *Idaho* E7 735
Portland, *Oregon* D3 175
Pullman, *Washington* C5 285
Rapid City, *S Dakota* D11 1,190
Rawlins, *Wyoming* F10 1,090
Redding, *California* G3 595
Reno, *Nevada* G4 750
Sacramento, *California* H3 755
Salem, *Oregon* D3 225
Salt Lake City, *Utah* G8 840
San Francisco, *California* H2 805
Sheridan, *Wyoming* D10 945
Spokane, *Washington* B5 280
The Dalles, *Oregon* D3 250
Tri-Cities, *Washington* C4 225
Twin Falls, *Idaho* F6 630
Vancouver, *BC* A3 140
Vernal, *Utah* G8 1,010
Walla Walla, *Washington* C5 270
Wenatchee, *Washington* C4 140
Wendover, *Utah* G6 805
Winnemucca, *Nevada* G5 710
Yakima, *Washington* C4 145
Yellowstone NP, *Wyoming* D8 780
Yosemite NP, *California* H4 925

Miles to Spokane

Baker City, *Oregon* D5 305
Banff, *Alberta* A6 350
Bellingham, *Washington* B3 365
Bend, *Oregon* E3 385
Billings, *Montana* D9 540
Boise, *Idaho* E6 425
Bozeman, *Montana* D8 395
Bryce Canyon NP, *Utah* H8 995
Burns, *Oregon* E4 395
Butte, *Montana* D7 315
Calgary, *Alberta* A7 410
Canyonlands NP, *Utah* H8 1,035
Casper, *Wyoming* E10 815
Cheyenne, *Wyoming* F11 995
Cody, *Wyoming* D9 610
Colorado Springs, *Colo* H11 1,160
Colville, *Washington* B5 70
Cranbrook, *BC* A6 190
Denver, *Colorado* G11 1,090
Ely, *Nevada* H6 805
Eugene, *Oregon* D2 465
Fort Collins, *Colorado* G10 1,035
Glacier NP, *Montana* B7 280
Grand Junction, *Colo* H9 1,005
Great Falls, *Montana* C7 405
Green River, *Wyoming* F9 845
Havre, *Montana* B8 515
Helena, *Montana* C7 310
Idaho Falls, *Idaho* E7 515
Jackson, *Wyoming* E8 595
Kamloops, *BC* A4 565
Kelowna, *BC* A4 260
Klamath Falls, *Oregon* F3 520
Lakeview, *Oregon* F4 540
Lander, *Wyoming* E9 755
Lethbridge, *Alberta* A7 450
Lewiston, *Idaho* C5 105
Longview, *Washington* C3 395
Medford, *Oregon* F2 625
Medicine Hat, *Alberta* A8 645
Miles City, *Montana* C10 685
Missoula, *Montana* C7 195
Moab, *Utah* H9 955
Olympia, *Washington* C3 330
Ontario, *Oregon* E5 370
Pendleton, *Oregon* D5 205
Pocatello, *Idaho* E7 560
Portland, *Oregon* D3 355
Pullman, *Washington* C5 75
Rapid City, *S Dakota* D11 910
Rawlins, *Wyoming* F10 970
Redding, *California* G3 775
Reno, *Nevada* G4 795
Sacramento, *California* H3 935
Salem, *Oregon* D3 405
Salmon, *Idaho* D7 335
Salt Lake City, *Utah* G8 720
San Francisco, *California* H2 990
Seattle, *Washington* B3 280
Sheridan, *Wyoming* D10 670
The Dalles, *Oregon* D3 270
Tri-Cities, *Washington* C4 135
Twin Falls, *Idaho* F6 550
Vancouver, *BC* A3 410
Vernal, *Utah* G8 890
Walla Walla, *Washington* C5 155
Wenatchee, *Washington* C4 170
Wendover, *Utah* G6 725
Winnemucca, *Nevada* G5 630
Yakima, *Washington* C4 205
Yellowstone NP, *Wyoming* D8 500
Yosemite NP, *California* H4 940

Washington

Scale 1: 1,400,000

| 0 | 10 | 20 | 30 | 40 | 50 Miles |

| 0 | 10 | 20 | 30 | 40 | 50 | 60 | 70 | 80 Kilometers |

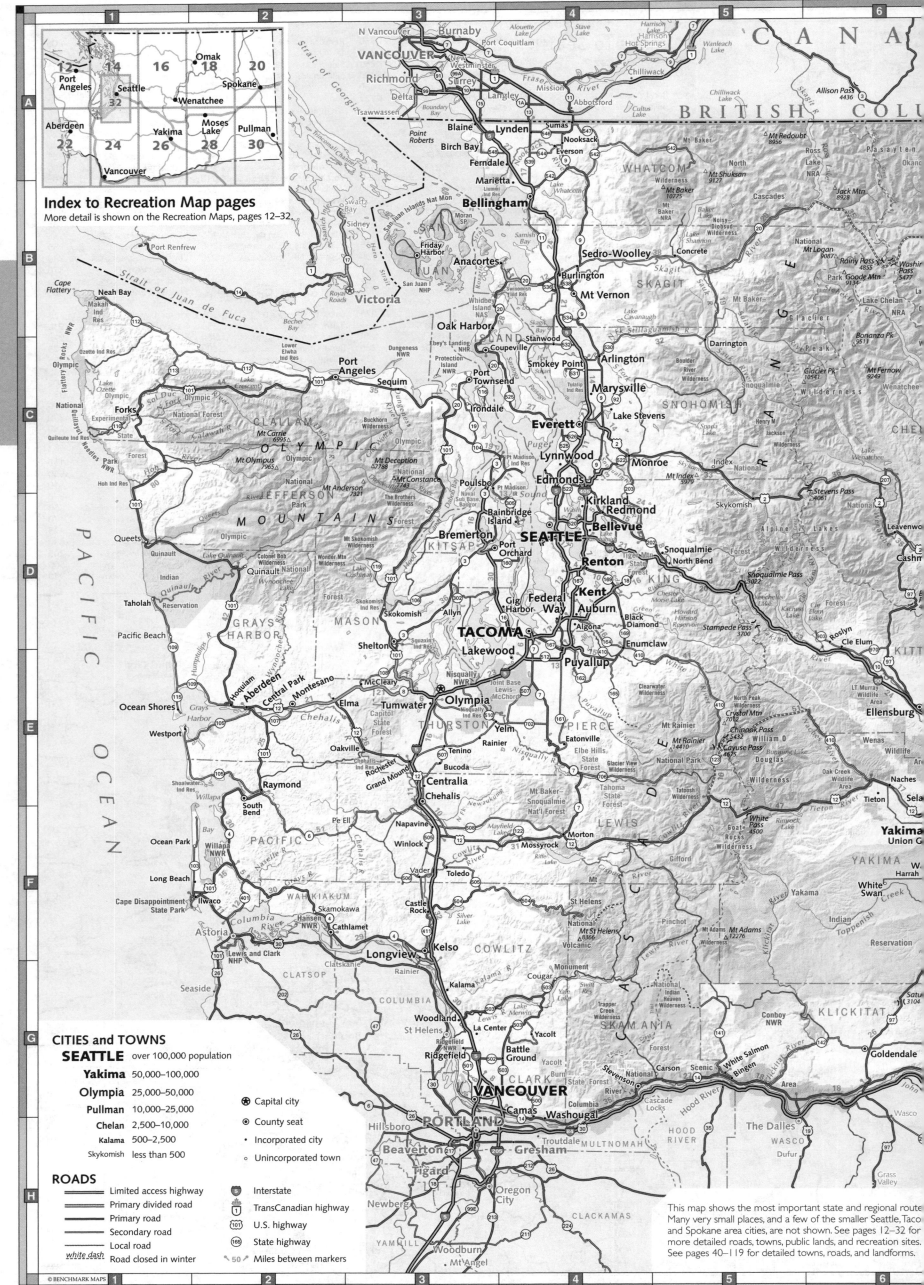

Index to Recreation Map pages
More detail is shown on the Recreation Maps, pages 12–32

| 12 | 14 | 16 | 18 | 20 |
Port Angeles — Seattle 32 — Omak — Spokane
Wenatchee
| 22 | 24 | 26 | 28 | 30 |
Aberdeen — Yakima — Moses Lake — Pullman
Vancouver

CITIES and TOWNS

SEATTLE over 100,000 population

Yakima 50,000–100,000

Olympia 25,000–50,000

Pullman 10,000–25,000

Chelan 2,500–10,000

Kalama 500–2,500

Skykomish less than 500

⊛ Capital city
◉ County seat
• Incorporated city
○ Unincorporated town

ROADS

Limited access highway
Primary divided road
Primary road
Secondary road
Local road
white dash Road closed in winter

Interstate
TransCanadian highway
U.S. highway
State highway
50 Miles between markers

This map shows the most important state and regional routes. Many very small places, and a few of the smaller Seattle, Tacoma, and Spokane area cities, are not shown. See pages 12–32 for more detailed roads, towns, public lands, and recreation sites. See pages 40–119 for detailed towns, roads, and landforms.

© BENCHMARK MAPS

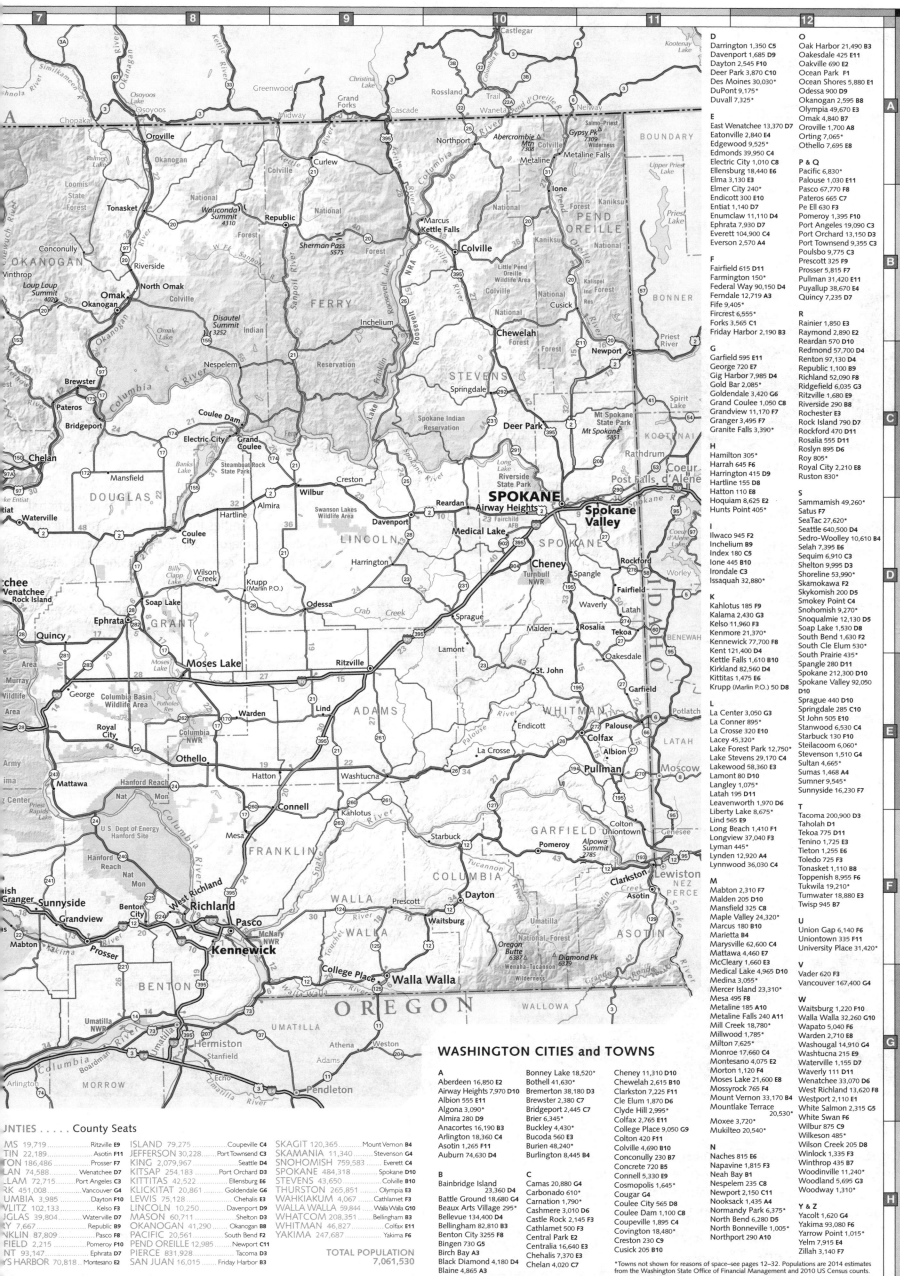

WASHINGTON

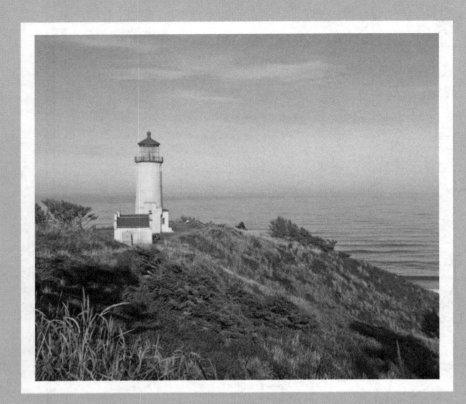

Cape Disappointment State Park

Situated along the Pacific Ocean, Cape Disappointment State Park has 2 miles of beach to wander, 2 lighthouses to explore, numerous trails to hike, and an interpretive center where you can learn about the history and culture of Cape Disappointment.

Recreation Map: Page 22, E3
Landscape Map: Page 95, F7

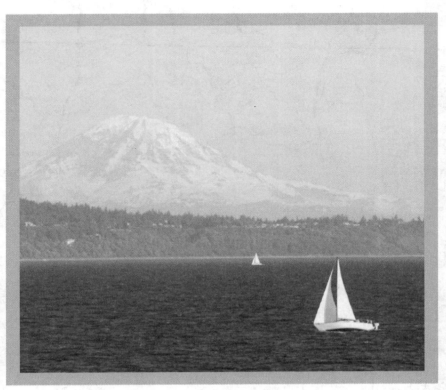

Puget Sound

Puget Sound offers a rich variety of recreational opportunities including sightseeing, hiking, kayaking, numerous boating activities, and whale watching. Snow-capped peaks provide picturesque backdrops for the perfect photo opportunity.

Recreation Map: Page 32, A3-G3
Landscape Map: Page 70, A1-G2

SCAN FOR REC RESOURCES

Olympic National Park

Olympic National Park is one of the most diverse parks you will ever find. From its beaches, to glacier-covered peaks, to rain forests, there is something for every type of nature enthusiast. Bring your hiking shoes because most of the park is accessible by trail only.

Recreation Map: Page 12, E3-G5
Landscape Map: Page 66, A8

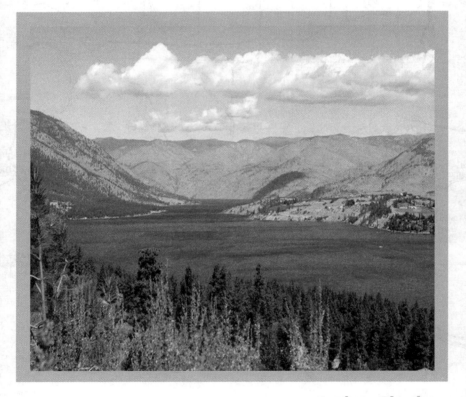

Lake Chelan

This narrow, 55-mile-long lake is the largest natural lake in Washington state. Known for water skiing it has several boat ramps and campgrounds scattered along its shores, making it a popular retreat for local recreationists.

Recreation Map: Page 16, D4-F6
Landscape Map: Page 59, E9

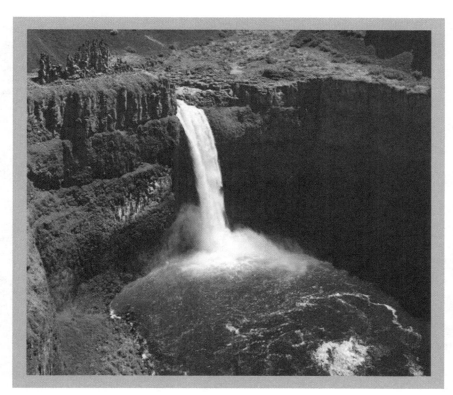

Palouse Falls State Park

Palouse Falls State Park is a hidden gem of the state park system. Far off the beaten path, the park boasts an impressive 198-ft waterfall, Palouse Falls. High volumes of water flow typically occur in spring and early summer.

Recreation Map: **Page 30, C2**
Landscape Map: **Page 105, A9**

Wine Country

Washington State is a rising star in the U.S. and world wine industry with great wineries located all over. But the highest concentration of wineries, due to climate, are found in the Columbia Basin. On any given weekend experience the world of Washington wine at several events, wine bars, and tasting rooms.

Recreation Map: **Pages 18, 28, & 30**
Landscape Map: **Pages 74-77, 88-92, 101-106**

Mt St Helens Nat'l Volcanic Monument

Mt St Helens is notoriously known for its explosive and devastating eruption on May 18, 1980. Attracting hikers and scholastics from far and wide, the now distinctive U-shape of Mt St Helens is one of the most recognizable landmarks in the country.

Recreation Map: **Page 24, E4**
Landscape Map: **Page 98, G3**

Stonehenge Memorial

This concrete replica of the ancient Stonhenge, located in England, was built as a memorial to the men of Klickitat County who died in World War I. Perched atop a bluff overlooking the Columbia River, it provides breathtaking views and amazing photo opportunities.

Recreation Map: **Page 26, C4**
Landscape Map: **Page 112, F6**

RECREATION

Recreation Map Legend

⊛ ⊚ State Capital, County Seat
○ ⊚ Notable Town
SEATTLE ○ 250,000–1,000,000
SPOKANE ○ 100,000–250,000
Yakima ○ 50,000–100,000
Olympia ○ 10,000–50,000
Ephrata ○ 2,500–10,000
Rainier ○ Fewer than 2,500
Lamont ○ Settlement or Locale
el 2068 Elevation in Feet

══════ Limited Access Highway
══════ Limited Access Highway, Toll
────── Primary Through Highway
────── Secondary Through Road
────── Paved Road
------ Unpaved and 4WD Road
🖌 25 🖌 Miles Between Markers

🛡5 🛡101 Interstate, U.S. Highway
62 N8 State, County Highway
25 Canadian Highway

Climate Station
Rest Area
Campground
Major Airport
Mountain Peak
Lighthouse
Forks ○ ⊚ Notable Town
RV Park
Fishing
Boating
Ski Area, Snopark /Winter Recreation
Hiking
Rafting
Amusement Park
Zoo
University
Natural Wonder
Museum
Stadium
Birdwatching
Whale Watching
★ Other Attraction

River
Stream
Intermittent Stream
Lake
Intermittent Lake

─ ·· ─ ·· International Boundary
─ · ─ · State Boundary
─ ── ─ County Boundary
K I N G County Name

Large public land parcels are labeled in colored type
Bureau of Land Management Land*
U.S. Forest Service
Wilderness
Military Land
State Land
State Park
National Park / Monument / Recreation Area
Wildlife Area
Indian Land
Bureau of Reclamation
HOKO 601 State Game Management Unit†

*Public Lands shown in this Atlas may include privately owned parcels within their boundaries. Public lands are also subject to changes and leasing. Please respect all landowners' rights, including permission to enter and pass. Please observe the basic rule of gates: leave them as you find them, whether open or closed.

†Game Management Unit boundaries shown are effective February, 2011 and are for general reference only. For precise boundary descriptions and the latest hunting rules and seasons, see the current Big Game Hunting pamphlet published yearly by the Washington Department of Fish and Wildlife. Washington residents may obtain a pamphlet from any dealer of fish and game licenses statewide. Out-of-state residents may order on-line at: www.wdfw.wa.gov/hunting, or by calling (360) 902-2515.

Recreation Maps

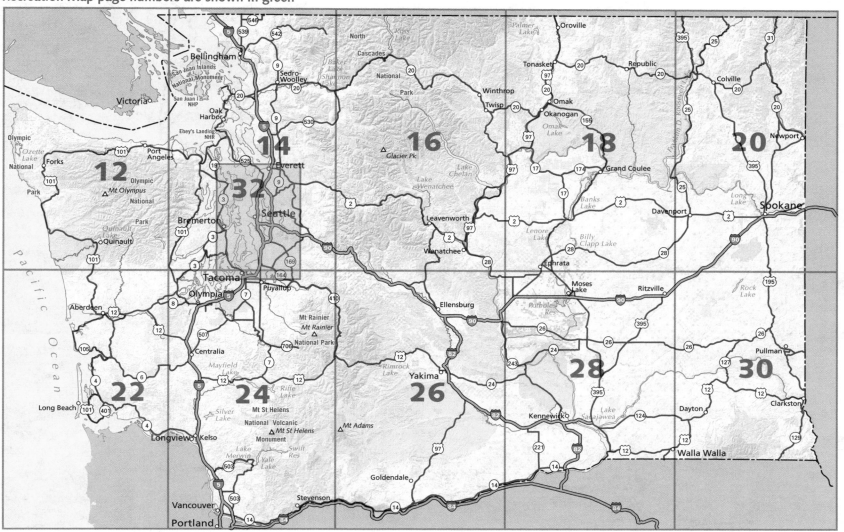

RECREATION

RECREATION

Legend:
Wilderness • State Parks • Bureau of Reclamation • Bureau of Land Management • National Parks/Monuments • State Game Management Unit
Forest Service • State Lands • Military Lands • Tribal Lands • Wildlife Areas • HOKO 601

Grid: 1 2 3 4 5 6 — A B C D E F G H

Vancouver Island and area

VANCOUVER ISLAND

Cassidy
Ladysmith
Blaineys
Saltair
Chemainus
Westholme
Vesuvius Bay
Crofton
Maple Bay
Ganges
Galiano
Lake Cowichan
Hayward
Duncan
Tzuhalem
Koksilah
Deerholme
Mayne
Pender Island
Port Washington
Cowichan Bay
Boatswain Bank
Cohwichan Station
Saturna
South Pender
Lyall Creek
Waldron
Cobble Hill
Deep Cove
Swartz Bay
Beaver Point
Fulford Harbour
Shawnigan Lake
Mill Bay
Bazan Bay
James Island
Sidney
Prevost
SAN JUAN
Cliffside
Saanichton
Tod
Bamberton
Elk Lake
Roche Harbor
Malahat
Prospect Lake
Kapoor
Glyno
Cordova Bay
San Juan Island Natl Historical Park (British Camp)
Friday Harbor
SAN JUAN ISLAND
Port Renfrew
Goldstream
Strawberry Bale
Lime Kiln State Park
Glen Lake
Belmont Colwood
Esquimalt
Cadboro Bay
San Juan Island National Historical Park (American Camp)
River Jordan
Shirley
Saseenos Station
Happy Valley
Lagoon
Victoria
ISLANDS 410
Sooke
East Sooke
Metchosin

WHATCOM
NORTH SOUND 407
Beach Grove
Tsawwassen Beach
Point Roberts
South Beach

STRAIT OF GEORGIA
GALIANO ISLAND
Trincomali Channel
SALTSPRING ISLAND
Haro Strait

CANADA
STRAIT OF JUAN DE FUCA
BRITISH COLUMBIA

Olympic Peninsula

PACIFIC OCEAN

Cape Flattery Lighthouse
Cape Resort
Neah Bay
Makah Indian Reservation
Makah Tribal Museum
Point of Arches
Cape Flattery
Cape Alava
Flattery Rocks National Wildlife Refuge
Sekiu
Clallam Bay
Pysht
HOKO 601
Ozette
Ozette Ind Res
Ozette Lake
Old Royal
DICKEY 602
Olympic National Park
SOL DUC 607
Sol Duc River
Beaver
Sappho
Klahowya
Olympic
PYSHT 603
Fairholm
Lake Crescent
Bear Creek
Shuwah
Klahanie
Quillayute
Forks
Forks Timber Museum
Mora
La Push
Quileute Ind Res
Three Rivers Resort
Rialto
Bogachiel State Park
Willoughby Creek
GOODMAN 612
Quillayute Needles National Wildlife Refuge
Hole in the Wall
Bonesome Creek
Hoh River Resort
CLEARWATER 615
Oil City
Hoh Ind Res
Destruction Island Lighthouse
Olympic National Park
Kalaloch
South Beach
Queets
Quinault Indian Res
Taholah
Copalis National Wildlife Refuge
Moclips
COPALIS 642
Humptulips
WYNOOCHEE 648

Lyre River Park
Crescent Beach & RV Park
Salt Creek
Salt Creek Rec Area
Joyce
Log Cabin Resort
Disque
Crescent
Ovington
Fairholme
Merrymere Falls
Olympic Hot Springs
Sol Duc
Happy Lake Ridge
CLALLAM
OLYMPIC
Mt Olympus 7965
Hoh Rain Forest Visitor Center
Hoh River
JEFFERSON
Solleks River
Yahoo Lake
Upper Clearwater
Queets River
Clearwater
North Fork
Graves Creek
Lake Quinault
Rain Forest Resort
Gatton Creek
Falls Creek
Quinault
Willaby Creek
Colonel Bob
Grove
Campbell Tree Grove
Amanda Park
Rain Forest
Neilton
QUINAULT RIDGE 638
Coho
Promised Land Park
GRAYS HARBOR

1. Peabody Creek
2. Black Ball Transport (ferry)
3. Fiero Marine Life Center
4. Victoria Rapid Transit Inc (ferry)

1. Rainbow's End
2. Sequim West
3. Museum & Art Ctr Sequim–Dungeness Valley

Port Angeles
Lower Elwha Ind Res
Elwha
Ramapo
Shadow
Mtn
Indian Creek Rec Area
Elwha Dam
Pioneer Memorial Mus
Museum at the Carnegie
Heart O' the Hills
Altair
Hurricane Ridge Picnic Area
Olympic
Hurricane Ridge Visitors Center
Deer Park
HURRICANE RIDGE
Olympic National Park
MOUNTAINS
Elwha River
Enchanted Valley
Olympic National Forest

COYLE 624
Dungeness National Wildlife Refuge
New Dungeness Lighthouse
Dungeness
Dungeness Rec Area
Olympic Game Farm
Sequim
Jamestown
Port Williams
Conestoga Quarters
KOA
Sequim Bay State Park
John Wayne Waterfront Resort
Seven Cedars Casino
Dungeness Forks
Buckhorn Wilderness
BUCKHORN
OLYMPIC Wilderness 621
Dosewallips
Dosewallips River
Elkhorn
The Brothers Wilderness
Collins
Duckabush River
National Forest
Lena Creek
Hamma Hamma
Mt Skokomish Wilderness
Wonder Mountain Wilderness
Staircase
Lake Cushman
Lake Cushman Resort
La Bar Horse Camp
Big Creek
Lilliwaup Creek
Melbourne Lake
Lilliwaup
Sunrise Resort
Rest-A-While
Hoodsport
Dewatto
SKOKOMISH 636
Skokomish Ind Res
Brown Creek
Oxbow
Grisdale
Potlatch
Potlatch State Park
Tahuya
MASON 633
Bayshore
Matlock
Matlock

Scale 1:600,000
0 5 10 15 20 25 30 40 50 Miles
0 5 10 15 20 25 30 40 50 Kilometers

State & National Parks ▲★🚶

Bogachiel State Park Camping and hiking, forested nature trail. 6 miles south of Forks on US 101. (360) 374-6356. parks.wa.gov **F2**

Olympic National Park Camping, hiking, and mountain climbing on the Olympic Peninsula from the Pacific Coast inland, including beaches, glacier-covered peaks, and rain forest. Much of the park is roadless and accessible by trail only. Port Angeles. (360) 565-3130. **E3-G5**

Potlatch State Park Camping, picnicking, boating, hiking. 12 miles north of Shelton on US 101. (360) 877-5361. **H6**

Sequim Bay State Park Camping, picnicking, hiking, fishing, boat launch, and beach access. 4 miles northeast of Sequim on US 101. 888-226-7688 or (360) 683-4235. **E6**

Forests & Wildlife Areas 🚶🐦

Dungeness National Wildlife Refuge A great spot for bird watching, with sightings of over 200 species. The area is accessible by trail. Parking is located at the entrance. Tours of the New Dungeness Lighthouse, located at the end of the spit, are conducted daily. On Dungeness Spit. (360) 457-8451. **D6**

Flattery Rocks National Wildlife Refuge Over 100 miles of shoreline, rocks, and reef. Along northern coast of Washington. Closed to public. Viewable by boat only. (360) 457-8451. **D1**

Olympic National Forest Forest land adjoining the Olympic National Park. Includes Buckhorn, The Brothers, Mount Skokomish, Colonel Bob, and Wonder Mountain wildernesses. Olympic Peninsula. (360) 956-2402. **E2–H5**

Quillayute Needles National Wildlife Refuge An offshore refuge and marine sanctuary. Accessible by boat only. (360) 457-8451. **E1–F2**

San Juan Islands National Wildlife Refuge Over 80 small islands where numerous bird species rest and nest, including bald eagles and double-crested cormorants. The islands are closed to public entry, but wildlife may be observed by boat. Around the San Juan Islands. (360) 457-8451. **B6–C6**

River Rafting 🛶

Dosewallips River Two sections of this river are run. The upper section from Elkhorn Campground to just above Wilson Creek is for expert boaters only. The lower run, from Wilson Creek to Hood Canal, is an intermediate run. Logs are a hazard on this river. **F6**

Dungeness River 3-mile-long, Class III–IV run from Gold Creek to Dungeness Forks campground. From the campground to the fish hatchery is a 5.5-mile-long, Class III run with numerous logjams requiring portages. The best time to enjoy this river is in early spring. **E6**

Elwha River Two runs are found on the Elwha River. The upper run is from Altaire Campground to the gauge approximately 4 miles from put-in. This is an intermediate run. The lower run, a Class II run, begins just off State Rte 112 and ends at the mouth of the river. **E5**

Hoh River A 20-mile Class II river run from Hoh Ranger Station to the Hoh Oxbow Campground. Logjams are a hazard, especially along the first 6 miles, above where the South Fork Hoh River enters. West side of Olympic Peninsula. **F3**

Queets River The Queets River is a Class II run with numerous Class I rapids. The run is 12 miles long from Queets Campground to just below Lyman Rapids. Logs may block the main channel. **G3**

Sol Duc River Three sections of the Sol Duc River can be rafted. The uppermost run is for expert boaters only. It is 9 miles long, from Sol Duc Hot Springs to Fibreboard Bridge. The middle section from Fibreboard Bridge to the hatchery is a 24-mile-long Class III run. The lower section is a 7.5-mile-long Class II–III run from the hatchery to Salmon Drive. **E2**

Boating & Fishing 🐟🚤

Hoh River The Hoh River is known for winter and summer steelhead and chinook. Public access is good, and there are several campgrounds along the river from the national park boundary to US 101. **F3**

Lake Quinault Lake Quinault is on the Quinault Indian Reservation, and you must have a tribal permit to fish here. Dolly Varden, char, lake cutthroat trout, and kokanee. **G4**

Neah Bay Ocean and strait access. Charter boats available. Fish for halibut, chinook and coho salmon and a variety of bottom fish. Check on salmon fishing restrictions. On State Rte 112. **D1**

Ozette Lake Canoeing. Camping along the north shore. Olympic National Park, near coast off Hoh–Ozetta Rd. **E1**

Port Angeles Public boat ramps are located in Port Angeles. Fish for chinook, coho, and pink salmon, halibut, lingcod, and various bottom fish. Coho and chinook season may be closed or restricted. **E5**

Queets River Winter steelhead is the catch for the Queets River, especially at the mouth of the Salmon River. Summer steelhead, chinook, and coho salmon are also known to be found in the Queets. **G3**

Ferries ★

Black Ball Ferry Line The *M.V. Coho* ferries vehicles and passengers from Port Angeles (360) 457-4491 to Victoria, BC. (250) 386-2202. www.cohoferry.com **E5**

Natural Wonders ★🚶👥

Dungeness Spit A 5.5-mile-long sand spit, one of the longest in the world. The spit is the northern land mass between the Strait of Juan de Fuca and Dungeness Bay, home of the New Dungeness Lighthouse. North of Sequim. (360) 457-8451. www.fws.gov **D6**

Enchanted Valley A 13-mile one-way hike from Graves Creek Campground along the East Fork of the Quinault River to the Enchanted Valley and on to the world's largest Western Hemlock. Olympic National Park. **G5**

Hoh Rain Forest At the visitor center is the Hall of Mosses Trail winding through an old growth rain forest of spruce, cedar, hemlock, and fir draped with numerous species of mosses, ferns, and lichens. The Spruce Nature Trail explains how a rain forest develops. Olympic National Park. **F3**

Hole in the Wall Natural Arch A natural arch. A 2-mile hike north of Rialto Beach. 2 miles north of Rialto Beach. **E1**

Hoodsport Trail Park Hiking trail along Dow Creek. 2 miles west of Hoodsport on State Rte 119. (360) 755-9231. **H6**

Hurricane Ridge Hurricane Ridge offers spectacular views of glaciated Mount Olympus and the Strait of Juan de Fuca. There is a visitor center, picnic area, and trailheads located at Hurricane Ridge. Olympic NP. **E5**

Marymere Falls 90-ft-high falls can be viewed on a 0.8 mile hike from Storm King Information Station. Off US 101 at Lake Crescent. **E4**

Olympic Hot Springs Hike approximately 1.5 miles to this former resort, now returned to its natural state. Olympic NP. **E4**

Point of Arches A series of water- and wind-worn arches. Accessible by trail only. Olympic NP in the coastal section. **D1**

Quinault Rain Forest A 2-mile hike through the forest leads to 90-ft-high falls along Falls Creek. Off US 101. **H4**

Historic Sites & Museums ★🏛

Forks Timber Museum Vintage logging and farming equipment exhibits. Historic photographs of the Forks area. Nature trail and picnic area. South of Forks on US 101. Friday/Saturday only in Winter. (360) 374-9663. **E2**

Museum and Arts Center in the Sequim–Dungeness Valley Displays depicting Coast Salish Indian and pioneer life, as well as natural history exhibits. 175 W Cedar, Sequim. (360) 683-8110. www.macsequim.org **E6**

Museum at the Carnegie Exhibits illustrating county history and Clallam and Makah Indian artifacts. 207 S Lincoln, Port Angeles. (360) 452-6779. **E5**

Notable Towns ○ ◉

Forks Westernmost incorporated city in the state. This logging town and center of outdoor recreation is named for the many rivers that come together nearby. Forks has become a tourist attraction for fans of Stephenie Meyer's *Twilight* series which is set in and around the town. 800-443-6757 or (360) 374-2531. www.forkswa.com **E2**

Friday Harbor Only incorporated city in San Juan County. Several shops, restaurants, and the Whale Museum are within walking distance of the ferry landing. (360) 378-5240 (San Juan Island Chamber of Commerce). www.sanjuanisland.org **C6**

Kalaloch, pronounced "klalock." Community with classic lodge built in 1953 along the coastal strip portion of Olympic National Park. 800-443-6757 or (360) 374-2531 (Forks Chamber of Commerce). **G2**

Port Angeles The largest city on the north side of the Olympic Peninsula. Ferry to Victoria, BC or drive the short distance to Olympic National Park. (360) 452-2363 (Port Angeles Regional Chamber of Commerce). www.portangeles.org **E5**

Roche Harbor This village on the northwest corner of San Juan Island started as a lime kiln company town and is now a resort community. English Camp unit of San Juan Island National Historic Park is a few miles to the south. (360) 378-5240 (San Juan Island Chamber of Commerce). www.sanjuanisland.org **C6**

Other Attractions ★🏛🐘⛳🪶

7 Cedars Casino Full casino and slots. Golf. On Scenic Hwy 101, Sequim. 800-458-2597 or (360) 683-7777. www.7cedarsresort.com **E6**

Cape Flattery Lighthouse Built in 1854, this is the northernmost lighthouse in the Western Contiguous United States. This lighthouse is not accessible. Off the Coast of Cape Flattery on Tatoosh Island. **C1**

Feiro Marine Life Center Marine life displays including a hands-on intertidal tank. City Pier, Port Angeles. (360) 417-6254. www.feiromarinelifecenter.org **E5**

New Dungeness Lighthouse Built in 1857 and renovated in 1927. Tours. Accessible by foot (check tide tables) or boat only. End of Dungeness Spit. One of a few lighthouses that allows families to be lighthouse keepers for a week. (360) 683-6638 www.newdungenesslighthouse.com **D6**

Olympic Game Farm This preserve is home to numerous animals used in television and films. There is a drive-through tour, a walking tour, and a petting zoo. Ward Rd, Sequim. 800-778-4295 or (360) 683-4295. olygamefarm.com **E6**

The Whale Museum Exhibits illustrating the biology and behavior of whales. First Street, Friday Harbor. (360) 378-4710. Report sightings to The Whale Hotline: 1-800-562-8832. www.whalemuseum.org. **C6**

Whale Watching Cape Flattery and Cape Alava are good places to watch migrating whales January through early February and in late March through April. (360) 452-8552 (Visitor's Bureau). **D1**

Information Resources

Highway Info, Mountain Pass Reports, and Ferry Schedules
Dial 511 or 800-695-7623. www.wsdot.wa.gov

National Recreation Reservation Service
Reservations for selected campgrounds. 877-444-6777 www.recreation.gov

Olympic National Forest Headquarters
1835 Black Lake Blvd, SW, Olympia 98512. (360) 956-2402
www.fs.usda.gov/olympic

Hood Canal Ranger District, Quilcene Office
295142 Hwy 101 S, PO Box 280, Quilcene 98376. (360) 765-2200

Pacific Ranger District, Forks Office
437 Tillicum Ln, Forks 98331. (360) 374-6522

Pacific Ranger District, Quinault Office
353 S Shore Rd, PO Box 9, Quinault 98575. (360) 288-2525

Olympic National Park Headquarters
600 E Park Av, Port Angeles 98362. (360) 565-3000. www.nps.gov/olym

Hoh Rain Forest Visitor Center
18113 Upper Hoh Rd, Forks 98331. (360) 374-6925

Olympic National Park Visitor Center
3002 Mt Angeles Rd, Port Angeles 98362. (360) 565-3130
(360) 565-3100 Wilderness Info Center (for trail info, permits)
(360) 565-3131 Recorded road and weather information

Washington Department of Natural Resources, Olympic Region
411 Tillicum Ln, Forks 98331. (360) 374-2800. www.dnr.wa.gov

Washington State Parks Information Center & Campground Reservations
(360) 902-8844, 888-226-7688. www.parks.wa.gov
(360) 902-8555 (Boaters Guide)
(360) 902-8600 (Environmental Learning Centers)

Washington Department of Transportation Ferry System
511 or 888-808-7977 or (206) 464-6400 (out of state).
wsdot.wa.gov/ferries

Hunting & Fishing

Washington Department of Fish and Wildlife, Coastal Region 6
48 Devonshire Rd, Montesano 98563. (360) 249-4628. wdfw.wa.gov

See map on page 29.

Campgrounds & RV Parks ▲🚐

See page **34** for the campground and RV park listings.

Climate

See explanation on page 31

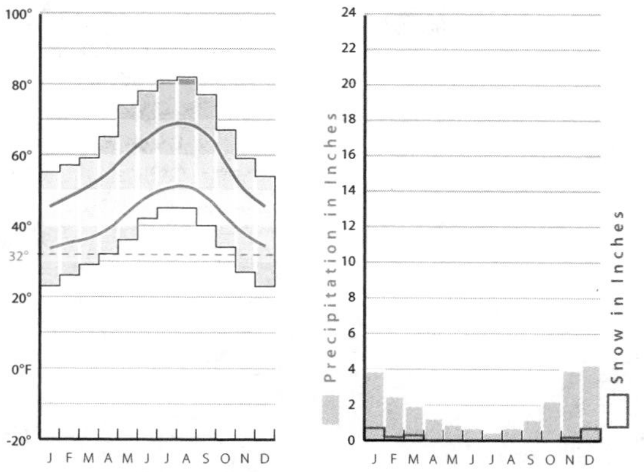

Port Angeles: el. 39 ft — 68 days with 25" precipitation, 2" of snow, 45 nights below freezing, 1 day above 90°

Jan (23°) 34°–45° (55°) **Apr** (32°) 39°–55° (65°)
July (45°) 51°–68° (81°) **Oct** (34°) 43°–58° (67°)

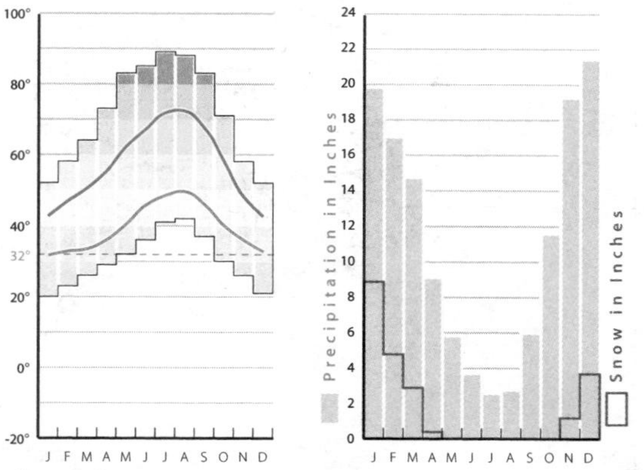

Grisdale: el. 436 ft — 156 days with 135" precipitation, 22" of snow, 92 nights below freezing, 3 days above 90°

Jan (20°) 32°–43° (52°) **Apr** (29°) 36°–55° (73°)
July (41°) 49°–72° (89°) **Oct** (30°) 40°–58° (71°)

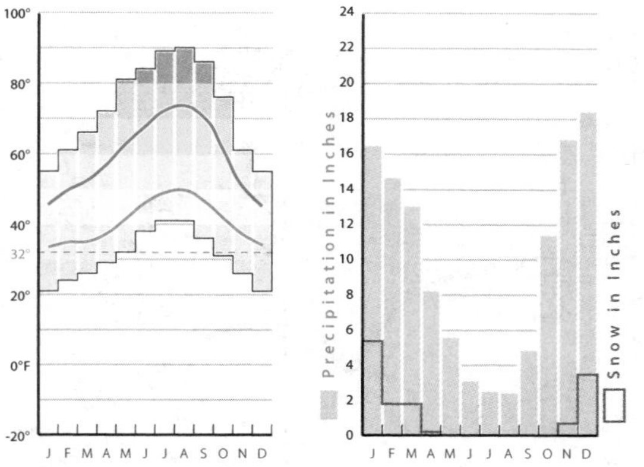

Forks: el. 351 ft — 154 days with 119" precipitation, 13" of snow, 67 nights below freezing, 4 days above 90°

Jan (21°) 34°–46° (55°) **Apr** (29°) 37°–57° (72°)
July (41°) 49°–72° (89°) **Oct** (31°) 42°–61° (76°)

Landscape Page Index

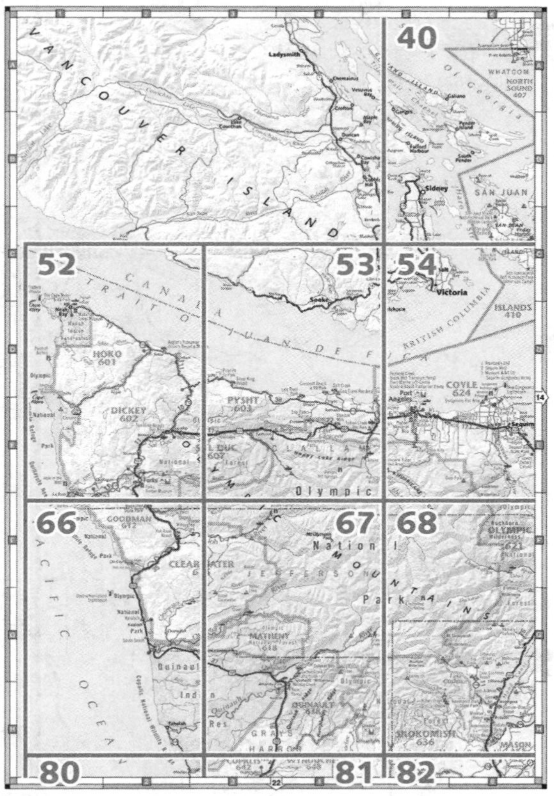

Landscape Page Numbers Are Shown in Blue

RECREATION

© BENCHMARK MAPS

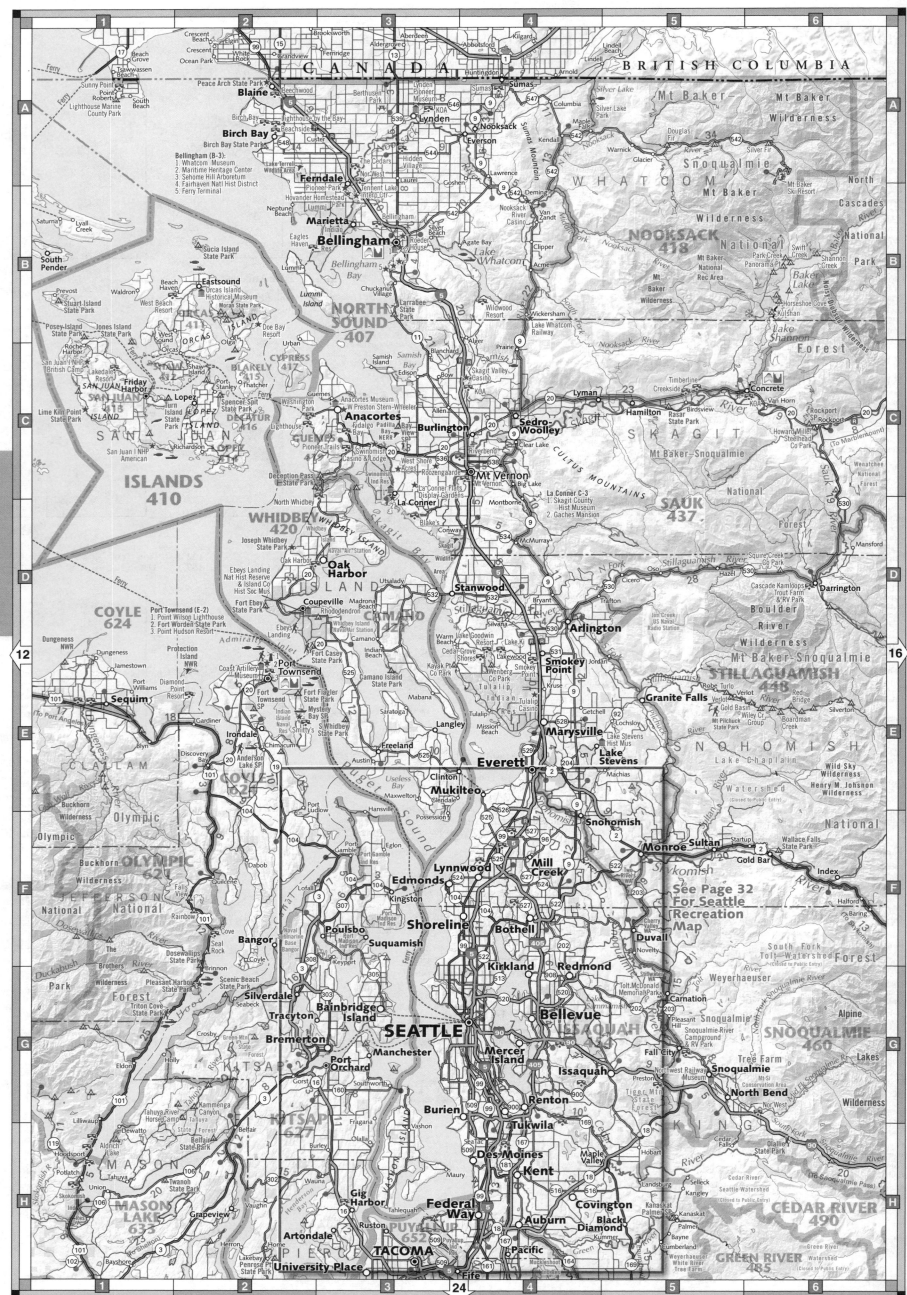

RECREATION

	Wilderness		State Parks		Bureau of Reclamation		Bureau of Land Management		National Parks/Monuments	HOKO 601	State Game Management Unit
	Forest Service		State Lands		Military Lands		Tribal Lands		Wildlife Areas		

Bellingham (B-3):
1. Whatcom Museum
2. Maritime Heritage Center
3. Sehome Hill Arboretum
4. Fairhaven Natl Hist District
5. Ferry Terminal

Port Townsend (E-2):
1. Point Wilson Lighthouse
2. Fort Worden State Park
3. Point Hudson Resort

La Conner C-3:
1. Skagit County Hist Museum
2. Gaches Mansion

See Page 32 For Seattle Recreation Map

© BENCHMARK MAPS

Scale 1:600,000

0   5   10   15   20   25   30   40   50 Miles
0   5   10 15 20 25 30   40   50 Kilometers

State & National Parks ▲★

Anderson Lake State Park Day use area with boat launch and hiking trails. South of Port Townsend. (360) 385-1259. **E2**
Bay View State Park Camping and picnicking. West of Burlington on Bayview–Edison Rd. (360) 757-0227. **C3**
Belfair State Park Beach access, camping, and picnicking. West of Belfair on State Rte 300. (360) 275-0668. **H2**
Birch Bay State Park Camping, picnicking, and hiking. South of Blaine on State Rte 548. (360) 371-2800. **A2**
Camano Island State Park Camping, picnicking, hiking, and mountain biking. Southwest of Stanwood on State Rte 532. (360) 387-3031. **E3**
Deception Pass State Park Camping, picnicking, hiking, mountain bike trail, boat launch, and underwater park. North of Oak Harbor. (360) 675-2417. **C2**
Dosewallips State Park Camping, hiking, and fishing. North of Brinnon. (360) 796-4415. **F2**
Fort Casey State Park Camping, hiking, underwater park, and interpretive area. South of Coupeville on State Rte 20. (360) 902-8844. **D2**
Fort Ebey State Park Camping, hiking, and mountain biking. South of Oak Harbor off State Rte 20. (360) 678-4636. **D2**
Fort Flagler State Park Camping, picnicking, hiking, boating. 1890s artillery fort. NE of Port Hadlock. (360) 385-1259. **E2**
Fort Townsend State Park Camping, hiking, swimming, and fishing at historic fort site. South of Port Townsend. (360) 385-3595. **E2**
Fort Worden State Park Camp, picnic, hike or fish, boat launch. See the Coast Artillery Museum, Marine Science Center, and Wilson Lighthouse. North of Port Townsend. (360) 344-4431. **D2**
Joseph Whidbey State Park Picnicking and beach combing. West shore of Whidbey Island. West of Oak Harbor. (360) 902-8844. **D2**
Kanaskat–Palmer State Park Camping, picnicking, hiking, and biking. Northeast of Enumclaw. (360) 886-0148. **H5**
Larrabee State Park Camping, hiking, and mountain biking. South of Bellingham on Chuckanut Dr. (360) 902-8844. **B3**
Lime Kiln Point State Park Picnicking, hiking; known for whale watching. On San Juan Island. (360) 378-2044. **C1**
Moran State Park Camping, picnicking, boat launch. Southeast of Eastbound. (360) 376-2326. **B2**
Mount Pilchuck State Park Day use area of hiking trails linking lakes and streams. Historic lookout. 8 miles east of Granite Falls. (360) 902-8844. **E5**
Mystery Bay State Park Picnic area and boat launch. On Marrowstone Island, on State Rte 116. (360) 385-1259. **E2**
Olallie State Park Picnicking, hiking. East of North Bend. (360) 902-8844. **H6**
Penrose Point State Park Camping, hiking, and biking. North of Longbranch. (253) 884-2514. **H2**
Pleasant Harbor State Park Beachcombing, fishing, boating, and scuba diving. South of Brinnon, on US 101. (360) 796-4415. **G1**
Rasar State Park Camping, hiking, picnicking along the Skagit River. East of Hamilton on Cape Horn Rd. (360) 826-3942. **C5**
San Juan Island National Historic Park Site of 1859 "Pig War" crisis. Hiking, picnicking, beach access. On San Juan Island. (360) 378-2240. **C1**
Scenic Beach State Park Camping, picnicking, and beach access. Northwest of Bremerton. (360) 830-5079. **G2**
South Whidbey State Park Camping, picnicking, and hiking. South of Greenbank off State Rte 525. (360) 331-4559. **E2**
Spencer Spit State Park Camping, wildlife viewing, and hiking. On salt marsh. Southeast of Port Stanley. (360) 468-2251. **C2**
Sucia Island Marine State Park Camping accessible by boat only. N of Orcas Island. (360) 376-2073. **B2**
Triton Cove State Park Picnicking, hiking, fishing, and boat launch. 8 miles south of Dosewallips on US 101. (360) 796-4415. **G1**
Twanoh State Park Camping, hiking, fishing, boat launch, picnicking. 8 miles west of Belfair on State Rte 106. (360) 275-2222. **H1**
Wallace Falls State Park Camping, hiking, and mountain biking along the Wallace River. 256-ft waterfall. Northeast of Gold Bar. (360) 793-0420. **F6**

Forest & Wildlife Areas 🐦🚶

Green Mountain State Forest Hiking and camping. On the Tahuya Peninsula, north of Tahuya SF. (360) 825-1631. www.dnr.wa.gov **G2**
Lake Terrell Wildlife Area Stopover for migrating ducks and other waterfowl. South of Birch Bay on Lake Terrell. (360) 385-4723. **A2**
Mt Baker National Recreation Area 8,600 acres offer hiking, horse trails, and snowmobiling. North of Concrete. (360) 856-5700. **B5**
Mt Baker–Snoqualmie National Forest Includes Mt Baker National Rec Area and Mt Baker, Glacier Peak, Boulder River, Henry M. Jackson, Wild Sky, Alpine Lakes, and Noisy–Diobsud wildernesses. (425) 783-6000. www.fs.usda.gov/mbs **A5–F6**
Padilla Bay National Estuarine Research Reserve Stopover for migratory birds. Interpretive center has educational displays, games, hands-on activities, and hiking trails. (360) 428-1558. www.padillabay.gov **C3**
Protection Island National Wildlife Refuge Refuge for thousands of birds including puffins, black oyster-catchers, and rhinoceros auklets. View by boat only, at least 200 yards from shore. (360) 457-8451. **E2**
San Juan Islands National Wildlife Refuge Observe wildlife by boat or ferry on 83 protected islands which serve as nesting areas for cormorants, puffins, and numerous shore birds. (360) 457-8451 www.fws.gov **B1–C2**
Skagit Wildlife Area Nesting and wintering area for numerous species of ducks, snow geese, and whistling swans. Off Skagit Bay. (360) 445-4441. **D3**
Tahuya State Forest 23,000-acre working forest. Offers camping, hiking, hunting, and boating. On the Tahuya Peninsula. (360) 825-1631. **G1**

Ski Areas ⛷

Mount Baker 8 lifts, 38 runs. Snowboarding, downhill, and nordic skiing. E of Bellingham. (360) 734-6771. Snow ph: (360) 671-0211 www.mtbaker.us **A6**

Boating & Fishing 🐟🚤

Admiralty Inlet Boat ramps are located at Fort Flagler and Fort Worden state parks. Chinook and coho salmon, halibut and various species of rockfish may be caught in this area. **E2**
Cascadia Marine Trail Kayak water trail, with camp sites, from Olympia to Point Roberts. Boating difficulty varies from easy to difficult. (206) 545-9161 (Wash. Water Trails Assoc.). www.wwta.org **A1–H3**
Lake Whatcom Boat ramp available at the city park at north end of lake. Fish for kokanee, cutthroat trout, and smallmouth bass. **B4**
Samish River Fish for fall coho, chinook salmon, and winter steelhead. **C4**
San Juan Islands Marine Area Fish for varieties of salmon, halibut, and rockfish. Boat ramps and moorage available. (360) 376-2073 (North of Orcas Island) and (360) 387-2044 (South of San Juan Island). **B1–C2**
Silver Lake Lake is stocked with rainbow trout annually. Fish for cutthroat. Occasionally a brook trout is caught. (360) 599-2776. **A5**

Ferries ★

San Juan Islands Shuttle Express Seasonal passenger ferry service from Bellingham to Orcas and San Juan Islands. Bellingham Cruise Terminal. 888-373-8522 or (360) 671-1137. www.orcawhales.com. **B3**
Victoria–San Juan Cruises Passenger ferry, *Victoria Star II*, runs from Bellingham to Victoria, BC, with stop at Roche Harbor. Bellingham Cruise Terminal. May–Oct. 800-443-4552 or (360) 738-8099. www.whales.com. **B3**
Washington State Ferries State-operated ferries serve the cities and towns in and around the Puget Sound. 888-808-7977 or (206) 464-6400 (Seattle). www.wsdot.wa.gov/ferries. **B3**

Historic Sites & Museums 🏛★

Anacortes Museum Exhibits depicting local and maritime history. Also has a research library. 1305 8th St, Anacortes. (360) 293-1915. **C3**
Ebey's Landing National Historic Reserve Historic area of buildings, farms, and military sites. Coupeville. (360) 678-6084. **D2**
Fairhaven National Historic District Area of preserved historic buildings. Bellingham. (360) 671-3990. www.fairhaven.com **B3**
Gaches Mansion Restored and furnished 1891 Victorian home and La Conner Quilt Museum. 703 2nd St, La Conner. (360) 466-4288. **C3**
Hovander Homestead Park Visit the restored and furnished 1903 house, barn, farm, zoo, and gardens. Nielsen Ave, Ferndale. (360) 384-3444. **B2**
Island County Museum Exhibits illustrating farming in the 1800s. Front and Alexander streets, Coupeville. (360) 678-3310. www.islandhistory.org **D2**
Lake Stevens Historical Museum Exhibits and photographs of area history. 124th Ave, Lake Stevens. (425) 334-1012. **E5**
Maritime Heritage Center Location of 1852 sawmill and a fish hatchery. 1600 C St, Bellingham. (360) 778-7195 **A2**
Northwest Railway Museum A collection of rail cars. Located at the Northern Pacific Snoqualmie Depot built in 1890. Railroad Ave and King St, Snoqualmie. (425) 888-3030. www.trainmuseum.org. **G5**
Orcas Island Historical Museum Exhibits about early island history. North Beach Rd, Eastbound. (360) 376-4849. www.orcasmuseum.org **B2**
Pioneer Park Thirteen log buildings dating 1870–1895. Cherry St, Ferndale. (360) 384-6461. www.ferndaleheritagesociety.com **A2**
Roeder House Built between 1903 and 1908. Tours available. Home of a cultural arts center. 2600 Sunset Drive, Bellingham. (360) 733-2900. **B3**
San Juan Historical Museum A collection of pioneer and "Pig War" memorabilia housed in a 2-story farmhouse. 405 Price St, Friday Harbor. (360) 378-3949. www.sjmuseum.org. **C1**
Skagit County Historical Museum Vintage farm implements and logging equipment. 501 S 4th St, La Conner. (360) 466-3365. www.skagitcounty.net **C3**
Whatcom Museum of History and Art Historic buildings with exhibits depicting regional history and displays of tools, toys, and clothing from the Victorian age. 121 Prospect St, Bellingham. (360) 778-8930. www.whatcommuseum.org **B3**

Notable Towns ○ ◉

Lynden An historic Dutch Village with a full-size windmill. Visit the Lynden Pioneer Museum and Berthusen Park. (360) 354-5995 (C of C). **A3**
Mt Vernon Commercial center for one of the largest bulb-growing regions in the nation. See Roozengaarde bulb garden, La Conner Flats Display Garden and West Shore Acres. (360) 248-8547 (C of C). **C4**
Port Townsend A National Historic Landmark. See St Paul's Church, the Rothschild House, Jefferson County Courthouse, and Jefferson County Historical Museum. (360) 385-2722 (C of C) **E2**

Other Attractions ★🏛

International Peace Arch Park Location of the Peace Arch built in the 1920s. Day use only. In Blaine. (360) 332-7165. www.peacearchpark.org **A2**
Lake Whatcom Railway Tour the countryside on a steam-powered train. N.P. Rd, Wickersham. (360) 441-0719. www.lakewhatcomrailway.com **B4**
Nooksack River Casino 5048 Mt Baker Hwy, Deming. 877-935-9300 or (360) 592-5472. www.nooksackcasino.com. **B4**
Sehome Hill Arboretum 165-acre reserve with 2 miles of trails to browse through the displays of native plants. Bellingham. (360) 778-7000. **B3**
Skagit Valley Casino Resort 5984 Darrk Ln, Bow. 877-275-2448 or (360) 724-7777. www.theskagit.com. **C4**
Swinomish Casino and Lodge 12885 Casino Dr, Anacortes. 888-288-8883. www.swinomishcasinoandlodge.com **C3**
Tennant Lake Natural History Interpretive Center Displays and nature walks around a bog. The Fragrance Garden, a section designed for the visually impaired, displays plants with distinctive smells and textures that are signed in Braille. Nielson Rd, Ferndale. (360) 384-3064. **A3**
Tulalip Casino 10200 Quil Ceda Blvd, Marysville. (360) 716-7162. www.tulalipcasino.com **E4**
Wenberg County Park Camping, swimming, boating, and fishing. Northwest of Everett, on Lake Goodwin. (425) 388-6600. **E4**
WT Preston A museum in a retired sternwheeler snag boat, used to clear logjams from Puget Sound. 7th St and R Ave, Anacortes. (360) 293-1915. **C3**

Information Resources

Highway Information and Mountain Pass Report
Dial 511 or 800-695-7623. www.wsdot.wa.gov
Mt Baker–Snoqualmie National Forest Headquarters
2930 Wetmore Ave, Suite 3A, Everett 98201. (425) 783-6000. www.fs.usda.gov/mbs
- **Darrington Ranger District Office**
  1405 Emens Ave N, Darrington 98241. (360) 436-1155
- **Mt Baker Ranger District Office**
  810 State Route 20, Sedro-Woolley 98284. (360) 856-5700 ext. 515
- **Skykomish Ranger District Office**
  74920 NE Stevens Pass Hwy, Skykomish 98288. (360) 677-2414
- **Snoqualmie Ranger District, North Bend Office**
  902 SE North Bend Wy, North Bend 98045. (425) 888-1421

National Recreation Reservation Service
Reservations for selected campgrounds. 877-444-6777 www.recreation.gov
Olympic National Forest Headquarters
1835 SW Black Lake Blvd, Olympia 98512. (360) 956-2402 www.fs.usda.gov/olympic
- **Hood Canal Ranger District Office**
  295142 Hwy 101 S, Quilcene 98376. (360) 765-2200

Outdoor Recreation Information Center, USFS/NPS
222 Yale Ave N (inside REI), Seattle 98109. (206) 470-4060
Washington Department of Natural Resources
- **Northwest Region Office**
  919 North Township St, Sedro-Woolley 98284. (360) 856-3500 www.dnr.wa.gov
- **South Puget Sound Region Office**
  950 Farman Ave N, Enumclaw 98022. (360) 825-1631

Washington State Parks Information Center
(360) 902-8844, 888-226-7688. www.parks.wa.gov
(360) 902-8555 (Boaters Guide)
(360) 902-8600 (Environmental Learning Centers)
(360) 902-8684 (Snopark and Winter Recreation Info)

Hunting & Fishing

Washington Department of Fish and Wildlife, North Puget Sound Region 4
16018 Mill Creek Blvd, Mill Creek 98012. (425) 775-1311. wdfw.wa.gov
See map on page 29

Campgrounds & RV Parks ▲🚐

See page **34** for campground and RV park information.
See pages **32** and **33** for recreation information for the Seattle area.

Climate

See explanation on page 31

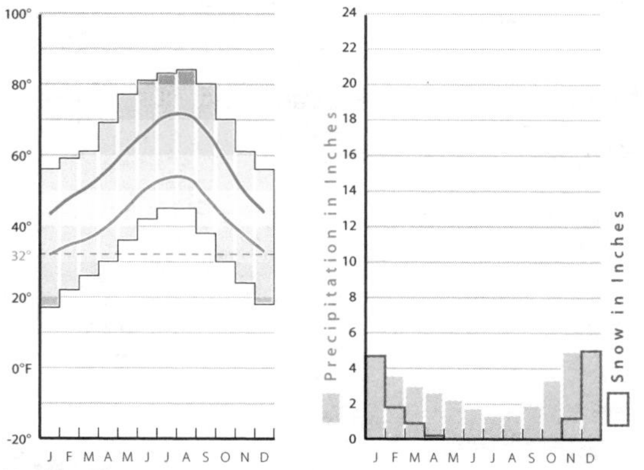

Bellingham: el. 148 ft — 74 days with 36" precipitation, 14" of snow, 63 nights below freezing, 1 day above 90°

Jan	(17°) 32°–43° (56°)	**Apr**	(30°) 40°–56° (69°)
July	(45°) 53°–71° (83°)	**Oct**	(30°) 42°–58° (70°)

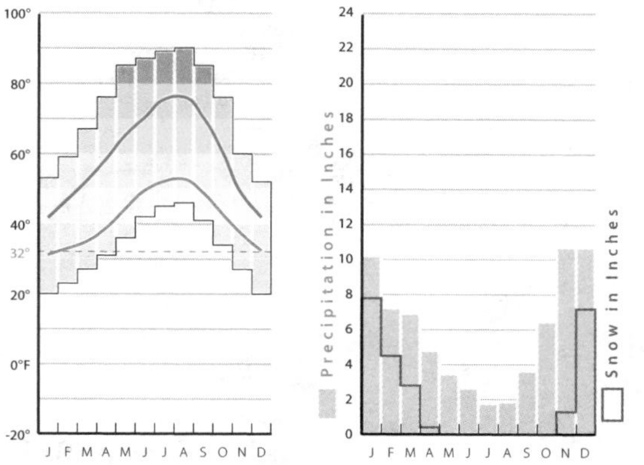

Concrete: el. 193 ft — 132 days with 71" precipitation, 24" of snow, 62 nights below freezing, 4 days above 90°

Jan	(20°) 31°–42° (53°)	**Apr**	(31°) 39°–58° (76°)
July	(45°) 52°–75° (89°)	**Oct**	(34°) 43°–60° (76°)

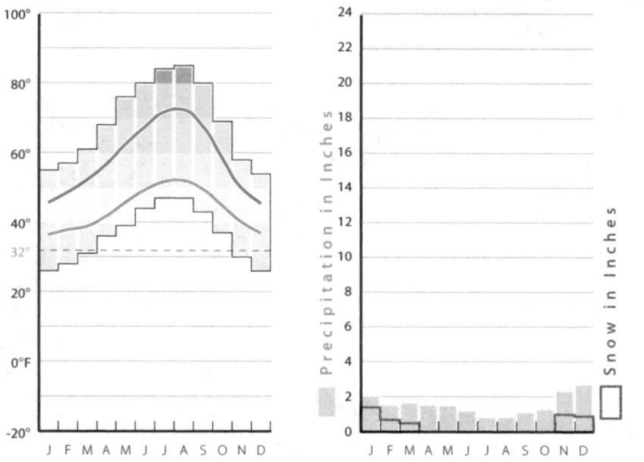

Port Townsend: el. 98 ft — 60 days with 19" precipitation, 5" of snow, 21 nights below freezing, 1 day above 90°

Jan	(26°) 37°–46° (55°)	**Apr**	(36°) 42°–57° (68°)
July	(47°) 52°–72° (84°)	**Oct**	(37°) 45°–59° (69°)

Landscape Page Index

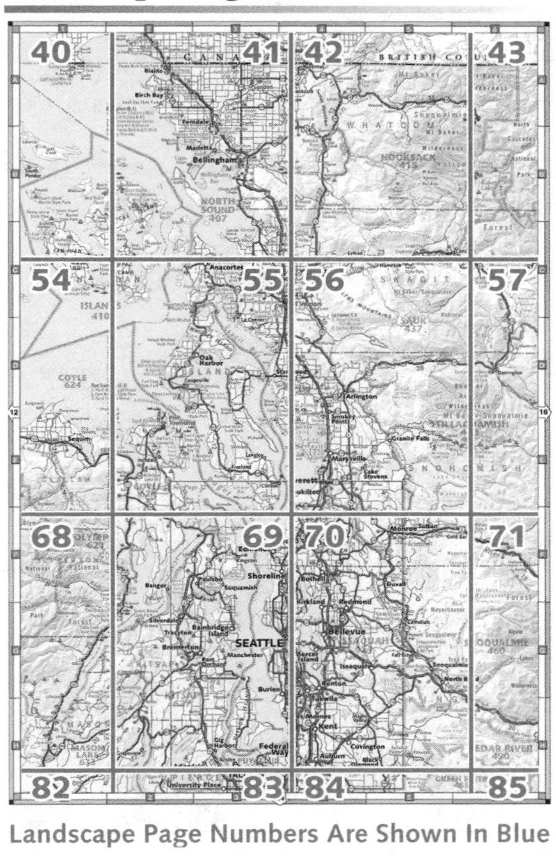

Landscape Page Numbers Are Shown In Blue

RECREATION

RECREATION

Wilderness
State Parks
Bureau of Reclamation
Bureau of Land Management
National Parks/ Monuments
State Game Management Unit

Forest Service
State Lands
Military Lands
Tribal Lands
Wildlife Areas

HOKO 601

Scale 1:600,000

© BENCHMARK MAPS

State & National Parks and Recreation Areas ▲★

Daroga State Park Camping, picnicking, and boat launching. North of Entiat on US 97. (509) 664-6380. **F6**
Lake Chelan National Recreation Area Accessible by boat or ferry. Ferry runs from the town of Chelan to Stehekin daily in the summer and on a limited schedule during the winter. Northeast of Wenatchee. (360) 854-7200. **C3–D4**
Lake Wenatchee State Park Camping, picnicking, hiking, fishing, and cross-country skiing trails. North of Leavenworth off US 2. (509) 763-3101. **F3**
Lincoln Rock State Park Camping, picnicking, and hiking. North of Wenatchee on US 2. (509) 884-8702. **G5**
North Cascades National Park 684,000 acres of high cascade country, from the Canadian border to Lake Chelan NRA. East of Concrete off State Rte 20. (360) 854-7200. **A1–C3**
Pearrygin Lake State Park Camping, fishing, boating, and snowmobiling. Northeast of Winthrop. (509) 996-2370. **C6**
Peshastin Pinnacles State Park Day use area with hiking. 2 miles west of Cashmere. (509) 884-8702. **G4**
Rockport State Park Old growth forest with intact ecosystem. West of Rockport on State Rte 20. (360) 902-8844. **C1**
Ross Lake National Recreation Area Camping, boating, and fishing. Northeast of Concrete on State Rte 20. (360) 854-7200. **A2**
Squilchuck State Park Group camping, hiking, mountain biking, and cross-country skiing. Southwest of Wenatchee. (509) 664-6373. **H5**
Twenty-Five Mile Creek State Park Camping, picnicking, and boat launching. Northwest of Chelan. (509) 687-3610. **E5**
Wenatchee Confluence State Park Camping, picnicking, hiking boat launching. North of Wenatchee on US 2. (509) 664-6373. **G5**

Forests & Wildlife Areas 🚶🦅

Chelan Butte Wildlife Area Hiking and hunting in 9,000 acres of state-managed land. South of Chelan State Park. (509) 686-3383. **F6**
Entiat Wildlife Area Hiking and hunting in state-managed area. Northwest of Entiat. (509) 686-3383. **G5–F6**
Mount Baker–Snoqualmie National Forest Includes all or portions of Mt Baker, Noisy-Diobsud, Glacier Peak, Henry M Jackson, Boulder River, Wild Sky, and Alpine Lakes wildernesses. (425) 783-6000. www.fs.usda.gov/mbs **A5–E6**
Okanogan–Wenatchee National Forest Located on the eastern slopes of the Cascade Range. Includes all or portions of Pasayten, Lake Chelan–Sawtooth, Glacier Peak, Henry M Jackson, and Alpine Lakes wildernesses. (509) 664-9200. **A1–C4**
Skagit River Bald Eagle Natural Area An area to observe bald eagles during the fall and winter months. East of Rockport. (360) 445-4441. **C1**
Swakane Wildlife Area Home to a herd of bighorn sheep. Hiking and hunting in state-managed area. Southwest of Entiat. (509) 686-3383. **G5**

Ski Areas & Snoparks ⛷❄

Badger Mountain 5 downhill runs, cross-country skiing, and snowshoeing. Only open weekends and holidays. SW of Waterville. (509) 745-8273. www.skibadgermt.com **G6**
Blewett Pass Snopark Area offers over 57 miles of snowmobiling and cross-country ski trails. On US 97, South of Leavenworth. (509) 674-4411. **H4**
Leavenworth Ski Hill Downhill and cross-country skiing with groomed trails. North of Leavenworth. (509) 548-5477 (Leavenworth Winter Sports Club). www.skileavenworth.com **G4**
Methow Valley 120 miles of groomed cross-country trails with varying degrees of difficulty, from easy to advanced. (509) 996-3287 (Methow Valley Sport Trails Association). Trail report: 800-682-5787. www.mvsta.com **C5**
Mission Ridge 35 runs on over 2,000 acres. SW of Wenatchee. (509) 663-6543. Snow phone: (509) 663-3200. www.missionridge.com **H5**
Salmon La Sac Snopark Snowmobiling and cross-country skiing. North of Cle Elum Lake. (509) 852-1100 (Cle Elum Ranger District). **H3**
Stevens Pass 37 runs, 15.5 miles of cross-country trails. Offering snowboarding and night skiing. Northwest of Leavenworth, on US 2. (206) 812-4510. Snow phone: (206) 634-1645. www.stevenspass.com **F3**
The Summit at Snoqualmie 4 ski areas with 65 downhill runs, groomed cross-country trails, terrain parks, and tubing center. Night skiing and snowboarding. (425) 434-7669. Snow phone: (206) 236-1600. www.summit-at-snoqualmie.com **H1**

River Rafting 🛶

Methow River Two sections of this river can be rafted. The first 10 miles is a Class II run. The lower section is an intermediate to advanced run with numerous Class III rapids. Commercial guide service available. **C5**
Middle Fork Snoqualmie River Two sections of the Middle Fork are rafted. The upper section, Taylor River to Concrete Bridge, is a Class II run. Below the bridge to Tanner is an advanced river run with many Class III rapids. Commercial guide services are available. **G1**
North Fork Skykomish River Run begins at Galena and ends at Index. This river run is for experienced boaters only. Commercial guide services are available. **F1**
Sauk River Raft from Bedal Campground to the White Chuck River, a Class III run. From the White Chuck River to Darrington is a more technical run for experienced boaters. Logjams are a hazard on both sections. Commercial raft guides are available. **D1**
Skagit River The upper section of the Skagit River, from Goodell Creek to Copper Creek, is a Class II run. Below Copper Creek to Rockport is an easier run. Commercial guides are available. Area known for fall and winter bald eagle watching. **C1**
Skykomish River From Index to Gold Bar is Class III run with one Class IV rapid. Commercial guide service available. **F1**
Wenatchee River Raft the upper section, Lake Wenatchee to US 2, a Class II run, and the lower section, Leavenworth to Monitor, a Class III run. Commercial guide service available for the lower section. **G4**

Boating & Fishing 🐟🚤

Fish Lake Boat launching and rentals available. Fish for rainbow and brown trout as well as largemouth and smallmouth bass. **F4**
Lake Chelan Known for water skiing. Fish for chinook salmon, rainbow trout, kokanee, and turbot, a freshwater lingcod. Several boat ramps. **E4**
Lake Wenatchee Boat ramps at the state park and Glacier View Campground. Waterskiing, canoeing, and fishing. Fish for kokanee and sockeye salmon. **F4**
Methow River Known for fly fishing for steelhead and trout. **C5**
Pearrygin Lake Known for good trout fishing. **C6**
Ross Lake Fish for rainbow trout primarily; however, Dolly Varden (must be released), cutthroat, and brook trout are also caught here. Boat ramp at north end of lake. Boat rentals available at Ross Lake Resort. **A3**
Wapato Lake Known for spring trout fishing. There are also largemouth bass, crappie, and bluegill. A public boat ramp is available. **E6**

Ferries ★

Lake Chelan Boat Company *The Lady of the Lake II* and the *Lake Express* provide passenger service to Stehekin. The *Lady of the Lake II* has scheduled stops at Field's Point and Lucerne, and flags stops, when water levels permit, at Manson, Prince Creek and Moore Point. US 97A, Chelan. (509) 682-4584. www.ladyofthelake.com. **F6**

Natural Wonders 🔭

Lake Chelan Occupying a glacier-carved valley, 55 miles long. One of the deepest lakes in the continental US. The deepest point in the lake is below sea level. North of US 97A. E5
Rainbow Falls Tour bus provides transportation to the 312-ft falls. 3.5 miles from Stehekin. D4
Trail of the Cedars A self-guided interpretive trail through old-growth cedar forest. Newhalem. B2

Historic Sites & Museums ★🏛

Blewett Site of an arrastra, a water-powered gold ore–grinding device used from 1861 to 1880. 10 mi south of US 2 on US 97. **H4**
Cashmere Museum and Pioneer Village Museum houses an extensive collection of Native American artifacts. The village is comprised of restored and furnished pioneer buildings. 600 Cotlets Way, Cashmere. (509) 782-3230. **G4**
Lake Chelan Museum Exhibits of historic memorabilia including collection of apple box labels. Woodin Ave, Chelan. (509) 682-5644. **F6**
North Cascades Smokejumper Base Active base for fire suppression efforts in the Northwest. Tours focus on the base, program history, and equipment. Methow Valley is considered the birthplace of smokejumping, which began here in 1939. South of Winthrop. (509) 997-9750. **H5**
Wenatchee Valley Museum & Cultural Center Displays and exhibits illustrate pioneer and Native American life in the region. 127 S Mission, Wenatchee. (509) 888-6240. www.wenatcheewa.gov **H5**
Shafer Museum Collection of historic buildings; including a log cabin built in 1897, a print shop, and general store. Displays of mining and farming equipment. Winthrop. (509) 996-2712. www.shafermuseum.com **C6**

Notable Towns ○ ◉

Winthrop A restored, historic town surrounded by national forest. With numerous year-round outdoor activities to enjoy, including skiing, rafting, and hiking. (509) 996-2125. www.winthropwashington.com. **C5**

Other Attractions ★🚶🏛

Hyak Lodge Remodeled bunkhouse serves as overnight accommodations and conference center. Snoqualmie Pass. (425) 434-5955. **H1**
Ladder Creek Falls and Garden A nature walk through a garden, started in the 1920s, of native plants set along pools and falls of Ladder Creek. Newhalem. (206) 386-4495. **B2**
Mill Bay Casino 455 Wapato Lake Rd, Manson. 800-648-2946 or (509) 687-6911. www.colvillecasinos.com. **F6**
Ohme Gardens Rocky bluffs are the backdrop for these alpine gardens. Paths wind through the park of meadows, ponds, and lush rain forest. N of Wenatchee on Alt US 97. (509) 662-5785. www.ohmegardens.com **G5**
Rocky Reach Dam Tour the dam and see exhibits on development of electricity on the Columbia River. Watch the migrating fish from the fish ladder viewpoint. North of Wenatchee on Alt US 97. (509) 663-7522. **G5**
Skagit Tours Tour of the Skagit River Project, which generates electricity for the city of Seattle. Tour includes visit to the generating facilities, a ride on an incline railway, and a boat cruise. Diablo. (360) 854-2589. **B2**
Slidewaters Water slides, spa, swimming pool, and arcade games. 102 Waterslide Dr, Chelan. (509) 682-5751. www.slidewaterswaterpark.com. **F6**
Snoqualmie Tunnel A 2.3-mile-long railway tunnel built between 1913 and 1914. Upon completion this was the world's longest electrified railway tunnel. Accessible by foot or bicycle. Bring a light source. Open May 1 to Nov 1. **H2**
Steam Locomotive A 1928-built steam engine. Used by Seattle City Light Railway. Newhalem. **B2**
Washington State Apple Commission Visitor's Center Free juice and apple tasting as well as displays and a video illustrating the development of the apple-growing industry in the state. 2900 Euclid Ave, Wenatchee. (509) 663-9600. www.bestapples.com **H5**

Information Resources

Bureau of Land Management, Wenatchee Field Office
915 North Walla Walla, Wenatchee 98801. (509) 665-2100
National Recreation Reservation Service
Reservations for selected campgrounds. 877-444-6777
www.recreation.gov
Highway Information and Mountain Pass Report
Dial 511 or 800-695-7623. www.wsdot.wa.gov
Mt Baker–Snoqualmie National Forest Headquarters
2930 Wetmore Ave, Suite 3a, Everett 98201. (425) 783-6000
www.fs.usda.gov/mbs
- **Darrington Ranger District Office**
  1405 Emens Ave N, Darrington 98241. (360) 436-1155
- **Skykomish Ranger District Office**
  74920 NE Stevens Pass Hwy, Skykomish 98288. (360) 677-2414
- **Snoqualmie Ranger District, Enumclaw Office**
  450 Roosevelt Av E, Enumclaw 98022. (360) 825-6585
  (425) 434-6111 Snoqualmie Pass Visitor Center

North Cascades National Park, Ross Lake and Lake Chelan NRA/ Mt Baker Ranger District Office
810 State Route 20, Sedro-Woolley 98284. (360) 854-7200
www.nps.gov/noca
- **North Cascades Visitor Center**
  502 Newhalem St, Newhalem 98283. (206) 386-4495
- **Wilderness Information Center**
  7280 Ranger Station Rd, Marblemount 98267. (360) 854-7245

Northwest Weather and Avalanche Center
7600 Sandpoint Wy NE, Seattle 98115. (206) 526-6677
Recorded message Oct 1-Apr 15. www.nwac.us
Okanogan–Wenatchee National Forest Headquarters
215 Melody Ln, Wenatchee 98801. (509) 664-9200.
www.fs.usda.gov/okawen
- **Chelan Ranger District Office**
  428 West Woodin Av, Chelan 98816. (509) 682-4900
- **Cle Elum Ranger District Office**
  803 W 2nd St, Cle Elum 98922. (509) 852-1100
- **Entiat Ranger District Office**
  2108 Entiat Wy, Entiat 98822. (509) 784-4700
- **Methow Valley Ranger District Office**
  24 W Chewuch Rd, Winthrop 98862. (509) 996-4003
  (509) 996-4000 Visitor Information Center, Hwy 20 (Summer only)
- **Naches Ranger District Office**
  10237 Hwy 12, Naches 98937. (509) 653-1401
- **Tonasket Ranger District Office**
  1 West Winesap, Tonasket 98855. (509) 486-2186
- **Wenatchee River Ranger District Office**
  600 Sherbourne, Leavenworth 98826. (509) 548-2550

Pacific Northwest Ski Areas Association
PO Box 758, La Conner 98257 877-533-5520. www.pnsaa.org
Washington State Parks Information Center & Campground Reservations
(360) 902-8844, 888-226-7688 www.parks.wa.gov
(360) 902-8555 (Boaters Guide)
(360) 902-8600 (Environmental Learning Centers)
(360) 902-8684 (Sno-park and Winter Recreation Info)

Hunting & Fishing

Washington Department of Fish and Wildlife, North Central Region 2
1550 Alder St NW, Ephrata 98823. (509) 754-4624. wdfw.wa.gov
Washington Department of Fish and Wildlife, Wenatchee District Office
3860 Chelan Hwy North, Wenatchee 98801. (509) 662-0452
See map on page 29.

Campgrounds & RV Parks ▲🚐

See page 34 for campground and RV park information.

Climate

See Explanation on page 31.

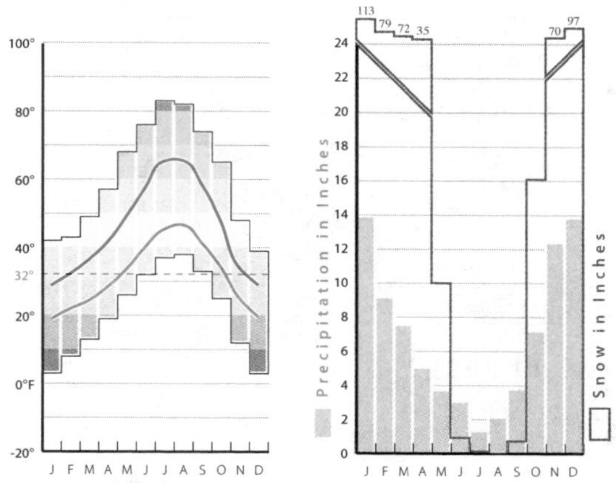

Stevens Pass: 138 days with 83" precipitation, 493" of snow,
el. 4072 ft — 199 nights below freezing, 0 days above 90°

Jan	(3°) 19°–29° (42°)	Apr	(19°) 28°–42° (57°)
July	(37°) 45°–65° (83°)	Oct	(25°) 34°–48° (65°)

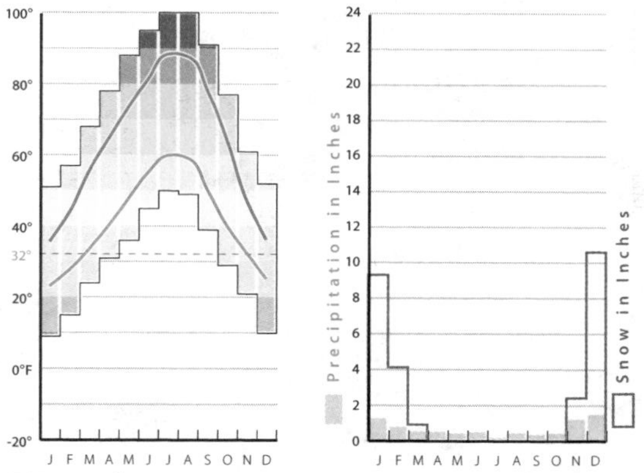

Wenatchee: 28 days with 9" precipitation, 27" of snow,
el. 640 ft — 110 nights below freezing, 37 days above 90°

Jan	(9°) 23°–36° (51°)	Apr	(31°) 40°–65° (78°)
July	(50°) 60°–88° (100°)	Oct	(29°) 40°–64° (77°)

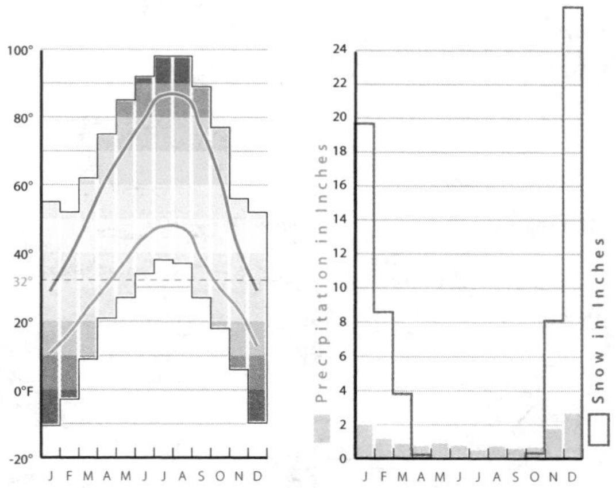

Winthrop: 43 days with 14" precipitation, 67" of snow,
el. 1755 ft — 197 nights below freezing, 31 days above 90°

Jan	(-12°) 11°–29° (43°)	Apr	(21°) 30°–62° (75°)
July	(38°) 48°–86° (98°)	Oct	(18°) 30°–62° (77°)

Landscape Page Index

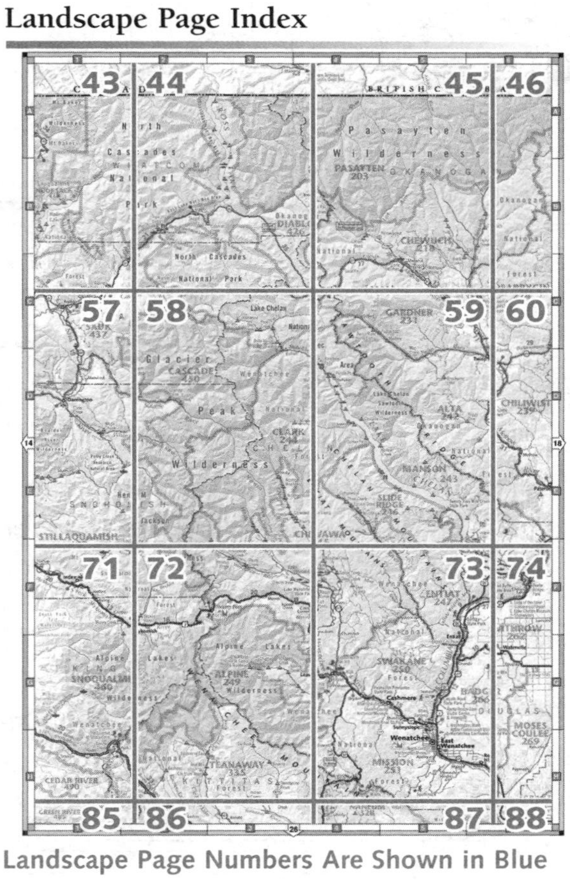

Landscape Page Numbers Are Shown in Blue

RECREATION

Wilderness | State Parks | Bureau of Reclamation | Bureau of Land Management | National Parks/Monuments | State Game Management Unit

Forest Service | State Lands | Military Lands | Tribal Lands | Wildlife Areas | HOKO 601

RECREATION

CANADA — BRITISH COLUMBIA

Pasayten Wilderness
PASAYTEN 203

Osoyoos Lake

Chopaka
Nighthawk
Oroville
Veteran's Memorial Park
River Oaks RV Resort
Osoyoos-Wenatchee National Forest
Okanogan-Wenatchee National Forest
Sun-Cove Resort & Guest Ranch
Cordell
Sonora Point
Enterprise

Bridesville
Rock Creek
Kettle Valley
West Midway
Midway
Myncaster
Boundary Falls
Anaconda
Grand Forks
West Grand Forks

Old Molson Museum
Molson
Molson School Museum
Chesaw WA
Chesaw
Toroda
Danville

Okanogan
Big Tree Botanical Area
Sitzmark Ski Area
Beth Lake
Lost Lake
Beaver Lake
Bodie
Empire Lake
Malo
Karamin

Deer Creek Nordic Snopark

SHERMAN 101

Loomis
Palmer Lake
North Fork Ninemile
Loomis
State SINLAHEKIN 215 Forest
Sinlahekin Wildlife Area
Spectacle Lake Resort
WANNACUT 209

Okanogan
CHEWUCH 218

Wenatchee National

PEARRYGIN 224

Havillah
Hishlands Cross-Country Snopark
Mt Bonaparte Lookout
Bonaparte Lake
Old Toroda

Wenatchee
Wauconda

OKANOGAN EAST 204

National Forest

Pollard
Black Beach Resort
Curlew Lake State Park
Torboy

Republic
Winchester
Sanpoil River Canyon
Nine Mile Falls
White Mtn Fire Interpretive Site
Sherman Pass Overlook

FERRY

Tonasket
Janis
Barker
Kerr
Oriole
Aeneas
Swan Lake
Long Lake
West Fork

Conconully
Conconully Lake
Conconully SP
Scotch Creek Wildlife Area
Margie's
Glenwood
Riverside
Brown Lake
Synarep
Crawfish Lake

National Forest
Methow Wildlife Area

POGUE 233
Pogue Mtn Wildlife Area
Omak
Cherokee
Eastside Park
Earl Precht Memorial RV
Okanogan Co Historical Mus
Legion City Park
SR 215
Okanogan
Okanogan Fairgrounds
Okanogan Bingo-Casino
St Marys Mission
Disautel

Colville

Indian

Loup Loup Ski Bowl
Loup Loup State Forest
Leader Lake
Twisp

Chilliwist
Chilliwist Wildlife Area
Malott
Omak Lake

Coyote Creek Rest Area

Reservation

CHILIWIST 239

Carlton

TIMENTWA FLAT

Nespelem
Colville Indian Agency
Buffalo Lake
Keller

GOLD MOUNTAIN RIDGE

Methow
Indian Dan Wildlife Area
Brewster
Columbia Cove
Fort Okanogan Interpretive Center

ALTA 242
Alta Lake State Park
Echo Valley Ski Area

Wenatchee National Forest

Pateros
Central Ferry Wildlife Area
Rocky Butte
Chief Joseph Park
Bridgeport State Park
Bridgeport
Chief Joseph Dam
Azwell

COLUMBIA RIVER

FOSTER CREEK 260

BIGBEND 248
Leahy

Grand Coulee RV Parks:
The King's Court RV
Coulee Playland Resort
Lakeview Terrace RV
Grand Coulee RV
Coulee Dam Casino
Koontzville
Belvedere
Seaton's Grove
Elmer City
Coulee Dam
Grand Coulee
Electric City
Banks Lake
Sun Banks Resort
Osborne
Steamboat Rock State Park
Spring Canyon

Franklin D Roosevelt Lake
Keller Ferry
The River Rue

National Recreation Area

CHELAN MANSON 243
Lake Chelan
Chelan
Lakeside
Chelan Falls
Chelan Butte Wildlife Area
Beebe

DOUGLAS

Mansfield
Sims Corner
Mold

Sherman
Lincoln

ROOSEVELT 133
Country Lane
Wilbur
Creston
Bell

WITHROW 262
Lamoine
Touhey
SAINT ANDREWS 254
St Andrews
Withrow
Withrow Moraine

Hanson
Hartline
Almira
Govan
Telford

LINCOLN

Swanson Lake Wildlife Area

Waterville
Supplee
Douglas
Farmer
Farmer

Banks Lake Wildlife Area

HARRINGTON 136

Badger Mtn Ski Area
BADGER 266
Alstown

Dry Falls Vis'Ctr
Coulee City
Coulee City Park
Sun Lakes-Dry Falls SP
Sun Lakes Park
Laurent's Sun Village Resort
Coulee Lodge Resort

BEEZLEY 272

MOSES COULEE 269

McCarteney
Blue Lake Resort
Lake Lenore Caves
Lenore Lake
Blue Lake

Columbia Basin WA

Billy Clapp Lake
Basin WA (Stratford Unit)
Wilson Creek

Crab Creek
Marlin

CHANNELED SCABLANDS

Palisades

Adco
Stratford
NCB SWA

Earl

Downs
Lamona
Nemo

GRANT

Rock Island
Appledale

Soap Lake
Lakeview Park
Grant County Historical Museum
Gloyd Seeps Wildlife Area

Odessa

Sylvan Lake

BEEZLEY 272
Colockum Wildlife Area
Ephrata
Oasis RV Park & Golf
Crater

MOSES COULEE HILLS
BEEZLEY HILLS

Quincy
Winchester
Batum
Jantz
Marcellus

© BENCHMARK MAPS

Scale 1:600,000

0 5 10 15 20 25 30 40 50 Miles

0 5 10 15 20 25 30 40 50 Kilometers

State & National Parks and Recreation Areas

Alta Lake State Park Camping, picnicking, hiking, water sports, and boat launch. Golfing nearby. Southwest of Pateros. (509) 923-2473. **E1**

Bridgeport State Park Camping, picnicking, and boat launch. Hiking trail to overlook. Northeast of Bridgeport on State Rte 17. (509) 686-7231. **E2**

Conconully State Park Camping, nature trail. Open weekends during off season. Dates back to 1910. NW of Omak on US 97. (509) 826-7408. **C2**

Curlew Lake State Park Camping, hiking, mountain biking, and wildlife viewing. In an area once an Indian campground. North of Republic. (509) 775-3592. **B5**

Lake Roosevelt National Recreation Area Camping, boating, fishing, water-skiing, and picnicking. North shore of the lake controlled by Colville Indian Res. Visitor Stations at Coulee Dam, and Spring Cyn. (509) 754-7800. **F5–F6**

Steamboat Rock State Park Camping, picnicking, hiking, mountain biking, horseback riding, and boat launching. South of Grand Coulee on State Rte 155. (509) 633-1304. **F4**

Sun Lakes–Dry Falls State Park Camping, picnicking, hiking, mountain biking, and boating. Dry Falls Visitor's Center includes exhibits on the formation of Grand Coulee. SW of Coulee City. (509) 632-5583. **G3**

Forests & Wildlife Areas

Columbia Basin Wildlife Area Northern extent of the wildlife area. Diverse landscape, including canyons, channeled scablands, and sand dunes. (509) 765-6641. www.wdfw.wa.gov **G3**

Colville National Forest Includes the Salmo–Priest Wilderness. Located in northeastern corner of the state. (509) 684-7000. **A6-C6**

Gloyd Seeps Wildlife Area Area of swamps. Bird watching, hunting, and hiking are some of the options here. West of Ephrata. (509) 765-6641. **H3**

Loomis and Loup Loup State Forests Camping, picnicking, hiking, boating, and fishing. North and West of Okanogan. (509) 684-7474. **A2**

Okanogan–Wenatchee National Forest On the eastern border of the North Cascades National Park. Includes the Pasayten Wilderness. North-central Washington. (509) 826-3275. www.fs.usda.gov/okawen **A1–C4**

Scotch Creek Wildlife Area Over 23,000 acres of sharp-tailed grouse and other bird species habitat. Boat launch available. (509) 826-4430. **C2**

Sinlahekin Wildlife Area Created in 1939, it is the oldest wildlife area in Washington. Winter range area for mule deer on a strip of state land in Sinlahekin Valley. South of Loomis. (509) 223-3358. **B2–C2**

Ski Areas & Snoparks

Deer Creek Nordic Snopark 6 miles of groomed cross-country trails. E of Curlew on FS Rd 61. (509) 775-7400. www.parks.wa.gov **A6**

Echo Valley Ski Area Downhill skiing, snow tubing, and more than 17 miles of cross-country trails. Day Lodge. NW of Chelan on Boyd District Road. (509) 687-3167 or (509) 682-3503. www.echovalley.org **E1**

Highlands Snopark Groomed cross-country ski trails, 15-space snopark. NE of Tonasket on FS Rd 3230. (509) 486-2186. **B3**

Loup Loup Ski Bowl 10 runs, 2 lifts for downhill skiing. 18 miles of nordic ski trails. E of Twisp on State Rte 20. (509) 557-3401. www.skitheloup.com **C1**

Sitzmark 19 downhill runs and 14 miles of cross-country ski trails. NE of Tonasket on Nealy Rd. (509) 485-3323. **A4**

Boating & Fishing

Banks Lake Water-skiing, swimming, and fishing are options here. Fish for largemouth and smallmouth bass, walleye, crappie, and trout. Between Coulee City and Grand Coulee. www.wdfw.wa.gov **G3**

Bonaparte Lake Good fishing for mackinaw. Rainbow trout and kokanee are also caught here. Public boat ramp at Bonaparte Lake Campground. Northeast of Tonasket off State Rte 20. **B4**

Conconully Lake Good fishing for rainbow trout in the spring. Boat ramps, boat rentals, and campgrounds are available. NW of Okanogan. **C2**

Curlew Lake Canoeing, fishing, and camping are options here. Good fishing for rainbow trout and largemouth bass. Boat ramps, boat rentals, and campgrounds are available around the lake. N of Republic on State Rte 21. **B5**

Omak Lake Boating, fishing, camping, and water-skiing. Colville Indian Reservation Fishing Permit is required. Known for Lahontan cutthroat trout. Colville Indian Reservation. (509) 634-8845. **D3**

Lake Roosevelt Numerous campgrounds and boat launches available. Water-skiing, sailboating, canoeing, swimming, and fishing are all available here. Fish for sturgeon, walleye, rainbow trout, and kokanee. East of Coulee Dam. **E4–F6**

Ferries ★

Keller Ferry Free ferry across Lake Roosevelt for those using State Rte 21. The *MV Sanpoil* was launched in 2013. The capacity of the vessel is 20 cars with a maximum vehicle size of 100 feet in length with a gross weight of 105,500 lbs. Ferry operates from 6:00 a.m. to Midnight, every day of the week. On Lake Roosevelt. 888-808-7977. **E5**

Natural Wonders

Big Tree Botanical Area Trail loops through old-growth pine. Off FS Road 32. (509) 486-2186. **A4**

Dry Falls An area of an ancient, post-glacial waterfall 3.5 miles wide and 400 feet high. In Sun Lakes–Dry Falls State Park. (509) 632-5583. **G3**

Empire Lake A vehicle-accessible alpine Lake. On FS Road 2150. **B5**

Nine Mile Falls Roadside viewpoint of falls and trail to a second viewpoint of falls. On FS Road 2053. **C5**

Sanpoil River Canyon Steep-walled canyon strewn with giant boulders. South of Republic on State Route 21. **C5**

Sherman Pass Overlook Scenic interpretive trail depicting the fire history of the area. East of Republic on State Route 20. **C6**

Withrow Moraine & Jameson Lake Drumlin Field Southern limit of the only Ice Age terminal moraine on the Waterville Plateau section of the Columbia Plateau. The drumlin field includes excellent examples of glacially-formed elongated hills.W of Coulee City on US Hwy 2. **G3**

Historic Sites & Museums ★

Fort Okanogan Interpretive Center Picnicking. Exhibits and overlook site of fur trading post on the Columbia River. East of Brewster. (509) 689-6665. **E2**

Grant County Historical Museum and Village Collection of Indian artifacts and turn-of-the-century tools, clothing, and household furnishings. The village is comprised of 29 buildings. 742 Basin St NW, Ephrata. (509) 754-3334. **H3**

Molson School and Old Molson Museums Tour pioneer classrooms, a library, and historic buildings from the 1900s. Molson. (509) 485-3292. **A3**

Okanogan County Historical Museum Local history museum. 1410 2nd Ave N, Okanogan. (509) 422-4272. www.okanoganhistory.org **C2**

Saint Mary's Mission Jesuit mission established in 1886 to minister to the Native Americans of the Colville Federation. East of Omak on Mission Rd. (509) 826-6401. **D3**

Notable Towns ○ ◉

Coulee Dam City is home to Colville Tribal Museum and Coulee Dam Casino. It is the only city in the state partially located in three counties. 800-268-5332 or (509) 633-3074 (Chamber of Commerce). **E5**

Ephrata Known as a horse trading center in the late 1800s, when herds of wild horses were prevalent in the area. In the early 1900s Ephrata became a trade center for ranchers in the area. Today the town's airport is popular with gliders and aerobatic planes. Glider contests are held here annually. Visit the Grant County Pioneer Village and Museum. (509) 754-4656 (Chamber of Commerce) or (509) 754-3334 (Museum). **H2**

Grand Coulee This town sprang into life in 1933 when work on the Grand Coulee Dam began. Thousands came here looking for work during the Depression. The dam is well worth a visit. 800-268-5332 or (509) 633-3074 (Chamber of Commerce). **E4**

Oroville The town gets its name from "oro," the Spanish word for gold. Although mining was important early on, agriculture has played a more important role in the area's economy over time, especially apple and pear orchards. 888-699-5969 (Oroville Chamber of Commerce). **A3**

Other Attractions ★

Chief Joseph Dam Tour the nation's second largest producer of hydroelectric power. East of Bridgeport. (509) 686-5501. **E2**

Chief Joseph Park Day use area with hiking trails and primitive boat launch. No vehicular access. N of Bridgeport off State Rte 173. (509) 686-2473. **E2**

Coulee Dam Casino 515 Birch St, Coulee Dam. 800-556-7492 or (509) 633-0766. www.colvillecasinos.com **E4**

Grand Coulee Dam A massive concrete dam on the Columbia River. Construction, which included two power plants, began in 1933 and was finished in 1942. A third power plant went online in 1974, making it the largest electric power-producing facility in the US. Tours are available. Laser light shows daily, Memorial Day through Labor Day. Visitor center open daily. East of Grand Coulee. (509) 633-9265 (Visitor Arrival Center). **E4**

Lake Lenore Caves Day use area with hiking trails. Site of rock overhang used as a shelter by Native Americans centuries ago. Area of geological and historic interest. North of Soap Lake. (509) 754-4624. **G3**

Mount Bonaparte Lookout Hike various trails to the top of Mount Bonaparte to historic fire lookout. (509) 486-2186. **B4**

Okanogan Bingo Casino 41 Appleway Rd, Okanogan. 800-559-4643 or (509) 422-4646. www.colvillecasinos.com **C3**

Osoyoos Lake Veteran's Memorial Park Camping, picnicking, and boat launch. North of Oroville on US 97. (509) 476-3321. **A3**

White Mountain Fire Interpretive Site Offers views of the 1988 burn area. Hiking and picnicking. East of Republic on State Route 20. **C6**

Information Resources

Colville National Forest Headquarters
765 S Main, Colville 99114. (509) 684-7000. www.fs.usda.gov/colville

Republic Ranger District Office
650 E Delaware Ave, Republic 99166. (509) 775-7400.

Confederated Tribes of the Colville Indian Reservation
888-881-7684 or (509) 634-2200 (Switchboard). www.colvilletribes.com

Fish and Wildlife Department
Nespelem 99155. 800-549-0028 or (509) 634-2110.

Parks and Recreation Department
Nespelem 99155. (509) 634-3145.

Highway Information and Mountain Pass Report
Dial 511 or 800-695-7623. www.wsdot.wa.gov

Lake Roosevelt National Recreation Area
1008 Crest Dr, Coulee Dam 99116. (509) 754-7880. www.nps.gov/laro

National Recreation Reservation Service
877-444-6777. Reservations for selected campgrounds. www.reserveusa.com

Northwest Weather and Avalanche Center
7600 Sandpoint Way NE, Seattle 98115. (206) 526-4666. Recorded message Oct 1–Apr 15. www.nwac.us

Okanogan–Wenatchee National Forests, Okanogan Valley Office
1240 S Second Ave, Okanogan 98840. (509) 826-3275. www.fs.usda.gov/okawen

Methow Valley Ranger District Office
24 W Chewuch Rd, Winthrop 98862. (509) 996-4003.
(509) 996-4000 Visitor Information Center (Summers only)

Tonasket Ranger District Office
1 W Winesap, Tonasket 98855. (509) 486-2186.

US Customs Service
(509) 476-2955 (Information on border crossings). cbp.gov

Washington Department of Natural Resources, Northeast Region
225 South Silke Rd, Colville 99414. (509) 684-7474. www.dnr.wa.gov

Washington Outfitters & Guides Association
125 Methrow Valley Hwy N #10, Twisp 98856. (509) 997-1080 www.woga.org

Washington State Parks Information Center & Campground Reservations
(360) 902-8844, 888-226-7688. www.parks.wa.gov
(360) 902-8555 (Boaters Guide)
(360) 902-8600 (Environmental Learning Centers Reservations)
(360) 902-8684 (Snopark and Winter Recreation Info)

Hunting & Fishing

Washington Department of Fish and Wildlife, North Central Region 2
1550 Alder St NW, Ephrata 98823. (509) 754-4624. www.wdfw.wa.gov
See map on page 29.

Campgrounds & RV Parks

See page 35 for campground and RV park information.

Climate

See Explanation on page 31

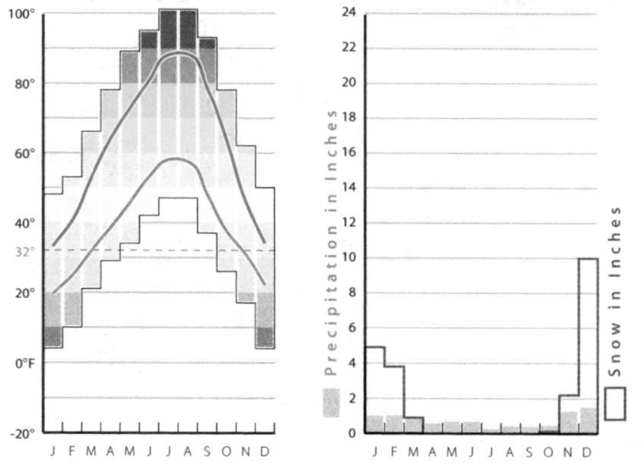

Bridgeport: el. 820 ft — 32 days with 10" precipitation, 22" of snow, 123 nights below freezing, 38 days above 90°
Jan (4°) 20°– 33° (48°) **Apr** (29°) 39°– 64° (78°)
July (47°) 58°– 88° (101°) **Oct** (26°) 38°– 64° (78°)

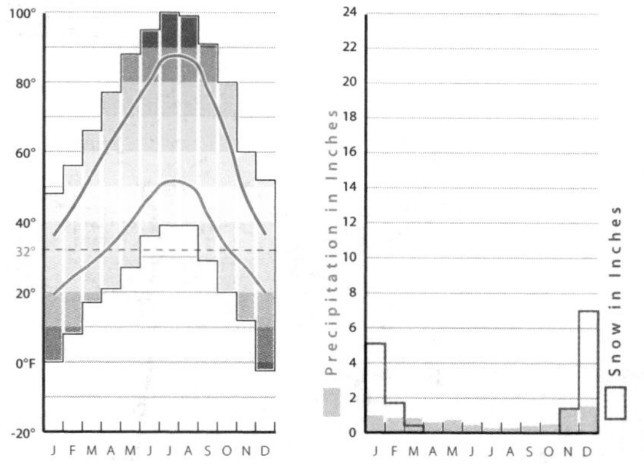

Odessa: el. 1542 ft — 36 days with 10" precipitation, 16" of snow, 164 nights below freezing, 34 days above 90°
Jan (0°) 19°– 36° (48°) **Apr** (21°) 33°– 63° (77°)
July (39°) 52°– 87° (100°) **Oct** (20°) 33°– 64° (80°)

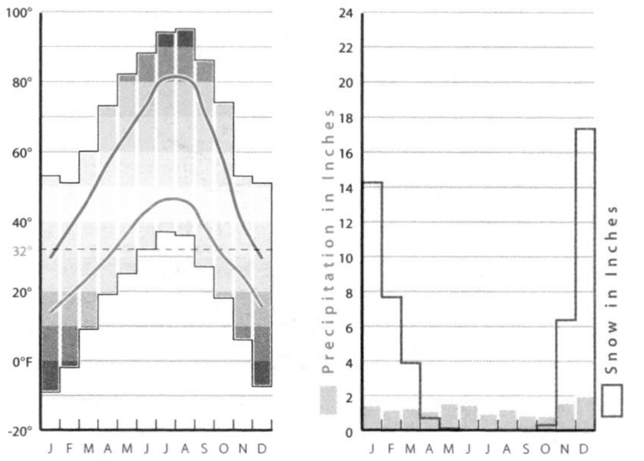

Republic: el. 2612 ft — 51 days with 16" precipitation, 51" of snow, 196 nights below freezing, 13 days above 90°
Jan (-9°) 14°– 29° (44°) **Apr** (19°) 30°– 57° (73°)
July (37°) 46°– 81° (94°) **Oct** (18°) 30°– 57° (74°)

Landscape Page Index

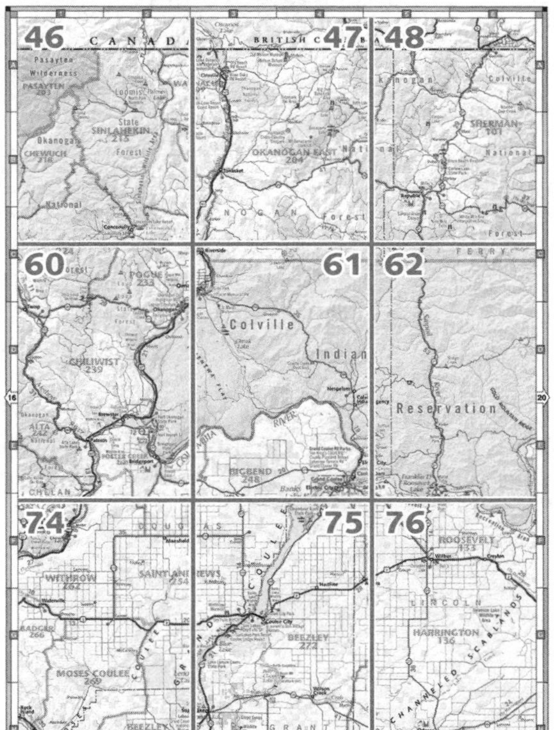

Landscape Page Numbers Are Shown in Blue

RECREATION

Legend: Wilderness · State Parks · Bureau of Reclamation · Bureau of Land Management · National Parks/Monuments · State Game Management Unit · Forest Service · State Lands · Military Lands · Tribal Lands · Wildlife Areas · HOKO 601

RECREATION

CANADA — BRITISH COLUMBIA

Okanogan — Colville National Forest · Recreation Area

KELLY HILL 105 · SHERMAN 101 · DOUGLAS 108 · ALADDIN 111 · SELKIRK 113 · HUCKLEBERRY 121 · 49 DEGREES NORTH 117 · MT SPOKANE 174 · ROOSEVELT 133 · HARRINGTON 136 · CHENEY 130 · MICA PEAK 127

Wenatchee · National · Forest · Colville · Indian Reservation · Spokane Indian Reservation · Franklin D Roosevelt Lake · Lake Roosevelt National Recreation Area · Columbia River · Huckleberry Range · Gold Mountain Ridge · Oregon City Ridge · Rainy Ridge · Onion Ridge

Priest Lake · Upper Priest Lake · Priest Wilderness · Colville National Forest · Pend Oreille · Selkirk Mountains

Counties / Regions: FERRY · STEVENS · PEND OREILLE · BOUNDARY · BONNER · LINCOLN · SPOKANE · ADAMS · WHITMAN · KOOTENAI · BENEWAH · IDAHO

Towns and sites: West Grand Forks · Grand Forks · Danville · Christina · Cascade · Gilpin · Laurier · Rossland · Silica · Casino · Columbia Gardens · Remac · Waneta · Paterson · Northport · Leadpoint · Metaline · Metaline Falls · Ione · Tiger · Nordman · Outlet Bay · Pierre Lake · Orient · Dulwich · Deer Creek · Kettle River · Boyds · Snag Cove · Bossburg · Evans · North Gorge · Onion Creek · Aladdin · Big Meadow Lake · Muddy Creek · Lost Creek · Blueslide · Ruby · Panhandle · Kamloops · Marcus · North Lake RV Park · Marcus Island · Echo · Kettle Falls · Sherman Creek Wildlife Area · St Paul's Mission · Douglas Falls Grange Park · Beaver Lodge Resort & RV Park · Flodelle Creek · Park Rapids · Crystal Falls · Locke · Browns Lake · Kalispel · Indian Reservation · South Skookum Lake · Kings Lake · Colville · Orin · Little Pend Oreille National Wildlife Refuge · Arden · Addy · Chewelah · Cusick · Usk · Skookum Creek · Marshall Lake Resort · Geophysical Nordic Snopark · Dalkena · Wolfred · Furport · Newport · Old American · Pioneer Park · Priest River · Thama · Inchelium · Rainbow Beach Resort · Rocky Point · Hartman's Log Cabin Resort · Meteor · Covada · Kewa · Gifford · Cloverleaf · Bluecreek · Winona Beach Resort · Silver Beach Resort · Waitts · Jump-Off Joe Lake Resort · Spokane Indian Bingo & Casino · 49 Degrees North Ski Area · Chewelah Mtn Nordic Ski Area · Penrith · Diamond Lake · Scotia · Tweedie · Edgemere · Harlem · Clagstone · Blanchard · Spirit Lake · Twin Lakes · Twinlow · Cedonia · Hunters · Daisy · Maud · Rice · Barnaby Island · Gifford Ferry · Covada · Wilmont Creek · Rogers Bar · Fruitland · Turk · Camas · Springdale · Loon Lake · Deer Lake Resort · Shore Acres Resort · Grays · Valley · Clayton · Deer Park · Denison · Chattaroy · Wild Rose · Buckeye · Mt Spokane State Park · Bear Creek Lodge · Rathdrum · Hayden · Post Falls · Coeur d'Alene · Liberty Lake · Enterprise (Boat In) · Crystal Cove · Detillion (Boat In) · Fort Spokane Historic Site · Two Rivers · Seven Bays · Porcupine Bay · Wellpinit · Columbia · Hawk Creek · Lincoln · Creston · Telford · Davenport · Mondovi · Reardan · Rocklyn · Omans · Gravelles · Earl · Bluestem · Waukon · Edwall · Harrington · Mohler · Downs · Lamona · Marcellus · Sprague · Sprague Lake Resort · Pifer · Four Seasons Campground · Fishtrap · Tyler · Medical Lake · West Medical Lake · East Medical Lake · Lakeland Village · Sun Cove Resort · Mallard-Bay Resort · Peaceful Pines · Cheney · Four Lakes · Marshall · Finch Arboretum · Airway Heights · Fairchild AFB · Fairchild Heritage Museum & Airpark · Overland · Ponderosa-Falls Resort · SPOKANE · Spokane Valley · Millwood · Country Homes · Nine Mile Falls · Riverside State Park · Bowl & Pitcher Formation · Turnbull NWR · Columbia Plateau Trail SP · Chapman Lake Resort · Spangle · Mt Hope · Waverly · Fairfield · Rockford · Worley · Plummer · Malden · Rosalia · Pandora · Willard · Latah · Spring Valley · Plaza

Long Lake · Long Lake Pictographs · Little Spokane River Natural Area & Indian Painted Rocks · Nine Mile Falls · Spokane House Interpretive Ctr

1. Downriver Golf Course & Snopark
2. Riverfront Park
3. Dishman Hills Conservancy
4. Valley Mission Park & Splash Down Waterpark
5. Spokane ORV Park & Spokane Co Raceway

1. Kettle Falls
2. Grandview Inn Motel & RV Park
3. Panorama RV Park

Spokane Plains Battlefield Heritage Site · Lincoln Co Hist Museum · Gonzaga Univ · Spokane Cheney Cowles Mem Museum

State routes shown: 3, 22, 25, 31, 20, 395, 2, 57, 211, 231, 292, 291, 26, 904, 902, 90, 195, 278, 58, 95, 41, 53, 54, 206, 27, 28, 21, 23, 24, 37, 34, 29

Scale 1:600,000 · 0 5 10 15 20 25 30 40 50 Miles · 0 5 10 15 20 30 40 50 Kilometers

© BENCHMARK MAPS

State Parks & National Recreation Areas ▲★

Columbia Plateau Trail State Park 130-mile long railbed trail. Picnicking and day use areas. Landscape created by Ice Age floods. Trailheads in Cheney, Amber Lake, and Martin Road. E of Sprague. (509) 646-9218. **H3-4**

Crawford State Park Picnicking. Guided tours explore 1,055 feet of Gardner Cave, third longest limestone cave in Washington. NW of Metaline Falls. (509) 238-4258. **A4**

Lake Roosevelt National Recreation Area A 130-mile-long lake formed by the Grand Coulee Dam. Recreational activities include camping, fishing, boating, swimming, and waterskiing. Visitor Contact Stations at Fort Spokane and Kettle Falls. (509) 754-7800. **F1–A3**

Mount Spokane State Park Camping, picnicking, hiking, and winter sports opportunities. NE of Spokane. (509) 238-4258. **E5**

Riverside State Park Camping, picnicking, hiking, mountain biking, snowmobiling, cross-country skiing, ORV area, and boat launch. Six miles NW of Spokane on White Parkway. (509) 465-5064. **F4**

Forests & Wildlife Areas 🚶🐦

Bighorn Sheep Viewing Area Bighorn sheep are common in the Hall Mountain area. The viewing area is located at the winter feeding station, northeast of Ione off Sullivan Lake Rd. (509) 446-7500. **B5**

Colville National Forest Includes the Salmo-Priest Wilderness. In the northeastern corner of Washington. (509) 684-7000. **A4–A5**

Dishman Hills Conservancy Area of hiking trails through the pine forest. East of Spokane. (509) 999-5100. www.dishmanhills.org **G5**

Flume Creek Mountain Goat Viewing Area View mountain goats, deer, and occasionally moose. NW of Metaline Falls. (509) 446-7500. **A4**

Little Pend Oreille National Wildlife Refuge Camping, hiking, fishing, and hunting are the primary activities here. Southeast of Colville off State Rte 20. (509) 684-8384. **C3**

Little Spokane River Natural Area and Indian Painted Rocks Abundant wildlife including a Great Blue Heron rookery in this historic fur trading area. Hiking trail leads to Indian pictographs. Also area to canoe or kayak with put-ins at Waikiki Rd and Indian Painted Rocks Trailhead. 6 miles north of Spokane. (509) 465-5064. **F4**

Sherman Creek Wildlife Area Hunt, hike or fish in this rugged, forested area. Most roads within the wildlife area are closed to vehicles. West of Kettle Falls off State Rte 20. (509) 738-4120. wdfw.wa.gov **B2**

Turnbull National Wildlife Refuge Known as a place to observe migrating waterfowl in the fall and spring. There is a self-guided auto tour through the refuge. South of Cheney. (509) 235-4723. www.fws.gov/turnbull **H4**

Ski Areas & Snoparks ⛷❄

49° North Mountain Resort 5 chairs, 75 marked trails, terrain park. E of Chewelah on FS Road 2902. (509) 935-6649. www.ski49n.com **D4**

Chewelah Mountain Nordic Ski Area 9 miles of groomed cross-country trails maintained and groomed by 49° North Mountain Resort. E of Chewelah on Flowery Trail Rd. (509) 935-6649. **D4**

Down River Golf Course Groomed cross-country ski trails and 80-space snopark. Golf course closed to golfing in winter. 3225 North Columbia Circle, Spokane. (509) 327-5269. **F4**

Flodelle/Tacoma Creek Snopark Seven miles of groomed snowmobiling trails. 19 miles E of Colville on State Hwy 20. (509) 684-7000. **C4**

Geophysical Nordic Snopark Over 6 miles of groomed cross-country ski trails and 20-space snopark. 10 miles NW of Newport. (509) 447-3129. **D5**

Kings Lake Snopark Groomed snowmobiling trails. East of Usk on County Road 3389. (509) 684-7000. **C5**

Mt Spokane Ski and Snowboard Park 5 lifts, 44 runs, and night skiing. 30 miles NE of Spokane. (509) 238-2220. Ski report: (509) 238-7974. www.mtspokane.com **E5**

Boating & Fishing 🐟🚤

Browns Lake Known for cutthroat fly fishing. There is a Forest Service campground with a boat ramp. Northeast of Usk. **C5**

Liberty Lake Fish for crappie, bluegill, perch, and various species of trout. Public boat ramp. East of Spokane. **G5**

Little Pend Oreille Lakes Chain of small lakes on the Little Pend Oreille River. Fish for cutthroat, rainbow, and brook trout. South of Ione. **B4**

Long Lake Fishing is not the best, but walleye, trout, northern pike, largemouth and smallmouth bass are caught here. No gasoline-powered craft allowed on lake. Northwest of Spokane. **F3**

Medical Lakes West Medical Lake is known as a top producer of rainbow trout. Medical Lake is known for brown trout fishing. Medical Lake has selective fishery regulations in place. There are public boat ramps at both lakes. South of Spokane. **G3**

Lake Roosevelt Numerous campgrounds, boat launching available. Fish for trout, walleye, perch, crappie, and catfish. Some campsites on the north, east and west shores of the north arm are on Indian reservation land; please observe signs. East of Coulee Dam. (509) 633-9441. **F1–A3**

Sullivan Lake Fishing, water-skiing, and sailing are the attractions here. Campgrounds and boat ramps are at the north and south ends of the lake. Fish for brown, brook, cutthroat, and rainbow trout. Southeast of Metaline Falls, on Sullivan Lake Rd. (509) 446-7500. **A5**

Ferries ★

Inchelium–Gifford Ferry Free ferry known as *GIF*, or the *Columbian Princess* crosses the Columbia River. Operated by the Colville Confederated Tribes. Call for hours and regulations. (509) 772-5473. **D2**

Natural Wonders ⛰

Bowl and Pitcher Formation View the unique Bowl and Pitcher basalt formation along the Spokane River, in Riverside State Park. **F4**

Devils Well A 20-ft diameter circular pond. SW of Newport off US 2. **E4**

Historic Sites & Museums 🏛★

Browns Lake Historic Civilian Conservation Corps Cabin Cabin built by the CCC in the 1930s. On FS Rd 5030, Browns Lake. **C5**

Northwest Museum of Arts & Culture Known locally as the *MAC*, it offers displays depicting the history of the mining, timber, and farming industries of the region. Next to the museum is the Campbell House, built in the late 1890s. 2316 W First Ave, Spokane. (509) 456-3931, 363-5315 (events hotline). www.northwestmuseum.org **G4**

Fairchild Heritage Museum and Airpark Exhibits illustrate the history and traditions of Fairchild Air Force Base and of military aviation. Exhibits review military flight from balloon usage during the Civil War to aircraft used in Operation Desert Storm. 100 E Bong St, Spokane. (509) 247-2100. **G3**

Fort Spokane Historic Site Built in the late 1800s to maintain peace between the settlers and Indians. A visitor center is located in the former guardhouse and an interpretive trail winds through the ruins of this old fort. On State Rte 25. (509) 754-7848. www.nps.gov/laro **E1**

Keller Heritage Center Museum & Park Includes a schoolhouse, cabin, sawmill, blacksmiths shop, and the museum of Indian and pioneer artifacts. 700 N Wynne St, Colville. (509) 684-5968. **C3**

Lincoln County Historical Museum A collection of Colville and Spokane Indian artifacts and a collection of pioneer furniture, clothing, and tools. Park St, Davenport. (509) 725-6711. **G2**

Log Flume Interpretive Trail A .5-mile loop trail illustrating logging practices during the 1920s, including the use of flumes, horses, and locomotives. West of Kettle Falls on State Rte 20 at East Portal Picnic Area. (509) 738-6111. **C2**

Long Lake Pictographs Indian rock paintings. On State Rte 291. **F3**

Mill Pond Historic Site An interpretive trail along a portion of the remnants of a 2-mile-long, wooden flume used to carry water to a hydroelectric station at Metaline Falls. East of Metaline Falls on Sullivan Lake Rd at Millpond Campground. (509) 446-7500. **A5**

Spokane House Interpretive Center Site of a trading post and first non-native structure in the Northwest. Located in Riverside State Park on Aubrey White Pkwy. (509) 466-4747 or (509) 465-5064. **F4**

St Paul's Mission Restored log church established in the mid-1800s. W of Kettle Falls on US 395. (509) 754-7800. **B2**

Stevens County Historical Society Museum Exhibits depicting pioneer life. Located in Keller Historical Park. Open May through September or by appointment. 700 N Wynne St, Colville. (509) 684-5968. **C3**

Notable Towns ○ ◉

Cheney One of the highest towns in the state at 2,400 feet. Top of the hill for trains climbing southwest from Spokane. Eastern Washington University is located here. The Turnbull National Wildlife Refuge is to the south. (509) 747-8480 (Chamber of Commerce). **G4**

Medical Lake Town located next to a lake that some claim has medicinal purposes. Eastern State Hospital is located here. There are a number of lakes in the area that offer fishing and boating. (509) 565-5000 City Hall. **G4**

Metaline Falls Northeastern most incorporated town in Washington State. Large cement plant, nearby Lake Sullivan. Parts of Kevin Costner's movie, The Postman, was filmed here. (509) 446-1721 (C of C). **B5**

Newport Pend Oreille County Historical Society Museum. Original townsite was on Idaho side of state line, now city of Oldtown. The cemetery is on an island bisected by state line but is completely in Newport per proclamation signed by President Harding. (509) 447-5812. **D6**

Other Attractions ★🐘🏛🎡

Bing Crosby Collection Collection of Bing Crosby memorabilia. Gonzaga University, 502 E Boone Ave, Spokane. (509) 313-3847. **G5**

Cat Tales Zoological Park Conservatory for big cats such as lions, tigers, and cheetahs. Educational programs and petting zoo. 17020 N Newport Hwy, Mead. (509) 238-4126. www.cattales.org. **F5**

Chewelah Casino US Hwy 395 and Smith Rd, Chewelah. 800-322-2788 or (509) 238-9845. www.chewelahcasino.com. **D3**

Crystal Falls Picnic area on Pend Oreille River with view of 80-ft. cascades. East of Colville on State Rte 20. (509) 684-8384. **C3**

John A Finch Arboretum 65 acres of gardens along Garden Springs Creek. Master Gardener tours available year round. (509) 624-4832. **G4**

Manito Park Stroll through the conservatory, Japanese garden, lilac garden, rose garden, or formal garden. Grand Blvd to Park Place, Spokane. (509) 625-6200. www.manitopark.org **G4**

Radar Dome ORV Area 26 miles of established off-road vehicle trails with access to over 100 miles of trails in the adjacent forest. Staging area at Clark Creek. East of Colville. (509) 684-7474. **C4**

Riverfront Park Set along the Spokane River, the site of Expo '74 is now a city park. Ride the hand-carved carousel built in 1909, ride the gondola over the Spokane River, see a movie at the IMAX theater, or skate at the Ice Palace. Howard St, Spokane. (509) 625-6601 or 625-6686 (IMAX). **F4**

Splash Down Waterpark Waterslides are the attraction here. Located in Valley Mission Park. 11123 E Mission Ave, Spokane. (509) 924-3079. **F5**

Spokane County ORV Park Four-wheel-drive, off-road, motorcycle, ATV, and go-kart events. Mar–Oct. User fee. N of Airway Heights, next to Spokane Raceway Park. (509) 456-4730 or (509) 224-9244 (Info Line). **G4**

Spokane County Raceway This motorsports park features a 2.5-mile road course and a quarter-mile drag strip. The track hosts NHRA events, as well as several driving schools for marque-specific clubs. N of Airway Heights. (509) 244-3333. www.spokanecountyraceway.com **G4**

Information Resources

Bureau of Land Management, Spokane District Office
1103 N Fancher, Spokane 99212. (509) 536-1200.
www.blm.gov/or/districts/spokane

Colville National Forest Headquarters and Ranger District Office
765 S Main, Colville 99114. (509) 684-7000. www.fs.usda.gov/colville

Newport Ranger District Office
315 N Warren, Newport 99156. (509) 447-7300

Sullivan Lake Ranger District Office
12641 Sullivan Lake Rd, Metaline Falls 99153. (509) 446-7500

Three Rivers Ranger District Office
255 W 11th, Kettle Falls 99141. (509) 738-7700

Confederated Tribes of the Colville Indian Reservation
888-881-7684 or (509) 634-2200 (Switchboard). www.colvilletribes.com

Fish and Wildlife Department
PO Box 150, Nespelem 99155. (509) 634-2110

Parks and Recreation Department
Nespelem 99155. (509) 634-3145

Highway Information and Mountain Pass Report
Dial 511 or 800-695-7623. www.wsdot.wa.gov

Lake Roosevelt National Recreation Area
1008 Crest Dr, Coulee Dam 99116. (509) 754-7800. www.nps.gov/laro

National Recreation Reservation Service
877-444-6777. Reservations for selected campgrounds.
www.reserveusa.com

Spokane Tribe of Indians
Wellpinit 99040. (509) 458-6500. www.spokanetribe.com

US Customs Service
(509) 476-2955 (Information on border crossings). cbp.gov

Washington Department of Natural Resources, Northeast Region
225 S Silke Rd, Colville 99114. (509) 684-7474 www.dnr.wa.gov

Washington State Parks Information Center & Campground Reservations
(360) 902-8844, 888-226-7688. www.parks.wa.gov
(360) 902-8555 (Boaters Guide)
(360) 902-8600 (Environmental Learning Centers Reservations)
(360) 902-8684 (Snopark and Winter Recreation Info)

Hunting & Fishing

Washington Department of Fish & Wildlife, Eastern Region 1
2315 N Discovery Place, Spokane Valley 99218. (509) 892-1001.
www.wdfw.wa.gov

See map on page 29.

Campgrounds & RV Parks ▲🚐

See page 35 for campground and RV park information.

Climate

See Explanation on page 31

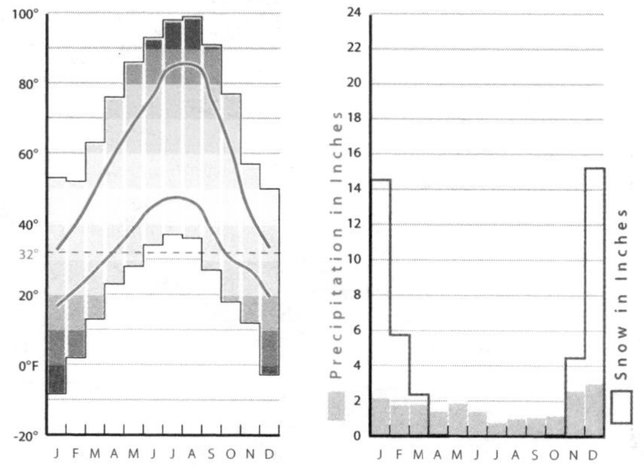

Chewelah: el. 1670 ft — 65 days with 21" precipitation, 43" of snow, 176 nights below freezing, 30 days above 90°

Jan (-7°) 17°– 33° (46°) Apr (23°) 33°– 60° (76°)
July (37°) 48°– 85° (98°) Oct (18°) 30°– 61° (77°)

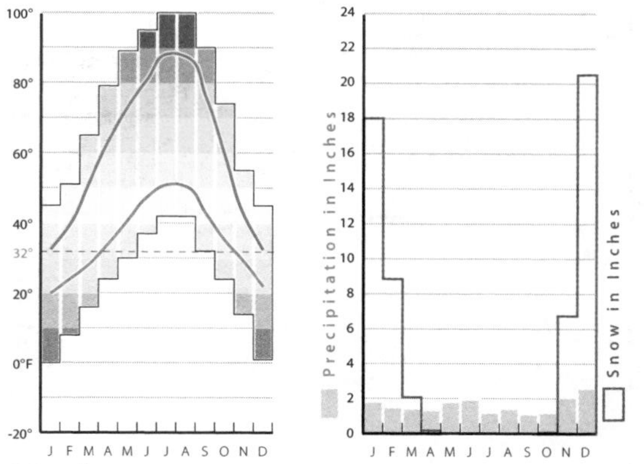

Northport: el. 1319 ft — 63 days with 20" precipitation, 57" of snow, 150 nights below freezing, 40 days above 90°

Jan (0°) 20°– 33° (45°) Apr (24°) 34°– 64° (79°)
July (42°) 51°– 88° (100°) Oct (24°) 35°– 60° (74°)

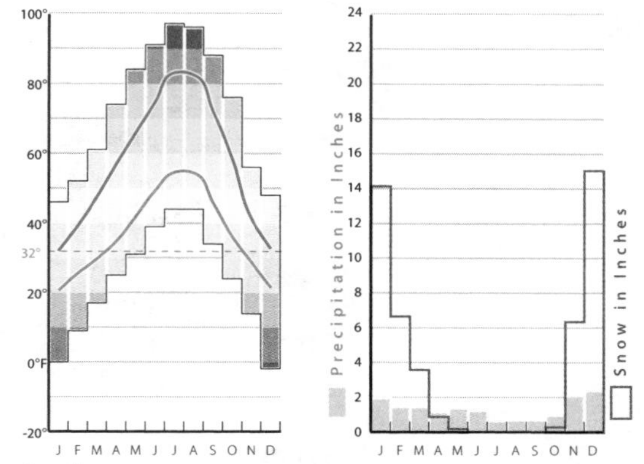

Spokane: el. 2356 ft — 50 days with 16" precipitation, 47" of snow, 139 nights below freezing, 19 days above 90°

Jan (0°) 21°– 32° (46°) Apr (25°) 35°– 57° (74°)
July (44°) 55°– 83° (97°) Oct (24°) 36°– 59° (76°)

Landscape Page Index

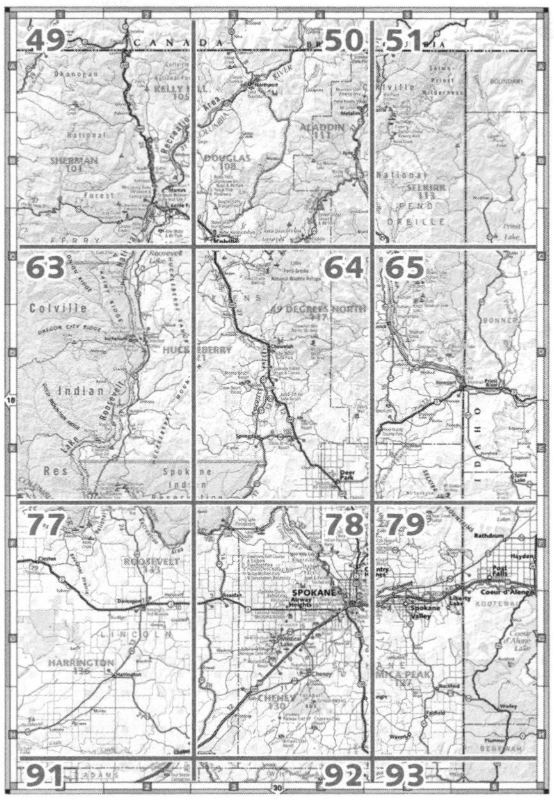

Landscape Page Numbers Are Shown in Blue

Wilderness | State Parks | Bureau of Reclamation | Bureau of Land Management | National Parks/ Monuments | HOKO 601 State Game Management Unit
Forest Service | State Lands | Military Lands | Tribal Lands | Wildlife Areas

RECREATION

RV Parks in Copalis Beach (A3):
Copalis Beach Surf & Sand RV Park
Driftwood Acres Ocean Campground
Dunes RV Resort
Echoes of the Sea Motel & CG
One O'Nine RV Park
Riverside RV Resort
Tidelands Campground

RV Parks in Ocean Shores (B3):
Quinault Maritime Resort
Yesterday's RV Park

RV Parks in Westport (B3):
American Sunset RV Resort
Holand Center RV Park
Pacific Motel & RV
Westport Inn
Islander Motel & RV
Kila Hana Camperland

RV Parks in Long Beach (E3):
Andersen's on the Ocean
Driftwood RV Park
Land's End RV Park
Pioneer RV Park
Sand Castle RV Park

RV Parks in Ilwaco (E3):
Beacon Charters & RV Park
Eagle's Nest Resort
Sou'Wester Lodge

PACIFIC OCEAN

North Beach Seashore Conservation Area
Long Beach Seashore Conservation Area

Key locations and features:

Quinault Indian Reservation
Moclips
Pacific Beach
Copalis Beach
Ocean City
Ocean Shores
Westport
Grayland
Tokeland
Bay Center
Nahcotta
Ocean Park
Long Beach
Ilwaco
Chinook
McGowan
Hammond
Warrenton
Astoria

GRAYS HARBOR
WYNOOCHEE 648
COPALIS 642
SATSOP 651
SKOKOMISH 636
Shelton
McCleary
Elma
Hoquiam
Aberdeen
Montesano
Central Park
Cosmopolis
MINOT PEAK 660
Oakville
Rochester
Grand Mound
CAPITOL PEAK 663
THURSTON
MASON
NORTH RIVER 658
FALL RIVER 672
LINCOLN 501
Raymond
South Bend
Menlo
Pe Ell
WILLIAMS CREEK 673
WILLAPA HILLS 506
RYDERWOOD 530
Ryderwood
GRAYS RIVER DIVIDE
LONG ISLAND 699
BEAR RIVER 681
LONG BEACH 684
Naselle
Cathlamet
WAHKIAKUM
COWLITZ
STELLA 504
LEWIS
PACIFIC
COLUMBIA RIVER
OREGON
Clatskanie
CLATSOP
COLUMBIA
Seaside
Gearhart
Cannon Beach
Vernonia
Nehalem
Manzanita
Wheeler
Rockaway Beach
Garibaldi
Bay City
Tillamook
TILLAMOOK
Forest Grove
Banks

Scale 1:600,000
0 5 10 15 20 25 30 40 50 Miles
0 5 10 15 20 30 40 50 Kilometers

© BENCHMARK MAPS

Recreation Guide

State Parks △ 🐦 ★

Cape Disappointment State Park Camping, picnic sites, hiking, mountain biking, boat launch, beach access, and tours of the North Head Lighthouse. 5 miles southwest of Ilwaco. (360) 642-3078. **E3**

Fort Columbia State Park National Historic Site with restored fort housing an interpretive center featuring exhibits of historic artillery. Southeast of Chinook. (360) 777-8221. **E3**

Grayland Beach State Park Camping, beach access, picnicking. In Grayland on State Rte 105. (360) 267-4301. **C3**

Griffiths–Priday Ocean State Park Day use area, for picnicking, fishing, beachcombing, and bird watching. Area also known for seasonal gray whale watching. West of Copalis Beach. (360) 902-8844. **A2**

Lake Sylvia State Park Camping, picnicking, hiking, fishing, and boat launch. 1 mile north of Montesano off US 12. (360) 249-3621. **B5**

Leadbetter Point State Park Hiking, kayak and canoe access, boat launch, viewpoint. At north end of Long Beach Peninsula on State Rte 103. (360) 642-3078. **D3**

Long Beach Seashore Conservation Area 29 miles of accessible shoreline from Leadbetter Point to Fort Canby State Park. Beach access at Oysterville, Ocean Park, Klipsan Beach, Cranberry Road, Bolstad, 10th Avenue, and Seaview. (360) 642-3078. **D2**

Loomis Lake State Park Day use area with beach access. North of Long Beach on State Rte 103. (360) 642-3078. **D3**

North Beach Seashore Conservation Area 22 miles of shoreline from the Quinault Indian Reservation to Grays Harbor. Beach access at Moclips, Analyde Gap, Roosevelt, Ocean City, Oyhut, Chance à la Mer, Taurus, and Damon Point. (360) 289-3553. **B2**

Ocean City State Park Camping, picnicking, hiking. 2 miles north of Ocean Shores on State Rte 115. (360) 289-3553. **B2**

Pacific Beach State Park Camping, picnicking, beach access. In Pacific Beach on State Rte 109. (360) 276-4297. **A2**

Pacific Pines State Park Day use area with hiking and beach access. North of Long Beach on State Rte 103. (360) 642-3078. **D3**

Rainbow Falls State Park Camping, hiking, and fishing. Bridge overlooks Rainbow Falls. Northeast of Pe Ell. (360) 291-3767. **C6**

Schafer State Park Camping and hiking. 12 miles northwest of Elma on Satsop River. (360) 482-3852. **A5**

Twin Harbors State Park Camping, picnicking, hiking to ocean. 3 miles south of Westport on State Rte 105. (360) 268-9717. **B3**

Westhaven State Park Beach access and trail to Westport Light State Park. North of Twin Harbors on State Rte 105. (360) 268-9717. **B2**

Westport Light State Park Trail to Westhaven State Park and beach access. West of Westport on State Rte 105. (360) 268-9717. **B3**

Forests & Wildlife Areas 🚶 🐦

Capitol State Forest Forested area developed for recreation activities including camping, hiking, horseback riding, and motor biking. (360) 577-2025. **B6**

Grays Harbor National Wildlife Refuge An 1,800-acre refuge of tidal flats, salt marshes, and woodlands. Exceptional viewing opportunities for North American shore birds, especially in mid-April. (360) 753-9467. www.fws.gov/graysharbor **B3**

Julia Butler Hansen National Refuge for the Columbian White-tailed Deer Mainland section of refuge is closed to visitors, however deer and other wildlife may be observed from the county road along the perimeter of the refuge. 46 Steamboat Slough Rd, Cathlamet. (360) 795-3915. www.fws.gov/jbh **E5**

Lewis and Clark National Wildlife Refuge Primary wintering area for tundra swan, geese, and duck. Includes 20 islands on 27 miles of the Columbia River. Shore birds and bald eagles are viewable by boat. (360) 795-3915. www.fws.gov/lc **E4**

Oyhut Wildlife Area Fishing, hunting, hiking, and bird watching on over 600 acres. South of Ocean Shores. (360) 533-5676. **B2**

Willapa National Wildlife Refuge The refuge includes one of the largest undisturbed estuaries on the West Coast. Boat to Long Island to view stands of old growth western red cedar. Headquarters located on US 101. NW of Naselle on US 101. (360) 484-3482. www.fws.gov/willapa **D3–E3**

Boating & Fishing 🐟 🚤

Chehalis River Fish the lower Chehalis River by boat or along the bank. Public boat ramps are located along the river. Fish for steelhead, chinook, coho, sea-run cutthroat, sturgeon, and largemouth bass. **B5**

Duck Lake There are two public boat ramps. Fish for rainbow and cutthroat trout, bluegill and crappie. **B3**

Grays Harbor North Jetty Fish for rockfish, surf perch, pile perch, lingcod, flounder, and coho salmon. **B3**

Humptulips River Fishing is good for winter steelhead and fall chinook. Other catches include coho and sea-run cutthroat trout. **A3**

Moclips River Fish for sea-run cutthroat trout. **A3**

Naselle River Fish for winter steelhead, fall run salmon and sea-run cutthroat trout. **D4**

Westport Harbor Charters for ocean fishing available. Fish for chinook, coho, albacore, halibut, and various species of rock fish. Boat ramp. 800-345-6223 or (360) 268-9422 (Chamber of Commerce). www.westportgrayland-chamber.org **B3**

Natural Wonders ⛰

Mima Mounds Natural Area Preserve Designated as a National Natural Landmark in 1966 by the National Park Service. Interpretive trail through mounded prairie. (360) 902-1600. www.dnr.wa.gov **B6**

Ferries ★

Puget Island Ferry Passenger and vehicle ferry service from Puget Island to Wesport, Oregon. Wahkiakum County has operated this ferry since 1962. State Rte 409, S of Cathlamet. (360) 795-3301. **E5**

Historic Sites & Museums 🏛 ★

Aberdeen Museum of History Collection of vintage farm and logging equipment. 111 E 3rd St, Aberdeen. (360) 533-1976 or (360) 532-1924 (Grays Harbor Chamber of Commerce). www.aberdeen-museum.org **B4**

Colbert House Restored and furnished 19th-century residence. Spruce and Quaker Streets, Ilwaco. (360) 642-3078. **E3**

Fort Columbia House Museum Restored fort commander's residence is now a military museum. In Fort Columbia State Park. (360) 777-8221. **E3**

Grays Harbor Historical Seaport Learning Center Visit the replica of the *Lady Washington*, a ship built in the late 1700s. Also visit boat-building exhibit. 712 Hagara St, Aberdeen. 800-200-5239 or (360) 532-8611. www.historicalseaport.org. **A4**

Hoquiam's Castle The restored and furnished mansion, now a bed and breakfast, built in 1897 for Robert Lytle, lumber magnate. 515 Chenault Ave, Hoquiam. (360) 533-2005. www.hoquiamcastle.com **A4**

Columbia Pacific Heritage Museum Exhibits of illustrating pioneer life in the area including Chinook Indian artifacts. There is also a scale model of an early 20th-century seaport. 115 SE Lake St, Ilwaco. (360) 642-3446. www.columbiapacificheritagemuseum.org **E3**

Lewis and Clark Interpretive Center Learn about the Lewis and Clark Expedition that covered over 7,000 miles and took over 2 years to complete. Fort Canby State Park. (360) 642-3029. **E3**

Mason County Historical Museum Exhibits depicting life at the turn of the century. 5th and Railroad Ave, Shelton. (360) 426-1020. **A6**

Pacific County Courthouse View the ornate stained-glass dome and historical paintings from the 1940s in this government office built in 1910. 300 Memorial Dr, South Bend. (360) 875-9328. **C4**

Pacific County Historical Society Museum Displays of Chinook Indian crafts, artwork, and exhibits illustrating the lumber, oyster, and fishing industries. US 101, South Bend. (360) 875-5224. www.pacificcohistory.org **C4**

Polson Park and Museum Museum is located in the mansion once owned by Arnold Polson. Exhibits chronicle the history of the Grays Harbor Area. 1611 Riverside Ave, Hoquiam. (360) 533-5862. www.polsonmuseum.org **A4**

Redmen Hall and River Life Interpretive Center Exhibits in old schoolhouse depict life along the Columbia River from the 1850s to the 1930s. 1394 W State Rte 4, Skamokawa. (360) 795-3007. **E5**

Wahkiakum County Historical Society Museum Collection of farming tools, guns, logging equipment, and artifacts from Northwest Indian tribes. 65 River St, Cathlamet. (360) 846-1604 or (360) 849-4353. **E5**

Willapa Seaport Museum Maritime museum with extensive displays of early military sea service, fishing, and timber industries. 310 Alder St, Raymond. (360) 942-4149. **C4**

Notable Towns ○ ◉

Cathlamet Established as a trading post in 1846, logging and fishing were the two main industries in this town along the Columbia River. Puget Island, in the middle of the Columbia River, is linked to Cathlamet by a bridge and to Westport, Oregon, by a ferry. (360) 795-9996. **E5**

Elma Incorporated in 1888. Located in the Chehalis River Valley, Elma hosts the Grays Harbor County Fair. The never-completed Satsop nuclear power plant is across the valley in the hills to the south. (360) 482-3055 (Chamber of Commerce). www.elmachamber.org **B5**

Ilwaco Important fishing port. Nearby attractions include Fort Canby State Park, Cape Disappointment Lighthouse, and the Lewis and Clark Interpretive Center. 800-451-2542 (Long Beach Peninsula Visitor's Bureau). www.funbeach.com **E3**

Oysterville Settled in 1854, now designated a National Historic District. Located on the Long Beach Peninsula, known for its 28 miles of sandy beach. 800-451-2542 (Long Beach Peninsula Visitor's Bureau). www.funbeach.com **D3**

Other Attractions ★ 🗼 🪶 ⌂ 🏛

Cape Disappointment Lighthouse Built in 1856, the oldest lighthouse in Washington. Tours are available through the Lewis and Clark Interpretive Center. (360) 642-3029. **E3**

Cranberry Demonstration Farm and Museum Observe the details of cranberry farming. Includes exhibits of old cranberry farming machinery. North of Long Beach on Pioneer Road. (360) 642-5553. www.cranberrymuseum.com **F3**

Grays Harbor Lighthouse (Westport Lighthouse) Built in 1898, it is the tallest lighthouse in Washington. The lighthouse is closed to the public, but can be viewed from outside the grounds. Westport. (360) 268-0078 (Westport Maritime Museum). www.wesportmaritimemuseum.com **B2**

Grays River Covered Bridge Covered bridge built in 1905. Just off Hwy 4 east of Grays River. **D5**

Little Creek Casino 91 W State Rte 108, Shelton. 800-667-7711 or (360) 427-7711. www.little-creek.com **A6**

Lucky Eagle Casino 188th St SW, Rochester. 800-720-1788 or (360) 273-2000. www.luckyeagle.com **C6**

North Head Lighthouse Built in 1898. Tours are available through the Lewis and Clark Interpretive Center. (360) 642-3029. **E2**

Ocean Shores Environmental Interpretive Center Exhibits illustrating the natural and human history of the Point Brown peninsula. 1033 Catala Ave SE. (360) 289-4617 or (360) 289-3553. **B3**

Shoalwater Bay Casino 4112 State Rte 105, Tokeland. (360) 267-2048. **C6**

Westport Maritime Museum Located in the former Coast Guard station. Exhibits include skeletons of various marine mammals and a children's learning area. 2201 Westhaven Dr, Westport. (360) 268-0078. www.wesportmaritimemuseum.com **B3**

Whale Watching See migrating gray whales along the coast January through early February and late March through April. Whale watching charters available or view from the coast at points such as North Head. **E3**

World Kite Museum and Hall of Fame Hundreds of kites from around the world, including a historical kite display. 303 Sid Snyder Dr, Long Beach. (360) 642-4020. wwwkitefestival.com. **E3**

Information Resources

Grays Harbor Tourism
800-621-9625. www.visitgraysharbor.com

Highway Information and Mountain Pass Report
Dial 511 or 800-695-7623. www.wsdot.wa.gov

Long Beach Peninsula Visitors Bureau
800-451-2542 or (360) 642-2400. www.funbeach.com

Washington Department of Natural Resources, Pacific Cascade Region
601 Bond Rd, Castle Rock 98611. (360) 577-2025 www.dnr.wa.gov

Washington Outfitters & Guides Association
125 Methrow Valley Hwy N #10, Twisp 98856. (509) 997-1080. www.woga.org

Washington State Parks Information Center & Campground Reservations
(360) 902-8844, 888-226-7688. www.parks.wa.gov
(360) 902-8555 (Boaters Guide)
(360) 902-8600 (Environmental Learning Centers)

Hunting & Fishing

Washington Department of Fish and Wildlife, Coastal Region 6
48 Devonshire Rd, Montesano 98563. (360) 249-4628. www.wdfw.wa.gov
See map on page 29.

Campgrounds & RV Parks △

See page 36 for list of campgrounds and RV Parks

Climate

See Explanation on page 31

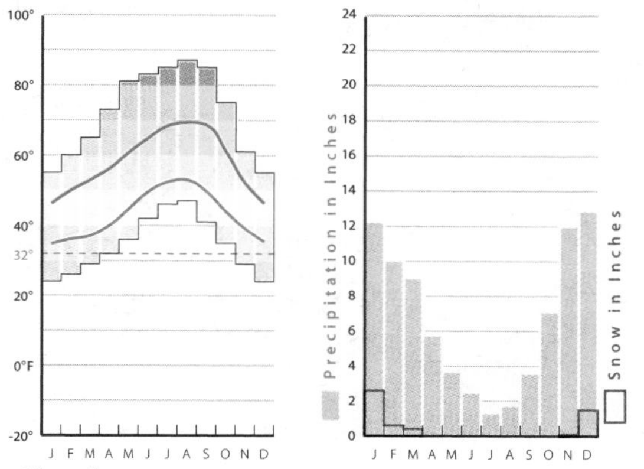

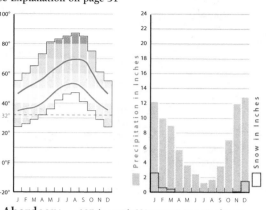

Aberdeen: el. 10 ft
137 days with 82" precipitation, 5" of snow, 43 nights below freezing, 2 days above 90°
Jan (24°) 35°– 46° (55°) **Apr** (32°) 40°– 56° (73°)
July (46°) 52°– 68° (85°) **Oct** (35°) 44°– 61° (75°)

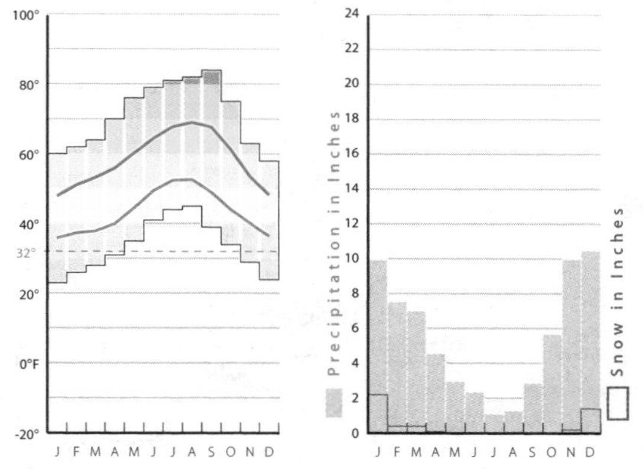

Astoria: el. 10 ft
128 days with 66" precipitation, 5" of snow, 37 nights below freezing, 1 day above 90°
Jan (23°) 36°– 48° (58°) **Apr** (31°) 40°– 56° (70°)
July (44°) 68°– 52° (81°) **Oct** (34°) 44°– 61° (75°)

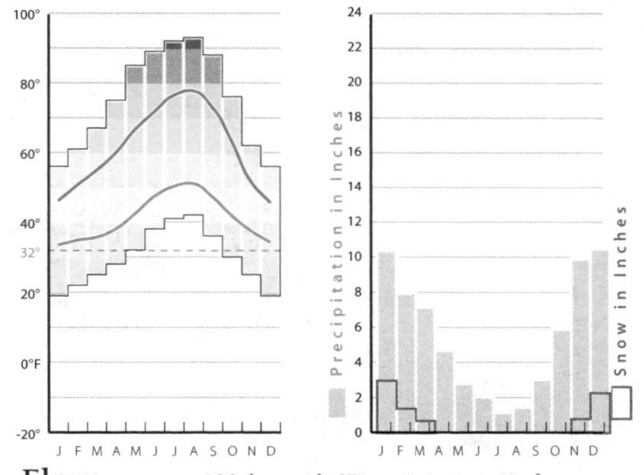

Elma: el. 69 ft
129 days with 67" precipitation, 8" of snow, 65 nights below freezing, 8 days above 90°
Jan (19°) 34°– 46° (56°) **Apr** (28°) 38°– 60° (75°)
July (41°) 51°– 77° (92°) **Oct** (30°) 42°– 63° (76°)

Landscape Page Index

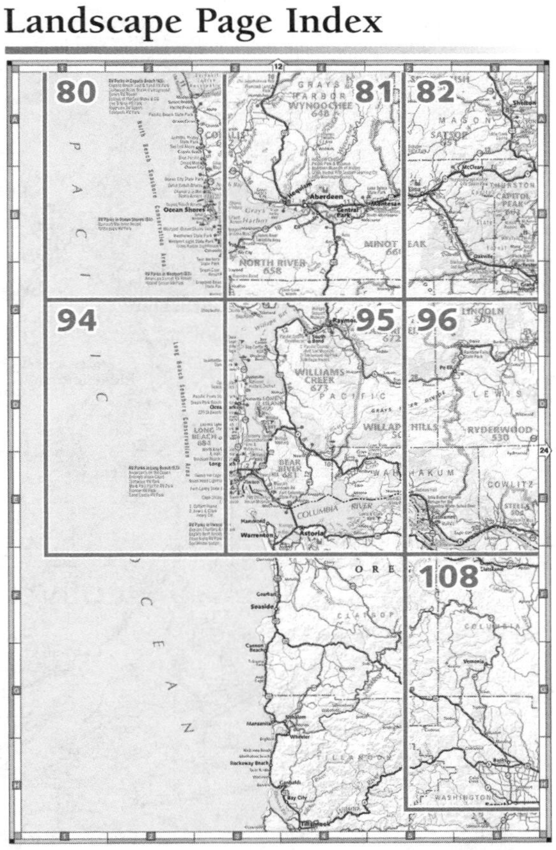

Landscape Page Numbers Are Shown in Blue

Legend

Wilderness	State Parks
Forest Service	State Lands
Bureau of Reclamation	Military Lands
Bureau of Land Management	Tribal Lands
National Parks/ Monuments	Wildlife Areas

HOKO 601 State Game Management Unit

RECREATION

Major places and features:

TACOMA, Pacific, Artondale, Home, Herron, KITSAP 627, Lakebay, Longbranch, Shelton, Bayshore, Dayton, Fife, Muckleshoot Ind Res, Sumner, Bonney Lake, Enumclaw, Buckley, South Prairie, Wilkeson, Carbonado, GREEN RIVER 485, Mt Baker, KING, ISSAQUAH 454, Snoqualmie

University Place, Lakewood, Puyallup, Parkland, Spanaway, Orting, Crocker, WHITE RIVER 653, Clearwater Wilderness, The Dalles, Norse Peak Wilderness

Steilacoom, DuPont, Fort Lewis, Elk Plain, Graham, Thrift, PUYALLUP 652, PIERCE, Mount Rainier National Park, MT RAINIER 14,411, Highest Point in Washington

Olympia, Lacey, Tumwater, DESCHUTES, Yelm, McKenna, Rainier, MASHEL 654, Eatonville, Elbe, Ashford, Longmire, Paradise, Cougar Rock

Oakville, Rochester, Tenino, Bucoda, Tono, Vail, THURSTON, SKOOKUMCHUCK 667, BLUE RIDGE, Mt Baker, Snoqualmie National Forest, Mineral, STORMKING 510, Gifford Pinchot National Forest, SOUTH RAINIER 513, Tatoosh

CAPITOL PEAK 663, GRAYS HARBOR, North Creek, Mima, LINCOLN 501, Centralia, Chehalis, Galvin, Napavine, MOSSYROCK 505, Morton, Randle, RANDLE 503, Goat Rocks Wilderness, PACKWOOD 516, Packwood

MASON, SATSOP 651, Kamilche

Winlock, Toledo, Vader, RYDERWOOD 530, Ryderwood, WINSTON 520, Packwood

WAHKIAKUM, Castle Rock, Silver Lake, STELLA 504, Stella, Oak Point, Eagle Cliff, Locoda, Quincy, Longview, Kelso, COWEEMAN 550, COWLITZ, GOWEEMAN, TOUTLE 556, MARGARET 524, Mt St Helens, LOO-WIT 522 Volcanic, Mt St Helens National Volcanic Monument, LEWIS RIVER 560, SKAMANIA, Mt Adams 12,276, Mt Adams Wilderness, CASCADE RANGE

Clatskanie, Alston, Rainier, Goble, Kalama, Columbia City, St Helens, Woodland, Yale, Cougar, Yale Lake, SIOUXON 572, Indian Heaven Wilderness, Trapper Creek Wilderness, Trout Lake, KLICKITAT

Vernonia, Scappoose, Ridgefield, Woodland, La Center, Battle Ground, Yacolt, WASHOUGAL 568, Amboy, Chelatchie, WIND RIVER 574, Carson, Stevenson, North Bonneville, Cascade Locks, White Salmon, Hood River

Forest Grove, Hillsboro, Banks, North Plains, VANCOUVER, Camas, Washougal, PORTLAND, Troutdale, Fairview, OREGON, MULTNOMAH, Columbia River Gorge National Scenic Area, HOOD RIVER, Mt Hood

Scale 1:600,000

0 5 10 15 20 25 30 40 50 Miles

0 5 10 15 20 25 30 40 50 Kilometers

© BENCHMARK MAPS

State & National Parks and Monuments

Battle Ground Lake State Park Considered a "miniature Crater Lake." Camping, picnicking, hiking, mountain biking, fishing, and boat launch. On Heissen Rd. (360) 687-4621. **G3**
Beacon Rock State Park Camping, picnicking, hiking, mountain biking, and boat launch. East of Vancouver on State Rte 14. (509) 427-8265. **H5**
Columbia River Gorge National Scenic Area Approximately 80 miles of the Columbia River canyon east of Washougal. Interpretive Center in Stevenson. (541) 308-1700. www.fs.usda.gov/crgnsa **H4**
Federation Forest State Park Picnicking and hiking. Over 600 acres of old growth. Location of the Catherine Montgomery Interpretive Center. Southeast of Enumclaw on State Rte 410. (360) 902-8844. **A6**
Flaming Geyser State Park Picnicking and hiking. Northeast of Enumclaw. (253) 735-8839. **A4**
Ike Kinswa State Park Camping, hiking, picnic sites, boat launch. On Mayfield Lake.(360) 983-3332. **D3**
Jarrell Cove State Park Camping, boating, and fishing. Boat docks available for overnight moorage. On Hartstine Island. (360) 426-9226. **A2**
Joemma Beach State Park Camping, picnicking, hiking, and boat launch. On Bay Rd. (253) 884-1944. **A2**
Lewis and Clark State Park Camping, picnic sites, hiking, mountain biking, and horseback riding. Southeast of Chehalis, off US 12. (360) 864-2643. **D2**
Millersylvania State Park Camping, picnicking, hiking. South of Olympia on State Rte 121. (360) 753-1519. **B2**
Mount Rainier National Park Camping, hiking, and fishing. Mount Rainier is highest point in the state. (360) 569-6608. www.nps.gov/mora **B5**
Mount St Helens National Volcanic Monument Hiking and sight-seeing in the area affected by the 1980 explosive volcanic eruption. (360) 449-7800. **E4**
Nolte State Park Picnic area, boat launch, and self-guided nature trail. Northeast of Enumclaw. (360) 825-4646. **A5**
Paradise Point State Park Camping, picnicking, and boat launch. South of Woodland. (360) 263-2350. **G2**
Seaquest State Park Camping, picnic sites, and interpretive trail. On state Rte 504. (360) 274-8633. **E2**
Tolmie State Park Day use area with fishing, swimming, and boating. Northeast of Olympia (360) 456-6464. **A2**

Forests & Wildlife Areas

Centennial Demonstration Forest Interpretive trail through the forest, past a beaver pond. West of Tumwater. 800-527-3305. **B1**
Charles L Pack Experimental Forest & Center for Sustainable Forestry Hike through old growth, managed forest, and second growth forest. North of Eatonville. (253) 692-4160. www.packforest.org. **B4**
Elbe Hills/Tahoma State Forests Areas of ORV trails, horse trails system, cross-country ski trails, campgrounds, and picnic areas. (360) 825-1631. **C4**
Gifford Pinchot National Forest Includes Mt Adams, Goat Rocks, Tatoosh, Glacier View, Indian Heaven, and Trapper Creek wildernesses. (360) 891-5000. **C5–G5**
Mount Baker–Snoqualmie National Forest Includes all or portions of Clearwater and Norse Peak wildernesses. (425) 783-6000. **A6**
Ridgefield National Wildlife Refuge The refuge preserves the Columbia River floodplain and manages agricultural land. Day use only; gate locked at dark. West of Ridgefield, on Columbia River. (360) 887-4106. **G2**
Shillapoo and Vancouver Lake Wildlife Areas Birdwatch for numerous species of birds including bald eagles and sandhill cranes. Area open for hunting and fishing. Northwest of Vancouver. (360) 906-6756. **G2**
Wolf Haven International Sanctuary for wolves that for one reason or another cannot be released into the wild. 3111 Offut Lake Rd, Tenino. (360) 264-4695 or 800-448-9653. www.wolfhaven.org. **B2**
Yacolt Burn State Forest Area managed by the state for its timber and recreation value. Northeast of Vancouver. (360) 577-2025. **G4**

Ski Areas & Snoparks

Mount Tahoma Ski Trails Snoparks, ski huts, and over 80 miles of cross-country ski trails, some which are groomed. Southeast of Elbe off State Rte 706. (360) 569-2451. skimtta.com (Mt Tahoma Trails Assoc). **C5**
Wind River Winter Recreation Area Groomed cross-country skiing trails. North of Carson on County Rd 30. (509) 395-3402 (Mt Adams Ranger District). **F5**

River Rafting

Colwitz River A float trip from La Wis Wis Campground to the town of Packwood with a few class II rapids. Possible log hazards. **C6**
Lewis River Crab Creek to the 9039 Road is a run for experts only. From the 9039 Road to Eagle Cliff Road is a class III run. Watch for log hazards on this river. North of Carson. (360) 247-3900. **F5**
Wind River This river is for expert boaters only. Over six miles of class III to class V rapids through a narrow gorge cut into the volcanic rocks. North of Carson. **G5**

Boating & Fishing

Coldwater Lake Formed by the eruption of Mt St Helens. Boat ramp at the south end of lake. Fish for cutthroat and rainbow trout. **E4**
Columbia River Fish for sturgeon, salmon, steelhead, and walleye. Public boat ramp at Beacon Rock State Park. **H4**
Lake Merwin Public boat ramp. Fish for coho salmon and kokanee. **F3**
Mayfield Lake Camping, boating, fishing, and water-skiing. Fish for tiger muskies, coho salmon, and rainbow trout. **D3**
Riffe Lake Fish for coho salmon, cutthroat, and brown trout. Public boat ramps and camping available. **D3-4**
South Fork Toutle River Fish for winter and summer steelhead. Stocked annually with steelhead. **E3**
Swift Reservoir Boat ramp. Lake is stocked with rainbow trout. **F4**
Yale Lake Public boat ramps. Fish for cutthroat trout and kokanee. **F4**

Natural Wonders

Ape Cave Tour a lava tube and learn how it was formed. Mt St Helens National Volcanic Monument. (360) 449-7800. **F4**
Big Four Ice Cave Picnic Area Explore a lava tube that served as a source of ice for the pioneers. Wear warm clothing and carry 2 light sources. On FS Road 24. (509) 395-3402. **F6**
Big Lava Bed Over 12 square miles of lava flow. See and explore various unique volcanic features. East of FS Road 66. (509) 395-3402. **G5**
Trail of Two Forests Interpretive trail through two forests separated by 2,000 years of age. Mt St Helens NVM. (360) 449-7800. **F4**

Historic Sites & Museums

Borst Family Homestead Visit 1857 Greek Revival-styled mansion and the Borst Granary blockhouse which served as a military post. Tours available. In Fort Borst Park, Johnson Rd, Centralia. (360) 330-7662. **C1**
Claquato Church Built in 1857. One of the oldest churches in the state. Southwest of Chehalis on Water Ave. (360) 748-8885. **C1**
Clark County Museum Exhibits depict pioneer life and display Chinook Indian artifacts. The basement is home to the SP & S Railway Museum. 1511 Main St, Vancouver. (360) 993-5679. www.cchmuseum.org **H2**
Ezra Meeker Mansion Built in the late 1880s. Features leaded stained glass windows, ceiling artwork and ornate handcrafted fireplaces. 312 Spring St, Puyallup. (253) 848-1770. www.meekermansion.org **A4**
Fort Cascades Historic Trail See Indian petroglyphs and other pioneer relics along the trail through the site of the fort. E of North Bonneville on State Rte 14. (541) 374-8820 or (503) 808-4508 (Corps of Engineers). **H5**
Fort Lewis Military Museum Collection of uniforms, military artifacts, and vehicles. Located in the historic Fort Lewis Inn. Open Wed–Sat. Fort Lewis. (253) 967-7206. www.fortlewismuseum.com **A2**
Fort Vancouver National Historic Site Site of the Hudson Bay Company's trading center in the mid-1800s and the first US military post in the Pacific Northwest. Visit Officers Row, 21 historic homes built from 1849 to 1901. 612 E Reserve St, Vancouver. (360) 816-6230. www.nps.gov/fova **H2**
John R Jackson House Historic Site Built in 1845, one of the oldest pioneer buildings north of the Columbia River. (360) 748-0831. **D2**
Layser Cave Interpretive Site A cave dwelling used by Native Americans for thousands of years until the eruption of Mt St Helens 3,500 years ago. All artifacts are protected by the Antiquities Act of 1906; do not remove them. Off FS Road 23. (360) 497-1100. **D5**
Lewis County Historical Museum Displays depicting pioneer life including a general store, blacksmith shop, pioneer kitchen, and Indian artifacts housed in an historic railroad depot. 599 NW Front Way, Chehalis. (360) 748-0831. www.lewiscountymuseum.org **C1**
Longmire Museum Collection of rocks, plants, and animals, as well as historic exhibits. Mt Rainier NP. (360) 569-6575. www.nps.gov/mora **C5**
Old Capitol Restored capitol building built in 1890s. Daily tours include Temple of Justice, Governor's Mansion, and Legislative building with a 287-ft diameter dome and Tiffany chandelier. Legion St, Olympia. (360) 586-8687. **A2**
Pearson Air Museum The oldest operating airport in the US. Exhibits illustrate the history of aviation. There is a children's hands-on activity center. 1115 East 5th St, Vancouver. (360) 816-6232. **H3**
Pioneer Farm Museum Tour a farm as it was in the 1880s, with hands-on activities such as farm chores done as they were 100 years ago. E of Eatonville on Ohop Valley Rd. (360) 832-6300. www.pioneerfarmmuseum.org **B4**
Pomeroy Living History Farm See life prior to electricity on a 1920s farmstead. Open the first weekend of the month July–October. 20902 NE Lucia Falls Rd, Yacolt. (360) 686-3537. www.pomeroyfarm.org **G3**
State Capital Museum A collection of historical documents, photographs, and pioneer and Northwest Indian artifacts. Housed in the Lord Mansion. 211 21st Av SW, Olympia. (360) 753-2580. www.washingtonhistory.org/visit/scm **B2**
Two Rivers Heritage Museum Local history displays of the paper and woolen industry and Native American history. 1 Durgan St, Washougal. (360) 835-8742. www.2rhm.com **H3**

Other Attractions

Bonneville Lock and Dam Visit electric generators and view migrating fish through underwater observation windows. East of North Bonneville. (509) 427-2181 (Washington Shore Visitor Center). **H5**
Chehalis–Centalia Railroad Steam train excursion in the Chehalis Valley. 1101 Sylvenus St, Chehalis. (360) 748-9593. www.steamtrainride.com **C1**
Columbia River Gorge Interpretive Center Exhibits illustrating the natural and human history of the gorge. 990 SW Rock Creek Dr, Stevenson. 800-991-2338. www.columbiagorge.org **G4**
Elbe Hills ORV Trails System of trails built for off-road, motorized recreation. Camping by reservation only. (360) 825-1631. **C4**
Evans Creek ORV Area Camping, off-road vehicle roads and trails. Bring your own water. South of Enumclaw on FS Road 7930. (360) 825-6585. **B5**
Hulda Klager Lilac Gardens Visit the gardens surrounding the 1889 Victorian home of Hulda Klager known for her work with hybrid lilacs. 115 S Pekin Rd, Woodland. (360) 225-8996. www.lilacgardens.com **G2**
Jones Creek ORV Area Picnic area at trailhead. Mountain bike and motorcycle trails. NE Lessard Rd. (360) 577-2025. **G3**
Matilda Jackson House Park Day use area with hiking trail. North of Marys Corner on State Rte 12. (360) 864-2643. **D2**
Mount Rainier Scenic Railroad Steam-powered train ride through the forest. South of Elbe. 888-783-2611 or (360) 569-7959. www.mrsr.com **C4**
Northwest Trek Wildlife Park View moose, bison, bears, and other wildlife native to the Northwest via a tram tour. 11610 Trek Dr E, Eatonville. (360) 832-6117. www.nwtrek.org. **B4**
Pendleton Woolen Mill Weaving done here since 1909. Mill tours and outlet store. 2 17th St, Washougal. 800-568-2480 or (360) 835-1118. **H4**
Wind River Nursery and Arboretum Working nursery established by the Forest Service in 1909. Visit historic buildings, dam, and interpretive trail. North of Carson on Hemlock Rd. (509) 395-3400. **G5**
Windsurfing & Kiteboarding Several popular windsurfing and kiteboarding spots along the Columbia River. (541) 386-9225 (Columbia Gorge Windsurfing Assoc). www.gorgewindsurfing.org **H4**

Information Resources

Gifford Pinchot National Forest Headquarters
10600 NE 51st Circle, Vancouver 98682. (360) 891-5000.
www.fs.usda.gov/giffordpinchot
Cowlitz Valley Ranger District Office
10024 Hwy 12, PO Box 670, Randle 98377. (360) 497-1100
Mt Adams Ranger District Office
2455 Hwy 141, Trout Lake 98650. (509) 395-3402
Highway Information and Mountain Pass Report
Dial 511 or 800-695-7623. www.wsdot.wa.gov
Mt Baker–Snoqualmie National Forest Headquarters
2930 Wetmore Ave, Suite 3A, Everett 98201. (425) 783-6000.
www.fs.usda.gov/mbs
Snoqualmie Ranger District, Enumclaw Office
450 Roosevelt Ave E, Enumclaw 98022. (360) 825-6585
Mount Rainier National Park
Tahoma Woods, Star Route, Ashford 98034. (360) 569-6608.
www.nps.gov/mora
Mount St Helens National Volcanic Monument Headquarters
42218 NE Yale Bridge Rd, Amboy 98601. (360) 449-7800.
www.fs.usda.gov/mountsthelens
Mount St Helens Visitor Center
3029 Spirit Lake Hwy, Castle Rock 98611. (360) 274-0962
National Recreation Reservation Service
877-444-6777. Reservations for selected campgrounds.
www.recreation.gov
Northwest Weather and Avalanche Center
7600 Sandpoint Wy NE, Seattle 98115. (206) 526-4666.
Recorded message Oct 1-Apr 15. www.nwac.us
Washington Department of Natural Resources Headquarters
1111 Washington St SE, PO Box 47000, Olympia 98504.
(360) 902-1000. www.dnr.wa.gov
Pacific Cascade Region
601 Bond Rd, Castle Rock 98611. (360) 577-2025
Washington State Parks Information Center & Campground Reservations
(360) 902-8844, 888-226-7688. www.parks.wa.gov
(360) 902-8555 (Boaters Guide)
(360) 902-8600 (Environmental Learning Centers)
(360) 902-8684 (Snopark and Winter Recreation Info)

Hunting & Fishing

Washington Department of Fish and Wildlife Headquarters
Natural Res Bldg, 1111 Washington St SE, Olympia 98501.
(360) 902-2200. www.wdfw.wa.gov
Washington Department of Fish and Wildlife, Southwest Region 5
2108 Grand Blvd, Vancouver 98661. (360) 696-6211
See map on page 29.

Campgrounds & RV Parks

See page 36 for the campground and RV park listings.

Climate

See explanation on page 31

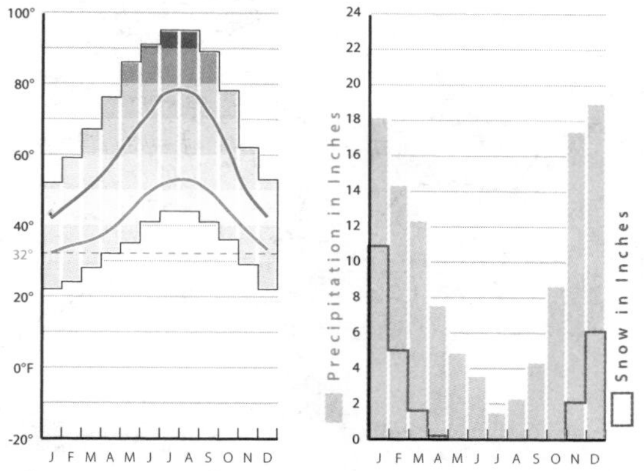

Cougar: 142 days with 114" precipitation, 26" of snow,
el. 659 ft — 52 nights below freezing, 12 days above 90°
Jan (22°) 32°–42° (52°) Apr (32°) 39°–57° (76°)
July (44°) 52°–78° (95°) Oct (36°) 44°–62° (78°)

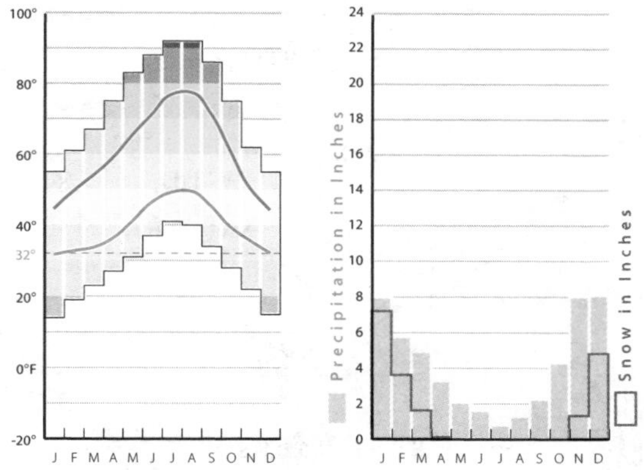

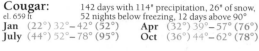

Olympia: 107 days with 51" precipitation, 19" of snow,
el. 194 ft — 86 nights below freezing, 6 days above 90°
Jan (14°) 32°–44° (55°) Apr (27°) 37°–59° (75°)
July (41°) 49°–77° (92°) Oct (28°) 39°–61° (75°)

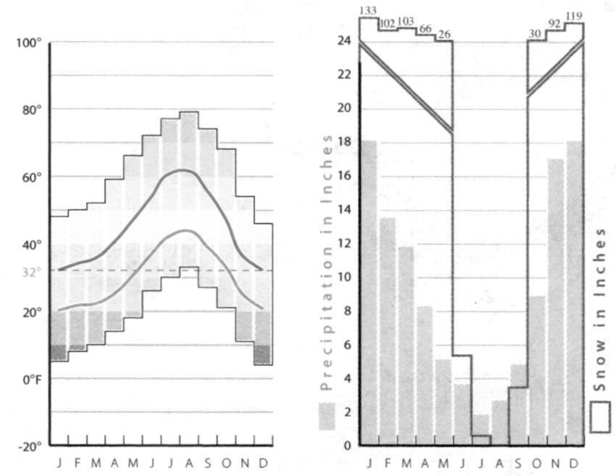

Paradise: 162 days with 116" precipitation, 683" of snow,
el. 5430 ft — 223 nights below freezing, 0 days above 90°
Jan (5°) 20°–32° (48°) Apr (14°) 25°–40° (59°)
July (30°) 42°–61° (77°) Oct (21°) 33°–47° (68°)

Landscape Page Index

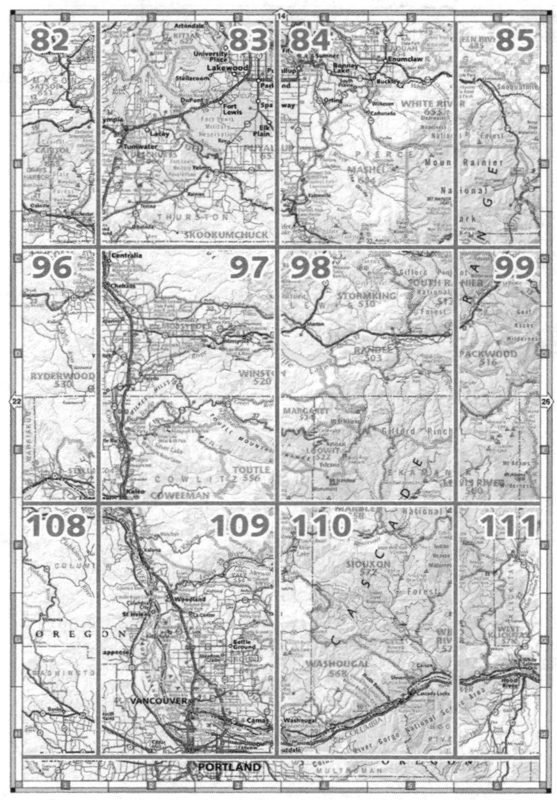

Landscape Page Numbers Are Shown in Blue

RECREATION

© BENCHMARK MAPS

Wilderness | State Parks | Bureau of Reclamation | Bureau of Land Management | National Parks/ Monuments | State Game Management Unit

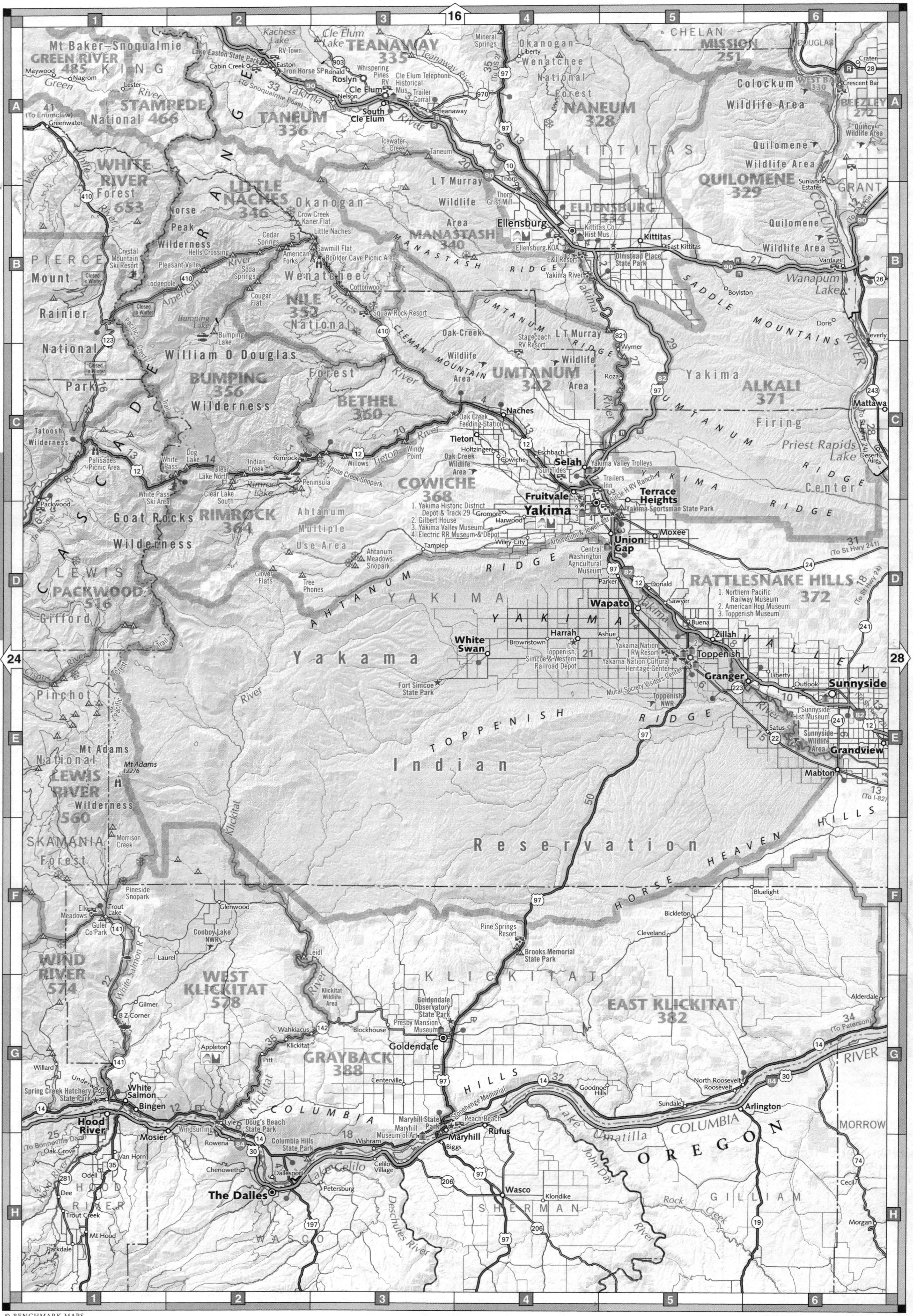

Forest Service | State Lands | Military Lands | Tribal Lands | Wildlife Areas

HOKO 601

RECREATION

Legend / Labels

Mt Baker–Snoqualmie

GREEN RIVER 485 KING

Maywood
Nagrom
Lester

STAMPEDE National 466

41 (To Enumclaw) Greenwater

WHITE RIVER Forest 653

Kachess Lake
Cle Elum Lake
Lake Easton State Park
Cabin Creek RV
Easton
Iron Horse SP
Ronald
Roslyn
Cle Elum
Nelson
South Cle Elum

TEANAWAY 335

Whispering Pines
Cle Elum Telephone Historical Mus.
Trailer Corral
Teanaway

Mineral Springs
Liberty

Okanogan– Wenatchee National Forest

CHELAN
MISSION 251

Colockum Wildlife Area

WEST BE 330

BEEZLEY 272

Crater
Crescent Bar

TANEUM 336

Thorp
Thorp Grist Mill

L T Murray

Wildlife Area

NANEUM 328

KITTITAS

ELLENSBURG 334

Ellensburg
Kittitas Co. Hist Mus
Ellensburg KOA
E&J Resort

QUILOMENE 329

Quilomene Wildlife Area

Quilomene Wildlife Area

Sunland Estates

LITTLE NACHES 346

Norse Peak Wilderness

Crow Creek
Kaner Flat
Little Naches
Cedar Springs
American Forks
Soda Springs

Okanogan– Wenatchee
Crystal Mountain Ski Resort
Hells Crossing
Pleasant Valley
Lodgepole

Sawmill Flat
Boulder Cave Picnic Area

MANASTASH 340

MANASTASH RIDGE

Kittitas
East Kittitas
Olmstead Place State Park
Yakima River

UMTANUM RIDGE

QUILOMENE

Vantage

Wanapum Lake

SADDLE MOUNTAINS

Doris
Boylston

90

27

Beverly

PIERCE

Mount Rainier National Park

123

Closed in Winter
410

Bumping Lake
William O Douglas
Bumping Lake

NILE 350 National

Cougar Flat
Squaw Rock Resort

BUMPING 356 Wilderness

BETHEL 360

Oak Creek
Cleman Mountain Wildlife Area

Stagecoach RV Resort

L T MURRAY RIDGE

UMTANUM 342

L T Murray Wildlife Area

Wymer
Roza

97
82

ALKALI 371

Firing

Yakima River

Mattawa
243

Priest Rapids Lake

RIDGE CENTER

RIDGE

Tatoosh Wilderness

Palisades Picnic Area

White Pass
13

Dog Lake
Clear Lake North
White Pass
Clear Lake South

Indian Creek
Rimrock
House Creek, Snopark

Peninsula
Rimrock Lake

Naches
Oak Creek Feeding Station
Tieton
Holtzinger
Oak Creek Wildlife Area
Cowiche

12

Eschbach
Selah
Yakima Valley Trolleys
Sundides

Central Washington Agricultural Museum

24

Goat Rocks Wilderness

RIMROCK 364

Ahtanum Multiple Use Area

Ahtanum Meadows Snopark
Clover Flats
Tree Phones

COWICHE 368

1. Yakima Historic District Depot & Track 29
2. Gilbert House
3. Yakima Valley Museum
4. Electric RR Museum & Depot

Fruitvale
Yakima
Gromore
Harwood

Trailers
Inn

Terrace Heights
Yakima Sportsman State Park
Moxee

Union Gap
Parker
Donald
Sawyer

12

RATTLESNAKE HILLS 372

1. Northern Pacific Railway Museum
2. American Hop Museum
3. Toppenish Museum

24
31 (To St Hwy 241)

LEWIS

PACKWOOD 516

Packwood
Gifford

AHTANUM RIDGE

YAKIMA

Tampico
Wiley City

YAKIMA VALLEY

Wapato
Harrah
Ashue
Buena
Zillah
Toppenish

241

Pinchot

Yakama

White Swan

Brownstown
Yakama Nation RV Resort
Yakama Nation, Simcoe & Western Railroad Depot

21

Yakama Nation Cultural Heritage Center
Mural Society Visitors Center
Toppenish NWR

Granger
223
Outlook
Liberty

Sunnyside
Sunnyside Hist Museum
Sunnyside Wildlife Area

82
241
12

28

LEWIS RIVER 560 Wilderness

Mt Adams
Mt Adams 12276

Morrison Creek

SKAMANIA Forest

Fort Simcoe State Park

TOPPENISH Indian

Reservation

TOPPENISH RIDGE

Satus
22
15

Grandview
Mabton
13 (To I-82)

HORSE HEAVEN HILLS

WIND RIVER 574

Pineside Snopark

Elk Meadows
Trout Lake
Guler Co Park
141

Glenwood

Conboy Lake NWR

Laurel

Pine Springs Resort

97

Bluelight

Bickleton
Cleveland

Alderdale
34

EAST KLICKITAT 382

WEST KLICKITAT 578

KLICKITAT

Leidl
Klickitat Wildlife Area

Brooks Memorial State Park

Goldendale Observatory State Park
Presby Mansion Museum

Goldendale

North Roosevelt
Roosevelt
30

Willard
141

B Z Corner
Gilmer
Appleton
142
Wahkiacus
Klickitat
Blockhouse

GRAYBACK 388

Centerville

97

14
32

Goodnoe Hills
Sundale

Arlington

MORROW

Spring Creek Hatchery State Park

White Salmon
Bingen

Lyle
Doug's Beach State Park
Columbia Hills State Park

Maryhill State Park
Maryhill Museum of Art
Maryhill
Rufus

Stonehenge Memorial
Peach Beach
Biggs

COLUMBIA

Wishram

John Day Lake

OREGON

GILLIAM

Hood River
Mosier
35
281
Odell
Dee
Van Horn
Rowena

30
14
18

Celilo
Celilo Village

Wasco
206

Klondike

Oak Grove

The Dalles
Dallesport
197
Petersburg

SHERMAN

Rock Creek

Morgan
19
74

Parkdale
Mt Hood

© BENCHMARK MAPS

Scale 1:600,000

0 5 10 15 20 25 30 40 50 Miles

0 5 10 15 20 25 30 40 50 Kilometers

State Parks www.parks.wa.gov

Brooks Memorial State Park and Environmental Learning Center Camping and hiking. North of Goldendale. (509) 773-4611. **F4**

Doug's Beach State Park A popular windsurfing site and (for those less adventurous) a windsurfing observation site. Picnic tables and shade trees line the shore. 3 miles east of Lyle. (509) 773-3141. **G2**

Fort Simcoe State Park Restored fort and buildings of the 9th Regiment's 1850s military post. Day use area. W of Toppenish. (509) 874-2372. **E3**

Goldendale Observatory State Park Largest reflecting telescope in the country open to public for group use. In Goldendale. (509) 773-3141. **G3**

Columbia Hills State Park Camping, fishing, and swimming. Native American petroglyphs located west of park. Call for petroglyph tour reservations. East of The Dalles Dam off State Rte 14. (509) 767-1159. **G2**

Iron Horse State Park A trail from the Columbia River, near Vantage to the Snoqualmie Pass. Open to hiking, biking, and horse back riding. (509) 773-2230. **A2**

Lake Easton State Park Camping, picnicking, hiking, and boat launch. West of Easton on Interstate 90. (509) 656-2230. **A2**

Maryhill State Park Camping, picnicking, hiking, boat dock, and boat launch. South of Goldendale on US 97. (509) 773-5007. **G3**

Olmstead Place State Park Preserved pioneer homestead of the 1870s. East of Ellensburg. (509) 925-1943. **B5**

Spring Creek Hatchery State Park Recently designated a state Park. 4 miles west of Bingen. (509) 773-3141. **G1**

Yakima Sportsman State Park Camping, picnicking, and boat launch. Pond fishing for kids under 15 years old. Day use area. Windsurfing area. East of Yakima. (509) 575-2774. **D5**

Forest & Wildlife Areas

Ahtanum Multiple Use Area Forested state managed trust lands. Recreation opportunities include camping, hiking, fishing, wildlife viewing, and snowmobiling. West of Yakima. (509) 925-8510. **D2**

Colockum Wildlife Area Hiking and hunting in area managed by the state. South of Wenatchee. (509) 663-6260. **A5**

Conboy Lake National Wildlife Refuge An area of previous wetlands, drained by a canal, now partially restored. Hiking, hunting, and fishing are the recreation options here. South of Glenwood. (509) 546-8300. **F2**

Gifford Pinchot National Forest Along the western slopes of the Cascade Range. Includes Mt Adams, Goat Rocks and Tatoosh wildernesses. (360) 891-5000. **D1–G1**

Klickitat Wildlife Area Fishing, boating, and wildlife viewing on approximately 14,700 acres. West of Goldendale. (509) 773-4459. **G3**

L. T. Murray Wildlife Area 106,400 acres of mixed forest, meadow, and sagebrush support winter elk herds and several species of raptors. Wildlife viewing and hunting opportunities. West of Ellensburg. (509) 902-2515. **B3–C4**

Oak Creek Wildlife Area This area provides good opportunities to see big horn sheep and elk, especially during winter feeding. SW of Ellensburg on US 12. (509) 653-2390. **C3–4**

Okanogan–Wenatchee National Forest Includes Norse Peak, William O Douglas, and Goat Rocks wildernesses. On the eastern slopes of the Cascade Range. (509) 664-9200. **B2–D2**

Quilomene Wildlife Area Dispersed camping (no campfires), hike, collect petrified wood or hunt in area of desert above the Columbia River Canyon. Northeast of Ellensburg. (509) 925-6746. **A6**

Toppenish National Wildlife Refuge A 1,900-acre preserve. Hunt or view wildlife. A stopover for various migrating shore birds. 6 miles south of Toppenish. (509) 546-8300. **E5**

Ski Areas & Snoparks

Crystal Mountain Resort 57 runs, 12 lifts, night skiing. SE of Enumclaw. (360) 663-3050. Snow phone: 888-754-6199. www.skicrystal.com **B1**

Pineside Snopark Groomed cross-country ski trails and 20-space snopark. N of Trout Lake on FS Road 82. (509) 395-3400 (Mt Adams RD). **F1**

White Pass 45 runs, 8 lifts, night skiing, and 11 miles of groomed cross-country trails. (509) 672-3101. Snow phone: (509) 672-3100. skiwhitepass.com **C1**

River Rafting

Tieton River An intermediate river trip from Rimrock to Windy Point. Commercial guides available. (509) 653-2205. **C2**

White Salmon River From BZ Corner to Northwestern Reservoir is a raft trip for experience boaters. Log jams are possible. Portage at Husum Falls. Commercial guide service available. North of White Salmon. (509) 395-3402. **G1**

Yakima River A scenic trip through the Yakima River Canyon from Ellensburg to the Roza Dam. **B4**

Boating & Fishing

Bumping Lake Camp, boat, water-ski, and fish. Boat ramp. Fish for kokanee, rainbow, and cutthroat trout. Off State Rte 410 on FS Road 1800. **B2**

Columbia River, above the Dalles Dam Lake Celilo is known for the most sturgeon catches of all the lakes on the Columbia. Also fish for steelhead, bass, and walleye. Good public access. **H3**

Rimrock Lake Camping, boating, water skiing, and fishing. Boat ramps are located on the north and south shores of the lake. Fish for kokanee and rainbow trout. Off State Rte 410 on FS Road 2000. **C2**

White Salmon River Fish for summer steelhead and spring chinook. **G1**

Natural Wonders

Boulder Cave Visit a cave over 300 feet in length, formed in the volcanic rock layers. Only known population of Pacific Western Big-Eared Bats in Washington. On State Rte 410. (509) 653-1401. **B3**

Mount Adams A 12,276-ft-high basalt and andesitic volcanic peak topped with glaciers. Surrounded by wilderness. N of Trout Lake. (509) 395-3402. **E1**

Palisades Picnic Area View the steep canyon wall of columnar basalt along the Clear Fork of the Cowlitz River. Popular whitewater area. On US 12. **C1**

Historic Sites & Museums

American Hop Museum Traces the history of the hop industry from early beginnings in 1700s New York, to present day in the Yakima Valley. 22 S B St, Toppenish. (509) 865-4677. www.americanhopmuseum.org **D5**

Central Washington Agricultural Museum A collection of vintage farm equipment located in Fulbright Park where demonstrations of the use of some of the equipment take place. 4508 Main St, Union Gap. (509) 457-8735. www.centralwaagmuseum.org **D4**

Cle Elum Historical Telephone Museum A collection of old telephones, switchboards, and other related equipment. Museum established in 1966. 221 E 1st St, Cle Elum. (509) 649-2880. **A3**

Gilbert House Tour the restored and furnished farmhouse built in 1898. Tours by appointment. 2109 W Yakima Ave, Yakima. (509) 248-0747. **C4**

Kittitas County Historical Museum Housed in the Cadwell Building, built in the late 1880s. Exhibits include Kittitas Indian artifacts, pioneer tools, and a mineral and rock collection. 114 E 3rd St, Ellensburg. (509) 925-3778. www.kchm.org **B4**

Maryhill Museum of Art A mansion built in the early 1900s houses varied collection of artwork and artifacts including sculptures by Auguste Rodin, antique chess sets, Indian baskets, and 18th-century Russian icons. Open mid-March through mid-November. 3 miles west of US 97 on State Rte 14. www.maryhillmuseum.org (509) 773-3733. **G3**

Northern Pacific Railway Museum A collection of rail and steam artifacts, photographs, and a restored telegraph office in a restored 1911 railroad depot. 10 Asotin Ave, Toppenish. (509) 865-1911. www.nprymuseum.org **D5**

Presby Mansion Museum Presby Mansion, built in 1902, is home to a collection of coffee mills, branding irons, brands, and-turn-of-the-century household items. 127 W Broadway St, Goldendale. (509) 773-4303. **G3**

Sunnyside Historical Museum Collection of Indian artifacts and displays of a pioneer kitchen and dining room. The Ben Snipe Cabin, built in 1859, is located across the street. 704 S 4th St, Sunnyside. (509) 837-6010. **E6**

Thorp Grist Mill Restored grist mill built in 1883. Southwest of Thorp. (509) 964-9640. www.thorp.org **B4**

Toppenish Museum A variety of exhibits including antique firefighting equipment and American Indian baskets. 1 S Elm St, Toppenish. (509) 865-3600. **D5**

Yakima Historic District, Depot and Track 29 Downtown historic district is located at First and Front streets. Track 29 is a series of rail cars converted into shops. (509) 575-3388 (Visitor Info Center). **C4**

Yakima Valley Museum Exhibits illustrating regional history and a collection of horse-drawn vehicles. 2105 Tieton Dr, Yakima. (509) 248-0747. www.yakimavalleymuseum.org **C3**

Notable Towns ○ ◉

Cle Elum Mining, ranching, and railroad town on the upper Yakima River is the first town of some size on I-90 east of Snoqualmie Pass. Iron Horse State Park–John Wayne Pioneer Trail follows the route of the former Milwaukee Road Railway through South Cle Elum. (509) 674-5958 (Cle Elum/Roslyn Chamber of Commerce). www.cleelumroslyn.org **A3**

Ellensburg National Historic District, consisting of numerous buildings built in the late 1880s after a fire destroyed much of the town in 1889. 888-925-2204 or (509) 925-2002 (Chamber of Commerce). www.kittitascountychamber.com **B4**

Goldendale Goldendale Observatory State Park is on north side of town. Maryhill Museum and Stonehenge replica are approximately 10 miles south of town. (509) 773-3400 (Chamber of Commerce). www.goldendalechamber.org **G3**

Roslyn Mining town near Cle Elum. Television series Northern Exposure was filmed here. (509) 674-5958 (Cle Elum/Roslyn Chamber of Commerce). www.cleelumroslyn.org **A3**

Toppenish Known as the city of murals. Dozens of large murals depicting the area's history adorn the outer walls of the buildings here. Tours are available. New murals are added each year between April and October. 800-863-6375 or (509) 865-3262 (C of C), (509) 865-6516 (Mural Soc). www.visittoppenish.com **D5**

Other Attractions

Stonehenge Memorial A concrete replica of the ancient Stonehenge, located in England, built as a memorial to the men of Klickitat County who died in World War I. (509) 773-3400 (Chamber of Commerce). **G4**

Toppenish, Simcoe and Western Railroad Locomotive ride from Harrah to White Swan. Harrah. (509) 865-1911. **D4**

Windsurfing and Kiteboarding on the Columbia River Doug's Beach and Horsethief Lake State Park, as well as others, are known as windsurfing spots along the Columbia River. (541) 386-9225 (Columbia Gorge Windsurfing Assoc). www.gorgewindsurfing.org **G2**

Yakama Nation Cultural Heritage Center The museum illustrates the history and traditions of the Yakama Nation. The library is a collection of material emphasizing Indian culture. The restaurant serves native foods. Off US Hwy 97, Toppenish. (509) 865-2800. www.yakamamuseum.com **D5**

Yakima Area Arboretum The arboretum includes an area of wetland, a Japanese Garden, and the Jewett Interpretive Center. 1401 Arboretum Drive, Yakima. (509) 248-7337. www.ahtrees.org **D4**

Yakima Valley Trolleys Ride in cars from the 1920s and '30s on an electric trolley from Yakima to Selah and return. Also visit the museum. 306 W Pine St, Yakima. (509) 249-5962. www.yakimavalleytrolleys.org **C4**

Information Resources

Bureau of Land Management, Wenatchee Field Office
915 North Walla Walla, Wenatchee 98801. (509) 665-2100
www.blm.gov

Gifford Pinchot National Forest Headquarters
10600 NE 51st Circle, Vancouver 98682. (360) 891-5000
www.fs.usda.gov/giffordpinchot

Mt Adams Ranger District Office
2455 Hwy 141, Trout Lake 98650. (509) 395-3402

Highway Information and Mountain Pass Report
Dial 511 or 800-695-7623. www.wsdot.wa.gov

National Recreation Reservation Service
877-444-6777. Reservations for selected campgrounds.
www.recreation.gov

Northwest Weather and Avalanche Center
7600 Sandpoint Wy NE, Seattle 98115. (206) 526-4666
Recorded message Oct 1-Apr 15. www.nwac.us

Okanogan–Wenatchee National Forest Headquarters
215 Melody Ln, Wenatchee 98801. (509) 664-9200
www.fs.usda.gov/okawen

Cle Elum Ranger District Office
803 W 2nd St, Cle Elum 98922. (509) 852-1100

Naches Ranger District Office
10237 Hwy 12, Naches 98937. (509) 653-1401

Washington Department of Natural Resources, Southeast Region
713 E Bowers Rd, Ellensburg 98926. (509) 925-8510 www.dnr.wa.gov

Washington State Parks Information Center
(360) 902-8844, 888-226-7688. www.parks.wa.gov
(360) 902-8555 (Boaters Guide)
(360) 902-8600 (Environmental Learning Centers)
(360) 902-8684 (Sno-park and Winter Recreation Info)

Hunting & Fishing

Washington Department of Fish and Wildlife, South Central Region 3
1701 S 24th Ave, Yakima 98902. (509) 575-2740. www.wdfw.wa.gov
See map on page 29.

Campgrounds & RV Parks

See page 37 for the campground and RV park listings.

Climate

See explanation on page 31

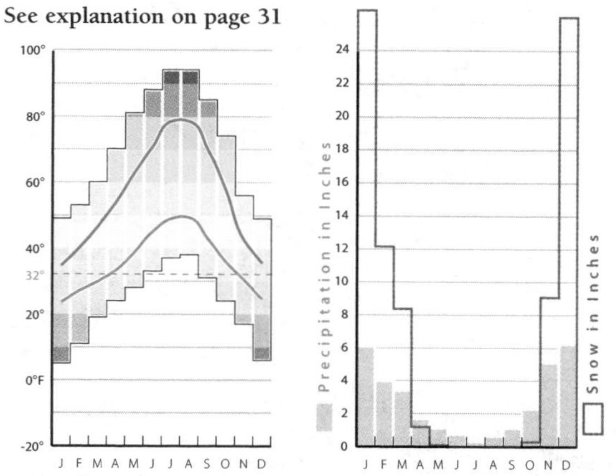

Appleton: el. 2336 ft — 74 days with 33" precipitation, 84" of snow, 147 nights below freezing, 11 days above 90°
Jan (5°) 24°– 35° (49°)   Apr (24°) 33°– 54° (70°)
July (37°) 49°– 79° (94°)   Oct (24°) 36°– 58° (74°)

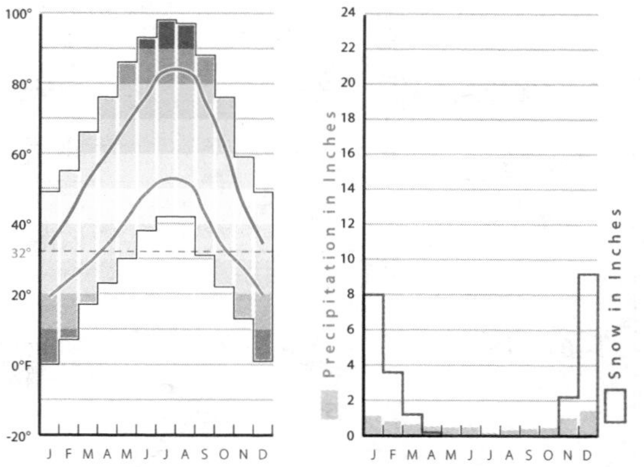

Ellensburg: el. 1480 ft — 30 days with 9" precipitation, 25" of snow, 159 nights below freezing, 22 days above 90°
Jan (0°) 19°– 34° (49°)   Apr (23°) 34°– 60° (76°)
July (42°) 53°– 84° (98°)   Oct (22°) 33°– 62° (76°)

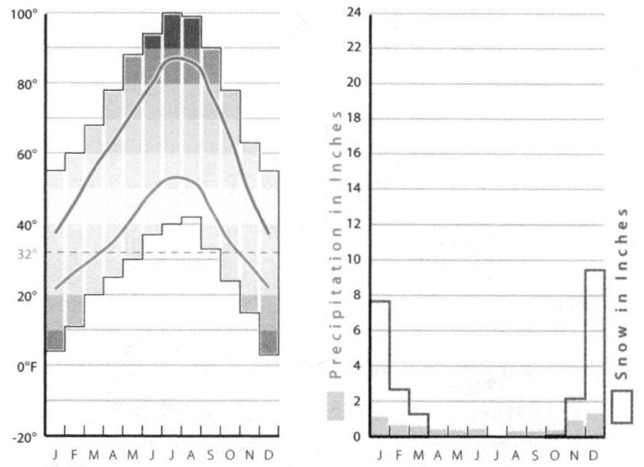

Yakima: el. 1063 ft — 25 days with 8" precipitation, 24" of snow, 145 nights below freezing, 32 days above 90°
Jan (4°) 22°– 38° (55°)   Apr (25°) 35°– 64° (78°)
July (40°) 53°– 87° (100°)   Oct (24°) 35°– 65° (78°)

Landscape Page Index

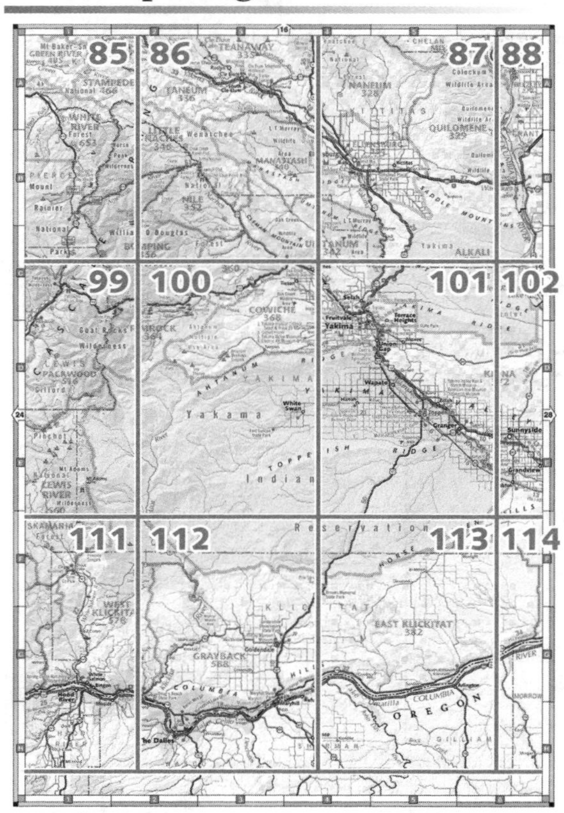

Landscape Page Numbers Are Shown In Blue

RECREATION

© BENCHMARK MAPS

Legend:
- Wilderness
- Forest Service
- State Parks
- State Lands
- Bureau of Reclamation
- Military Lands
- Bureau of Land Management
- Tribal Lands
- National Parks/Monuments
- Wildlife Areas
- HOKO 601 — State Game Management Unit

RECREATION

Counties / Areas:
CHELAN, DOUGLAS, KITTITAS, GRANT, ADAMS, LINCOLN, FRANKLIN, BENTON, WALLA WALLA, KLICKITAT, YAKIMA, MORROW, GILLIAM, UMATILLA

Game Management Units:
- BEEZLEY 272
- DESERT 290
- RITZVILLE 284
- WAHLUKE 278
- ALKALI 371
- RINGOLD 379
- KAHLOTUS 381
- RATTLESNAKE HILLS 372
- HORSE HEAVEN 373
- EAST KLICKITAT 382
- PRESCOTT 149

Wildlife Areas:
- Colockum Wildlife Area
- Quilomene Wildlife Area 329
- Whiskey Dick Wildlife Area
- Quincy Lake Wildlife Area
- Winchester Wasteway Wildlife Area
- Shady Tree
- North Columbia Basin Wildlife Area - Gloyd Seeps Unit
- Gloyd Seeps Wildlife Area
- Potholes Wildlife Area
- Seep Lakes Wildlife Area
- Crab Creek Wildlife Area
- Sunnyside Wildlife Area
- Rattlesnake Slope Wildlife Area

Cities / Towns:
Quincy, Winchester, Crater, Crescent Bar, Moses Lake, George, Royal City, Smyrna, Mattawa, Warden, Ritzville, Moody, Batum, Jantz, Marcellus, Schrag, Lind, Ralston, Paha, Providence, Cunningham, Hatton, Othello, Connell, Kahlotus, Wacota, Ruxby, Matthew, Mesa, Eltopia, Windust, Sheffler, Eureka, Lamar, Harsha, Climax, Fishhook Park, Charbonneau Park, Sandy Heights, Richland, West Richland, Benton City, Kennewick, Pasco, Burbank, Tri-Cities, Finley, Wallula, Lowden, Touchet, Walla Walla, College Place, Milton-Freewater, Umapine, Helix, Athena, Weston, Adams, Cayuse, Thorn Hollow, Mission, Pendleton, Rieth, Gibbon, Sunnyside, Grandview, Mabton, Outlook, Liberty, Prosser, Whitstran, Gibbon, Badger, Chaffee, Paterson, Plymouth, Umatilla, Irrigon, Hermiston, Stanfield, Echo, Westland, Hinkle, Holdman, Boardman, Crow Butte Park, Alderdale, Cecil, Morgan, Ione, Stanford

Features:
- Gorge Amphitheater
- Wild Horse
- Gingko Petrified Forest State Park
- Vantage
- Wanapum Dam & Heritage Center
- Wanapum Lake
- Priest Rapids Lake
- Potholes Reservoir
- Columbia NWR
- Sage Hills Golf Club & RV Resort
- Royal City Golf Course
- Saddle Mountain Unit
- Hanford Reach National Monument
- Wahluke Unit
- B & C Reactors
- McGee Ranch Riverlands Unit
- Fitzner-Eberhart Arid Lands Ecology Reserve Unit
- Hanford Reservation - US Dept of Energy
- Ligo Observatory
- Juniper Dunes Wilderness (Restricted Access)
- Scooteney Reservoir
- Horn Rapids RV Resort
- Horn Rapids ORV Park
- Rattlesnake Slope Wildlife Area
- Columbia River Exhibition of History, Science & Technology
- The REACH
- Wright's Desert Gold
- Sacajawea State Park
- Ice Harbor Lock & Dam & Visitor Ctr
- McNary NWR
- Tri-Cities
- Madame Dorian Mem Park
- Pierce's Green Valley
- McNary Lock and Dam & Pacific Salmon Vis Ctr
- Umatilla NWR
- Umatilla National Wildlife Refuge
- Umatilla Ordnance Depot (No Public Access)
- Power City
- Boardman Bombing Range (No Public Access to Boardman Bombing Range)
- Lake Umatilla
- Lake Wallula
- Lake Sacajavea
- Lake West
- Wine Country
- Benton Co Historical Museum
- Beach RV Park
- Three Rivers

RV Parks in Moses Lake:
Cascade Campground, Desert Oasis RV Park, Grant County Fairgrounds, Suncrest Resort

1. East Benton Co Hist Museum
2. Franklin Co Hist Museum
3. WA State Railroad Museum

OREGON

Scale 1:600,000

0 5 10 15 20 25 30 40 50 Miles
0 5 10 15 20 25 30 40 50 Kilometers

State Parks & National Monuments △★

Ginkgo Petrified Forest State Park Area of petrified trees, a result of burial in the mud of a shallow lake and then covered by a lava flow. Interpretive center has samples of petrified ginkgo, found only in a few places in the world; as well as fir, spruce, and cedar. Interpretive trail passes through petrified forest. North of Vantage off I-90. (509) 856-2700. **B1**

Hanford Reach National Monument Along the last free-flowing stretch of the Columbia River, providing spawning habitat for salmon. Plutonium reactors stand along the river, remnants of WWII and the Cold War. No longer in production, these reactors are now being dismantled, and the lands and waters are being cleaned. Includes Saddle Mountain NWR. (509) 546-8300. www.fws.gov/hanfordreach **C2–D3**

Potholes State Park Camping, picnicking, hiking, fishing, and boating. Boat launch available. Southwest of Moses Lake on State Rte 262. (509) 346-2759. **B3**

Sacajawea State Park and Interpretive Center Regional displays of Native American culture and the Lewis and Clark Expedition. Boat launch, moorage, and hiking trails. East of Pasco. (509) 545-2361. **E4**

Wanapum Recreational Area Camping, swimming, fishing, and boating. Boat launch and hiking trails. 3 miles south of Vantage off I-90. Open seasonally. (509) 856-2700. **B1**

Forests & Wildlife Areas ☘🏃

Columbia National Wildlife Refuge An area of diverse arid landscapes, canyons, channeled scablands, sand dunes, and flatlands. Lakes, seeps, and marshes provide habitant for numerous species of waterfowl. (509) 546-8300. www.fws.gov/columbia **B2**

Desert Wildlife Area Approximately 35,000 acres of wetlands and desert uplands support diverse recreation opportunities. Wetlands provide a breeding ground for numerous waterfowl species. (509) 765-6641. **B3**

McNary National Wildlife Refuge Managed grasslands, marshes, cropland, and open water along the Pacific flyway, a migration route of numerous species of waterfowl. Over 200 species of birds. Environmental Education Center (EEC) and refuge headquarters located in Burbank. South of Pasco. (509) 546-8300. www.fws.gov/mcnary **E4**

Potholes Wildlife Area The Potholes Reservoir area. Canoe, boat, fish, and hunt in and around the lake. Southwest of Moses Lake. (509) 765-6641. **A3**

Quincy Lake Wildlife Area Explore the mesas, box canyons, potholes, and lakes cut into 15,000 acres of eroded lava flows. Bird watching, hunting, and fishing are some of the recreation opportunities in the area. South of Quincy. (509) 765-6641. **A1**

Seep Lakes Wildlife Area Channeled scablands created by ancient glacial floods dominate this 4,887-acre reserve. Fish and bird watch in and around the numerous small lakes. South of Potholes Reservoir. (509) 765-6641. **B3**

Sunnyside–Snake River Wildlife Area Area for nesting waterfowl and home to Canada geese in late winter to early spring. Service roads are open to hiking, biking, and horse back riding. S of Grandview. (509) 545-2027. **E1**

Umatilla National Wildlife Refuge Hiking, hunting, fishing, and wildlife viewing are some of the options here. On the Columbia River. (509) 546-8300. www.fws.gov/umatilla **G2**

Whiskey Dick Unit, L.T. Murray Wildlife Area Hiking, hunting, wildlife and wildflower viewing. 15 mi NE of Ellensburg. (509) 925-6746. **A1**

Winchester Reservoir Wildlife Area Grassy uplands surround this shallow lake. Waterfowl use the area on their migration along the Pacific Flyway. The lake is stocked with trout, making fishing excellent. West of Moses Lake. (509) 765-6641. **A2**

Boating & Fishing 🐟 ⛵

Columbia River Numerous boat launches available at Wanapum and Priest Rapids lakes, along the Hanford Reach, lakes Wallula and Umatilla. **B1**

Lake Sacajawea, Lower Snake River Fish for steelhead and smallmouth bass. Public boat ramps are available at Sacajawea State Park, Charbonneau and Windust parks. **E5**

Potholes Reservoir Boating, fishing, and water-skiing. Boat ramp at state park. Fish for perch, crappie, walleye, and trout. North of Othello. **B3**

Historic Sites & Museums 🏛 ★

Benton County Historical Museum A variety of exhibits and displays from American Indian artifacts to a collection of women's dresses dating from the 1840s to the 1920s. 1000 Paterson Ave, Prosser. (509) 786-3842. **E2**

East Benton County Historical Museum Exhibits depict local history, and include a petrified wood floor. 205 Keewaydin Dr, Kennewick. (509) 582-7704. www.ebchs.org **E4**

Hanford Reach Interpretive Center (The REACH) Exhibits illustrating the natural, scientific, and cultural history of the tri-cities region. 1943 Columbia Park Trail, Richland. (509) 943-4100. visitthereach.org **E4**

Franklin County Historical Museum. Exhibits portray local history. 305 N 4th Ave, Pasco. (509) 547-3714. franklincountyhistoricalsociety.org **E4**

Lewis & Clark National Historic Trail Journeying westward down the Snake River, the Corps of Discovery camped at present day Sacajawea State Park before continuing down the Columbia River. On their return, Lewis & Clark traded canoes for horses near The Dalles, then proceeded to Clarkston along an Indian cutoff trail. East of Wallula Gap. **E4**

Moses Lake Museum & Art Center Collection of Indian artifacts and exhibits on local history. 401 S Balsam St, Moses Lake. (509) 764-3830. **A3**

Washington State Railroads Historical Society Museum Exhibits and displays on the history of Washington railroads, including rail cars, steam, and diesel engines. Library. Closed in Winter. 122 N Tacoma St, Pasco. (509) 543-4159. www.wsrhs.org **E4**

Notable Towns ○ ◎ ◉

George Located about halfway from Seattle and Spokane on Interstate 90. Visit the nearby Gorge Amphitheatre, host to outdoor concerts. View the Wild Horse sculptures at vista points off I-90 between Vantage and George. (509) 785-3831 (AgFARMation Visitor Information). **A1**

Sunnyside Asparagus Capital of the Yakima Valley. Location of the Darigold Dairy Fair, which offers tours of the cheese factory. 800-457-8089. **E1**

Tri-Cities Together, the cities of Kennewick, Pasco, and Richland abound in recreation and cultural activities like Columbia Park, company town architecture, wine tasting, boating, and wildlife viewing. (509) 736-0510. **E4**

Other Attractions ★ 🏛

Grant County Off-Road Vehicle Area Area of dunes designated for ORV use. South of Moses Lake and east of Beverly. (509) 754-2011 ext 2931. www.tourgrantcounty.com **C1, B3**

The Gorge Amphitheatre Beautiful, 20,000+ seat concert venue. It is known for its spectacular views of the Columbia Gorge Canyon and Columbia River. It offers terraced lawn seating and concert-friendly weather. (509) 785-6262 www.livenationvenue.com/gorge-amphitheater **A1**

Ice Harbor Dam A self-guided tour of the powerhouse, locks, and fish ladders. Seasonal. On Snake River, East of Pasco. (509) 547-2048. **E4**

LIGO Observatory The Laser Interferometer Gravitational-Wave facility seeks to detect and measure ripples in the fabric of space-time, thereby proving the existence of gravitational waves and furthering Einstein's general theory of relativity. Tours on the 2nd Saturday of each month. NW of Richland. (509) 372-8106 (General Info), (509) 372-8248 (Tours). **D3**

Three Rivers Children's Museum A museum with hands-on activities for children. 650 George Washington Way, Richland. (509) 946-5437. **E3**

Wanapum Dam and Heritage Center Visit the dam, tour the powerhouse, and see fish travel up the fish ladder. The heritage center has exhibits illustrating Wanapum Indian history and culture. 15655 Wanapum Village Ln SW, Beverly. (509) 754-5088 ext 2571. www.wanapum.org **B1**

Information Resources

Army Corps of Engineers, Walla Walla District
201 N Third St, Walla Walla 99362. (509) 527-7020.
www.nww.usace.army.mil

Bureau of Land Management, Wenatchee Field Office
915 North Walla Walla, Wenatchee 98801. (509) 665-2100.
www.or.blm.gov

Highway Information and Mountain Pass Report
Dial 511 or 800-695-7623. wsdot.wa.gov

National Recreation Reservation Service
877-444-6777. Reservations for selected campgrounds.
www.recreation.gov

Washington Department of Natural Resources, Southeast Region
713 E Bowers Rd, Ellensburg 98926. (509) 925-8510. www.dnr.wa.gov

Washington State Parks Information Center
(360) 902-8844, 888-226-7688 www.parks.wa.gov
(360) 902-8555 (Boaters Guide)
(360) 902-8600 (Environmental Learning Centers Reservations)

Hunting & Fishing

Washington Department of Fish and Wildlife, North Central Region 2
1550 Alder St NW, Ephrata 98823. (509) 754-4624. wdfw.wa.gov

Washington Department of Fish and Wildlife, South Central Region 3
1701 S 24th Ave, Yakima 98902. (509) 575-2740. wdfw.wa.gov
See map below.

Campgrounds & RV Parks △🚐

See page 37 for the campground and RV park listings.

Climate

See explanation on page 31

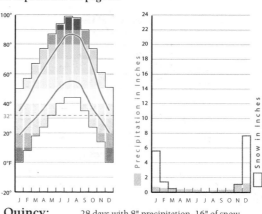

Quincy: 28 days with 8" precipitation, 16" of snow,
el. 1273 ft 141 nights below freezing, 31 days above 90°
Jan (0°) 19°– 35° (50°) **Apr** (24°) 37°– 64° (77°)
July (44°) 55°– 87° (99°) **Oct** (24°) 36°– 64° (77°)

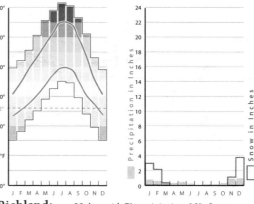

Richland: 23 days with 7" precipitation, 10" of snow,
el. 374 ft 89 nights below freezing, 46 days above 90°
Jan (10°) 27°– 41° (59°) **Apr** (30°) 41°– 67° (81°)
July (50°) 60°– 90° (103°) **Oct** (28°) 41°– 67° (82°)

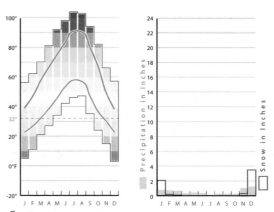

Smyrna: 26 days with 8" precipitation, 6" of snow,
el. 561 ft 127 nights below freezing, 48 days above 90°
Jan (5°) 23°– 39° (56°) **Apr** (27°) 39°– 67° (81°)
July (46°) 58°– 91° (104°) **Oct** (24°) 36°– 67° (82°)

Landscape Page Index

Landscape Page Numbers Are Shown In Blue

Department of Fish & Wildlife Regions and Offices

RECREATION

RECREATION

Legend:
- Wilderness
- Forest Service
- State Parks
- State Lands
- Bureau of Reclamation
- Military Lands
- Bureau of Land Management
- Tribal Lands
- National Parks/ Monuments
- Wildlife Areas
- HOKO 601 State Game Management Unit

LINCOLN

SPOKANE

Coeur d'Alene Indian Reservation

BENEWAH

Sprague
Pifer
Four Seasons
Lamont
Marcellus
Ritzville
Paha
Ralston
Benge
Washtucna
Hooper
Revere
Ewan
St John
Lancaster
Winona
Endicott
Thera
Diamond
LaCrosse
Pampa
Jerita
Hay
Dusty
Wilcox
Mockonema
Codger Pole
Colfax
Risbeck
Parvin
Shawnee
Fallon

WHITMAN
STEPTOE 139
Steptoe Butte State Park
Garfield
Elberton
Glenwood

Rosalia
Malden
Pine City
Balder
Thornton
Oakesdale
Belmont
Cashup

Latah
Spring Valley
Fairbanks
Lone Pine
Tekoa
Willard
Benewah
Tensed
De Smet
Sanders

Farmington
Barron Historic Flour Mill
Roy Chatters Printing & Newspaper Museum (Boomerang Museum)
Palouse
Potlatch Junction
Onaway
Potlatch

PALOUSE RANGE
LATAH

RITZVILLE 284
ADAMS

ESQUATZEL 381
FRANKLIN
Kahlotus
Wacota
Ruxby
Matthew
Lake Herbert West
Starbuck

Palouse Falls State Park
KOA Lyons Ferry Park
SNAKE RIVER
Central Ferry
Peyton
Ridpath

ALMOTA 142
Penawawa
Ping
Almota
Boyer Park & Marina
Illia
Lower Granite Lock and Dam Visitor Center
Mayview
Gould City

Pullman
Busby
Staley
Johnson
Colton
Uniontown
Leon

Moscow
Howell
Joel
Cornwall
Blaine
Genesee

MAYVIEW 145
GARFIELD
Pomeroy
Garfield Co Courthouse & Museum
Marengo
MARENGO 163
Turner
Govello
Ronan
Patit
Alto
COLUMBIA

PEOLA 178
The Last Resort
W.T. Wooten Wildlife Area
Boundary & Rose Springs
Peola
Rose Springs

Chief Timothy Park
Hillview
Silcott
Clarkston
Clarkston Heights
Lewiston
Lapwai
North Lapwai
Sweetwater
Webb
Lewiston Orchards

PRESCOTT 149
Lamar
Harsha
Climax
Prescott
Dayton Historic Depot & Museum
Lewis & Clark Trail State Park
Dayton
Columbia County Courthouse
Huntsville
Waitsburg
Bruce Memorial Museum
Dixie
Minnick

TOUCHET
WALLA WALLA
Walla Walla Regional Airport
BLUE CREEK 154
Whitman Mission National Historic Site
Walla Walla
Fort Walla Walla Museum
Four Seasons RV Resort
College Place
Kooskooskie

DAYTON 162
Mountain Home Park
Mountain Top
Camp Wooten State Park & Environmental Learning Center
TUCANNON 166
Tucannon
Umatilla
Stentz Spring
Big Spring
Godman
Touchet Corral
Snopark
Bluewood

COUSE 181
ASOTIN
Asotin
Asotin Museum
Asotin Creek Wildlife Area
Cloverland
Anatone
LICK CREEK 175
MOUNTAIN VIEW 172
Field Springs State Park
Hells Canyon
Heller Bar

National
Forest
MOUNTAINS
Wenaha-Tucannon Wilderness
WENAHA 169
MILL CREEK WATERSHED 157
GRANDE RONDE 186
Chief Joseph Wildlife Area
Grouse

NEZ PERCE

Milton-Freewater
Umapine
Athena
Weston
Adams
Duncan
Cayuse
Thorn Hollow
Gibbon

BLUE
OREGON
Wenaha

Troy
Paradise
Flora
Promise
Maxville
Looking Glass
Kimmell

UMATILLA
UNION
WALLOWA
Tollgate
Bingham Springs

Elgin
Minam
Wallowa

HELLS CANYON
Imnaha

© BENCHMARK MAPS

Scale 1:600,000

0 5 10 15 20 25 30 40 50 Miles
0 5 10 15 20 30 40 50 Kilometers

State Parks www.parks.wa.gov

Camp Wooten State Park & Environmental Learning Center Popular group use park, located on the Tucannon River. Offers nature study and camp and recreational facilities by reservation only. Northeast of Walla Walla on FS Road 47. (509) 843-1080, (360) 902-8600 (ELC). **E3**

Fields Spring State Park and Environmental Learning Centers Camping, hiking, bird watching, winter activities, and group use of Wo-He-Lo and Puffer Butte ELCs, by reservation. South of Anatone on State Rte 129. (509) 256-3332, (360) 902-8600 (ELCs). **F5**

Lewis and Clark Trail State Park Camping, picnic area with kitchen, shelter, and nature trail mark the passage of the Corps of Discovery in May 1806. Interpretive programs in August. US 12, E of Waitsburg. (509) 337-6457. **E2**

Palouse Falls State Park Picnicking, camping, and hiking on the Palouse River. View of Palouse Falls, a 198-ft falls in a steep walled canyon. Northwest of Starbuck off State Rte 261. (509) 646-9218. **C2**

Steptoe Butte State Park Day use only picnic area. Bird watchers and hang gliders are afforded excellent views from atop 3,612-ft Steptoe Butte. North of Colfax. (509) 456-5064. **B5**

Forests & Wildlife Areas

Asotin Creek Wildlife Area Major elk calving and winter range on 13,158 acres. Hiking, hunting, and fishing. Access SW of Asotin. (509) 758-3151. **F6**

Chief Joseph Wildlife Area Bighorn sheep, elk, turkey, and pheasant have been reintroduced. Hiking, hunting, and fishing. Much of the area is accessible by foot only. South of Asotin. (509) 758-3151. **F6**

Umatilla National Forest Located in the Blue Mountains. Includes the Wenaha–Tucannon Wilderness. (541) 278-3716. **E4–F6**

W. T. Wooten Wildlife Area Set along the Tucannon River, a wintering area for elk. Hiking, hunting, fishing, and view wildlife viewing. East of Dayton. (509) 758-3151. **E4**

Ski Areas & Snoparks

Boundary and Rose Springs Snoparks 47 miles of groomed trails for snowmobiling and cross-country skiing. Large snowplay area nearby. Peola Rd, S of Pomeroy. (509) 843-1891. **E4**

Fields Spring State Park Over 7 miles of groomed cross-country trails, a 50-space snopark, and a tubing hill. State Rte 129, S of Clarkston. (509) 256-3332. **F5**

Ski Bluewood 24 downhill runs, 2 chair lifts, and snowboarding. Southeast of Dayton on North Touchet Road. (509) 382-4725. Snow phone: (509) 522-4110. www.bluewood.com **F3**

Touchet Corral Snopark 56 miles of groomed trails for snowmobiling. SE of Dayton off FS Road 64. (509) 382-4334 (Blue Mtn Snowmobile Club). **F3**

Boating & Fishing

Grand Ronde River Fish for steelhead, catfish, and bass. South of Clarkston on State Rte 129. **F5**

Snake River Three narrow, long lakes in this section of river; Lake Herbert West, Lake Bryan, and Lower Granite Lake. Water-ski, sail, boat, or fish these lakes. Fish for steelhead, bass, and white sturgeon. Camping and boat ramps available at Lyons Ferry, Central Ferry, Chief Timothy, and Wawawai county parks. Clarkston. **D1**

Natural Wonders

Hells Canyon The Snake River gorge is the deepest gorge in North America. This area of the gorge is under the administration of the Hells Canyon National Recreation Area. **G6**

Palouse Falls The water of the Palouse River cascades nearly 200 feet off of a columnar basalt cliff. Palouse Falls State Park. **C2**

Historic Sites & Museums

Asotin County Historical Museum Collection of Native American and pioneer artifacts. 215 Filmore St, Asotin. (509) 243-4659. **E6**

Barron Historic Flour Mill A timber structure houses the milling and sifting equipment used from the late 1800s to the 1930s. 103 E Jackson, Oakesdale. (509) 285-4020. **A5**

Bruce Memorial Museum Furnished, restored mansion built in 1883. Open weekends in summer and by appointment. Waitsburg. (509) 337-6157. **E2**

Columbia County Courthouse Oldest courthouse in Washington. Built in 1887 and still in use today. Dayton. (509) 382-4541. www.columbiaco.com **E3**

Dayton Historic Depot and Museum Built in 1881, depot is now home to a collection of railroad memorabilia, pioneer furniture, and historic phones. 222 E Commercial St, Dayton. (509) 382-2026. www.daytonhistoricdepot.org **E3**

Fort Walla Walla Museum Fourteen furnished historic buildings and five buildings housing pioneer farm implements and machinery. Interpretive events. 755 Myra Rd, Walla Walla. (509) 525-7703. **F1**

Garfield County Courthouse and Museum Victorian era courthouse built in 1901. Museum houses regional pioneer memorabilia. 708 Columbia St, Pomeroy. (509) 843-3814. **D4**

Lewis & Clark National Historic Trail West and eastbound routes met just west of Clarkston. Home of the Nez Perce Indians, who befriended and provided supplies for Lewis & Clark. Clarkston and Walla Walla. **E3**

Washington State University On campus is anthropology and art museums and an insect collection. Home to Beasley Coliseum, Cougars football, and a creamery. 225 N Grand Ave, Pullman. (509) 335-3564 or (509) 355-5586 (Tours), (509) 335-1910 (Art Museum Tours), (509) 335-7275 (Parking). **C5**

Notable Towns ○ ◉

Clarkston Gateway to Hells Canyon and the Snake River, Lewis & Clark stopped nearby in 1805. Recreation possibilities include fishing, hiking, boating, rafting, and wildlife viewing. 800-933-2128 (C of C). **D5**

Walla Walla This area in the western foothills of the Blue Mountains is known for sweet onions and hosts the Walla Walla Sweet Onion Harvest Festival. Offers wine tasting, skiing, and hiking. (509) 525-0850 (C of C) or (509) 526-3117 (Wine Alliance). www.wallawalla.org **F1**

Other Attractions ★ ☖

Codger Pole Fifty years after a 1938 football game between Colfax and St. John, the players, all in their late-60s, played it again. Renowned woodcarver Jonathan LaBenne memorialized the 52 players in cedar, carving whimsical caricatures of each on five 65-foot poles. Main St, Colfax. (509) 397-3712 (Chamber of Commerce). www.colfaxchamber.com **B5**

Hells Canyon Take a jet-boat ride up the deepest gorge in North America, or help deliver mail on a two-day journey. Several excursions are available. South of Clarkston. (509) 758-7712 (Chamber of Commerce). **G6**

Lower Granite Lock and Dam Visitor Center Tours of fish ladder, viewing area, and dam. North of Pomeroy. (509) 751-0240. **C4**

Roy Chatters Printing and Newspaper Museum (Boomerang Museum) Vintage printing presses and a large collection of Whitman County newspapers. By appointment only. Main St, Palouse. (509) 878-1742. **B5**

Information Resources

Army Corps of Engineers, Walla Walla District
201 N Third St, Walla Walla 99362. (509) 527-7020.
www.nww.usace.army.mil

Bureau of Land Management, Spokane District Office
1103 N Fancher, Spokane 99212. (509) 536-1200. www.or.blm.gov

Hells Canyon National Recreation Area
2535 Riverside Drive, PO Box 699, Clarkston 99403. (509) 758-0616.
www.fs.usda.gov/hellscanyon

Highway Information and Mountain Pass Report
Dial 511 or 800-695-7623. www.wsdot.wa.gov

National Recreation Reservation Service
877-444-6777. Reservations for selected campgrounds.
www.recreation.gov

Northwest Weather and Avalanche Center
7600 Sandpoint Wy NE, Seattle 98115. (206) 526-4666.
Recorded message Oct 1-Apr 15. www.nwac.us

Umatilla National Forest Headquarters
2517 SW Hailey Av, Pendleton OR 97801. (541) 278-3716.
www.fs.usda.gov/umatilla

    Walla Walla Ranger District Office
    1415 W Rose St, Walla Walla 99362. (509) 522-6290.

    Pomeroy Ranger District Office
    71 W Main, Pomeroy 99347. (509) 843-1891.

Washington Department of Natural Resources, Southeast Region
713 E Bowers Rd, Ellensburg 98926. (509) 925-8510. www.dnr.wa.gov

Washington State Parks Information Center & Campground Reservations
(360) 902-8844, 888-226-7688. www.parks.wa.gov
(360) 902-8555 (Boaters Guide)
(360) 902-8600 (Environmental Learning Centers Reservations)
(360) 902-8684 (Snopark and Winter Recreation Info)

Hunting & Fishing

Washington Department of Fish & Wildlife, Eastern Region 1
8702 N Division St, Spokane 99218. (509) 892-1001. www.wdfw.wa.gov
See map on page 29.

Campgrounds & RV Parks

See page **37** for the campground and RV park listings.

Climate

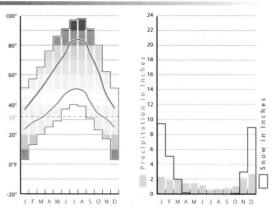

Colfax: 60 days with 19" precipitation, 29" of snow,
el. 1955 ft   133 nights below freezing, 21 days above 90°
Jan (3°) 24°–37° (51°)   **Apr** (25°) 36°–59° (76°)
July (40°) 50°–83° (97°)   **Oct** (23°) 34°–62° (80°)

Landscape Page Index

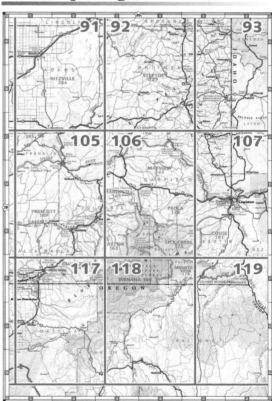

Landscape Page Numbers Are Shown In Blue

Explanation of the Climate Graphs Shown on Pages 13–33

Temperature and precipitation information is shown for representative climate stations in all parts of the state. The bar graphs show monthly information. Average and extreme values for four months are given in the four-line summary below each graph. The summary also gives the elevation of the climate station (which may be slightly different from the elevation of the town), total annual precipitation and snowfall, and the annual number of days with more than one-tenth of an inch of precipitation, with frost, and with temperatures over 90 degrees.

The 31 stations graphed show the general range of climates. They do not include high mountain locations, where snowfall can be much higher than at any of the graphed stations, and low temperatures much more severe. Note that many Cascade passes are closed by snow during much of the year—always inquire locally

Data furnished by George Taylor, Oregon Climate Service, Oregon State University.

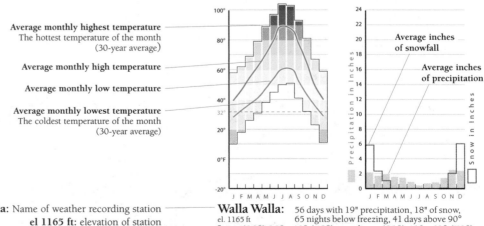

Walla Walla: Name of weather recording station
    el 1165 ft: elevation of station
56 days: average number of days in the year with more than one-tenth of an inch of precipitation
19" precipitation: average annual precipitation including water content of snow
18" of snow: average annual snowfall
65 nights: average number of nights below freezing
41 days: average number of days above 90°

Note: all figures are 30-year averages

Walla Walla: 56 days with 19" precipitation, 18" of snow,
el. 1165 ft   65 nights below freezing, 41 days above 90°
Jan (10°) 28°–40° (58°)   **Apr** (31°) 41°–63° (79°)
July (50°) 61°–89° (104°)   **Oct** (32°) 44°–65° (81°)

Temperature ranges for January, April, July and October. Bold blue numbers give the average extreme low temperatures—the coldest night you may expect during that month. The lighter blue numbers give the low temperatures averaged for the entire month. Bold red numbers give the average extreme high temperature—the hottest afternoon you may expect during that month. The light red numbers give the afternoon high temperatures averaged for the entire month.

Wilderness | State Parks | Bureau of Reclamation | Bureau of Land Management | National Parks/Monuments
Forest Service | State Lands | Military Lands | Tribal Lands | Wildlife Areas

Seattle/Tacoma

14

JEFFERSON

Port Ludlow
Oak Bay
Port Townsend
Austin
Midvale Corner
WHIDBEY ISLAND
Clinton
Columbia Beach
Everett
Machias
Lake Stevens

Hansville
Maxwelton
Glendale
Possession
Mukilteo
Boeing Aircraft Plant (World's Largest Building)
Mukilteo
Snohomish
Roosevelt

SNOHOMISH
Fairmont
Lake Serene
Silver Lake
Monroe

Shine Tidelands State Park
Port Gamble
Eglon
Port Gamble Historic District & Museum
Port Gamble S'Klallam Ind Res
Mill Creek
Clearview
Maltby

Kitsap Memorial State Park
Kingston
Striebels Corner
Appletree Cove
Lynnwood
Edmonds
Woodway
Seattle Heights
Edmonds Museum
Two Rivers WA

Vinland
Port Madison
Mountlake Terrace
Brier
Lake Pleasant

Indianola
Port Madison Ind Res
Shoreline
Bothell
Kenmore
Woodinville
Hollywood
Duvall
Cherry Valley WA

Naval Submarine Base Bangor
Poulsbo
Suquamish
Old Man House Park
Suquamish Museum
Suquamish Clearwater Casino
Lake Forest Park
St Edward State Park
Juanita
Novelty

Scandia
Keyport
Naval Undersea Warfare Center
Seabold
Bloedel Reserve
Fay Bainbridge Park
Nordic Heritage Museum
Shilshole Bay
Hiram M Chittenden Locks & Fish Ladder
Discovery Park
Woodland Park Zoo
Burke Museum of Natural History & Culture
Kirkland
Redmond
Stillwater WA
Bridle Trails State Park
Marymoor Museum
Yarrow Point
Hunts Point
Ames Lake

Silverdale
BAINBRIDGE ISLAND
Bainbridge Gardens
Island Center
Bainbridge Island
Bainbridge Island Hist Museum
Murden Cove
West Pt Lighthouse
Maritime Heritage Ctr
KeyArena
Seattle Center/Space Needle
Pike Place Market
SEATTLE
Medina
Clyde Hill
WA Park Arboretum
Bellevue
Inglewood
Pine Lake

Dyes Inlet
Fairview
Illahee
Brownsville
Tracyton
Seattle Aquarium
CenturyLink Field/Safeco Field
Harbor Island
Beaux Arts Village
Trailer Inns
Beaver Lake

Naval Reserve
Chico
Erlands Point
Rocky Point
Outdoor Recreation Information Center
Klondike Gold Rush NHP
Mercer Island
Newcastle
Eastgate
Lake Sammamish State Park
Issaquah
High Point

Bremerton
Kitsap County Hist Museum
Puget Sound Navy Museum
USS Turner Joy
Manchester
Blake Island State Park
Fauntleroy
Museum of Flight
Kennydale
Cougar Mtn Zoo
Issaquah Village
Issaquah Highlands Recreation Club
Tiger Mtn State Forest

Gorst
Port Orchard
Annapolis
Colby
South Colby
Southworth
White Center
Riverton Heights
Boulevard Park
Skyway
Renton
Tukwila
Renton Hist Mus
Squak Mtn State Park
Blue Sky Parks & Resorts

KITSAP
Bethel
Long Lake
Cedarhurst
Colvos
Cove
Vashon
Sea-Tac
Orillia
Burien
Normandy Park
SeaTac
Fairwood

Wildwood
Fragaria
Olalla
Lisabeula
Burton
Fern Heath
Maury
Des Moines
KOA
East Hill
Lake Youngs
Hobart
Walsh Lake

Glenwood
Burley
Tramp Harbor
Zenith
Saltwater State Park (Day Use)
Woodmont Beach
Kent
Lake Meridian
Maple Valley
Landsburg

Stansberry Lake
Burley Lagoon
Crescent Lake
Wauna
Dockton
Harbor Heights
Redondo
Poverty Bay
Lakota
Adelaide
Meredith
Christopher
Emerald Downs Racetrack
Georgetown
Lake Sawyer
Covington

Kopachuck State Park
Forest Beach
Gig Harbor RV Resort
Gig Harbor
Point Defiance Park
Tahlequah
Dash Point State Park
Browns Point
Federal Way
Rhododendron Species Foundation
Wild Waves Theme Park
Muckleshoot Casino
Auburn
White River Valley Hist Museum
Muckleshoot Indian Res
Black Diamond
Franklin
Hanging Gardens
Green River Gorge
Cumberland

Artondale
Arletta
Midway
Ruston
Commencement Bay
Wright Park & Seymour Botanical Conservatory
Puyallup
Algona
Pacific

PIERCE
McNeil Island Prison
Rosedale
Cromwell
Wollochet
TACOMA
Washington State History Mus
Tacoma Dome
Fircrest
University Place
Indian Res
Milton
Edgewood
Mucklesloot
Enumclaw

Yoman
Steilacoom
Lakewood
Midland
Manitou
Hillsdale
Majestic Mobile Manor
North Puyallup
Fife
Sumner
Bonney Lake
Lake Tapps
Upper Mill

24

© BENCHMARK MAPS

Scale 1:270,000

0 5 10 15 Miles
0 5 10 15 20 Kilometers

Recreation Guide

State Parks www.parks.wa.gov

Blake Island State Park Camping, hiking, and mountain biking. Accessible by boat only. Scheduled tour boat departs Seattle. Moorage buoys available. (360) 731-8330, (360) 902-8844 (Moorage Info). **E2**

Bridle Trails State Park Over 25 miles of hiking and equestrian trails. 3 miles north of Bellevue. (425) 649-4275. **D5**

Dash Point State Park Camping, picnicking, hiking, and biking. Northeast of Tacoma on State Rte 509. (360) 902-8444. **G3**

Illahee State Park Camping, picnicking, hiking, beach access, and boat launch. Northeast of Bremerton on State Rte 306. (360) 478-6460. **D1**

Kitsap Memorial State Park Camping and picnicking. North of Poulsbo on State Rte 3. (360) 779-3205. **B1**

Kopachuck State Park Camping, picnicking, hiking, swimming, and clamming. Southwest of Rosedale. (253) 265-3606. **G1**

Lake Sammamish State Park Picnicking, hiking, swimming, and boat launch. Northwest of Issaquah off Interstate 90. (425) 649-4275. **E6**

Manchester State Park Camping, picnicking, hiking, and beach access. Northeast of Port Orchard. (360) 871-4065. **E2**

Saint Edward State Park Former seminary. Hiking, tennis, and fishing. South of Kenmore. (425) 823-2992. **C4**

Saltwater State Park Camping, picnicking, hiking, and boat launch. South of Des Moines on State Rte 509. (360) 902-8444. **F3**

Shine Tidelands State Park West end of the Hood Canal Bridge. (360) 902-8444. **B1**

Squak Mountain State Park Day use hiking area. South of Issaquah. (360) 902-8444. **E5**

Forest & Wildlife Areas

Green River Gorge Conservation Area Hike or boat through gorge of hanging gardens and historical sites. On the Green River between Kanaskat–Palmer and Flaming Geyser state parks. (253) 931-3930. **G6**

Tiger Mountain State Forest State-managed lands providing various recreation opportunities including hiking, biking, horseback riding, and parasailing. Also an area of timber cutting. Southeast of Issaquah. (360) 825-1631. **E6**

Ferries

Clipper Vacations The high-speed passenger ferry *Victoria Clipper IV* operates between Victoria and Seattle. Service to the San Juan Islands from Seattle also available. Pier 69, Seattle. 800-888-2535. www.clippervacations.com **D4**

Washington State Ferries Numerous state-operated car and passenger only ferries serve the cities and towns in and around the Puget Sound. 888-808-7977 (In Washington only) or (206) 464-6400 (Seattle). www.wsdot.wa.gov/ferries. **D4**

Historic Sites & Museums

Bainbridge Island Historical Museum A collection of photographs and artifacts illustrating the area's history. Located in the restored 1908 Island Center School. 215 Ericksen Ave NE, Bainbridge Island. (206) 842-2773. **D2**

Burke Museum of Natural History and Culture Exhibits include a fine collection of anthropological displays. Tours. NE 17th Ave and 45th Ave, Seattle. (206) 543-5590. www.burkemuseum.org **D4**

Edmonds Museum Exhibits and displays covering the history of Edmonds. Located in the former, 1910, City Hall. 118 N 5th Ave, Edmonds. (425) 774-0900. www.historicedmonds.org **B3**

Imagine Children's Museum Hands-on interactive exhibits for playful learning. 1502 Wall St, Everett. (425) 258-1006. www.imaginecm.org. **A4**

Kitsap County Historical Museum Displays of pioneer and Coast Salish Indian artifacts. 280 4th St, Bremerton. (360) 479-6226. **B1**

Klondike Gold Rush National Historical Park Visitor center contains photographs, displays of turn-of-the-century mining hardware, and gold panning demonstrations illustrate the Klondike gold rush. 319 2nd Ave S, Seattle. (206) 220-4240. www.nps.gov/klse **E4**

Maritime Heritage Center Center includes Center for Wooden Boats, where over 100 wooden boats and replicas are displayed. The Northwest Seaport features tours of the *Wawona* sailing schooner and the *Arthur Foss* tugboat. 1002 Valle St, Seattle. (206) 447-9800. **D3**

Marymoor Museum A collection of artifacts and photographs related to area history. Located in the Clise Mansion, built as a hunting lodge for a Seattle businessman, in Marymoor Park. 6046 W Lake Sammamish Pkwy NE, Redmond. (425) 885-3684. **D5**

Museum of Flight Exhibits illustrate the history of flight. The Great Gallery Complex contains more than 40 aircraft, including a DC-3 and a 1926 Swallow. 9404 E Marginal Way S, Seattle. (206) 764-5720. **E4**

Naval Undersea Museum Collection of naval memorabilia with an emphasis on submarine technology and history. Keyport. (360) 396-4148. **C1**

Nordic Heritage Museum Exhibits illustrating the immigration and cultural contributions of the Scandinavian people to the Pacific Northwest from the 18th century to the present. 3014 NW 67th St, Seattle. (206) 789-5707. www.nordicmuseum.org **C3**

Old Man House Park Replica of an Indian shelter. Day use only. South of Suquamish. (360) 598-3311. **C2**

Point Defiance Park Nearly 700 acres on Point Defiance. Attractions include the Camp 6 Logging Museum, which offers train rides; Fort Nisqually, the reconstructed and restored Hudson Bay Co outpost; and the Zoo and Aquarium, where polar bears, whales, and sea otters can be observed. Tacoma. (253) 305-1000 (Metro Parks Tacoma). **G2**

Port Gamble Historic Museum Exhibits tracing the history and growth of the town. (360) 297-8074. **B2**

Puget Sound Navy Museum Exhibits and displays depicting US naval history. 251 First St, Bremerton. (360) 627-2270. **E1**

Renton History Museum Exhibits trace the city's history, including the coal mining and lumbering eras. 235 Mill Ave S, Renton. (425) 255-2330. **E4**

Suquamish Museum Displays and exhibits trace the history of the Puget Sound Indians. 6861 NE South St, Suquamish. (360) 394-8499. **C1**

Washington State History Museum Displays illustrate the state's past and present. 1911 Pacific Ave, Tacoma. 888-238-4373. www.wshs.org **H2**

White River Valley Museum Exhibits depict local area history. 918 H St SE, Auburn. (253) 288-7433. www.wrvmuseum.org **G4**

Notable Towns ○ ◉

Gig Harbor A fishing village with waterfront specialty shops. Charter boat fishing and charter sailboating available. (253) 851-6865. **G1**

Port Gamble The designated National Historic District includes more than 30 restored Victorian buildings. Also visit the Port Gamble Historic Museum, where exhibits trace the history and growth of the town. 800-337-0580 (Visitor and Convention Bureau). **B2**

Snohomish A quaint Victorian town established in 1859. Known as the antique capital of Washington State. (360) 568-2526 (C of C). **A4**

Other Attractions

Bainbridge Gardens Gardens, nursery, and nature trail located on historic site from the 1920s. 9415 Miller Rd, Bainbridge Island. (206) 842-5888. **D2**

Bloedel Reserve Woodlands, meadows, ponds, and formal gardens on a 150-acre estate. Reservations required. 7571 NE Dolphin Dr, Bainbridge Island. (206) 842-7631. www.bloedelreserve.org **C2**

Boeing Tour Center (Boeing 747, 767, 777, 787 Production Facility) Tour of aircraft assembly plant and video presentation. World's largest building. Everett. 800-464-1476 or (360) 756-0086. www.boeing.com **A4**

Cougar Mountain Zoo This zoo is devoted primarily to threatened and endangered species. 19525 SE 54th St, Issaquah. (425) 391-5508. **E5**

Discovery Park Over 500 acres of forest, meadows and canyons with nature trails. Also the location of the Daybreak Star Indian Cultural Center, an environmental learning center, and the West Point Lighthouse. 3801 Discovery Park Blvd, Seattle. (206) 386-4236. **D3**

Emerald Downs Racetrack Horse racing and simulcast betting. April–Sept. 2300 Emerald Downs Dr, Auburn. 888-931-8400 or (253) 288-7000. www.emeralddowns.com **G4**

Fort Ward Park Coast artillery fort on Rich Passage. Boat ramp and picnic area. On Bainbridge Island, south of Winslow. (206) 842-4041. **D2**

Hiram M Chittenden Locks, Dam and Fish Ladder Visitor center exhibits illustrate the history and operation of the locks. Fish ladder can be observed through viewing window. 3015 NW 54th St, Seattle. (206) 783-7059. **D3**

KeyArena Home to the Seattle Storm WNBA basketball team. Seattle Center, Seattle. (206) 684-7200, 800-462-2849 or (206) 283-3865 (Tickets). **D3**

Marine Science Center Educational exhibits on marine life. Hands-on tidal tanks. 18743 Front St NE, Poulsbo. (360) 598-4460. www.poulsbomsc.org **C1**

Mukilteo Lighthouse A wood frame lighthouse built in 1906 that is still in service using the original Fresnel lens light. Open for tours on weekend afternoons. North of Mukilteo off State Rte 525. (425) 513-9602. **A4**

Muckleshoot Casino 2402 Auburn Way S, Auburn. 800-804-4944 or (253) 804-4444. www.muckleshootcasino.com **G5**

Pike Place Market A marketplace for everything from produce and seafood to arts and crafts. 1st Ave & Pike St, Seattle. (206) 682-7453. www.pikeplacemarket.org **D3**

CenturyLink Field Home to the Seattle Seahawks football team. 800 Occidental Ave South, Seattle. 1-888-NFL-HAWK (tickets) or (206) 381-7582 (tours). **D3**

Rhododendron Species Botanical Garden View over 2,000 varieties of rhododendron in this 24-acre garden. Located on the Weyerhaeuser HQ campus. Weyerhaeuser Way South, Federal Way. (253) 838-4646. **G4**

Safeco Field Home to the Seattle Mariners baseball team. 1250 First Ave South, Seattle. (206) 346-4001 (tickets) or (206) 346-4241 (tours). **D3**

Seattle Aquarium Observe a variety of aquatic life including sea birds and mammals. Exhibits include an underwater dome, coral reef, tidal pool, and sea otters. Pier 59, 1483 Alaskan Way, Seattle. (206) 386-4300. **D3**

Space Needle at Seattle Center The symbol of the 1962 World's Fair. An observation deck is located over 500 feet above the ground. Dining is available in the restaurant at the top of the structure. 305 Harrison St, Seattle. 800-937-9582 or (206) 905-2100. www.spaceneedle.com **D3**

Suquamish Clearwater Casino 15347 Suquamish Way NE, Suquamish. (360) 598-8789 (casino) or (360) 598-8700 (resort). **C2**

Tacoma Dome Home to concerts, sporting events, and exhibitions. 2727 East D St, Tacoma. (253) 272-3663. www.tacomadome.org **H3**

USS Turner Joy Self-guided tours of US naval destroyer in service from 1959 to 1982. Bremerton Waterfront. (360) 792-2457. **E1**

Washington Park Arboretum A variety of plants from all corners of the world. The traditional Japanese Garden occupies 3.5 acres and features Japanese maples, azaleas, ferns, and other plants; centered on a teahouse and pond. Seattle. (206) 543-8800. **D4**

West Point Lighthouse Built in 1881. Although now automated, much of the lighthouse's original equipment is on display here. Located in Discovery Park, Seattle. (206) 386-4236. **D3**

Wild Waves Theme Park Waterslides, wave pool, river raft ride, and children's pool. Enchanted Parkway South, Federal Way. (253) 661-8000. **G4**

Woodland Park Zoo Visit animals from a variety of habitats, including bears, gorillas, monkeys, hippopotamuses, and lions. Exhibits include the Tropical Rain Forest, the African Savanna, and the Trail of Vines. 601 N 59th St, Seattle. (206) 548-2500. www.zoo.org **D3**

Wright Park and Seymour Botanical Conservatory Park is landscaped with a collection of exotic plants. The Seymour Conservatory is a glass-and-steel structure built in 1907 and contains tropical trees, ferns, shrubs, and other flowering plants. 3rd & G Sts, Tacoma. (253) 591-5330. **G3**

Information Resources

Highway Information and Mountain Pass Report
Dial 511 or 800-695-7623. www.wsdot.wa.gov

Mt Baker–Snoqualmie National Forest Headquarters
2930 Wetmore Ave, Suite 3A, Everett 98201. (425) 783-6000. www.fs.usda.gov/mbs

National Weather Service
(206) 526-6087 Forecast. www.nws.gov

Outdoor Recreation Information Center, USFS/NPS
222 Yale Ave N (inside REI), Seattle 98109. (206) 470-4060

Washington Department of Natural Resources, South Puget Sound Region
950 Farma St N, Enumclaw 98022. (360) 825-1631. www.dnr.wa.gov

Washington State Ferries
(206) 464-6400 (Seattle), 1-888-808-7977 (Statewide), 800-843-3779 (Info Message)

Washington State Parks Information Center & Campground Reservations
(360) 902-8844, 888-226-7688. www.parks.wa.gov
(360) 902-8555 (Boaters Guide)
(360) 902-8600 Environmental Learning Center

Washington Trails Association
705 2nd Ave, Suite 300, Seattle 98104. (206) 625-1367. www.wta.org

Hunting & Fishing

Washington Department of Fish and Wildlife, North Puget Sound Region 4
16018 Mill Creek Blvd, Mill Creek 98012. (425) 775-1311. www.wdfw.wa.gov

See map on page 29.

Campgrounds & RV Parks

See page 37 for list of campgrounds and RV Parks.

Climate

See explanation on page 31

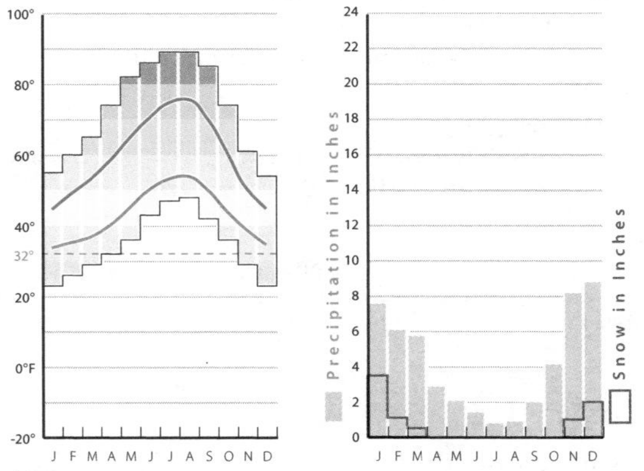

Bremerton: 100 days with 52" precipitation, 8" of snow,
el. 161 ft 46 nights below freezing, 3 days above 90°

Jan	(23°) 34°–45° (55°)	Apr	(32) 40°–58° (74°)
July	(47°) 53°–75° (89°)	Oct	(36°) 44°–60° (74°)

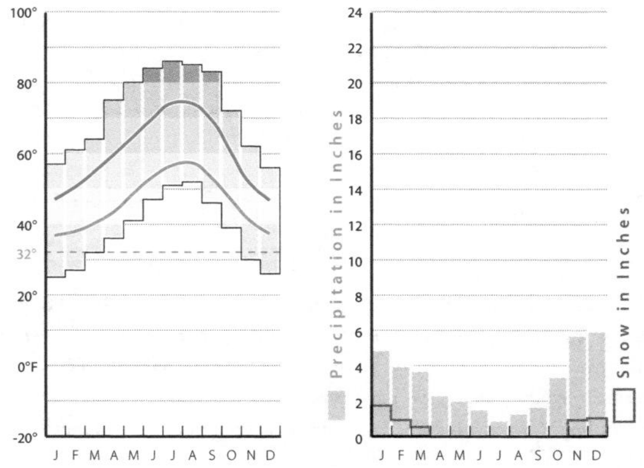

Seattle: 93 days with 37" precipitation, 5" of snow,
el. 20 ft 23 nights below freezing, 2 days above 90°

Jan	(25°) 37°–47° (57°)	Apr	(36°) 43°–59° (75°)
July	(51°) 57°–74° (86°)	Oct	(39°) 47°–60° (72°)

Landscape Page Index

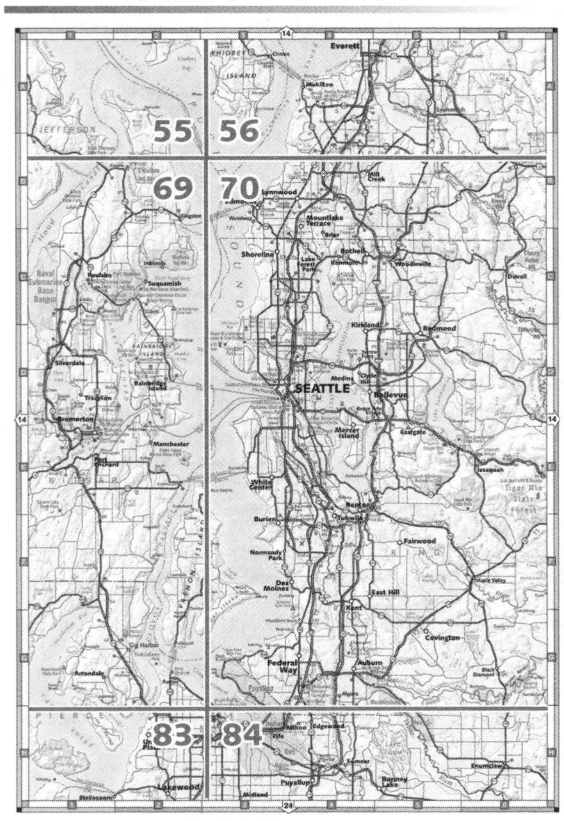

Landscape Page Numbers Are Shown In Blue

RECREATION

Explanation

Recreation Maps show selected campgrounds and RV parks. These are listed below for each page, in alphabetical order.

All campgrounds are shown on the more detailed Landscape pages.

Campgrounds

10–number of sites **W**–drinking water **H**–hookups **PH**–partial hookups **S**–showers **D**–dump station **TH**–trailhead

RV Parks

10–number of sites **FH**–full hookups **PH**–partial hookups **NH**–No hookups **C**–cable/satellite TV **L**–laundry **D**–dump station **NT**–no tents **NP**–no pets **NS**–no showers

Page 12

Campgrounds

Altair. Olympic NP. **30, W,** picnic area, hiking. (360) 565-3130. **E5**

Bear Creek. DNR. **10,** hiking, fishing. (360) 374-6131. **E2**

Big Creek. Olympic NF. **23, W,** picnic shelter, hiking. (360) 765-2200. **G6**

Bogachiel State Park. 42, W, PH, S, D, group site, hiking, rain forest nature trail. (360) 374-6356. **F2**

Brown Creek. Olympic NF. **20, W,** picnic area, fishing. (360) 765-2200. **H5**

Campbell Tree Grove. Olympic NF. **31,** picnic area, hiking, fishing. On edge of the Colonel Bob Wilderness. No fee. (360) 288-2525. **G4**

Coho. Olympic NF. **56, W, D, TH,** boat ramp, picnic area, hiking. On the shore of Wynoochee Lake. (360) 765-2200. **H4**

Collins. Olympic NF. **16,** hiking, fishing. (360) 765-2200. **F6**

Deer Park. Olympic NP. **14,** picnic sites, hiking. No RVs. Closed mid-Fall to mid-June. (360) 565-3130. **E6**

Dosewallips. Olympic NP. **30,** walk-in only camping, picnic sites, hiking. (360) 565-3130. **F6**

Dungeness Forks. Olympic NF. **10.** Tents only. (360) 765-2200. **E6**

Dungeness Recreation Area. 66, W, D, S, hiking trails. (360) 683-5847. **E5**

Elkhorn. Olympic NF. **20, W,** hiking, biking. (360) 765-2200. **F6**

Elwha. Olympic NP. **40, W,** picnic sites, hiking. (360) 565-3130. **E5**

Fairholme. Olympic NP. **88, W,** picnic area, boat ramp, evening programs in summer (inquire at ranger station). (360) 565-3130. **E3**

Falls Creek. Olympic NF. **31, W,** hiking, boat ramp. (360) 288-2525. **G4**

Gatton Creek. Olympic NF. **5,** hiking. (360) 288-2525. **G4**

Graves Creek. Olympic NP. **30, W,** picnic area, hiking. (360) 565-3130. **G5**

Hamma Hamma. Olympic NF. **15,** hiking, fishing. (360) 765-2200. **G6**

Heart o' the Hills. Olympic NP. **102, W,** picnic area, hiking, evening programs in summer (inquire at ranger station). (360) 565-3130. **E5**

Hoh. Olympic NP. **88, W, D,** picnic area, hiking, evening programs in summer (inquire at visitor center). (360) 565-3130. **F3**

Kalaloch. Olympic NP. **170, W, D,** group camp, evening programs. Reservations required in Summer. 800-365-2267, (360) 565-3130. **G2**

Klahanie. Olympic NF. **20, W,** hiking, fishing. (360) 374-6522. **E2**

Klahowya. Olympic NF. **58, W,** boat ramp, fishing. (360) 374-6522. **E3**

LeBar Creek Horse Camp. Olympic NF. **13,** equestrian camping only. (360) 765-2200. **H5**

Laney. Olympic NF. **10,** hiking, fishing, rustic. Tents only. (360) 765-2200. **G5**

Lena Creek. Olympic NF. **13, W,** hiking, fishing. (360) 765-2200. **G6**

Lyre River. DNR. **11, W,** sheltered picnic area. (360) 374-6131. **D4**

Mora. Olympic NP. **94, W, D,** group camp area (by reservation only), hiking, evening programs in summer. (360) 565-3130. **E1**

North Fork. Olympic NP. **9,** recommended for tents only. (360) 565-3130. **G4**

Oxbow. Olympic NF. **30,** hiking, fishing, rustic. Tents only. (360) 765-2200. **H5**

Ozette. Olympic NP. **15, W,** picnic area, boat ramp, hiking. (360) 565-3130. **D1**

Potlatch State Park. 73, W, H, S, D, hiking, boating. (360) 877-5361. **H6**

Queets. Olympic NP. **20,** picnic area, hiking. (360) 565-3130. **G3**

Salt Creek Rec Area. 92, W, S, hiking, picnic area. (360) 928-3441. **D4**

Sequim Bay State Park. 64,W, H, S, group site, playground, day use area, boat launch, beach access. 888-226-7688, (360) 683-4235. **E6**

Sol Duc. Olympic NP. **82, W, D,** group site, day use area, boat launch, beach access, evening programs in summer. (360) 565-3130. **E4**

South Beach. Olympic NP. **55,** hiking. Seasonal. (360) 565-3130. **G2**

Staircase. Olympic NP. **47, W,** hiking. (360) 565-3130. **G5**

Upper Clearwater. DNR. **9,** picnic area, fishing. (360) 374-6131. **G3**

Willaby Creek. Olympic NF. **21, W,** hiking, fishing, boat ramp. (360) 288-2525. **G4**

RV Parks

Al's RV Park. East of Port Angeles. **35 FH, C, L, NS,** fishing, hiking. (360) 457-9844. **E5**

Angler's Hideaway. Sekiu. **31 FH, C, L,** pavilion. Reservations required. $100 pet deposit. (360) 963-2750. www.anglershideaway.com **D2**

Cape Resort. Neah Bay. **39 FH, C, L, D.** (360) 645-2250. **C1**

Conestoga Quarters RV Park. East of Port Angeles. **36 FH, D,** fire rings. 800-808-4637 or (360) 452-4637. **E6**

Crescent Beach and RV Park. West of Port Angeles. **41 FH, L,** fishing, saltwater beach, sports field. 866-690-3344 or (360) 928-3344. **D4**

Elwha Dam RV Park. East of Port Angeles. **39 FH, C, L,** fire rings, playground, badminton, horseshoes. (360) 452-7054. **E5**

Forks 101 RV Park. Forks. **36 FH, C, L,** Wi-Fi, April–Sept. (360) 374-5073. **E2**

Glen Ayr RV Park and Motel. Hoodsport. **36 FH, C, L,** rec room, sports field, horseshoes. 866-877-9522, (360) 877-9522. **H6**

Hoh River Resort and RV Park. Southeast of Forks. **18 FH, C,** fire rings. (360) 374-5566. **F2**

John Wayne's Waterfront Resort. Sequim. **41 FH, C, L, NT,** rec room with internet, groups. (360) 681-3853. **E6**

Lake Cushman Resort. 13, W, PH, cabins, group site, tents, fishing, swimming, boat launch. 800-588-9630 or (360) 877-9630. www.lakecushman.com **G6**

Log Cabin Resort and RV Park. On Lake Crescent. **38 FH, L, D,** fire rings, playground, sports field. (360) 928-3325. www.logcabinresort.net **E4**

Lonesome Creek RV Park. La Push. **42 FH, L, D, S,** fire rings, wood, rec room. (360) 374-4338. **F1**

Lyre River Park. West of Port Angeles. **100 (55 FH, 27 PH), L, D,** rec room, sports field, horseshoes. (360) 928-3436. **D4**

Olson's Resort & Marina. Sekiu. **50 FH, L, D,** open camping area, boat launch, fishing, moorage. (360) 963-2311. **D2**

Peabody Creek RV Park. Port Angeles. **35 (32 FH), L.** (360) 457-7092 **D5**

Port Angeles–Sequim KOA. Port Angeles. **90 (20 FH, 51 PH), L,** Wi-Fi, rec room, swimming pool, playground, sports field. 800-562-7558. **E6**

Rain Forest Resort Village. On Lake Quinault. **31 PH, L, NT,** pavilion, boating. 800-255-6936, (360) 288-2535. www.rainforestresort.com **H4**

Rainbow's End RV Park. Sequim. **40 FH, C, L, D,** fire rings, rec room, sports field, horseshoes. (360) 683-3863. www.rainbowsendrvpark.com **D6**

Rest-A-While RV Park. Hoodsport. **96 FH, C, L,** rec room, sports field, store, marina, boat launch. (360) 877-9474. www.restawhile.com **H6**

Salt Creek RV Park. Port Angeles. **65 (55 FH), L, D.** Par 3 golf course. (360) 928-2488. www.olypen.com/scrv **E4**

Sequim West RV Park. Sequim. **27 (22 FH), C, L.** 800-528-4527. **D6**

Shadow Mountain RV Park. West of Port Angeles. **40 FH, L, D,** fire rings, Wi-Fi, playground, basketball, horseshoes, store. 877-928-3043. **E5**

Sunrise–Dow Creek Resort. Hoodsport. **90 (17 FH, 44 PH),** rec room, volleyball, hiking, fishing. (360) 877-5022. www.sunriseresorts.com **H6**

Three Rivers Resort. Forks. **9. FH, PH, L.** (360) 374-5300. **F3**

Welcome Inn RV Park. Port Angeles. **35 FH, C, L, D, NT,** rec room. 800-357-1553, (360) 457-1553. **E5**

Page 14

Campgrounds

Bay View State Park. 76, W, PH, S, D, group site, picnic area, swimming, bird watching. 888-226-7688, (360) 757-0227. **C3**

Birch Bay State Park. 169, W, PH, S, D, TH, group site, picnic area, hiking, boating, boat launch. 888-226-7688, (360) 371-2800. **A2**

Camano Island State Park. 88, W, S, D, picnicking. (360) 387-3031. **E3**

Deception Pass State Park. 315, W, S, D, TH, group site, hiking, biking, boating, boat launch. 888-226-7688, (360) 675-2417. **C2**

Doe Bay Resort. 30, W, S, walk-in sites, cabins, hostel, kitchen area, hot tub, sauna, store, cafe. (360) 376-2291. www.doebay.com **B2**

Douglas Fir. Mt Baker–Snoqualmie NF. **29, W, TH,** fishing, hiking. 877-444-6777, (360) 856-5700. **A5**

Falls View. Olympic NF. **30, W,** hiking, picnic area. (360) 765-2200. **F1**

Fort Casey State Park. 35, W, PH, S, boat ramp, day use area. (360) 678-4519. **D2**

Fort Ebey State Park. 50, W, PH, S, TH, group site, mountain bike trails, fishing, hiking. 888-226-7688, (360) 678-4636. **D2**

Fort Flagler State Park. 116, W, PH, S, D, TH, group site, day use area, beach combing. March–October. 888-226-7688, (360) 385-1259. **E2**

Fort Worden State Park. 80, W, H, S, D, hiking, biking. (360) 344-4400. **D2**

Gold Basin. Mt Baker–Snoqualmie NF. **87, W, S,** group site, picnic area, hiking. Open mid-May–September. 877-444-6777, (360) 436-1155. **E6**

Horseshoe Cove. Mt Baker–Snoqualmie NF. **38, W,** group sites, picnic area, hiking, fishing, boat ramp. 877-444-6777, (360) 856-5700. **B6**

Howard Miller Steelhead Park. 60, W, PH, S, D, playground, fishing, boat launch, picnic area. (360) 853-8808. **C6**

Jones Island State Park. 24, W, primitive sites, group area. Accessible only by boat; boat buoys and floats available. (360) 378-2044. **C1**

Kanasket–Palmer State Park. 44, PH, W, S, D, group site, picnic area, hiking, mountain bike trails. 888-226-7688, (360) 886-0148. **H5**

Kayak Point County Park. 30, W, PH, yurts, group sites, boat pier, picnic area, fishing, boating. (360) 652-7992. **E4**

Larrabee State Park. 85, W, H, S, D, group site, day use area, hiking, biking, horse trails. 888-226-7688, (360) 676-2093. **B3**

Lighthouse Marine County Park. 30, W, S, boat launch, group site, picnic sites, whale watching. (360) 945-4911. **A1**

Moran State Park. 151, W, S, D, hiking, boat launch, group site, day use area. Reservations necessary in summer. 888-226-7688, (360) 376-2326. **B2**

Old Fort Townsend State Park. 44, W, S, D, group site, day use area, playground, hiking. Historic fort was built in 1859. (360) 385-3595. **E2**

Panorama Point. Mt Baker–Snoqualmie NF. **15, W,** fishing, boat ramp. Open mid-May to mid-September. 877-444-6777, (360) 856-5700. **B6**

Park Creek. Mt Baker–Snoqualmie NF. **12,** fishing. Open mid-May to mid-September. 877-444-6777, (360) 856-5700. **B6**

Penrose Point State Park. 82, W, S, D, hiking and biking. 888-226-7688, (206) 884-2514. **H2**

Rainbow. Olympic NF. **9, W,** all group sites. (360) 765-2200. **F1**

Rasar State Park. 38, W, PH, S, D, TH, group site, hiking, fishing. 888-226-7688, (360) 826-3942. **C5**

Red Bridge. Mt Baker–Snoqualmie NF. **16,** fishing, hiking. 877-444-6777, (360) 436-1155. **E6**

Scenic Beach State Park. 70, W, S, D, group site, day use area, beach combing, swimming. 888-226-7688, (360) 830-5079. **G2**

Seal Rock. Olympic NF. **41, W,** boat launch. May–Sept. (360) 765-2200. **F2**

Shannon Creek. Mt Baker–Snoqualmie NF. **19, W,** fishing, boat ramp. Open mid-May to mid-September. 877-444-6777, (360) 856-5700. **B6**

Silver Fir. Mt Baker–Snoqualmie NF. **20, W,** fishing. Open mid-May to mid-September. 877-444-6777, (360) 856-5700. **A6**

Silver Lake Park. 62, W, H, fishing, picnic area, group site, cabins, lodge, boat launch, boat rentals, horse facilities. (360) 599-2776. **A4**

South Whidbey State Park. 54, W, PH, S, TH, group site, hiking. Open mid-March to mid-October. 888-226-7688, (360) 331-4559. **E2**

Spencer Spit State Park. 37, W, D, 3 group camps, 7 walk-in beach sites. Open March–October. (360) 468-2251. **C2**

Squire Creek County Park. 34, W. (360) 435-3441. **D6**

Stuart Island State Park. 18, W, overnight moorage. Only enter harbor from east end; west end has rocks and reefs. (360) 376-2073. **B1**

Sucia Island State Park. 60, W, group camping, picnicking. Buoys for overnight moorage. Accessible by boat only. (360) 376-2073. **B1**

Swift Creek Campground. Mt Baker–Snoqualmie NF. **50, H, L, D,** picnic area, boat ramp, dock, rentals. 425-783-6000. **B6**

Tahuya River Horse Camp. DNR. **11, W,** picnic area, hiking, horse trails, staging area. Camping by permit only. (360) 825-1631. **G1**

Tolt McDonald Memorial Park. 40, W, PH, S, TH, group sites, cabins, walk-in sites. (206) 205-5434. **G5**

Turlo. Mt Baker–Snoqualmie NF. **18, W,** hiking, fishing. 877-444-6777, (360) 436-1155. **E5**

Verlot. Mt Baker–Snoqualmie NF. **25, W,** picnic area, hiking, fishing. Open May–October. 877-444-6777, (360) 436-1155. **E5**

Wallace Falls State Park. 2, W, hiking and mountain bike trails. (360) 793-0420. **F6**

Wenberg County Park. 70, W, PH, S, D, Wi-Fi, swimming, boat launch, playground, day use area, hiking. (425) 388-6600. **E4**

Wiley Creek Group. Mt Baker–Snoqualmie NF. Hiking, fishing. Groups only, reservations required. 877-444-6777, (541) 338-7869. **E6**

RV Parks

Beachside RV Park. Birch Bay. **72 (61 FH), L, D, NT,** rec room, Wi-Fi, horseshoes. 800-596-9586, (360) 371-5962. www.beachsidervpark.com **A2**

Beachwood Resort. Blaine. **250 FH, L,** pools, clubhouse, horseshoes, playground. (360) 371-5006. www.mybeachwoodresort.com **A2**

Bellingham RV Park. Bellingham. **56 FH, C, L, D, NS,** rec room. 888-372-1224, (360) 752-1224. www.bellinghamrvpark.com **B3**

Birch Bay Resort Park. Birch Bay. **60 FH, 64 PH, C, L, D, NT,** rec room, sports field. (360) 371-7922. www.birchbayrvresort.com **A2**

Blake's RV Park and Marina. Southeast of La Conner. **50 (28 FH, 9 PH), L,** boat ramp and dock, playground. (360) 445-6533. **D3**

Burlington–Anacortes KOA. N of Burlington. **102 (50 FH, 27 PH), C, L, D,** Wi-Fi, groups, rec hall, pool, playground, sports field. 800-562-9154. **C4**

Cascade Kamloops Trout Farm and RV Park. Darrington. **38 FH, C, L, D,** fire rings, Wi-Fi, rec hall, pond fishing. (360) 436-1003. **D6**

Cedar Grove Shores RV Park. West of Lakewood. **48 FH, 12 PH, C, L, D, NT,** rec room, group sites, sports field, horseshoes. 866-342-4981. **E3**

The Cedars RV Resort. Ferndale. **70 FH, 57 PH, C, L, D,** fire rings, rec room, pool, playground, sports field, horseshoes, hiking. (360) 384-2622. **A3**

Concrete–Grandy Creek KOA. 170 (50 FH, 84 PH), L, D, Wi-Fi, cabins, pool, rec room. Mid-March–Oct. 888-562-4236, (360) 826-3554. **C6**

Cove RV Park. Brinnon. **26 FH, C, L,** rec area. (360) 796-4723. **G2**

Creekside RV Park. West of Concrete. **33 (25 FH), C, L, D,** fire rings, rec room, sports field, horseshoes. (360) 826-3566. **C5**

Diamond Point RV Resort. Sequim. **70 FH, C, D,** Wi-Fi, hiking, fishing, horseshoes, clubhouse. (360) 681-0590. www.kmresorts.com **E2**

Eagles Haven RV Park. Southwest of Lummi. **43 FH, C, L, D,** Wi-Fi, playground, group site, sports field. (360) 758-2420. **B2**

Fidalgo Bay Resort. Anacortes. **204 FH, C, L, D,** Wi-Fi, clubhouse, rec hall, beachfront. 800-727-5478, (360) 293-5353. www.fidalgobay.com **C3**

Hidden Village RV Park & Campground. Lynden. **42, FH, PH, C, L, D,** Wi-Fi, groups sites, pool, rec room, sports field, fishing. 800-843-8606, (360) 398-1041. www.hvrv.com **A3**

Kulshan. 108, W, H, D, picnic area, fishing, boat ramp. (360) 853-8341. **B6**

Lake Goodwin Resort. West of Lakewood. **109 (69 FH, 15 PH), L, D,** Wi-Fi, gas station, sports field. 800-242-8169. www.lakegoodwinresort.com **D3**

Lake Ki RV Park. West of Lakewood. **57 FH, 4 PH, L, D,** fire rings, sports field. (360) 652-0619. **D4**

Lakedale Resort. San Juan Island. **8, FH, PH,** tents, swimming, canvas cabins, boat rental, sports field. 800-617-2267. www.lakedale.com **C1**

Lighthouse by the Bay RV Resort. Birch Bay. **100 FH, L, D, S,** Wi-Fi, playground, rec room. (360) 371-5603. www.lighthousebythebay.com **A2**

Lighthouse RV Park. Anacortes. **33 FH, C, L, NT.** (360) 293-3344. **C2**

Lynden–Bellingham KOA. Lynden. **160 (60 FH, 35 PH), L, D,** rec room, pool, sports field, horseshoes, playground, hiking. 800-562-4779. **A3**

Mount Vernon RV Park. Mount Vernon. **262 FH, C, L, D, NT,** rec room, horseshoes. (360) 428-8787. **C4**

Nor'West RV Park. Ferndale. **27 FH, C, L, NT, D,** horseshoes, hiking, playground. (360) 384-5038. **A3**

Nor'West RV Park. North Bend. **27 FH, C, L, NT.** (425) 888-9685. **G6**

North Whidbey RV Park. North of Oak Harbor on Deception Pass. **100, FH, C,** group sites, cabins, rec pavilion, playground. 888-462-2674, (360) 675-9597. www.northwhidbeyrvpark.com **D2**

Oak Harbor City Beach Park. Oak Harbor. **85 (55 PH), D,** sports field, fishing, swimming, tennis, horseshoes. (360) 679-5551. **D2**

Pioneer Trails Campground & RV Resort. Anacortes. **98 FH, C, L, D,** Wi-Fi, playground, sports field, rec room, horseshoes, picnic area. (360) 293-5355. www.pioneertrails.com **C2**

Point Hudson Resort and Marina. Port Townsend. **46 FH, L, D, NT,** rec pavilion. 800-228-2803. **D2**

Riverbend RV Park. West of Mount Vernon. **145 (90 FH), C, L, D,** rec room, sports field, horseshoes, fishing, picnic pavilion. (360) 428-4044. **C4**

Smokey Point RV Park. Smokey Point. **97 FH, C, L, S, D,** Wi-Fi, rec hall, horseshoes. (360) 653-8804. www.smokeypointrv.com **E4**

Snoqualmie River RV Park & Campground. Fall City. **123 (92 PH), C, D,** fishing, rec pavilion, sports field. (425) 222-5545. www.srcghsg.com **G5**

Smitty's RV Park. Nordland. **44 FH, NT.** (360) 385-2165. **E2**

Sumas RV Park. Sumas. **51 FH, C, L, D,** fire rings, sports field. (360) 988-8875. www.sumasrvpark.com **A3**

Sunny Point RV Resort Park. Point Roberts. **50 (24 PH), L, D,** Wi-Fi, sports field, playground. (360) 945-1986. www.sunnypointroberts.com **A1**

Timberline RV Resort. West of Concrete. **39 FH, L,** fire rings, rec room, horseshoes. (360) 826-3131. **C5**

Washington Park (City Park). Anacortes. **68 (46 PH), L, D,** playground, boat ramp, picnicking. (360) 293-1927. **C2**

West Beach Resort. Orcas Island. **50 (24 PH), L,** cabins, swim beach, store, marina, boat rentals. 877-937-8224. www.westbeachresort.com **B1**

Wildwood Resort. Sedro-Woolley. **157 (75 FH, 4 PH),** rec hall, sports field, playground, swimming, boat launch, cabins, marine fuel. (360) 595-2311. www.wildwood-resort.net **B4**

Page 16

Campgrounds

Beckler River. Mt Baker–Snoqualmie NF. **27, W,** picnic area, fishing. Open May–September. 877-444-6777, (360) 677-2414. **F2**

Bedal. Mt Baker–Snoqualmie NF. **21,** hiking, beachfront, boat launch, fishing. 877-444-6777, (360) 436-1155. **E2**

Beebe Bridge Park. 46, W, PH, D, picnic shelters, playground, swimming, boating, boat launch, horseshoes. (509) 661-8000. **F6**

Beverly. Wenatchee NF. **14,** picnic area. (509) 852-1100. **H3**

Blackpine Horse Camp. Wenatchee NF. **10, W, TH,** corral, horse trail, picnic area, fishing. (509) 548-2550. **G3**

Black Pine Lake. Okanogan NF. **23, W,** hiking, boat ramp, picnic area, fishing. (509) 996-4003. **D5**

Buck Creek. Mt Baker–Snoqualmie NF. **20,** picnic area, hiking, fishing. 877-444-6777, (360) 436-1155. **D2**

Buck Lake. Okanogan NF. **7,** fishing, boat ramp. (509) 996-4003. **C5**

Cayuse Horse Camp. Wenatchee NF. **14, W,** picnic area, hiking, corral, horse trails. (509) 852-1100. **H3**

RECREATION

Chatter Creek. Wenatchee NF. 12, W, group site (by reservation only), hiking. (509) 548-2550. G3

Chewuch. Okanogan NF. 16, fishing. May–Sept. (509) 996-4003. B6

Chiwawa Horse Camp. Wenatchee NF. 21, W, TH, horse trails, hiking. (509) 664-9200. E4

Cle Elum River. Wenatchee NF. 23, group site (by reservation only), picnic area, hiking, fishing. 877-444-6777, (509) 852-1100. H3

Clear Creek. Mt Baker–Snoqualmie NF. 13, fishing, hiking. 877-444-6777, 360) 436-1155. D1

Colonial Creek. Ross Lake NRA. 142, W, D, boat ramp. (360) 854-7200. B3

Cottonwood. Wenatchee NF. 25, W, hiking, fishing. (509) 784-4700. E4

Daroga State Park. 45, W, PH, S, D, TH, group site, picnic area, hiking, boat launch. 888-226-7688, (509) 664-6380. F6

Denny Creek. Mt Baker–Snoqualmie NF. 34, W, group site. Bridge has weight restrictions. 877-444-6777, (360) 825-6585. H1

Early Winters. Okanogan NF. 13, W, fishing. (509) 996-4003. Apr–Nov. C5

Eightmile. Wenatchee NF. 45, W, group area (by reservation only), hiking, fishing. (509) 548-2550. G3

Entiat Park. 56 (31 FH), W, S, D, boat launch, swimming, playground. 800-736-8428. G5

Flat. Okanogan NF. 12, W, fishing. Pack-in/pack-out. (509) 996-4003. B6

Foggy Dew. Okanogan NF. 13, fishing, hiking. (509) 996-4003. D6

Fox Creek. Wenatchee NF. 16, W, picnic area, fishing, hiking, mountain biking. May–September. (509) 784-4700. E4

Friends Landing. Montesano. 19 PH, D, pavilion, playground, boat ramp, boating, fishing. (360) 249-5117. www.gofriendslanding.com B4

Glacier View. Wenatchee NF. 23, W, TH, picnic area, hiking, boat launch, walk-in sites. May–September. (509) 548-2550. F3

Goodell Creek. Ross Lake NRA. 21, W, raft launch. (360) 854-7200. B2

Goose Creek. Wenatchee NF. 29, W, TH, picnic area, hiking, motorcycle trails. (509) 548-2550. F4

Harlequin. Lake Chelan NRA. 7, TH, group site, picnic shelter, horse stable, hose trail, hiking. Permit required. (360) 854-7200. D4

Hozomeen. Ross Lake NRA. 75, W, boat ramp. Pack-in/pack-out. (360) 854-7200. A3

Ida Creek. Wenatchee NF. 10, W, fishing and hiking. (509) 548-2550. G3

Johnny Creek. Wenatchee NF. 65, W, hiking. May–Sept. (509) 548-2550. G3

Kachess. Wenatchee NF. 152, TH, group sites, picnic area, hiking, swimming, boating. May–Sept. 877-444-6777, (509) 852-1100. H2

Ken Wilcox Horse Camp. Wenatchee NF. 19, picnic area, hiking. (509) 852-1100. H4

Klipchuck. Okanogan NF. 46, W, hiking, fishing. (509) 996-4003. C4

Lake Chelan State Park. 144, W, H, S, D, boat launch. April–October. 888-226-7688, (509) 687-3710. F5

Lake Creek. Wenatchee NF. 18, W, hiking. (509) 784-4700. F3

Lake Wenatchee State Park. 197, W, S, D, group site, day use area, boat launch, cross-country skiing. 888-226-7688, (509) 763-3101. F3

Lincoln Rock State Park. 94, W, H, S, D, day use area, boat launch, hiking, biking. 888-226-7688, (509) 884-8702. G5

Lone Fir. Okanogan NF. 27, W, interpretive trail. (509) 996-4003. C4

Marble Creek. Mt Baker–Snoqualmie NF. 23, fishing. 877-444-6777, (360) 856-5700. C2

Meadows. Okanogan NF. 14. (509) 996-4003. B4

Mineral Springs. Wenatchee NF. 7, W, group site, fishing. 877-444-6777, (509) 852-1100. H4

Money Creek. Mt Baker–Snoqualmie NF. 25, W, hiking, fishing. 877-444-6777, (360) 677-2414. F1

Nason Creek. Wenatchee NF. 73, W, group site, picnic area. (509) 548-2550. F4

Newhalem Creek. Ross Lake NRA. 111, W, D, hiking, fishing. May–October. (360) 854-7200. B2

North Fork. Wenatchee NF. 8, W, fishing. (509) 784-4700. May–Sept. E4

Owhi. Wenatchee NF. 22, TH. canoeing, hike-in only. (509) 852-1100. H2

Pearrygin Lake State Park. 153, W, H, S, D, group site, boat launch, swimming, fishing. 888-226-7688, (509) 996-2370. C6

Poplar Flat. Okanogan NF. 16, W, picnic area. (509) 996-4003. C5

Prince Creek. Wenatchee NF. 6, TH, picnic area, hiking, water-skiing, floating dock, boat-in or hike-in only. Ferry flag stop. (509) 682-4900. E5

Purple Point. Lake Chelan NRA. 6, W, hiking, picnic area. (360) 854-7200. D4

Rainy Creek. Wenatchee NF. 10, hiking, fishing. (509) 548-2550. F3

Red Mountain. Wenatchee NF. 10, picnic area, hiking, fishing. May–September. (509) 852-1100. H3

Rock Island. Wenatchee NF. 22, W, hiking, fishing. (509) 548-2550. G3

Salmon La Sac. Wenatchee NF. 69, W, picnic area, hiking, fishing. 877-444-6777, (509) 852-1100. H3

Schaefer Creek. Wenatchee NF. 10, fishing. (509) 548-2550. E3

Silver Falls. Wenatchee NF. 31, W, group site (by reservation only), picnic shelter, hiking. (509) 784-4700. E4

Squilchuck State Park. group site, hiking, mountain biking. (509) 664-6373. H5

Sulphur Creek. Mt Baker–Snoqualmie NF. 20, hiking, picnicking. 877-444-6777, (360) 436-1155. D2

Swauk. Wenatchee NF. 22, W, picnic area, hiking. (509) 852-1100. H4

Tinkham. Mt Baker–Snoqualmie NF. 47, W. May–September. 877-444-6777, (360) 825-6585. H1

Troublesome Creek. Mt Baker–Snoqualmie NF. 25, W. 877-444-6777, (360) 677-2414. E2

Tumwater. Wenatchee NF. 86, W, group area (by reservation only), shelter, fireplace. May–September. 800-274-6104, (509) 548-2550. G4

Twenty-Five Mile Creek State Park. 67, W, H, S, D, group site, picnic area, fishing, boating, boat launch, dock. 888-226-7688, (509) 687-3610. E5

War Creek. Okanogan NF. 10, W, fishing. (509) 996-4003. C5

Weaver Point. Lake Chelan NRA. 22, W, picnic area, hiking, fishing. (360) 854-7200. D4

Wenatchee Confluence State Park. 59, W, H, S, D, TH, group site, hiking, biking, boat launch, swimming. 888-226-7688, (509) 664-6373. G5

Wenatchee River County Park. Chelan County. 43, W, H, S, D, playground. (509) 667-7503. www.wenatcheeriverpark.org G4

Wish Poosh. Wenatchee NF. 34, W, picnic area, swimming, boating, boat launch. (509) 852-1100. H3

RV Parks

Alpine RV Park. Marblemount. 26 (22 FH), L, NS, sports field. (360) 873-9002. C1

Alpine View RV Park. Leavenworth. 33 (16 FH), L, D, tent sites, pet-friendly. (509) 548-8439, 888-548-8439. www.alpineviewrvpark.com G4

Big Twin Lake Campground. South of Winthrop. 89 (21 FH, 26 PH), D, fire rings, Wi-Fi, boat ramp and dock. (509) 996-2650. C5

Blu–Shastin RV Park. Hwy 97, S of Leavenworth. 86 FH, L, C, fire rings, rec hall, swimming pool, sports field. 888-548-4184. www.blushastin.com G4

Country Town Motel & RV Resort. Carlton. 20 FH, L, putting green, game room, library, store. 800-658-5249. D6

Icicle River RV Resort. South of Leavenworth. 102 FH, 13 PH, C, L, NT, fire rings, rec hall, sports field. (509) 548-5420. www.icicleriverrv.com G4

Pine–Near RV Park. Winthrop. 45 (24 FH), L, D. (509) 996-2391. C6

Pine Village Kampground KOA. East of Leavenworth. 135 (60 FH, 45 PH), C, L, D, rec room, pool, playground, sports field. 800-562-5709. G4

Riverbend RV Park. North of Twisp. 75 (55 FH), L, D, fire rings, rec hall, sports field. 800-686-4498, (509) 997-3500. www.riverbendrv.com D6

Silverline Resort. North of Winthrop. 122 (28 FH, 24 PH), boat ramp and dock, sports field. (509) 996-2448. www.silverlineresort.com C6

Wilderness Village. Rockport. 30 FH, C, L, Wi-Fi, club room, fishing, river access. (360) 873-2571. www.wildernessvillagervpark.com C1

Winthrop–North Cascades NP KOA. South of Winthrop. 99 (16 FH, 53 PH), L, D, Wi-Fi, rec room, pool, playground, sports field. 800-562-2158. www.methownet.com/koa C6

Page 18

Campgrounds

Alta Lake State Park. 123, W, PH, S, group site, hiking, picnic area, boat launch, fishing. April–Oct. 888-226-7688, (509) 923-2473. E1

Beaver Lake. Okanogan NF. 11, W, boat ramp, group site, fishing, hiking. May–Sept. (509) 486-2186. F3

Beth Lake. Okanogan NF. 14, picnic area, boat ramp. (509) 486-2186. A4

Bonaparte Lake. Okanogan NF. 27, W, group site, boat ramp, picnic area, hiking, fishing platform, winter recreation. May–Sept. (509) 486-2186. B4

Bridgeport State Park. 34, W, PH, S, D, group site, picnic area, hiking, boat launch, swimming. March–Oct. 888-226-7688, (509) 686-7231. E2

Chopaka Lake. DNR, Loomis SF. 8, W, boat ramp, sheltered picnic site, fishing. (509) 684-7474. A2

Conconully State Park. 59, W, PH, S, D, boat launch, picnic area, snowmobile trail to town. April–Oct. 888-226-7688, (509) 826-7408. C2

Coulee City Park. 110, W, H, S, D, playground, swimming, boat launch and dock. April–October. (509) 632-5331. G3

Crawfish Lake. Okanogan NF. 19, boat ramp, picnic area. (509) 486-2186. C3

Curlew Lake State Park. 82, W, H, S, D, boat launch, dock, biking, wildlife viewing. (509) 775-3592. B5

Keller Ferry. Lake Roosevelt NRA. 55, W, D, group sites, playground, boat dock and launch, marine fuel. 877-444-6777, (509) 633-9441. E5

Keller Park. Colville IR. 15, W, picnicking, swimming. (509) 633-9441. E5

Kerr. Okanogan NF. 13, fishing, winter recreation. (509) 486-2186. B2

Leader Lake. DNR, Loup Loup SF. 14, boat launch, picnic sites, fishing. (509) 684-7474. D2

Legion City Park. 20, W, S, picnic area, gazebo. (509) 422-3600. C2

Long Lake. Colville NF. 12, W, boat launch. (509) 775-7400. C5

Lost Lake. Okanogan NF. 19, W, group site, picnic area, hiking, boat ramp, fishing, boating (non-motorized). (509) 486-2186. A4

Loup Loup. Okanogan NF. 25, W, group picnic area, mountain bike trails. May–November. (509) 996-4003. C1

North Fork Ninemile. DNR, Loomis SF. 11, W, picnic sites. (509) 684-7474. A2

Oriole. Okanogan NF. 10, fishing. May–Nov. (509) 486-2186. C2

Osoyoos Lake State Veteran's Memorial Park. 86, W, H, S, D, boating, fishing, swimming, boat launch. Apr–Oct. 888-226-7688, (509) 476-3321. A3

Spring Canyon. Lake Roosevelt NRA. 87, W, D, group area, playground, boat dock and launch, visitor station. 877-444-6777, (509) 633-9441. E5

Steamboat Rock State Park. 162, W, H, S, D, group site, day use area, boat launch, hike, bike, horse trails. 888-226-7688, (509) 633-1304. F4

Sun Lakes–Dry Falls State Park. 191, W, H, S, D, group site, day use area, boat launch, hike, bike trails. 888-226-7688, (509) 632-5583. G3

Swan Lake. Colville NF. 25, W, TH, group area, picnic shelter, boat launch, fishing, swimming, hike, bike trails. (509) 775-7400. C5

RV Parks

Bell RV Park. Wilbur. 30 FH, L, D, S, Wi-Fi. (509) 647-5888. F5

Black Beach Resort. Northeast of Republic, on Curlew Lake. 112 FH, 8 PH), L, D, fire rings, boat ramp, dock, playground. (509) 775-3989. B5

Blue Lake Resort. SW of Coulee City. 100 FH, D. fire rings, playground, sports field. (509) 632-5364. www.bluelakeresortwashington.com G3

Bonaparte Lake Resort. Tonasket. 29 FH, L, S, cabins, store, boating, fishing, gas. (509) 486-2828. www.bonapartelakeresort.com B4

Carl Precht Memorial RV Park. Omak. 78 (68 FH), S, D. (509) 826-1170 C3

Columbia Cove RV Park. Brewster. 29 FH, swimming, fishing, boat launch. (509) 689-3464. E2

Coulee Lodge Resort. West of Coulee City. 40 (23 FH), L, D, boat ramp, dock, rentals, sports field. (509) 632-5565. www.couleelodgeresort.com G3

Coulee Playland Resort. On Banks Lake. 65 (39 FH, 18 PH), L, D, Wi-Fi, rec pavilion, boat ramp, dock. 888-633-2671, (509) 633-2671. www.couleeplayland.com E4

Country Lane RV Park. Wilbur. 31 (27 FH), C, L, D, pool, rec room, Wi-Fi, store. (509) 647-0100. F5

Glenwood RV Park. Riverside. 20 FH, L. (509) 826-1121. C2

Grand Coulee RV Park. Grand Coulee. 35 (23 FH, 8 PH), C, L, D, picnic area, Wi-Fi. (509) 633-0750. F4

Jack's RV Park & Motel. Conconully. 54 FH, C, L, D, fire rings, swimming pool, horseshoes. 800-893-5668, (509) 826-0132. C2

The King's Court RV Park. Grand Coulee. 32 FH, C, L, D, Wi-Fi. 800-759-2608, (509) 633-3655. www.kingscourtrv.com E4

Lakeview Terrace RV Park. Grand Coulee. 20, S, L. (509) 633-2169. E4

Laurent's Sun Village Resort. Coulee City. 96 (80 FH, 16 PH), L, D, store, cabins, boat launch, moorage, rentals. 888-632-5664, (509) 632-5664. G3

Liars Cove Resort. Conconully. 35 FH, C, L, D, cabins, group area, boat ramp, dock. 800-830-1288, (509) 826-1288. www.liarscoveresort.com C2

Margie's RV Park. Riverside. 53 (23 FH, 24 PH), L, D, S, pavilion, horseshoes, fire rings. (509) 826-5810. www.margies-rvpark.com C3

Marina RV Park. Bridgeport. 58 FH, C, S, D. (509) 686-4747. E2

Oasis RV Park and Golf. South of Ephrata. 89 (28 FH, 40 PH), C, L, D, fire rings, Wi-Fi, fish pond, hiking, swimming pool, sports field. 877-754-5102, (509) 754-5102. www.oasisrvandgolfresort.com H2

Okanogan County Fairgrounds RV Park. Okanogan. 64 FH, 44 PH, groups, building rentals, kitchens, horse stalls. (509) 422-1621. D2

Sonora Point. East of Loomis. 46 (34 FH, 12 PH), NS, fire rings, rec hall, boat ramp and dock, sports field. (509) 223-3700. B2

River Oaks RV Resort. Oroville. 48 FH, L, S, NT. (509) 476-2087. A3

The River Rue RV Park. On Lake Roosevelt. 74 (39 FH, 12 PH), L, D, S, swimmimg, hiking, store. www.riverrue.com (509) 647-2647. F5

Shady Pines Resort. Conconully. 23 FH, boat dock, boat rentals, swimming, fishing. 800-552-2287, (509) 826-2287. www.shadypinesresort.com C2

Spectacle Lake Resort. E of Loomis. 33 FH, C, L, D, boat ramp, dock, fishing, swimming, rec rooom. (509) 223-3433. spectaclelakeresort.com B2

Sun Banks Resort. Electric City. 230 (20 FH, 40 PH), L, S, boating, swimming, fishing, sports field. 888-822-7195. www.sunbanksresort.com F4

Sun Cove Resort & Guest Ranch. Southeast of Oroville. 27 (19 FH), L, D, S, rec hall, pool, boat ramp, dock, store. (509) 476-2223. A3

Sun Lakes Park Resort. SW of Coulee City. 144 FH, L, D, pool, boat ramp, dock, sports field, hiking, store, mini golf. (509) 632-5291. G3

Winchester RV Park. Republic. 32 FH, L, D, S, pavilion, cabins, horseshoes, fishing, hiking, sports field. (509) 775-1039. B5

Page 20

Campgrounds

Big Meadow Lake. Colville NF. 17, picnic area, hiking, fishing, boat launch, wildlife viewing. (509) 684-7000. B4

Browns Lake. Colville NF. 18, TH, picnic area, ORV trails, hiking, canoeing. (509) 447-7300. C5

Canyon Creek. Colville NF. 12, hiking, fishing. (509) 738-7700. C2

Cloverleaf. Lake Roosevelt NRA. 9, W, picnic area, boat dock, boat-in or hike-in only. (509) 633-9441. D2

Columbia. Spokane IR. 25, 4 shelters. (509) 458-6500. E1

Deer Creek. Colville NF. 9, TH, picnic area, hiking, bike and horse trails, winter recreation. (509) 738-7700. A1

Detillion. Lake Roosevelt NRA. 12, W, boat-in only, picnic area, boat dock. (509) 633-9441. E2

Douglas Falls Grange Park. DNR. 8, W, sports field, picnic area, boat dock, horseshoe pits, falls viewpoint. (509) 684-7474. B2

Enterprise. Lake Roosevelt NRA. 13, boat-in only. (509) 633-9441. E2

Evans. Lake Roosevelt NRA. 43, W, D, group site, picnic area, boat launch, dock. 877-444-6777, (509) 633-9441. E1

Flodelle Creek. DNR. 8, W, mountain biking, motorcycling, hiking, fishing. (509) 684-7474. C4

Fort Spokane. Lake Roosevelt NRA. 67, W, D, group sites, picnic area, boat ramp and dock, marine dump station. 877-444-6777, (509) 633-9441, (509) 633-3836 (Visitor Center). F1

Gifford. Lake Roosevelt NRA. 42, W, D, group site, picnic area, boat launch, dock. 877-444-6777, (509) 633-9441. D2

Haag Cove. Lake Roosevelt NRA. 16, W, dock, picnic area. (509) 633-9441. C2

Hawk Creek. Lake Roosevelt NRA. 21, W, boat ramp and dock, picnic area, hiking. (509) 633-9441. F1

Hunters. Lake Roosevelt NRA. 39, W, D, group sites, picnic area, boat launch, dock. 877-444-6777, (509) 633-9441. E2

Kamloops. Lake Roosevelt NRA. 17, W, boat dock. (509) 633-9441. B2

Kettle Falls. Lake Roosevelt NRA. 76, W, S, D, group site, picnic area, boat launch, boat dock, marina. 877-444-6777, (509) 633-9441, (509) 738-6266 (Visitor Station), (509) 738-6121 (marina). C2

Kettle River. Lake Roosevelt NRA. 13, W, boat dock. (509) 633-9441. B2

Lake Ellen. Colville NF. 11, fishing, boat launch. (509) 738-7700. C2

Long Lake. DNR. 9, W, picnic area, hiking, fishing, boat launch, nearby pictographs. (509) 684-7474. F3

Marcus Island. Lake Roosevelt NRA. 27, W, picnic area, boat launch, boat dock, water skiing. (509) 633-9441. B2

Mill Pond. Colville NF. 10, W, TH, picnic area, hiking, boat launch. (509) 446-7500. A5

Mt Spokane State Park. 8, W, groups, hike, horse trails. (509) 238-4258. E5

Noisy Creek. Colville NF. 19, W, TH, hiking, wildlife viewing, fishing, boat launch, swimming area. (509) 446-7500. B5

North Gorge. Lake Roosevelt NRA. 12, W, boat launch, dock. (509) 633-9441. B2

Panhandle. Colville NF. 13, W, boat ramp, picnic area, ORV trails. (509) 447-7300. C5

Pend Oreille County Park. 17, W, picnic area, old growth forest trails. (509) 447-4821. www.pendoreilleco.org E5

Pierre Lake. Colville NF. 15, boat ramp, fishing. (509) 738-7700. A2

Pioneer Park. Colville NF. 17, W, picnic area, hiking, wildlife viewing, swimming, boat launch. (509) 447-7300. D6

Porcupine Bay. Lake Roosevelt NRA. 31, W, D, boat launch, dock. (509) 633-9441. F2

Riverside State Park. 32, W, S, D, group site, boat launch, hiking, ATV, cross-country ski trails. 888-226-7688, (509) 456-5064. F4

Rocky Point. Colville IR. 10. (509) 634-3145. D1

Rogers Bar. Colville IR. 25. (509) 634-3145. E1

Sheep Creek. DNR. 11, W, picnic area, interpretive site. (509) 684-7474. A3

Skookum Creek. DNR. 10, W, picnic area. (509) 684-7474. D5

Snag Cove. Lake Roosevelt NRA. 9, W, boat ramp and dock, picnic area. (509) 633-9441. B2

South Skookum Lake. Colville NF. 25, W, picnic area, ORV trails, hiking, fishing, swimming, boat launch. (509) 447-7300. C5

Sullivan Lake, East and West. Colville NF. 48, W, two campgrounds, group site, picnic area, swimming, fishing, boat ramp. (509) 446-7500. B5

Wilmont Creek. Colville IR. 15. (509) 634-3145. E1

RV Parks

Alderwood RV Express. N of Spokane on US 2. 105 FH, C, L, D, pool, rec room. 888-847-0500, (509) 467-5320. www.alderwoodrv.com F5

Bear Creek Lodge. On Mt Spokane. 12 PH, D, restaurant, groups, store, lodge, snow tubing, trails. (509) 238-9114. www.bearcreeklodgewa.com F5

Beaver Lodge Resort & RV Park. SW of Tiger. 45 (11 FH, 6 PH), L, cabins, pavilion, boating, fishing. (509) 684-5657. www.beaverlodgeresort.org C4

Blueslide Resort. Blueslide. 45 (15 FH, 3 PH), L, D, fishing, hiking, rec hall, pool, sports field, boat dock. (509) 445-1327. www.blueslideresort.com C5

Chapman Lake Resort. South of Cheney. 50 (9 PH), NT, cabins, boat launch. (509) 523-2221. H4

Deer Lake Resort. N of Loon Lake. 82 (65 FH), L, D, S, pavilion, boat dock, boat rental, fuel, cabins. (509) 233-2081. www.deerlakeresort.com E4

Four Seasons Campground. W of Sprague. 38 (29 FH, 9 PH), D, pool, boat ramp, rentals, store. (509) 257-2332. fourseasonscampground.com H2

Grandview Inn Motel & RV Park. Kettle Falls. 23 FH, L, C, S, pavilion, sports field, pool, horseshoes, fishing. 888-488-6733, (509) 738-6733. C2

Hartman's Log Cabin Resort. Inchelium. **32 FH, L, NS,** boat ramp, swimming, fishing, marina, fuel. (509) 722-3543. hartmanslogcabin.com **D1**

Hico Village Northpointe RV Park. N of Spokane on Nevada St. **30 FH, L, D,** rec room, Wi-Fi, playground. (509) 466-0600. **F5**

Klink's Williams Lake Resort. SW of Cheney. **20 FH, 55 PH, D, S,** Wi-Fi, rec room, fire rings, sports field, boat ramp, dock, rentals. 800-274-1540, (509) 235-2391. www.klinksresort.com **H4**

Jump Off Joe Lake Resort & RV Park. On Jumpoff Joe Lake. **22 FH, L,** boat ramp and dock, fishing, swimming. Apr–Oct. (509) 937-2133. **E4**

Mallard Bay Resort. Clear Lake. **3 FH, 46 PH,** pavilion, playground, boat ramp and dock, fishing. (509) 299-3830. **G3**

Marshall Lake Resort. NW of Newport on Marshall Lake. **50 FH, C, L, S,** fire rings, boat dock, boat rentals. (509) 447-4158. **D5**

Moonlight RV Park. W of Diamond Lake on State Hwy 211. **32 (15 FH, 17 PH),** fishing, swimming, playground, horseshoes. (509) 447-0631. **E5**

Mt Linton RV Park. Metaline. **40 FH, L, D, C, S,** Wi-Fi. (509) 446-4553. **A4**

North Lake RV Park. N of Kettle Falls. **77 FH, L, C, D,** rec hall, pool, playground, sports field, hiking. (509) 738-2593. **B2**

Old American Kampground. Newport. **100 FH, C, L, D,** clubhouse, hot tub, swimming, hiking, marina. (509) 447-3663. **D6**

Overland Station RV Park. Southwest of Spokane. **32 FH.** (509) 747-1703. **G4**

Panorama RV Park & Storage. Kettle Falls. **61 FH, C, L, D,** rec hall, horseshoes. 800-227-6352, (509) 738-6831. **C2**

Peaceful Pines RV Park & Campground. Cheney. **17 FH, 10 PH, D, C,** Wi-Fi. 800-985-2966, (509) 235-4966. www.peacefulpinesrv.com **G4**

Ponderosa Falls RV Resort. SW of Spokane. **165 FH, C, L, D, S,** pool, store. 800-494-7275, (509) 747-9415. **G4**

Rainbow Beach Resort. Inchelium. **19 (16 FH), L,** boating. (509) 722-5901. **D1**

Seven Bays. Northwest of Davenport. **35, FH, L, S,** fishing, boat launch, boat fuel, store, marine dump station. (509) 725-1676. **F1**

Shore Acres Resort. Loon Lake. **25 FH, D, C, S, NT,** cabins, marina, boat rentals. 800-900-2474, (509) 233-2474. www.shoreacresresort.com **E4**

Silver Beach Resort. NW of Valley. **51 FH, L, D, S, NT,** boat ramp, dock, boat rentals, swimming. (509) 937-2811. www.silverbeachresort.net **D3**

Spokane KOA. East of Spokane. **196 (82 FH, 83 PH), L, D, C, TH,** Wi-Fi, rec room, pool, sports field. 800-562-3309, (509) 924-4722. **G5**

Spokane RV Resort at Deer Park Golf Club. Deer Park. **125 FH, C, L, NT,** rec room, pool, hiking. 877-276-1155. www.spokanervresort.com **E4**

Sprague Lake Resort. W of Sprague. **31 FH, L,** boat ramp, dock, boat rentals, horseback riding, fishing. (509) 257-2864. www.spraguelakeresort.com **H2**

Sun Cove Resort. South of Medical Lake. **17 (8 FH, 9 PH), C, S, D,** fire rings, boat ramp and dock, fishing, boat rentals. (509) 299-3717. **G4**

Trailer Inn's RV Park. 4th Ave, Spokane. **96 FH, C, L,** Wi-Fi, playground, rec room. 800-659-4864, (509) 535-1811. www.trailerinnsrv.com **G5**

Two Rivers Marina & RV Park. N of Davenport. **101 FH, C, L, D,** boat launch, marina, playground. Casino. 800-722-4031, (509) 722-4029. **F1**

Upper Columbia RV Park. Northport. **22 FH, D,** groups, store, fishing, playground. Apr–Oct. (509) 732-4367. www.uppercolumbiarv.com **A3**

Wild Rose RV Park. Colbert. **54 FH, L,** rec hall. (509) 276-8853. **F4**

Winona Beach Resort. On Waitts Lake. **49 FH, 5 PH, D,** cabins, fishing, playground, boat ramp, dock, rentals. 888-271-4693, (509) 937-2231. **D3**

Page 22

Campgrounds

Cape Disappointment State Park. 220, W, H, S, D, 5 group camps, boat ramp, hiking, biking. 888-226-7688, (360) 642-3088. **E2**

Fall Creek. DNR, Capitol SF. **8, W, TH,** horse ramp, mountain biking, horse trails. (360) 577-2025. **B6**

Grayland Beach State Park. 100, W, H, D, S, horse riding on beach. 888-226-7688, (360) 267-4301. **C3**

Lake Sylvia State Park. 35, W, S, D, group site, day use area, boat launch, hiking. 888-226-7688, (360) 249-3621. **B5**

Margaret McKenny. DNR, Capitol SF. **25, W,** hiking, mountain biking, horse trails. (360) 577-2025. **B6**

Middle Waddell. DNR, Capitol SF. **24, W,** ORV staging area, mountain biking, motorcycle trails. (360) 577-2025. **B6**

Mima Falls. DNR, Capitol SF. **5, W, TH,** picnic area, hiking, mountain biking, horse trails. (360) 577-2025. **B6**

Ocean City State Park. 178, W, H, S, D, group site. 888-226-7688, (360) 289-3553. **B2**

Pacific Beach State Park. 60, W, PH, S, D, picnicking, beach combing. (360) 276-4297. **A2**

Porter Creek. DNR, Capitol SF. **16, W,** hiking, mountain biking, motorcycle and horse trails. (360) 577-2025. **B6**

Promised Land Park. 17, W, picnic and kitchen area. (360) 533-7000. **E5**

Rainbow Falls State Park. 53, S, D, group site, playground, nature trail, day use area. (360) 291-3767. **C6**

Schafer State Park. 56, W, PH, S, D, day use area, hiking, mountain biking. 888-226-7688, (360) 482-3852. **A5**

Skamokawa Vista Park. 34, W, D, S, yurts, playground, swimming, fishing, boating. (360) 795-8605. **E5**

Twin Harbors State Park. 266, W, H, S, D, picnicking, hiking to ocean, horse riding on beach. 888-226-7688, (360) 268-9717. **B3**

RV Parks

American Sunset RV Resort. Westport. **118 FH, L, S,** Wi-Fi, rec hall, pool, sports field, store. 800-569-2267, (360) 268-0207. **B3**

Andersen's on the Ocean. Long Beach. **54 FH, L, D, C, S,** Wi-Fi, playground, groups. 800-645-6795, (360) 642-2231. andersensrv.com **E3**

Artic RV Park & Campground. Artic. **12 FH, 11 PH, L, D, S,** fire rings, fishing, rec room, sports field, hiking. (360) 533-4470. **B4**

Bay Center KOA. South of Bay Center. **65 (10 FH, 30 PH), L, D, C,** fire rings, Wi-Fi, rec room, playground, sports field. 800-562-7810. **C3**

Bayshore RV Park. Tokeland. **41 FH, C, D,** beach, clubhouse, Wi-Fi. 800-638-7555, (360) 267-2625. **C3**

Beacon Charters & RV Park. Ilwaco. **60 FH, C.** (360) 642-2138. **E3**

Blue Pacific Motel & RV Park. Ocean City. **13 FH, 6 PH, L, S, C,** fire rings, sports field, horseshoes. (360) 289-2262. **A2**

Copalis Beach Surf and Sand RV Park. Copalis Beach. **41 FH, 6 PH, C, L, D,** fire rings, rec hall, horseshoes. 800-867-2707, (360) 289-2707. **A3**

Driftwood Acres Ocean Campground. Copalis Beach. **39 (5 FH, 15 PH), D,** fire rings, sports field. (360) 289-3484. **A3**

Driftwood RV Park. Long Beach. **56 FH, L, NT, C, S,** Wi-Fi, pet area. 888-567-1902, (360) 642-2711. www.driftwood-rvpark.net **E3**

The Dunes RV Resort. Copalis Beach. **38 (28 FH, 3 PH), D, S,** playground, sports field, rec room. 877-386-3779, (360) 289-3873. **A3**

Eagle's Nest Resort. Ilwaco. **110 FH, C, L, D,** fire rings, rec hall, pool, restaurant, playground, hiking, mini golf. (360) 642-8351. **E3**

Echoes of the Sea Motel & Campground. Copalis Beach. **38 (30 PH), D.** 800-578-3246, (360) 289-3358. **A3**

Elma RV Park. Elma. **104 PH, C, L, D,** Wi-Fi, clubhouse, pets welcome, volleyball. 866-211-3939, (360) 482-4053. www.elmarvpark.com **B5**

Fishermans Cove RV Park. Ilwaco. **44 FH, D, C, S, L.** (360) 642-3689. **E3**

Friends Landing. Montesano. **28 (10 FH), D,** pavilion, playground, boat ramp, boating, fishing. (360) 249-5117. **B3**

Grizzly Joe's RV Park. Westport. **35 FH, C, L, D, NT,** rec hall, boat dock. (360) 268-5555. **B3**

Holand Center RV Park. Westport. **80 FH, C, L, NT.** (360) 268-9582. **B3**

Ilwaco KOA. Ilwaco. **164 (34 FH, 80 PH), L, D.** (360) 642-3292. **E3**

Islander Motel, Charters & RV Park. Westport. **56 (44 FH), C, L, D, S, NT,** swimming pool, boat dock. (360) 268-9166. westport-islander.com **B3**

Jolly Rogers Fishing Camp. Westport. **25 FH, C, D,** fire rings, boat dock, fishing, crabbing. (360) 268-0265. **B3**

Kenanna RV Park. South of Grayland. **108 (89 FH), C, L, D, S,** rec hall, playground, hiking. 800-867-3515. www.kenannarv.com **C3**

Kila Hana Camperland. Westport. **86 (53 FH, 33 PH), C, L, D,** fire rings, rec room. (360) 268-9528. www.kilahana.com **B3**

Land's End RV Park. Long Beach. **50 (42 FH, 8 PH), C, L, D, S,** fishing, playground. (360) 642-3253. **E3**

MaRV's RV Park. East of Cathlamet. **20 FH, C, D, L,** rec hall. (360) 795-3453. **E5**

Mauch's Sundown RV Park. Chinook. **42 FH, C, L, D, S.** (360) 777-8713. **C4**

Ocean Bay Mobile & RV Park. Ocean Park. **36 FH, C, D, NS.** (360) 665-6933. **D3**

Ocean Mist RV Park. Ocean City. **95 FH, 10 PH, C, L, D,** hot tub, beach access. Membership. (360) 289-3656. **A2**

Ocean Park Resort. Ocean Park. **83 (70 FH, 6 PH), C, L, D, S,** Wi-Fi, rec hall, pool, playground. 800-835-4634. www.opresort.com **D3**

One O'Nine RV Park and Campground. Copalis Beach. **20 FH, C,** fire rings. (360) 289-2608. **B3**

Pacific Motel & RV Resort. Westport. **80 FH, C, L, D,** Wi-Fi, fire rings, rec hall, swimming pool. (360) 268-9325. **B3**

Pioneer RV Park. Long Beach. **34 FH, C, NT, S.** (360) 642-3990. **E3**

Quinault Maritime Resort. Ocean Shores. **63 (48 FH), C, L, D,** boat ramp and dock. 800-742-0414, (360) 289-0414. **B3**

River's End Campground & RV Park. Chinook. **80 (18 FH, 57 PH), C, L, D,** fire rings, rec hall, sports field. (360) 777-8317. **E3**

Riverside RV Resort. Copalis Beach. **56 FH, C, D, S,** rec hall, sports field, boat ramp. 800-500-2111, (360) 289-2111. **B3**

Safe Harbor RV Park. Chinook. **33 FH, L, D.** (360) 777-8247. **E3**

Sand Castle RV Park. Long Beach. **48 (38 FH), C, L, D, NT,** fishing, clamming. (360) 642-2174. www.sandcastlerv.com **E3**

Sou'Wester Lodge, Cabins & RV Park. Ilwaco. **45 (25 FH), L, S,** pavilion. (360) 642-2542. www.souwesterlodge.com **E3**

Spencer Lake RV Park. Shelton. **40 FH, C, L, D,** dock, boat ramp, fishing. (360) 426-3178. www.spencerlake.com **A6**

Tidelands Campground. Copalis Beach. **76 (11 FH, 26 PH), C, D, S,** fire rings, fishing, sports field. (360) 289-8963. www.tidelandsresort.com **A3**

Timberland RV Park. West of Raymond. **29 (24 FH), C, D, S.** 888-431-1720, (360) 942-3325. www.timberlandrvpark.com **C4**

Totem RV Park. Westport. **76 (46 FH, 21 PH), L, D, C, S,** pavilion, biking, surfing. 888-868-3678, (360) 268-0025. **B3**

Westgate Motor & Trailer Court. Ocean Park. **39 FH, C, D, NT, NS,** rec room, sports field, horseshoes. (360) 665-4211. **D3**

Westport Inn. Westport. **75 FH, C, L, D, NT,** rec room, horseshoes, gym, hiking. 800-572-0177, (360) 268-0111. www.westportwamotel.com **B3**

Willapa Harbor Golf & RV. Raymond. **20 PH, D, NT, C, S.** Wi-Fi, fire pits. 877-735-9407, (360) 942-2392. **C4**

Yesterdays RV Park. Ocean Shores. **37 FH, C, D.** (360) 289-9227. **B3**

Page 24

Campgrounds

Adams Fork. Gifford Pinchot NF. **23, W.** 877-444-6777, (360) 497-1100. **E6**

Alder Lake. 173 (in 4 campgrounds), W, picnic area with shelter, boat launch, fishing. (360) 569-2778. **C4**

Battle Ground Lake State Park. 46, W, S, D, hiking, mountain biking, swimming, equestrian trails. 888-226-7688, (360) 687-4621. **G3**

Beacon Rock State Park. 29, W, S, D, hiking, biking, equestrian trails, boat launch, group camp (200 guests). 888-226-7688, (509) 427-8265. **H5**

Beaver. Gifford Pinchot NF. **24, W,** group site, hiking, fishing, berry picking. 877-444-6777, (509) 395-3400. **G5**

Beaver Bay. PacifiCorp. **63, W, S,** boat ramp, picnic area. (503) 813-6666. **F4**

Big Creek. Gifford Pinchot NF. **29, W,** picnic area. (360) 497-1100. **C4**

Blue Lake Creek. Gifford Pinchot NF. **11, W,** picnic area, ORV trails. 877-444-6777, (360) 497-1100. **D6**

Corral Pass. Mt Baker–Snoqualmie NF. **20,** hiking. (360) 825-6585. **B6**

Cougar. PacifiCorp. **45, S.** No RVs or trailers. (503) 813-6666. **F4**

Cougar Rock. Mt Rainier NP. **173, W, D,** group site. 800-365-2267, 877-444-6777, (360) 569-2211. **C5**

Cultus Creek. Gifford Pinchot NF. **50,** picnic area, berry picking, hiking. (509) 395-3400. **F5**

The Dalles. Mt Baker–Snoqualmie NF. **45, W, TH,** 2 group sites, picnic area, fishing. 877-444-6777, (360) 825-6585. **A6**

Elbe Hills ORV. Elbe Hills SF. **6, TH,** picnic area with shelter, ORV trails. (360) 569-2451 or 825-1631. **C4**

Evans Creek ORV Area. Mt Baker–Snoqualmie NF. **23, W, TH,** mountain biking, motorcycle trails, picnic area. 877-444-6777, (360) 825-6585. **B5**

Falls Creek Horse Camp. Gifford Pinchot NF. **4,** hiking, horse ramp, horse trails. No large trailer turnaround. (509) 395-3400. **F5**

Forlorn Lakes. Gifford Pinchot NF. **25,** fishing. (509) 395-3400. **F6**

Goose Lake. Gifford Pinchot NF. **18,** picnic area, fishing, boat launch. 877-444-6777, (509) 395-3400. **F6**

Green River Horse Camp. Mt St Helens NVM. **8.** (360) 449-7800. **E4**

Horseshoe Lake. Gifford Pinchot NF. **11,** hiking, fishing. (360) 497-1100. **E6**

Ike Kinswa State Park. 103, W, H, S, D, boat launch. 888-226-7688, (360) 983-3402. **D3**

Ipsut Creek. Mt Rainier NP. Hike-in only, no vehicle access. (360) 569-2211. **B5**

Iron Creek. Gifford Pinchot NF. **98, W.** 877-444-6777, (360) 497-1100. **D5**

Joemma Beach State Park. 23, W, picnic shelter, boat launch. (253) 884-1944. **A2**

Kalama Horse Camp. Mt St Helens NVM. **17, TH,** 7 family campsites, 2 group sites, picnic area, shelter, hiking, corrals. (360) 449-7500. **E3**

Keenes Horse Camp. Gifford Pinchot NF. **13,** corrals. (360) 497-1100. **E6**

La Wis Wis. Gifford Pinchot NF. **115, W,** picnic area. 877-444-6777, (360) 497-1100. **C6**

Lake Merrill. DNR. **9, W,** picnic area, boat ramp. (360) 577-2025. **F3**

Lewis and Clark State Park. 40, W, PH, S, group site, hiking, biking, horse trails. April–October. (360) 864-2643. **D2**

Lewis River Horse Camp. Mt St Helens NVM. **9, W.** (360) 449-7800. **E5**

Lower Falls. Gifford Pinchot NF. **44, W,** picnic area, group site, hiking, mountain biking, horseback riding. (360) 449-7800. **E5**

Millersylvania State Park. 168, W, PH, S, D, hiking. (360) 753-1519. **B2**

Moss Creek. Gifford Pinchot NF. **17, W.** 877-444-6777, (509) 395-3400. **G6**

North Fork. Gifford Pinchot NF. **32, W,** group sites. 877-444-6777, (360) 497-1100. **D5**

Ohanapecosh. Mt Rainier NP. **188, W, D,** group site, hiking. May–October. 800-365-2267, 877-444-6777, (360) 569-2211. **C6**

Oklahoma. Gifford Pinchot NF. **18, W,** hiking. 877-444-6777, (509) 395-3400. **G6**

Panther Creek. Gifford Pinchot NF. **32, W,** group area. 877-444-6777, (509) 395-3400. **G5**

Paradise Creek. Gifford Pinchot NF. **42, W.** 877-444-6777, (509) 395-3400. **F5**

Paradise Point State Park. 76, W, S, D, hiking. (360) 263-2350. **G2**

Peterson Prairie. Gifford Pinchot NF. **29, W,** group site. 877-444-6777, (509) 395-3400. **F6**

Rock Creek. Yacolt Burn SF. **19, W,** picnic area with shelter, horse ramp, horseback riding, mountain biking, hiking. (360) 577-2025. **G4**

Sahara Creek. Elbe Hills SF. **18, W, TH,** picnic area with shelter, bicycle and horse trails. (360) 825-1631. **C4**

Seaquest State Park. 88, W, H, S, D, group site, hiking. 888-226-7688, (360) 274-8633. **E2**

Silver Springs. Mt Baker-Snoqualmie NF. **55, W,** group site, hiking, fishing. 877-444-6777, (360) 825-6585. **B6**

Sunset Falls. Mt St Helens NVM. **18,** fishing, hiking. (360) 449-7800. **G4**

Swift. Pacific Power and Light. **93, W,** boat ramp, picnic area. (503) 813-6666. **F4**

Takhlakh Lake. Gifford Pinchot NF. **53,** picnic area, hiking trails. 877-444-6777, (360) 497-1100. **E6**

Tillicum. Gifford Pinchot NF. **15,** group site, hiking, mountain biking, berry picking. (509) 449-7800. **F5**

Tower Rock. Gifford Pinchot NF. **21, W.** 877-444-6777, (360) 497-1100. **D5**

Trout Lake Creek. Gifford Pinchot NF. **17,** fishing. (509) 395-3400. **F6**

Walupt Lake. Gifford Pinchot NF. **42, W, TH,** hiking, fishing, boating. 877-444-6777, (360) 497-1100. **D6**

Walupt Lake Horse Camp. Gifford Pinchot NF. **7, W.** (360) 497-1100. **D6**

White River. Mt Rainier NP. **112, W,** hiking. (360) 569-2211. **B6**

RV Parks

99 RV Park. N of Vancouver. **95 FH, L, S,** rec room. (360) 573-0351. **G3**

American Heritage KOA. S of Tumwater. **99 (24 FH, 50 PH), L, S, D,** rec hall, pool, playground, sports field, bike rentals, pavilion, store. May–September. (360) 943-8778. **B1**

Barrier Dam Campground. South of Salkum. **27 PH, D, S,** fire rings, sports field, hiking. (360) 985-2495. www.barrierdam.com **D2**

Beacon Rock Resort. Skamania. **50 FH, L, C, D,** pool. (509) 427-8473. **H5**

Big Fir RV Park. East of Ridgefield. **70 (37 FH), C, D,** sports field, horseshoes. (360) 887-8970. **G3**

Bridge RV Park & Campground. White Salmon. **50 (35 FH), C, L, D,** sports field. (509) 493-1111. www.bridgerv.com **G6**

Brookhollow RV Park. East of Kelso. **132 FH, C, L, NT, S,** Wi-Fi, rec room, gym, hiking. 800-867-0453. www.brookhollowrvpark.com **F2**

Camp Kalama RV Park. Kalama. **164 (65 FH, 49 PH), C, L, D,** rec hall, boat ramp, fishing, hiking. 800-750-2456. www.kalama.com/~campkalama **F2**

Camp Lakeview. Kappwsin. **54 (19 FH, 20 PH), C, L, D,** hiking, fishing, swimming, boating, boat ramp. No alcohol. (360) 879-5426. **B4**

Cascade Peaks RV Resort. Randle. **400 (120 FH, 280 PH), L, D,** pools, pavilion, hot tub, sauna, playground, store. 866-255-2931, (360) 494-9202. www.cascadepeakscamping.com **D5**

Cedars RV Park. Southwest of Silver Lake. **26 FH, C, L.** (360) 274-5136. **E2**

Columbia Riverfront RV Park. NW of Woodland. **76 FH, C, L, NT,** Wi-Fi, pool, playground. 800-845-9842. columbiariverfrontrvpark.com **F2**

Columbus Park. West of Tumwater. **30 FH, C, L, D,** playground, pavilion, boat ramp, dock, fishing, sports field. 866-848-9460, (360) 786-9460. **B1**

Cougar RV Park. Cougar. **14 FH, 7 PH,** fire rings. (360) 238-5224. **F4**

Harmony Lakeside RV Park. N of Mossyrock. **58 FH, 32 PH, C, D, S, L,** rec hall, boat ramp, dock. (360) 983-3804. harmonylakesidervpark.com **D3**

Harrison RV Park. West of Centralia. **35 FH, 9 PH, L, C, D, S,** Wi-Fi, rec hall, sports field, dog area. (360) 330-2167. www.harrisonrvpark.com **C1**

Jantzen Beach RV Park. Hayden I., Ore. **169 FH, C, L, NT,** rec hall, pools, playground. 800-443-7248, (503) 289-7626. www.jantzenbeachrv.com **H2**

Lake Mayfield Resort and Marina. SE of Silver Creek. **69 (48 FH, 2 PH), D,** sports field, boat ramp, dock. (360) 985-2357. lakemayfield.com **D3**

Lewis and Clark Campground & RV Park. W of North Bonneville. **20 FH, 20 PH, L, D,** sports field, horseshoes. (509) 427-4630. **H5**

Lewis River RV Park. Northeast of Woodland. **89 (25 FH, 51 PH), L, D,** fire rings, pavilion, swimming pool, hiking. (360) 225-9556. **F2**

Lone Fir Resort. Cougar. **34 FH, C, L, S,** pavilion, pool, playground, horseshoes. (360) 238-5210. www.lonefirresort.com **F4**

Mahaffey's Campground. Kalama. **27 (13 FH, 10 PH).** (360) 673-3867. **F2**

Majestic Manor RV Park. Puyallup. **88 FH, C, L, D, S,** pool, store, Wi-Fi, rec hall. 800-348-3144, (253) 845-3144. majesticrvpark.com **A4**

Maple Grove RV Resort. Randle. **52 FH, 68 PH, C, L, D,** Wi-Fi, rec hall, pool, golf, playground, fishing, horseshoes. (360) 497-2742. **D5**

Midway RV Park. North of Centralia. **60 FH, C, L, D, NT, S,** Wi-Fi, rec hall. 800-600-3204, (360) 736-3200. **C1**

Mount St Helens KOA. NE of Castle Rock. **88 (48 FH), C, L, D, S,** Wi-Fi, rec room, playground. (360) 274-8522. **E2**

Mounthaven Resort. E of Ashford. **16 FH, L, D, NT, S,** cabins, fire rings, playground. 800-456-9380, (360) 569-2594. www.mounthaven.com **C5**

Offut Lake Resort. Tenino. **62 (31 FH, 16 PH), C, L, D, S,** cabins, pavilion, playground, boating, fishing, store. (360) 264-2438. **B2**

Olympia Campground. South of Tumwater. **99 (28 FH, 46 PH), L, D, NS,** rec room, swimming pool, playground, bike rental. (360) 352-2551. **B2**

Outback RV Park. Rochester. **58 FH, C, L,** playground, groups, Wi-Fi, rec hall. (360) 273-0585. www.outbackrvpark.com **C1**

Packwood RV Park & Campground. Packwood. **87 FH, C, L, D, S,** fire rings, horseshoes. (360) 494-5145. www.packwoodrv.com **D6**

Peppertree West Motor Inn & RV Park. Centralia. **42 FH, C, L, D, S,** rec hall, golf. (360) 736-1124. **C2**

River Oaks RV Park. SW of Toledo. **25 FH, 12 PH, D, NT, L, S,** sports field, boat ramp, dock, fishing. (360) 864-2895. **D2**

Silver Lake Resort. Silver Lake. **36 (22 PH),** fire rings, sports field, boat ramp, dock, boat rentals, fishing. (360) 274-6141. **E2**

South Prairie Creek RV Park. South Prairie. **110 FH, C, L,** Wi-Fi. (360) 897-8465. www.southprairiecreekrvpark.com **A4**

Toutle River RV Resort. Castle Rock. **306 FH, C, L.** (360) 274-6208. **E2**

Van Mall RV Park. Vancouver. **101 FH, C, L, NT, S,** rec hall, playground, sports field. (360) 891-1091. www.vancouverrvparks.com **H3**

Vancouver RV Park. NE 13th St, Vancouver. **160 FH, C, L,** rec hall. 877-756-2972, (360) 695-1158. www.vanmallrv.com **H3**

Woodland Shores RV Park. East of Woodland, on Lewis River. **57 FH, C, L,** Wi-Fi, rec hall. 800-481-2224, (360) 225-2222. **F2**

Page 26

Campgrounds

American Forks. Wenatchee NF. **16,** shelter. (509) 653-1401. **B2**

Brooks Memorial State Park. 45, W, H, D, S, group site, hiking, bird watching, bike riding. (509) 773-4611. **F4**

Bumping Lake. Wenatchee NF. **45, W,** picnic area, boating, hiking, fishing, marina nearby. 877-444-6777, (509) 653-1401. **B2**

Cedar Springs. Wenatchee NF. **14, W,** picnic area, hiking, fishing. 877-444-6777, (509) 653-1401. **B2**

Clear Lake North. Wenatchee NF. **36,** group area (reservations required), picnic area, hiking, fishing. (509) 653-1401. **C2**

Clear Lake South. Wenatchee NF. **31, W,** picnic area, canoeing, boat launch. (509) 653-1401. **C2**

Columbia Hills State Park. 14, W, H, D, boat launch. (509) 767-1159. **H3**

Cottonwood. Wenatchee NF. **16, W.** 877-444-6777, (509) 653-1401. **B3**

Cougar Flat. Wenatchee NF. **12, W,** picnic area, hiking. 877-444-6777, (509) 653-1401. **B2**

Crow Creek. Wenatchee NF. **15, TH,** picnic area, hiking and motorcycle trails. (509) 653-1401. **B2**

Dog Lake. Wenatchee NF. **8, TH,** picnic area, hiking. (509) 653-1401. **C2**

Guler County Park. 45, W, S, picnic area, groups. (509) 773-4616. **F1**

Hause Creek. Wenatchee NF. **42, W,** picnic area. 877-444-6777, (509) 653-1401. **C3**

Hells Crossing. Wenatchee NF. **18, W,** picnic area, hiking. 877-444-6777, (509) 653-1401. **B2**

Icewater Creek. Wenatchee NF. **15, W, TH,** picnic area, hiking, mountain bike and motorcycle trails. (509) 852-1100. **A3**

Indian Creek. Wenatchee NF. **39, W,** dispersed camping, picnic area, on Rimrock Lake. 877-444-6777 or (509) 653-1401. **C2**

Kaner Flat. Wenatchee NF. **49, W, TH,** group area (reservations required), picnic area, motorbike trails. (509) 653-1401. **B2**

Lake Easton State Park. 137, W, H, S, D, group site, hiking, cross-country skiing, boat launch. 888-226-7688 or (509) 656-2230. **A2**

Little Naches. Wenatchee NF. **17, W.** 877-444-6777, (509) 653-1401. **B3**

Lodgepole. Wenatchee NF. **34, W,** picnic area, hiking. 877-444-6777, (509) 653-1401. **B1**

Maryhill State Park. 70, W, H, S, D, group site, boat launch. 888-226-7688, (509) 773-5007. **G3**

Morrison Creek. Gifford Pinchot NF. **12.** (509) 395-3400. **E1**

Peninsula. Wenatchee NF. **60,** picnic area, boat ramp. (509) 653-1401. **C2**

Pleasant Valley. Wenatchee NF. **16, W, TH,** picnic area, shelter, hiking. 877-444-6777, (509) 653-1401. **B1**

Sawmill Flat. Wenatchee NF. **23, W,** shelter, picnic area. 877-444-6777, (509) 653-1401. **B3**

Soda Springs. Wenatchee NF. **26, W,** picnic area, 2 shelters, mineral springs. 877-444-6777, (509) 653-1401. **B2**

Taneum. Wenatchee NF. **13, W,** picnic area, hiking, equestrian trails. (509) 852-1100. **A3**

Tree Phones. DNR. **14, W, TH,** picnic area, group area and shelter, motor bike, mountain bike, horse trails. (509) 925-8510. **D2**

White Pass Lake (Leech Lake). Wenatchee NF. **10, TH,** picnic area, hiking, biking, horseback riding, boat launch. (509) 653-1401. **C1**

Willows. Wenatchee NF. **16, W.** 877-444-6777, (509) 653-1401. **C3**

Windy Point. Wenatchee NF. **15, W,** rafting take-out for Tieton River run. 877-444-6777, (509) 653-1401. **C3**

Yakima Sportsman State Park. 67, W, H, S, D, boat launch. 888-226-7688, (509) 575-2774. **D5**

RV Parks

Circle H RV Ranch. Yakima. **64 FH, C, L, D, S,** Wi-Fi, rec room, pool, horseshoes, playground. (509) 457-3683. **C5**

Elk Meadows RV Park & Campground. Trout Lake. **63 (44 FH, 19 PH), L, D,** pavilion. 877-395-2400, (509) 395-2400. elkmeadowsrvpark.com **F1**

Ellensburg KOA. Ellensburg. **140 (12 FH, 88 PH), L, D,** Wi-Fi, rec room, pool, playground, sports field, boat ramp. 800-562-7616. **B4**

Peach Beach RV Park. 82 (21 FH, 51 PH), D, playground, sports field, boat ramp, fishing. (509) 773-4927. **G4**

Pine Spring Resort–Satus Pass. NE of Goldendale. **22 (12 FH), C, NS,** fire rings, sports field, hiking. (509) 773-4434. **F4**

E & J Resort. 79 FH, C, L, D, NP, NT, rec room, swimming pool. 888-889-9870. **B4**

RV Town. Northeast of Easton. **19 FH, 52 PH, L, D, S,** fire rings, playground, sports field, pool, store. (509) 656-2360. **A2**

Squaw Rock Resort. Naches. **25 FH, 39 PH, D, L, S,** Wi-Fi, rec hall, pool, fishing. 800-546-2848 or (509) 658-2926. **C3**

Stagecoach RV Park. NW of Selah. **29 (24 FH), L,** horseshoes, hiking, sports field, playground. (509) 697-9650. **B4**

Sun Tides RV Park. W of Fruitvale, on Hwy 12. **60 FH, L, D, NT, S,** golf. (509) 966-7883. www.suntidesgolf.com **C4**

Trailer Corral RV Park & Cabins. East of Cle Elum. **24 (14 FH, 8 PH), C, L, D, S,** fishing, golf. (509) 674-2433. **A3**

Trailer Inns RV Park. Yakima. **135 FH, C, L,** Wi-Fi, group area, rec hall, pool, playground. 800-659-4784, (509) 452-9561. trailerinnsrv.com **C5**

Whispering Pines RV Park. Cle Elum. **9 FH, 26 PH, C, L, D,** fishing, picnicking. (509) 674-7278. **A3**

Yakama Nation RV Resort. West of Toppenish. **125, FH, L, D, NS,** rec hall, sports field, swimming pool, playground. 800-874-3087. **D5**

Yakima River RV Park. Ellensberg. **36 (15 FH),** fishing. (509) 925-4734. **B4**

Page 28

Campgrounds

Charbonneau Park. Corps of Engineers. **54, W, PH, D, S,** picnic area, marina, swimming. 877-444-6777 or (509) 547-7020. **E5**

Crow Butte Park. 50, W, S, H, D, hiking, boat launch. (509) 875-2644. March–October. www.crowbutte.com **G1**

Fishhook Park. Corps of Engineers. **53, W, PH, D, S,** picnic area with shelter, boat launch, swimming. 877-444-6777 or (509) 547-7020. **E5**

Hood Park. Corps of Engineers. **67, W, PH, S, D,** boat ramp, boating. 877-444-6777, (509) 547-7020. **E4**

Madame Dorion Memorial Park. 15, W, D, picnic area, boat launch. (509) 546-8300. **F5**

Potholes State Park. 121, W, H, S, D, group site, boat launch, playground. 888-226-7688, (509) 346-2759. **B3.**

Wanapum Recreation Area. 50, W, H, S, hiking, boat launch. (509) 856-2700. **B1**

Windust Park. Corps of Engineers. **24, W,** picnic area with shelter, playground, boat launch, dock. 877-444-6777, (509) 547-7020. **D6**

RV Parks

Beach RV Park. South of Benton City. **40 FH, C, D, L, S,** Wi-Fi (509) 588-5959. www.beachrv.net **E3**

Cascade Campground. Moses Lake. **85 (34 FH), D,** boating, moorage, playground. No alcohol. April–September. (509) 764-3805. **A3**

Crescent Bar Resort. W of Quincy. **60 (26 PH), L, D, S,** boat ramp, dock, sports field, tennis. (509) 787-1511 x21. www.crescentbarresort.com **A1**

Desert Oasis RV Park. Moses Lake. **34 FH, C, L, D.** (509) 764-5319. **A3**

Grant County Fairgrounds. Moses Lake. **56 FH, 188 PH, D, S,** Wi-Fi, indoor arena, stall rentals. (509) 765-3581 x22. www.gcfairgrounds.com **A3**

Horn Rapids RV Resort. Richland. **225 FH, C, L, D, NT,** clubhouse, pool, spa, store. 866-557-9637, (509) 375-9913. hornrapidsrvresort.com **E3**

Lakefront RV Park. Southwest of Moses Lake. **63 (47 FH), C, L, D, S,** rec room, playground, boat ramp and dock, boat rentals. (509) 765-8294. **A3**

MarDon Resort. South of Moses Lake. **273 (127 FH, 49 PH), L, D,** fire rings, rec room, playground, sports field, boat ramp and dock, boat rentals. 800-416-2736, (509) 346-2651. www.mardonresort.com **B3**

Pierce's Green Valley RV Park. W of Touchet. **30 (20 PH),** fishing, golf, swimming. Blues Fest in Sept. (509) 394-2387. piercesgreenvalley.com **E5**

Riviera Trailer Village. West of Pasco. **20 FH, L, NT, S,** golf, rec room, swimming pool. (509) 547-3521. **E4**

Royal City Public Golf Course. East of Royal City. **12 PH, D, NT.** (509) 346-2052. **B2**

Sage Hills Golf Club & RV Resort. Warden. **48 FH, L,** clubhouse, rec room, pool, golf. 888-628-3066, (509) 349-2603. www.sagehills.com **B4**

Sandy Heights RV Resort. Pasco. **185 FH, C, L, D,** Wi-Fi, clubhouse, pool, sports field. 877-894-1357. **E4**

Shady Tree RV Park. George. **44 FH, L.** (509) 785-2851. **A2**

Suncrest Resort. Moses Lake. **82 FH, L,** Wi-Fi, spa, pool, playground. (509) 765-0355. www.suncrestresort.com **A3**

Tri-Cities RV Park. Kennewick. **143 FH, C, L, D, NT.** (509) 783-2513. **E4**

Vantage Riverstone Resort. Vantage. **120 (60 FH), L, D, S,** Wi-Fi, pool, store, boat moorage, playground. (509) 856-2800. www.visitvantage.com **B1**

Wild Horse Campground. S of Quincy. **200, PH.** Gorge concerts. (509) 398-0543. www.wildhorsecampground.com **A1**

Willows Trailer Village. Southeast of Moses Lake. **65 FH, L, D,** playground, sports field. (509) 765-7531. **B3**

Wine Country RV Park. Prosser. **134 (125 FH), C, L,** Wi-Fi, store, pool, playground. 800-726-4969. www.winecountryrvpark.com **E2**

Wright's Desert Gold Motel & RV Park. S of Richland. **87 FH, C, L, NT, S,** Wi-Fi, store, rec room, pool. (509) 627-1000. wrightsdesertgold.com **E3**

Page 30

Campgrounds

Chief Timothy Park. 66, W, H, S, D, boat launch, hiking, mountain bike trails. (509) 758-9580. **D5**

Fields Spring State Park. 20, W, S, D, picnic area, hiking, mountain biking, bird watching, winter recreation. (509) 256-3332. **F5**

Godman. Umatilla NF. **8, TH,** cabins, picnic area, shelter. (509) 843-1891. **F3**

Lewis and Clark Trail State Park. 24, W, S, D, group site, picnic area with kitchen shelter, nature trail. (509) 337-6457. **E2**

Palouse Falls State Park. 11, W, picnic area with shelter, bird watching, hiking. (509) 646-9218. **C2**

Tucannon. Umatilla NF. **18,** picnic area, fishing. (509) 843-1891. **F3**

RV Parks

Boyer Park & Marina. South of Colfax. **28 PH, W, S, L, D,** moorage, boat ramp and dock. (509) 397-3208. **C4**

City of Pullman RV Park. Pullman. **24 FH, C, D, NS,** non-flushing toilets. (509) 338-3227. www.pullman-wa.gov **C5**

Granite Lake RV Resort. Clarkston. **75 FH, C, L, NS, NT.** 800-989-4578, (509) 751-1635. **D6**

Hillview RV Park. Clarkston. **103 FH, C, L, D, NT.** (509) 758-6299. **D5**

KOA Lyons Ferry Marina. Northwest of Starbuck on Snake River. **60 (18 FH),** boat ramp and dock. (509) 399-8020. **D1**

The Last Resort. S of Pomeroy. **36 (24 FH, 12 PH), L, D,** picnic pavilion, store. 800-562-3417, (509) 843-1556. www.thelastresortrv.com **D6**

RV Resort Four Seasons. Walla Walla. **89 FH, L, NT,** rec room. (509) 529-6072. **F1**

Page 32

Campgrounds

Blake Island State Park. 49, W, S, D, biking, hiking, scuba diving. Access by boat only. Moorage buoys. April–Oct. (360) 731-8330. **E2**

Dash Point State Park. 141, W, H, S, D, group site, picnic area, hiking, biking. 888-226-7688, (253) 661-4955. **G3**

Fay Bainbridge Park. 41, S, W, D, boating, day use area. (206) 842-3931. **D2**

Flowing Lake County Park. 30, W, PH, picnic area. (360) 568-2274. **A6**

Illahee State Park. 30, PH, W, S, D, group site, day use area, hiking, boat launch. April–September. (360) 478-6460. **D1**

Kitsap Memorial State Park. 39, PH, W, S, D, group site, day use area, kitchen shelter, hiking. 888-226-7688, (360) 779-3205. **B1**

Manchester State Park. 50, W, S, D, group site, day use area, hiking and mountain bike trails. 888-226-7688, (360) 871-4065. **E2**

RV Parks

Blue Sky RV Parks & Resorts. West of Snoqualmie. **51 FH, C, L, D, NT,** pavilion. (425) 222-7910. www.blueskypreston.com **E6**

Eagle Tree RV Park. Poulsbo. **88 FH, C, L, NT, S,** Wi-Fi, picnic area, clubhouse. (360) 598-5988. www.eagletreerv.com **C1**

Gig Harbor RV Resort. NW of Gig Harbor. **109 (93 FH), C, L, D,** rec hall, swimming pool, playground, horseshoes. (253) 858-8138. **G1**

Issaquah Highlands Recreation Club. Issaquah. **200 PH, C, L, D,** rec room, hiking. (425) 392-2351. **E5**

Issaquah Village RV Park. Issaquah. **58 FH, C, L, D, NT,** Wi-Fi, playground, hiking. 800-258-9233, (425) 392-9233. **E5**

Lake Pleasant RV Park. N of Bothell, on lake. **186 FH, 10 PH, C, L, D,** rec room, playground, hiking. 800-742-0386, (425) 487-1785. **B4**

Lakeside RV Park. Northwest of Mill Creek. **159 (150 FH), C, L,** playground, horseshoes, hiking. 800-468-7275, (425) 347-2970. **B4**

Majestic Mobile Manor RV. Puyallup. **118 FH, C, L, D, S,** Wi-Fi, rec room, pool. 800-348-3144, (253) 845-3144. www.majesticrvpark.com **H3**

Port Ludlow RV Park. Port Ludlow. **37, FH, L, D.** (360) 437-0513. **A1**

Seattle–Tacoma KOA. Southeast of Sea-Tac. **138 FH, 19 PH, C, L, D,** rec room, swimming pool, playground. 800-562-1892, (253) 872-8652. **F4**

Trailer Inns. S of Bellevue. **90 FH, C, L, NT,** Wi-Fi, rec room, pool, playground. 800-659-4684 or (425) 747-9181. www.trailerinnsrv.com **E5**

Twin Cedars RV Park. North of Lynnwood. **70 FH, C, L, D,** Wi-Fi, rec room. (425) 742-5540. **B4**

Landscape Map Legend

❋ ◉ State Capital; County Seat

SEATTLE ○ 250,000–1,000,000

SPOKANE ○ 100,000–250,000

Yakima ○ 50,000–100,000

Olympia ○ 10,000–50,000

Ephrata ○ 2,500–10,000

Rainier ○ Fewer than 2,500

Lamont ○ Settlement or Locale

Page ▫ Abandoned Settlement or Railroad Siding

el 4004 Elevation in Feet

River, Rapid and Waterfall

Stream

Intermittent Stream

Canal with Tunnel

Lake, Reservoir

Intermittent Lake

Glacier

Spring

4872 Elevation in Feet

Limited Access Highway

Limited Access Highway, Toll

Four-Lane Divided Highway

Primary Through Highway

Secondary Through Highway

Other Paved Road

Unpaved Road

Four-Wheel Drive Road

Other Road (Unclassified*)

Pacific Crest Trail

Other Trail

Ferry

16 17 Interchanges, Exit Numbers

Railroad with Tunnel

🛡 (395) Interstate, U.S. Highway

(120) (S22) State, County Highway

20 E31 Forest Service, BLM Route

52 Indian Land Route

(17) 25 Canadian Highway

State, International Boundary

County Boundary

▣ Rest Area

▪ Point of Interest, Historic Site

▪ Golf Course

🗼 Lighthouse

△ ⌣ Mountain Peak, Pass

⤢ ⊙ Gate, Trailhead

✈ Airport with Scheduled Service

✦ ✦ Military, Other Airport

🏓 △ Picnic Area, Campground

⛴ Boat Ramp

⚒ Mine/Quarry

⛷ ❄ Ski Area, Snopark/Winter Recreation

4004 Elevation in Feet

National Park Boundary

Indian Reservation Boundary

Military Reservation Boundary

US Forest Service Boundary

State Park Boundary

Wildlife Area Boundary

Land Use and Vegetation:

Forest	Cropland	Built-Up Area
Wetland	Grassland	Barren	Lava

* Other Roads in urban areas are typically paved public streets. In rural areas they include local backroads, rough 4WD routes, private roads, and logging roads.
Some of these roads are useable, but others are closed to public use, or seasonally impassible, or both. Inquire locally before attempting to drive "Other Roads."

Landscape Maps

Landscape Map page numbers are shown in blue
Metro Map page numbers are shown in purple

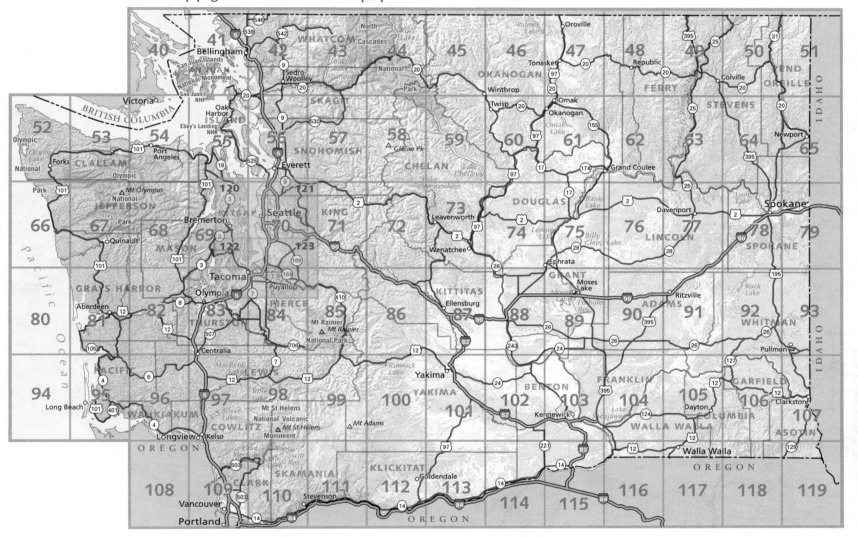

Also See Recreation Page 12

Scale 1:200,000

0 · · · 5 · · · 10 · · · 15 Miles

0 · · 5 · · 10 · · 15 · · 20 Kilometers

STRAIT OF GEORGIA

STRAIT OF CANADA

WHATCOM

BRITISH COLUMBIA

123°30' 123°20' 123°10'

49°00'

48°50'

48°40'

48°30'

VALDES ISLAND
Porlier Pass
Vernaci Point
Dionisio Point
North Galiano
Reid Island
KUPER ISLAND
Houston Passage
Wallace Island
Fernwood
Dock Point
Vesuvius Bay
Osborn Bay
St Mary Lake
Booth Bay
Crofton
Ganges
Trincomali Channel
GALIANO ISLAND
Parker Island
Montague Harbour
Gossip Island
Galiano
Georgina Point
Mayne
Edith Point
Gulf
MAYNE ISLAND
Bennett Bay
SALTSPRING ISLAND
Ganges Harbour
Long Harbour
Captain Passage
PREVOST ISLANDS
Islands
National
Winter Cove
Sansum Narrows
Maple Bay
Maple Bay
Quamichan Lake
Tzuhalem
Maple Mtn
Baynes Peak 1950
Cusheon Lake
BOLD BLUFF
Mt Sullivan 2306
Musgrave
Bruce Peak
Fulford Harbour
REGINALD HILL
Fulford Harbour
Beaver Point
Beaver Point
Eleanor Point
Point Liddell
Port Washington
Hope Bay
Otter Bay
Pender Island
PENDER ISLAND
Port Browning
Bedwell Harbour
South Pender
Wallace Point
Saturna
Lyall Creek
Lyall Creek
SATURNA ISLAND
BROWN RANGE
Monarch Head
Taylor Point
Savage Point
TUMBO ISLAND
Tumbo Channel
East Point
Park
Reserve
Plumper Sound
Swanson Channel
Navy Channel
Cowichan Bay
Cowichan Bay
Boatswain Bank
Cobble Hill
Cobble Hill
Shawnigan Lake
Shawnigan Lake
Mill Bay
Mill Bay
Cliffside
Old Baldy Mtn
Mt Wood
Bamberton
Mt Jeffrey
Malahat
VANCOUVER ISLAND
Cape Keppel
Satellite Channel
Moses Point
Deep Cove
Deep Cove
Patricia Bay
Warrior Point
Coles Bay
SAANICH PENINSULA
Swartz Bay
Sidney
Victoria International Airport
Port of Entry (24 hours)
Bazan Bay
Saanichton
Brentwood Bay
Keating
Tod
Elk Lake
Prospect Lake
Prospect Lake
Cordova Bay
Cordova Bay
Royal
Glyno
Colquitz
Strawberry Vale
Mt Douglas
Gordon Head
Arbutus Cove
Cadboro Bay
Mt Tolmie
Goldstream
Langford Station
Glen Lake
Colwood
Esquimalt
Belmont
Victoria
PIERS ISLAND
Colburne Passage
Shute Passage
COAL ISLAND
Brethour Island
Sidney Spit
SIDNEY ISLAND
James Island
JAMES ISLAND
Cordova Channel
Saanichton Bay
Cowichan Head
Hughes Passage
D'ARCY ISLAND
GOOCH ISLAND
PORTLAND ISLAND
Isabella Point
MORESBY ISLAND
Pelorus Point
Pt Fairfax
Prevost Passage
Moresby Passage
Swanson Channel
HARO STRAIT
SAN JUAN BOUNDARY PASS
Turn Point
STUART ISLAND
Stuart Island Marine State Park
Prevost Cem
Satellite Island
JOHNS ISLAND
Spieden Channel
SPIEDEN ISLAND
Green Point
Sentinel Island
New Channel
Cactus Islands
Flattop Island
San Juan
SAN JUAN ISLAND
Roche Harbor
Roche Harbor
English Camp
San Juan Island National Historical Park
Friday Harbor
Mt Dallas 1090
Lime Kiln Point State Park
Viewpoint
Bellevue Point
Lighthouse
Trout Lake
False Bay
Bailer Hill
Cattle Point
WALDRON ISLAND
Skipjack Island
Point Hammond
Fishery Point
North Bay
Sandy Point
Cowlitz Bay
San Juan Islands National Monument
CHATHAM ISLANDS
Discovery Island
Mary Todd I
Deltaport
TSI Terminal Systems & Railyard
Roberts Bank
Ferry Terminal
Tsawwassen
Beach Grove
Boundary Bay
Point Roberts
South Beach
Lighthouse Marine County Park
Boat Ramp

Tsawwassen–Nanaimo Ferry 2 Hours
Tsawwassen–Swartz Bay Ferry 1 Hour 35 Minutes
Sidney–Anacortes Ferry 3 Hours

In Friday Harbor
1. The Whale Museum
2. San Juan Historical Museum
3. Fairgrounds

© BENCHMARK MAPS

Scale 1:200,000

15 Miles

20 Kilometers

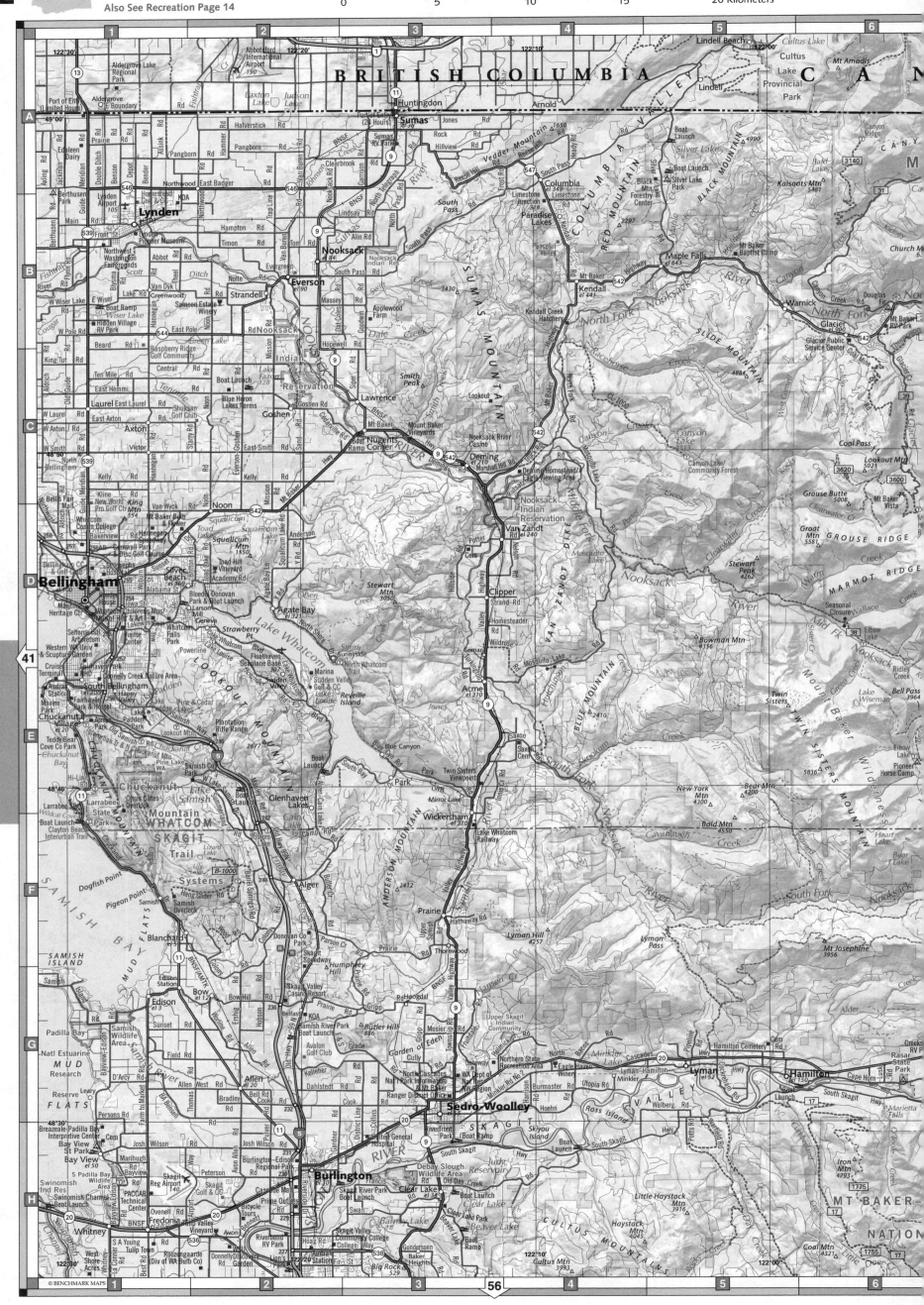

LANDSCAPE

Also See Recreation Page 16

Land Use and Vegetation

Forest
Wetland
Cropland
Grassland
Other
Built-Up Area

Land Ownership (Other public/tribal lands are named)

State Land (blue highlight)
BLM Land (yellow highlight)

LANDSCAPE

BRITISH COLUMBIA

© BENCHMARK MAPS

Scale 1:200,000

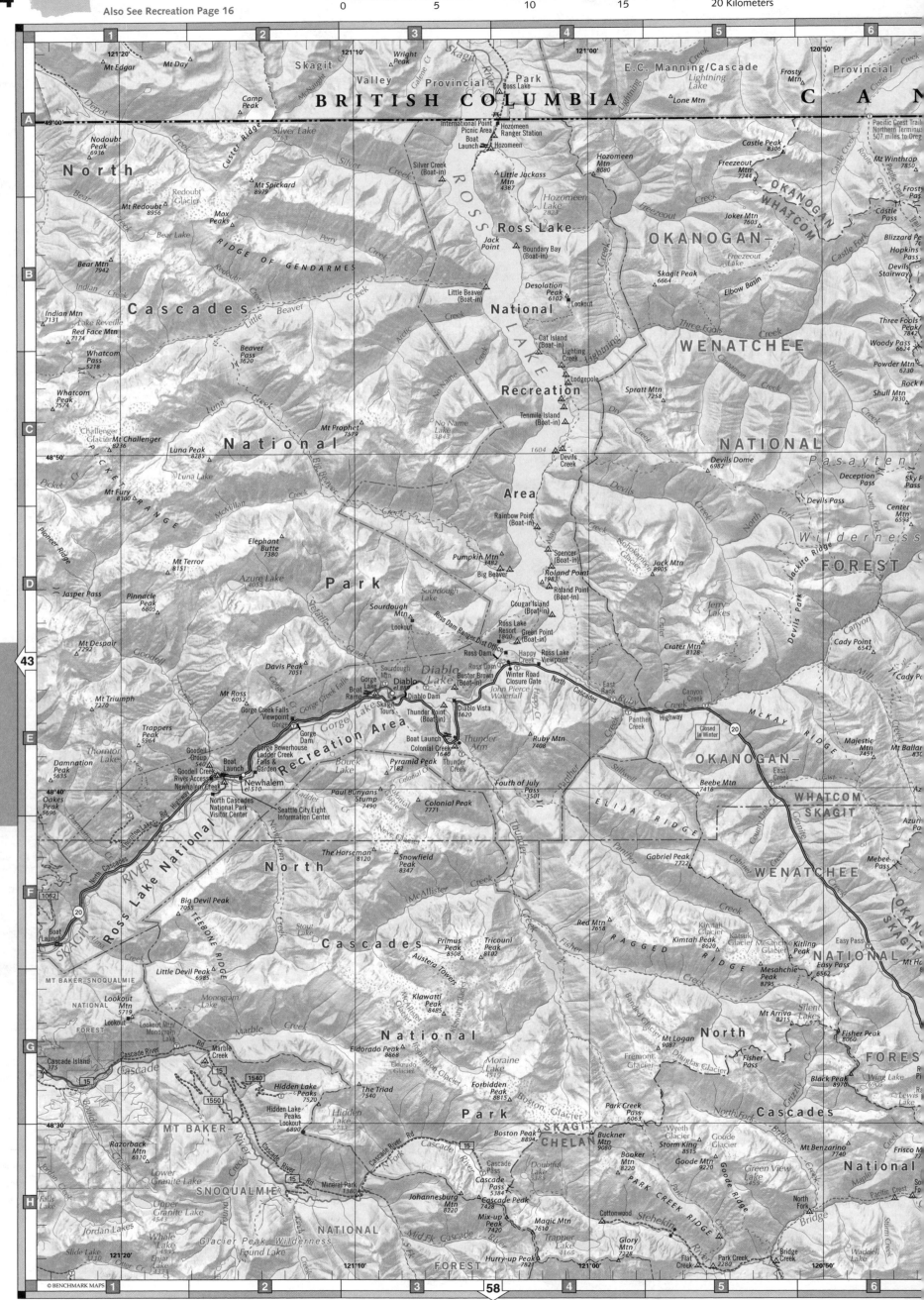

Land Use and Vegetation

- Forest
- Wetland
- Cropland
- Grassland
- Other
- Built-Up Area

Land Ownership (Other public/tribal lands are named)

- State Land (blue highlight)
- BLM Land (yellow highlight)

LANDSCAPE

BRITISH COLUMBIA

CANADA

Cathedral Provincial Park

OKANOGAN–

WENATCHEE

Pasayten Wilderness

NATIONAL FOREST

OKANOGAN–WENATCHEE NATIONAL FOREST

Methow Valley

Winthrop

Mazama

METHOW VALLEY

Selected place and feature labels:
Monument 83 Lookout, Holdover Ridge, Ptarmigan Ridge, Bunker Hill 7239, Sheep Mtn 8274, Quartz Mtn 7550, Peeve Pass, Cathedral Ridge, Orthodox Mtn, Remmel Lake, Cathedral Peak 8601, Haystack Mtn, Wolframite Mtn 8137, Apex Pass, Apex Mtn 8297, Tungsten Lake, Saddle Peak 7620

Smoky Mtn 7580, Soda Peak 7762, Lake of the Pines, Holman Peak, Buckskin Point 7361, Big Hidden Lake, White Lakes, Tatoosh Buttes 7245, Middle Mtn 6791, Ashnola Mtn 7780, Whistler Pass, Corral Lake, Larch Pass, Van Peak 7665, Andrew Pass, Andrew Peak 8301, Airview Lake, Four Point Lake, Cornwell Lake, Cal Peak 7489, Glory Lake, Peepsight Mtn 8146, Crazy Man Pass, Peepsight Lake, Remmel Mtn 8685

Gold Ridge, Buckskin Ridge, Point Defiance 7403, Ptarmigan Peak 8614, Dot Mtn 8220, Middle Hidden Lake, First Hidden Lake 4301, Island Mtn 7040, Dollar Watch Mtn 7679, Dollar Watch Pass, Many Trails Peak 8240, Three Fools Pass, Diamond Point 7916, Fox Lakes, Fawn Lake, Preston Ridge, Black Lake Ridge, Vic Meadow

Pasayten Wilderness, Osceola Peak 8587, Mt Carru 8595, Mt Lago 8745, Freds Lake 6507, Mt Rolo 8096, Shellrock Pass, Blackcap Mtn 8397, Monument Peak 8592, Ferguson Lake 6631, Lost Peak 8464, Lucky Pass, Nanny Goat Mtn 7700, Billy Goat Mtn 7633, Burch Mtn 7782, Eightmile Pass, Mt Barney 7828, Kidney Lake, Crystal Lake, Obstruction Peak 7940, Black Lake 3982, Wellie Peak 6620

Pasayten Peak 7850, Wildcat Mtn 7958, Lake Mtn 8371, Three Pinnacles 8095, Pistol Peaks 7802, West Craggy 8366, Big Craggy Peak 8470, Sherman Peak 8204, Farewell Peak 7439, Ike Mtn 7186, Doe Mtn 7154, Crystal Lake

Tamarack Peak 7290, Haystack Mtn 7203, Robinson Pass, Devils Peak 8081, Robinson Mtn 8726, Beauty Peak 7935, McLeod Mtn 8099, Sunrise Peak 8144, Burgett Peak 7367, Honeymoon, Camp Four 2391

Harts Pass 6198, Slate Peak 7440, Lookout, Meadows 6260, Scramble Point, Setting Sun Mtn 7253, Last Chance Point 7046, Ballard, Lost River Resort Airport 2415, Yellowjacket Snopark, Monument Creek, Sweetgrass Butte 6109, Ruffed Grouse, Lamb Butte 5545, Chewuch

Glacier Pass, Hancock Ridge, Deadhorse Point, Rattlesnake, River Bend, Lost River Winery, Driveway Butte 5982, Early Winters Wildlife Area, Goat Peak 7001, Goat Wall Viewpoint, Banker Pass 4750, Cub Pass 4800, Nice, Paul Mtn 4210, Falls Creek, Lookout, First Butte 5491

Holliway Mtn 8020, Straight Ridge, The Needles, Flaggs Mtn 7380, Delancy Ridge, Mazama Cross Country Ski Trails, Klipchuck 2940, Early Winters Visitor Center, Winter Road Closure Gate, Early Winters Inn, Mazama, Fawn Peak 6577, Buck Mtn 4490, Buck Lake 3247, Boat Ramp, Eightmile Snopark

Tower Mtn 8444, Golden Horn, Granite Pass, Lone Fir 3640, Vasiliki Ridge, Silver Star Mtn 8876, Snagtooth Ridge, Cedar Creek, Early Winters 2190, Freestone Inn, Goat Creek Snopark, Rendezvous Mtn 5480, Rendezvous Cross Country Ski Trails, Rendezvous Pass 3980, Frank Burge Seed Orchard, Boulder Creek Snopark, Ramsey Peak 5316

Granite Pass, Cutthroat Lake, Cutthroat Peak 7865, Washington Pass Overlook Trail, Washington Pass 5477, Early Winters Spires 7807, Kangaroo Ridge, Sandy Butte 6022, Weeman Bridge, Rendezvous, Lewis Butte 5346, Wildlife, Methow, Sullivan Pond

Stiletto Peak 7684, Copper Pass, Lincoln Butte 7065, Twisp Mtn 7161, Twisp Pass, North Lake, Blue Lake, Gibert Mtn 8023, Abernathy Peak 8321, McKinney Mtn 6469, Storey Peak 7821, North Gardner Mtn 8974, Gardner Mtn 8897, Milton Mtn 7152, Sun Mtn Cross Country Ski Trails, Winthrop, Pearrygin Lake St Park

NATIONAL FOREST, Hock Mtn 7750, Beaver Lake, Crescent Mtn 7816, Gilbert, Scatter Lake 7017, Sawtooth Ridge, Shelokum Lake 6347, Lake Chelan–Sawtooth Wilderness, Abernathy Ridge, Midnight Mtn 7480, Thompson Ridge, Sun Mtn, Methow Valley Visitor Center, Winthrop National Fish Hatchery, Methow Valley State Airport, N Cascades Smokejumper Base, Davis Lake, Big Twin Lake Campground, Pine-Near RV Park, Bear Creek, Lester Rd

Twisp Mtn, Hock Mtn, Twisp River Horse Camp 4440, South Creek, Midnight Mtn, Moccasin Lake

Also See Recreation Page 16

Scale 1:200,000

0 5 10 15 Miles

0 5 10 15 20 Kilometers

LANDSCAPE

Land Use and Vegetation

- Forest
- Wetland
- Cropland
- Grassland
- Other
- Built-Up Area

Land Ownership (Other public/tribal lands are named)

- State Land (blue highlight)
- BLM Land (yellow highlight)

Also See Recreation Page 18

BRITISH COLUMBIA

OKANOGAN

OKANOGAN-WENATCHEE NATIONAL FOREST

WENATCHEE NATIONAL FOREST

OKANOGAN-WENATCHEE NATIONAL FOREST

Colville Indian Reservation

Oroville
Tonasket
Riverside
Osoyoos
Bridesville
Molson
Chesaw
Wauconda
Enterprise
Ellisforde
Janis
Barker
Cherokee
North Omak
Synarep
Havillah

LANDSCAPE

Scale 1:200,000

0   5   10   15 Miles

0   5   10   15   20 Kilometers

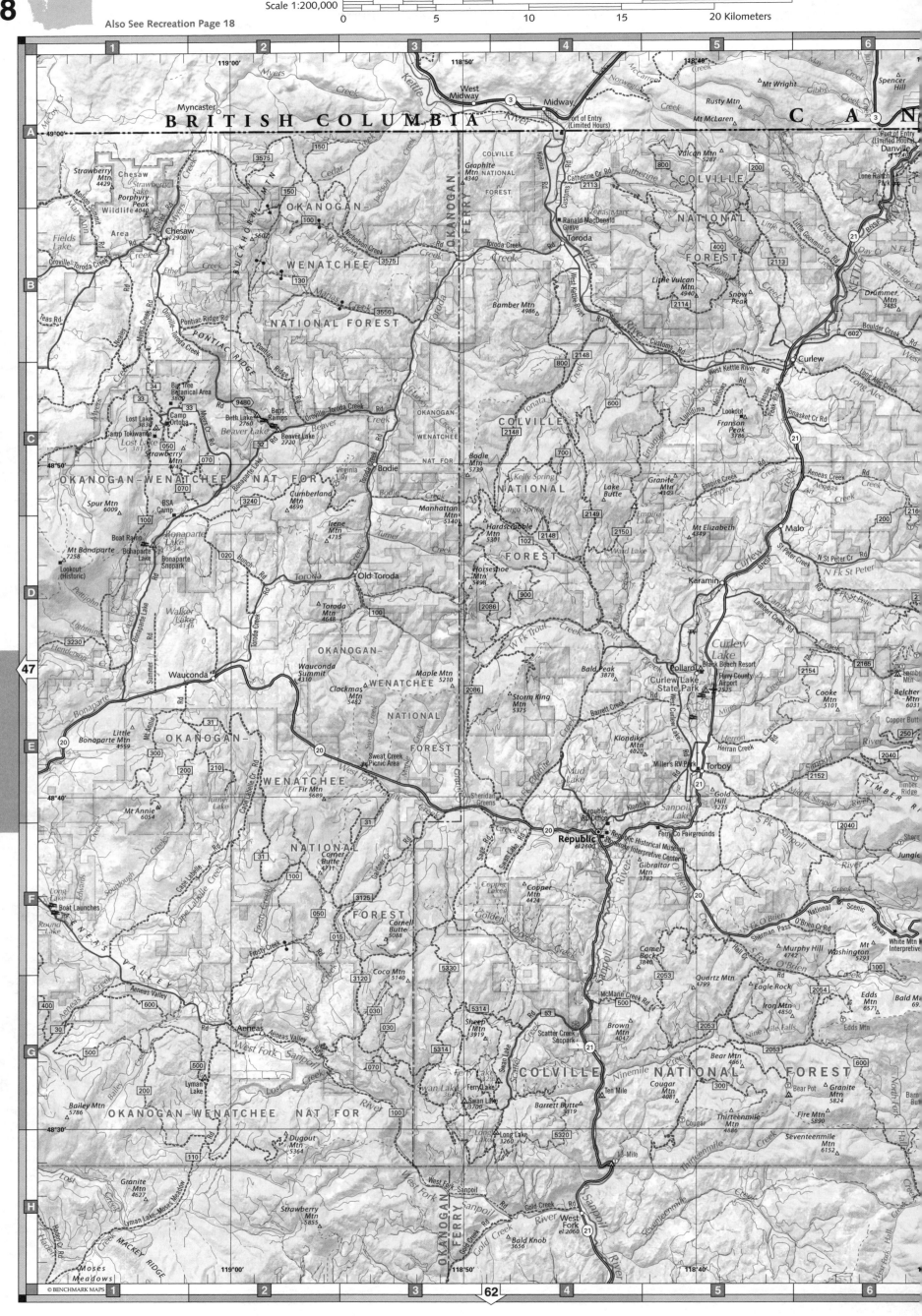

LANDSCAPE

47

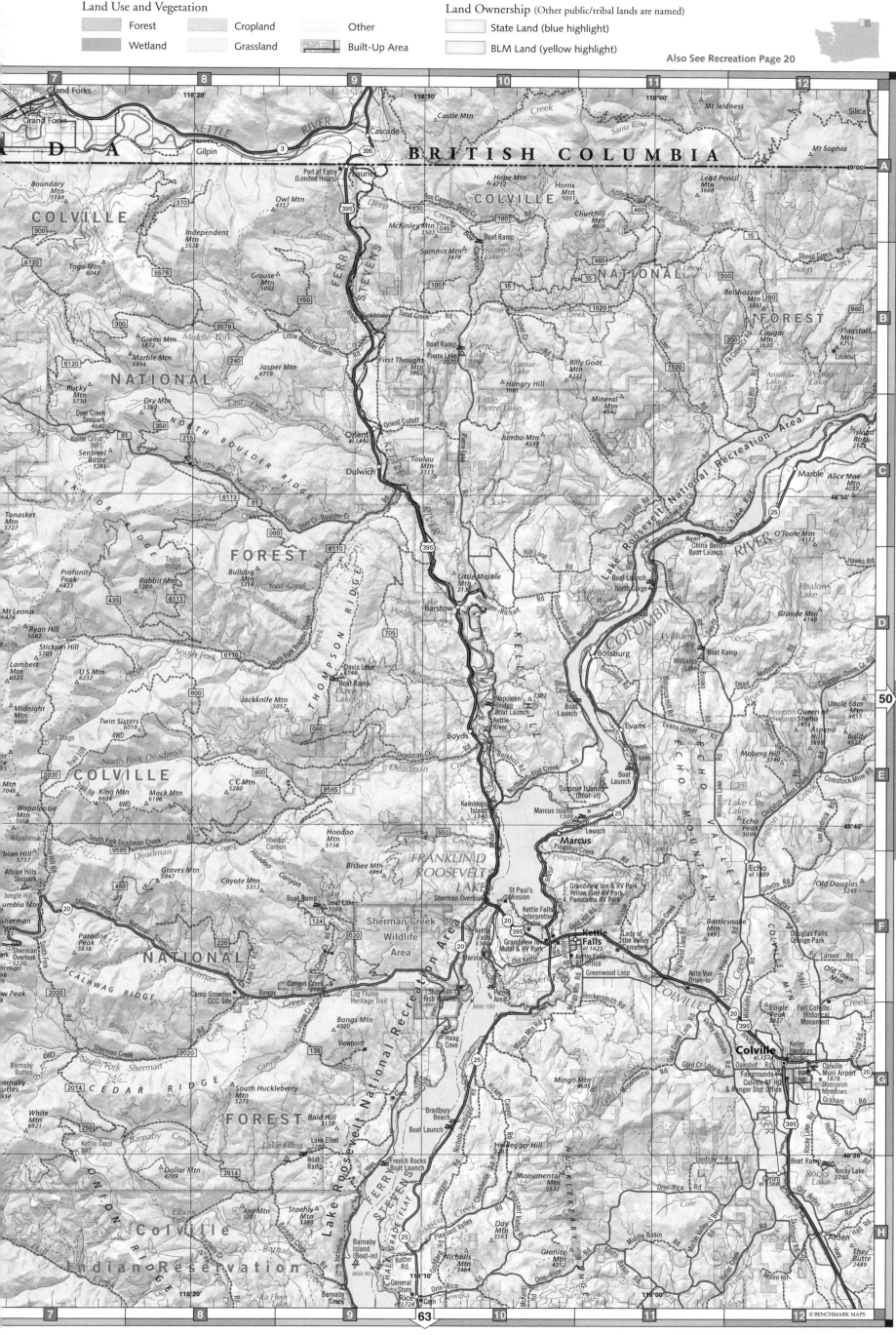

Land Use and Vegetation

Forest   Cropland   Other

Wetland   Grassland   Built-Up Area

Land Ownership (Other public/tribal lands are named)

State Land (blue highlight)

BLM Land (yellow highlight)

Also See Recreation Page 20

LANDSCAPE

BRITISH COLUMBIA

COLVILLE

NATIONAL   FOREST

COLVILLE   NATIONAL   FOREST

Grand Forks
West Grand Forks
Gilpin
Cascade
Laurier
Port of Entry (Limited Hours)

Boundary Mtn 5184

Togo Mtn 6043
Green Mtn 5872
Marble Mtn 5994

Independent Mtn 5538

Owl Mtn 4757

Castle Mtn
Bitter Creek
Mt Jeldness
Silica
Mt Sophia

Hope Mtn 4712
Horns Mtn 5051
Churchill Mtn 4605
Lead Pencil Mtn 3668
Cougar Mtn 3630
Flagstaff Mtn 4255

Rocky Mtn 5730
Dry Mtn 5380
Jasper Mtn 4719
Grouse Mtn 5092

Deer Creek Snopark
Kettle Crest NRT
Sentinel Butte 5281

Little Boulder
Little Boulder Creek

First Thought Mtn 3962

Pierre Lake
Lamar Lake
Hungry Hill 3681
Billy Goat Mtn 4232

Belshazzar Mtn 3931
Ansaldo Lake 3121
Peboon Lake

Tonasket Mtn 5727

Taylor Ridge

Profanity Peak 6423
Rabbit Mtn 5380

Bulldog Mtn 5218

Orient el 1440
Orient Cutoff
Toulou Mtn 3313
Dulwich

Jumbo Mtn 4539

Mineral Mtn 4542

Island Rock 2132

Marble
Alice Mae Mtn 4037

FOREST

Mt Leona 5474
Ryan Hill 5682
Stickpin Hill 5703
Lambert Mtn 6525
US Mtn 6232
Jackknife Mtn 5057
Twin Sisters 6019

Midnight Mtn 6660
Old Stage

Little Marble Mtn 2132

Renner Lake
Hodgson
Barstow

Bossburg

Williams Lake
Grande Mtn 4149

O'Toole Mtn 4112
Hawks Rd
Phalon Lake

Davis Lake 3548
Davis Lake

Napoleon Bridge Boat Launch
Kettle River

China Bend Boat Launch
North Gorge

Uncle Sam Mtn 4455
Peterson Queen of Sheba 3933
Aspend Hill 3895
Baldy 4523
Moberg Hill 3740

King Mtn 6634
Mack Mtn 6196
Wapaloosie Mtn 7018

COLVILLE   NATIONAL

C C Mtn 5280

Boyds

Evans

Lake City Lakes
Echo Peak 3099
Comstock Mine Rd

Kamloops Island 1340
Marcus Island 1300

Echo el 1889
Old Douglas 5245

FRANKLIN D ROOSEVELT LAKE

Hoodoo Mtn 5158

Bisbee Mtn 4964
Coyote Mtn 5313

Trout Lake 3060

Sherman Pass
Paradise Peak 5838

Sherman Overlook
Sherman

SCALAWAG RIDGE

NATIONAL

Camp Growden CCC Site

St Paul's Mission
Sherman Overlook

Marcus
Pingston Creek
Pingston

1. Grandview Inn & RV Park
2. Yellow Pine RV Park
4. Panorama RV Park

Battlesnake Mtn 3493

Douglas Falls Grange Park

Kettle Falls Interpretive Center
Kettle Falls el 1625
Grandview Inn Motel & RV Park
Marina
Kettle Falls RD Office
Old Kettle
Greenwood Loop
Lady of the Valley Cemetery
Auto Vue Drive-In

Fort Colville Historical Monument

Old Town Mtn

Eagle Peak

Sherman Creek Wildlife Area

Canyon Creek Trail

Log Flume Heritage Trail

Byway

Bangs Mtn 4020

Viewpoint

Sherman Creek
Camp

Sherman Creek Fish Hatchery
Picnic Area
Mile 100

Meyers

Hockersmith Rd

Colville el 1635
Oakshot
Fairgrounds
Colville NF HQ & Ranger Dist Office

Keller Heritage Center
Colville Muni Airport 1878

Dominion Meadows
Graham

CEDAR   RIDGE

Haag Cove

South Huckleberry Mtn 5273

Bald Hill 3110

Bradbury Beach

Boat Launch

White Mtn 6921

Kettle Crest NRT

Lake Ellen 2280
Lake Ellen

Dollar Mtn 4709

French Rocks Boat Launch

Barnaby Island (Boat-in)

Barnaby Creek

General Store Rice el 1724

Colville   Indian Reservation

Elbow Lake

Ant Mtn 3291
Staehly Mtn 3380

Nicholls Mtn 3484

Granite Mtn 4252

Bradbury
Mingo Mtn 4695
Heidegger Hill

Monumental Mtn 5532

Day Mtn 3563

Orin el 1568

Boat Ramp
Rocky Lake 2220

Arden
The Butte 2449
Arden Hill

Also See Recreation Page 20

Scale 1:200,000

0 5 10 15 Miles
0 5 10 15 20 Kilometers

LANDSCAPE

49

BRITISH COLUMBIA

Mt Jeldness
Silica
Baldy Mtn
Lake Mtn
Violin Lake
Tarnarac Mtn
Mt Sophia
Port of Entry (24 Hours)
Paterson
Waneta
Port of Entry (Limited Hours)
PEND D'OREILLE RIVER
C A N

Lead Pencil Mtn 3668
Grouse Mtn 3427
Mitchell Mtn 3709
Cedar Creek
Red Top Mtn 4660
6270
Crawford State Park Gardner Ca
Hooknose Mtn 7210

COLVILLE

NATIONAL

Big Sheep
Sheep Creek
Beishazzar Mtn 3031
Flagstaff Mtn 4755
Cougar Mtn 3630
Lookout
Upper Columbia RV Park
Grass Mtn 3379
Stone Mtn 4700
7078
Abercrombie Mtn 7308
Hooknose Mtn 7210
COLVILLE

FOREST

Ansaldo Lake 3121
Pepoon Lake
Northport el 1320
Silver Crown Mtn 2943
Black Canyon
Lime Creek Mtn 4739
Leadpoint el 2735
Silver Creek
Gladstone Mtn
075
Mountain Goat Viewing Area

Island Mtn 2795
Bodie Mtn 3790
Black Hawk Mtn 3470
STODDARD MOUNTAIN 3759
Deep Lake
Boat Ramp
Sherlock Peak 6365
Linton Mtn 6214
Mt Linton RV Park
Pend O
NATIONAL

Marble
Island Rock 2122
Alice Mae Mtn 4037
Grange
Smackout Creek
Smackout Camp
Speller Camp
Baldy Mtn 5901
Metaline el 2020
420
Lost Lake
31

O'Toole Mtn 4112
Quinns Meadows
Frederickson Hill 3135
Smackout Camp
300
FOREST

Ryan China Bend Boat Launch
Phalon Lake
Grande Mtn 4149
Onion Creek el 2460
Blue Ridge
Goldfield Mill
421 430
Smackout Pass
Boat Ramp
Box Canyon Dam

Boat Launch North Gorge
Williams Lake
Boat Ramp
Williams Lake
Uncle Sam Mtn 4655
Onion Mtn 4949
Mt Rogers 5557
Aladdin
Huckleberry Mtn 5472
Cement Hill
Edgewater
Ione el 2090
450

Queen of Sheba 3933
Aspend Mill 3897
Baldy 4523
Green Mtn 5463
Rabbit Mtn 3841
Aladdin Mtn 5015
Big Meadow Lake
Seldom Seen Mtn 5205
200
Muddy Creek Snopark
Dennis Rd
Ione Muni Airport 2707

Moberg Hill 3740
COLVILLE
Gillette Mtn 5770
7015
Blacktail Butte 5426
Tiger el 2099
Hanks Butte
20

Comstock Mine Rd
Lake City Lakes
Echo Peak 3099
Irish Mtn 4314
BON AYRE RIDGE
NATIONAL
Thomas Mtn 4890
Green Mtn 5015
Crater Lake
Boat Ramp Lake Leo 3180
Nile Lake

Echo el 1889
Old Douglas 5245
100
Little Roundtop 3842
Lake Thomas
Lake Thomas 3180
Lake Heritage
Granite Peak 5238
Lost C

Rattlesnake Mtn 3493
Douglas Falls Grange Park
Larsen Rd
9411
South Fork Mill Creek
Beaver Lodge Resort
Lake Gillette 3120
Sherry Lake
COLVILLE

COLVILLE MTN
Old Town Mtn
Aladdin
Old Dominion 5773
9411
Little Twin Lakes Boat Ramp
Twin Lakes
Coffin Lake 4099
423

COLVILLE
Eagle Peak 4637
Fort Colville Historical Monument
Stevens Co Historical Museum
The Knob 3252
Old Dominion
Black Lake
Boat Ramp
Radar Dome
Frodelle Creek 3760
Timber Mtn 5474

Colville el 1524
Oakshot Rd
Colville Muni Airport
Washington Dept of Nat Res NE Reg Office
Grange
Park Rapids el 2905
Lookout
NATIONAL

Colville Fairgrounds & Golf Course
Graham
White Mud Lake
Boat Ramp
Crystal Falls
Little Pend Oreille
2615

Colville National Forest HQ & RD Office
Lindsay Rd
Rocky Lake 2220
Boat Ramp
Hatch Lake
Starvation Lake
Blacktail Mtn 4257
Olson Peak 5610
2615

Orin el 1568
Arden
The Butte 2449
Castle Rock 3082
Little Pend Oreille National Wildlife Refuge HQ
McDowell Lake
National
Wildlife Refuge
448
Boulder Mtn 4668
9521

Arden Hill
Bayley Lake
Calispell Peak 6855
FOREST
629

© BENCHMARK MAPS

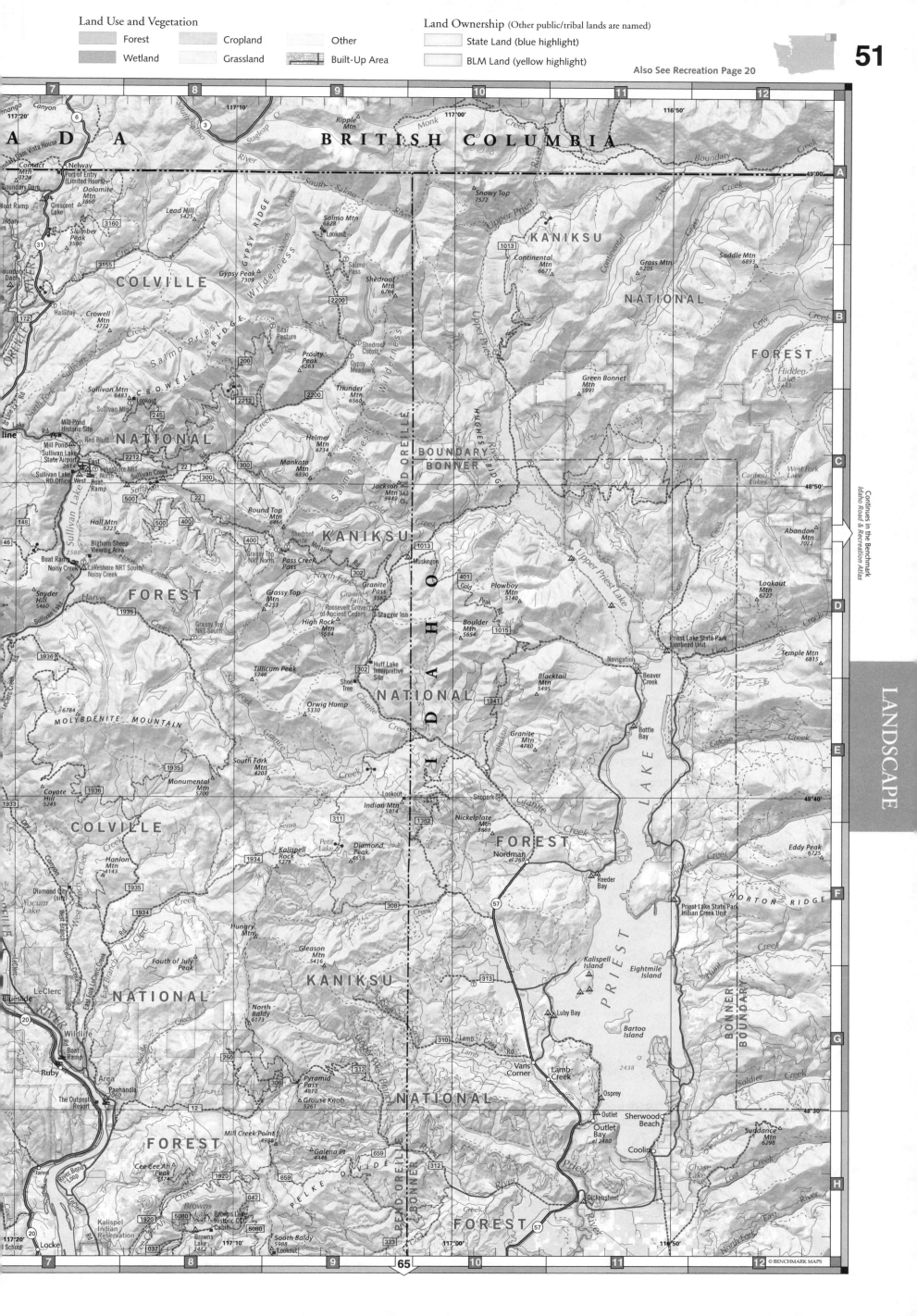

Also See Recreation Page 12

Scale 1:200,000

0 5 10 15 Miles
0 5 10 15 20 Kilometers

LANDSCAPE

CANADA

STRAIT OF

Juan de Fuca Provincial

Tatoosh Island
Cape Flattery Lighthouse 80
Cape Flattery
Kydikabbit Point
Koitlah Point
Cape Loop
Waadah Island
Neah Bay
US Coast Guard Station
Bahokus Peak 1380
Cape Flattery
Cape Flattery Rd
Neah Bay
Cape Resort
Makah Museum
Radio Towers
Bullman Beach Inn
Waatch

Makah Indian Reservation

48°20'

Waatch Point
Hobuck Beach
Waatch Peak 1350
Anderson Point
Portage Head
Makah National Fish Hatchery
Cheeka Peak 1620
Sooes Peak 1940
Shipwreck Point NRCA
Shipwreck Point
Chito Beach Resort
Kydaka Point
Eagle Point
Sekiu River
Hoko River/ Cowan Ranch State Park
Boat Ramp
Sekiu Point
Sekiu Airport 350
Sekiu el 80
Slip Point
Boat Ramp
US Coast Guard Reservation
Clallam Bay County Park
Clallam Bay
Eagle Crest Way
Clallam Bay Corrections Center

Coastal trail hikes limited by tides
Shi-Shi Beach
Point of Arches
Washburn Hill 796

Olympic National Park

Flattery Rocks National Wildlife Refuge

Sekiu Mtn 1940
Stolzenberg Mtn 2128
Old Royal
Ellis Mtn 2673

OLYMPIC

NATIONAL FOREST

Bodelteh Islands
Tskawahyah Island
Cape Alava
Ozette Island
Ozette 180
Ranger Station
Boat Ramp
Manny's Prairie
Ozette Indian Reservation
48°10'

Nelson Hill 1180
Beaver Hill 1091
Deadmans Hill
Sappho el 480
Bear Creek
Blue Heron Lodge

Boat Ramp
Deer Point
Swan Bay
Dickey Lake 193
Lake Pleasant County Park
Lake Pleasant
Beaver
Salmon Hatchery Interpretive Center
Boat Ramp
Mary Clark

Sand Point
Ranger Station (Seasonal)
Coastal trail hikes limited by tides

Olympic National Park

OZETTE LAKE

Garden Island
Preachers Point
Tivoli Island
Allens Bay 29

Shuwah
Fishing Access & Boat Ramp
Sol Duc Cabin
Gunderson Mtn 1235

OLYMPIC RIDGE

Yellow Banks
Norwegian Memorial
Kayostia Beach
Carroll Island

Wentworth Lake

48°00'

Sea Lion Rock
Jagged Island
Olympic National Park
Cape Johnson
Chilean Memorial

Hackleberry Lodge
Rayonier Forest Products

PRAIRIE
Klahanie

Forks
Olympic Natl Forest Pacific RD Office
Transit Center NPS Info Center
Forks 101 RV Park
Forks Timber Museum & Visitor Center
Hosp

OLYMPIC

NATIONAL

FOREST

Quillayute Needles National Wildlife Refuge
Dahdayla Island
Cake Rock 102
Hole in the Wall
Rialto Beach
Mora Ranger Station
Quillayute State Airport
Mtn View Cabins
Quillayute
Manitau Lodge
Three Rivers Resort
Olympic Natural Resources Center
Bogachiel Hatchery

La Push
Tribal Center
James Island
First Beach
Lonesome Creek RV Park
Crying Lady Rock
Cakesosta
Quileute Indian Reservation
Levendecker Co Park
Bogachiel State Park
Anderson Homestead Wildlife Area

Second Beach
Quillayute Needles
Teahwhit Head
Strawberry Bay
Giants Graveyard
Strawberry Point

CLALLAM
JEFFERSON

Olympic National Park

Boat Ramp

Park

© BENCHMARK MAPS

Land Use and Vegetation

Forest
Wetland
Cropland
Grassland
Other
Built-Up Area

Land Ownership (Other public/tribal lands are named)

State Land (blue highlight)
BLM Land (yellow highlight)

Also See Recreation Page 12

VANCOUVER ISLAND

Goldstream
Langford Station
Glen Lake
Colwood
Happy Valley
Braemar Heights
Trap Mtn 2333
Saseenos Station
Milnes Landing
Broom Hill
Otter Point
Sooke
Shirley
Eldus
Sooke Bay
East Sooke
Sooke Basin
Muir Point
Parsons Point
Sooke Inlet
Possession Point
Donaldson Island
Beachy Head
Sheringham Point
Orveas Bay
Otter Point
Weir Beach
William Head
Parry Bay
Pedder Bay
Canadian Forces Ammunition Depot
Rocky Point
Cape Calver
Smith Head
Church Point
Bentinck Island
Race Rocks
Becher Bay
Eemdyk Passage

BRITISH COLUMBIA

JUAN DE FUCA

Pillar Point
Pillar Point County Park
Boat Ramp
Boat Ramp
San Simon Point
Jordan River

Low Point
Crescent Beach RV Park
Salt Creek Rec Area
Crescent Bay
Striped Peak 1166
Observatory Point
Lower Elwha Klallam Indian Res
Angeles Point
Whiskey Creek Beach Resort
Murdock Creek Access
Lyre River Park
Point Crescent
Camp Hayden
Striped Peak Lookout
Boat Ramp
Freshwater Bay Park
Lower Elwha
Sadie Creek
Disque
Joyce
Freshwater Bay
Casino
Elwha Wildlife Area
William R Fairchild Intl Airport 288
Coville
Lower Elwha Hatchery
Edgewood
Ramapo
Piedmont
Log Cabin Resort
East Bench
Shadow Mtn RV Park
Eden
Dan Kelly
RV Park
Crescent
Pyramid Mtn 3725
Devil Point
East Rd Beach
Lake Sutherland
Indian Creek Rec Area
Lake Aldwell
Viewpoint
OLYMPIC NATIONAL FOREST
Mt Muller 3748
Fairholme
Camp David Jr
North Shore
Olympic Park Institute
Snug Harbor Boat Launch
South Shore Rd
Granny's RV Park
Elwha
Little River
North Point 1340
Kloshe Nanitch Viewpoint
Aurora Ridge
Fairholme
Lake Crescent
Barnes Point
Mt Storm King 4525
Maple Grove
Indian Creek Rec Area
McDonald Mtn
Ovington
Maple Point
Lake Crescent Lodge
Storm King Ranger Station
Marymere Falls
OLYMPIC NATIONAL FOREST
Madison Falls
Wildcat Mtn 3150
La Poel
Barnes Point
BALDY RIDGE
Mt Baldy 4680
Elwha
Little River Trail
Sourdough Mtn 4625
Aurora Peak 4725
Lizard Head Peak 5300
HAPPY LAKE RIDGE
Hughes Creek
ELWHA RIVER RANGE
Elwha Ranger Station
Altair
Griff Creek
Boat Ramp
Hurricane Hill 5757
Windy Arm
Lake Mills
Olympic Hot Springs
Observation Point
Hurricane Ridge Picnic Area
Whiskey Bend
Elwha River
Hurricane Ridge Visitors Center

OLYMPIC MOUNTAINS

Calawah River
Eagle Ranger Station (Summers Only)
Sol Duc Hot Springs Resort
Sol Duc 1650
Boulder Lake Shelter
Crystal Ridge
Boulder Lake
Boulder Peak 5579
Everett Peak 5180
Mt Appleton 5956
Olympic Hot Springs
Pine Mtn 3766
Sol Duc Falls
Mt Carrie 6995
Slide Peak 4310
Hidden Lake
Deer Lake Ranger Station (Seasonal)
Appleton Pass
Humes Ranch
Misery Peak 3564
Ring Lake
Blackwood Lake
Lunch Lake
Seven Lakes
Long Lake
Morgenroth Lake
Ranger Station (Seasonal)
Mt Fitzhenry 6075
Sugarloaf Mtn 3365
Seven Lakes Basin Ranger Station (Seasonal)
Bogachiel Peak 5474
HIGH DIVIDE
Carrie Glacier
Lillian River
LONG RIDGE

National Park

Green Peak 4582
Hoh Lake
Olympus Ranger Station (Seasonal)
Fairchild Glacier
Stephen Peak 6410
Dodger Point 5760
BAILEY RANGE
Nation's Largest Subalpine Fir
Ludden Peak 5828

CLALLAM / JEFFERSON

Hoh Rain Forest Visitor Center
Hoh 550
Hoh River
Mt Tom

© BENCHMARK MAPS

LANDSCAPE
54

Scale 1:200,000

0 5 10 15 Miles

0 5 10 15 20 Kilometers

LANDSCAPE

CANADA

BRITISH COLUMBIA

STRAIT OF JUAN DE FUCA

San Juan

Eagle Point | South Beach
San Juan Is
National Histo

Chatham Islands

Discovery Island
Seabird Point
Mary Todd Island
Cattle Point
Ross Bay
Trail Islands
Staines Point
Clover Point
Plumper Passage

Victoria

Esquimalt
BC Parliament
Maccaulay Point
Victoria Harbour

Goldstream
Langford Station
Glen Lake
Belmont
Colwood
Happy Valley
Lagoon

Metchosin
Albert Head
Parry Bay

Sooke Basin
Weir Beach
William Head
Pedder Bay

48°20'
Becher Bay
Canadian Forces Ammunition Depot Rocky Point
Smith Head
Cape Calver
Church Point
Bentinck Island
Race Rocks
Fernbyk Passage

Port Angeles–Victoria Ferry (90 Minutes)

Seattle–Victoria Ferry (Passenger Only)

123°20'

123°10'

DUNGENESS SPIT

New Dungeness Lighthouse
Dungeness National Wildlife Refuge
Dungeness Bay
Cline Spit Co Park
Dungeness Town
Dungeness Landing Co Park
Marine Dr
Dungeness Recreation Area
Lower Dungeness Wildlife Area
Boat Ramp
Dungeness Wildlife Area
E-Anderson Rd
WSU Martin Gardners Demonstration Center
Marilyn Nelson Co Park
Jamestown
Herd Creek Hatchery
Olympic Game Farm
Man Wheeler Co Park
Port William

48°10'
Observatory Point
Boat Ramp
Lower Elwha Klallam Indian Res
Angeles Point
Freshwater Bay Park
Freshwater Bay
Lower Elwha
Coville
Elwha Wildlife Area
Casino
William R. Fairchild Intl Airport
Lower Elwha Hatchery
Edgewood Dr
Ediz Hook
Picnic Area
Boat Launch
Port Angeles Coast Guard Air Station
Port Angeles Harbor
Port of Entry (limited hours)
Fiero Marine Life Center
Port Angeles
Olympic Discovery Trail
Al's RV Park
Viewpoint
Green Point
Port Angeles Gun Club
Olympic Cellars
Finn Hall Rd
Woodcock Rd
Sky Ridge
Olympic Golf & CC
Port Williams
Marlyn Nelson Co Park
Port Willia
Panorama Vista Beach Acc

53
112
101

Elwha
Dan Kelly Rd
RV Park
Camaraderie Cellars
Fairgroun
Lincoln Park
Olympic Nat Forest HQ
Olympic NP Visitor Center & HQ
Pioneer Memorial Mus
Verne Samuelson
Olympic Golf Club
Olympic Cellars
Motorcycle Track
Port Angeles Speedway
KOA
Port Angeles RV Park
R Corner
Conestoga Quarters RV Park
Robin Hill Farm
Kitchen-Dick Rd
Carlsborg
Carlsborg Rd
Sequim
Museum & Art Ctr
Washington St
W Sequim Bay
Sequim Bay Resort
Sequim Disc
Marina

Lake Aldwell
Viewpoint
Black Diamond Winery
Black Diamond Rd
Hardinger Winery
Peninsula Jr College
Cedars @ Dungeness
Olympic Paradise RV Park
Atterberry Rd
Costco
Three Waters Co Park
Silberhorn Rd
Neuharth Winery
Visitor Center
Happy Vly
Sequim Bay St Park
Louella

Indian Creek Rec Area
Boat Ramp
Little River
Elwha
THE FOOTHILLS
Little River
Mt Pleasant 2638
Dietz Rd
Township Line
Lost Mountain Winery
Lost Mountain Rd
Bell Hill 1006
Happy Valley
Burnt Hill

OLYMPIC NATIONAL FOREST
Mt Baldy 4680
McDonald Mtn
Madison Falls
Elwha
Elwha Ranger Station
Altair
Griff Creek
Wildcat Mtn 3750
Lake Rd
Heart O' the Hills
Entrance Station
First Top 5510
Second Top 6005
Lake Angeles
Burnt Mtn 4910
Round Mtn 3540
Maletti Hill 1625
Gellor Rd
King Hill
Little Oklahoma
Olsen
Dungeness Hatchery
Jamestown Skalallam Ind Res
Ced
Cas

48°00'
Boat Ramp
Windy Arm
Lake Mills
Observation Point
Whiskey Bend
Hurricane Hill Picnic Area
Hurricane Ridge Visitors Center
Hurricane Hill 5757
Mt Angeles 6454
KLAHHANE RIDGE
Steeple Rock
Obstruction Peak
Blue Mtn 6007
Slab Camp
Dungeness Forks
2870
2875
2855
2860
Johnny Come Lately Rd
Jimmycomelately
OLYMPIC
Bear Mtn 3460
284

Olympic
Humes Ranch
Eagle Point 6247
Maiden Peak 6434
Obstruction Peak 6450
Green Mtn 5622
Deer Park Ranger Station (Summers Only)
Deer Park 5325
East Crossing
2870
28

Mt Fitzhenry 6075

National
Elk Mtn 6764
Maynard Peak 5065
NATIONAL

Carrie Glacier
Mt Carrie 6995
Fairchild Glacier
Windfall Peak 5978
Buckhorn Wilderness
Tyler Peak 6364
River Shelter
Tubal Cain
2870
Mt Zi 2855

Park
Grand Lake
Moose Lake
Grand Valley
Greywolf Mtn 7218
Gray Wolf River
Silver Creek Shelter
Bon

Stephen Peak 5410
Dodger Point 5760
Elkhorn Ranger Station (Seasonal)
Grand Pass
Lillian Glacier
Cameron Creek
River Shelter
Tubal Cain
Mt Townsend 6280
Sink Lake Shelter
27

Nation's Largest Subalpine Fir
CLALLAM
JEFFERSON
Ludden Peak 5828
McCartney Peak 6784
Mt Walkinshaw 7378
Tubal Cain Mine
Buckhorn Wilderness
FOREST

Hoh River
O'Neil Pass

123°30'
123°20'
123°10'

© BENCHMARK MAPS

Land Use and Vegetation

Forest
Wetland
Cropland
Grassland
Other
Built-Up Area

Land Ownership (Other public/tribal lands are named)

State Land (blue highlight)
BLM Land (yellow highlight)

Also See Recreation Page 14

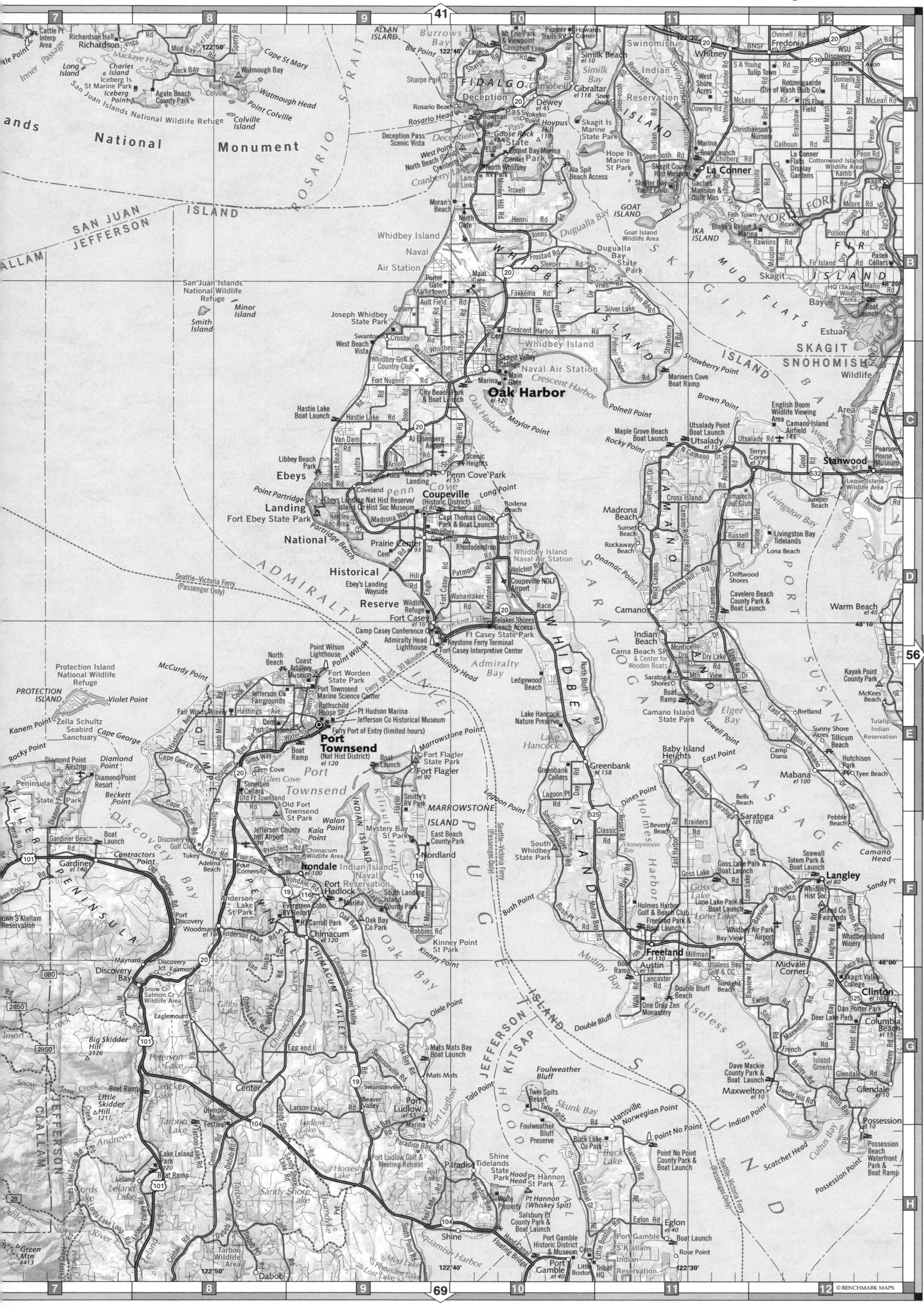

LANDSCAPE

Major labels (map):

San Juan Islands National Wildlife Refuge · National Monument · Rosario Strait · Deception Pass State Park · Fidalgo Island · La Conner · Swinomish Indian Reservation · Skagit Island · Whidbey Island · Naval Air Station · Oak Harbor · Ebeys Landing · Coupeville · Fort Ebey State Park · Ebeys Landing National Historical Reserve · Fort Casey · Keystone Ferry Terminal · Admiralty Bay · Port Townsend · Fort Worden State Park · Fort Flagler State Park · Marrowstone Island · Indian Island Naval Reservation · Port Hadlock · Irondale · Chimacum · Discovery Bay · Protection Island National Wildlife Refuge · Miller Peninsula State Park · Gardiner · Camano Island · Camano Island State Park · Stanwood · Warm Beach · Saratoga Passage · Greenbank · Freeland · Langley · Clinton · Columbia Beach · Possession Beach Waterfront Park · Port Ludlow · Port Gamble · Hood Canal · Foulweather Bluff · Point No Point · Puget Sound

© BENCHMARK MAPS

Also See Recreation Page 14

Scale 1:200,000

0   5   10   15 Miles

0   5   10   15   20 Kilometers

LANDSCAPE

Mt Vernon

La Conner

Stanwood

North Stanwood

Arlington

Smokey Point

Granite Falls

Marysville

Lake Stevens

Langley

Clinton

Everett

In Everett
1. Amtrak Station
2. Childrens Museum
3. Comcast Arena
4. Everett Mem Stadium

US Naval Station &
USS Abraham Lincoln

Mukilteo

Snohomish

Mill Creek

Monroe

SKAGIT FLATS

SKAGIT

SNOHOMISH

Tulalip Indian Reservation

CULTUS MOUNTAINS

SNOQUALMIE NATIONAL FOREST

MT BAKER

FRAILEY MOUNTAIN

WHIDBEY ISLAND

CAMANO ISLAND

PORT SUSAN

SARATOGA PASSAGE

PUGET SOUND

SKAGIT BAY

POSSESSION SOUND

KITSAP

ISLAND

SNOHOMISH

© BENCHMARK MAPS

Land Use and Vegetation

Forest Cropland Other

Wetland Grassland Built-Up Area

Land Ownership (Other public/tribal lands are named)

State Land (blue highlight)

BLM Land (yellow highlight)

Also See Recreation Page 16

57

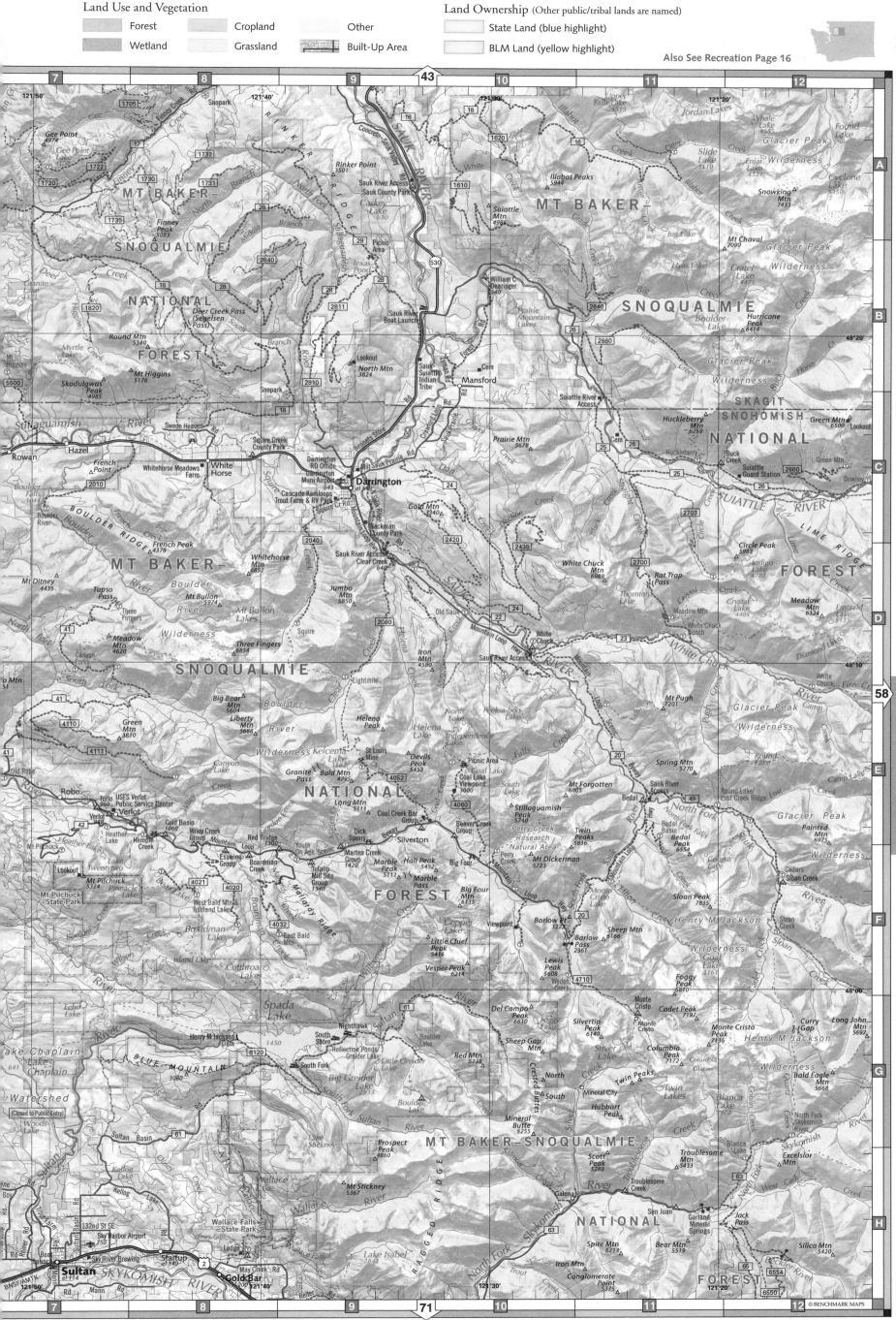

LANDSCAPE

Also See Recreation Page 16

Scale 1:200,000

0   5   10   15 Miles

0   5   10   15   20 Kilometers

44

LANDSCAPE

57

72

© BENCHMARK MAPS

Land Use and Vegetation

- Forest
- Wetland
- Cropland
- Grassland
- Other
- Built-Up Area

Land Ownership (Other public/tribal lands are named)

- State Land (blue highlight)
- BLM Land (yellow highlight)

LANDSCAPE

OKANOGAN-CHELAN

WENATCHEE

NATIONAL FOREST

OKANOGAN-WENATCHEE

CHELAN MOUNTAINS

TYEE RIDGE

Okanogan-Chelan Sawtooth Wilderness

Lake Chelan-Sawtooth Wilderness

Lake Chelan National Recreation Area

Stehekin

Twisp

Carlton

Manson

Lake Chelan State Park

Twenty-Five Mile Creek State Park

Big Buck Wildlife Area

Methow Valley Ranger District Office

© BENCHMARK MAPS

Also See Recreation Page 16

Scale 1:200,000

0 5 10 15 Miles
0 5 10 15 20 Kilometers

46

LANDSCAPE

59

Grid references: 1 2 3 4 5 6 / A B C D E F G H

Place names and features (as labeled on map):

METHOW VALLEY

Twin Lakes, Big Twin Lake Campground, North Cascades Smokejumper Base, Methow Valley State Airport, Moccasin Lake, Davis Lake, Boat Ramp, Campbell Lake Boat Launch

Methow Wildlife Area, Big Buck Wildlife Area

Twisp, el 1614, Methow Valley Ranger District Office, Twisp Municipal Airport, Riverbend RV Park

OKANOGAN WENATCHEE NATIONAL FOREST

Lookout Mtn 5515, McClure Mtn 4580, Golden Doe Wildlife Area

Finley Canyon Rd, Finley Mtn 4570, Thrapp Mtn 4266

LOUP LOUP STATE FOREST, Loup Loup Ski Bowl 7760, Loup Loup Pass 4020, Little Buck Mtn 5375, Bear Mtn 5460, Beaver Mtn 6381, Buck Mtn 6135, North Summit Snopark, South Summit Snopark, Woody Mtn 4585, Cook Mtn 3902

Buzzard Lake Wildlife Area, Wright Mtn 4321, Reed Mtn 4153, Rock Lakes 3800, Leader Lake, Boat Ramp, Spaulding Lake, Harris Mtn 2420

Chiliwist Wildlife Area, Malott, Soap Lake Mtn 2615, Rattlesnake Point 2406, Dent Mtn 3138, Davis Cyn Rd, Soap Lake 1169, Little Soap Lake

Carlton, el 1120, Country Town Motel & RV Resort, Texas Creek Wildlife Area, Mt Leecher 5020, Lookout

Foggy Dew, South Fk Gold Cr Snopark, Hungry Mtn 4616, Gold Ridge, Middle Fork Ridge, Rainy Creek

Methow, el 1153, Hunter Mtn 3468, Knowlton Knob 3852, Bald Knob 3487, Buckhorn Mountain 3268, Indian Dan Wildlife Area, Paradise Hill Rd, Rat Lake Boat Ramp

Monse, Monse Bridge Rd, Okanogan Wildlife Area, Cameron Lake

Brewster, el 820, Anderson Field Airport, Lake Pateros, Fort Okanogan Overlook, Fort Okanogan Interpretive Center, Cassimer Bar Fish Hatchery, Bridgeport Bar WA, Washburn Island Wildlife Area, La Grange

Pateros, el 780, Boat Ramp, Alta Lake, Alta Lake State Park, Goat Mtn 5329, Black Canyon Snopark

OKANOGAN WENATCHEE NATIONAL FOREST

Red Butte 5525, Oss Peak 5549, Parrish Peak 5496, Fox Peak 6213, Poison Spring, Cooper Mtn 5867, Squaw Creek Ridge

Central Ferry Wildlife Area, Rocky Butte el 810, Downing, Chief Joseph Park, Fish Hatchery

Bridgeport, el 829, Bridgeport State Park, Viewpoint, Bridgeport Wildlife Area

LAKE CHELAN, Twenty-Five Mile Creek State Park, Fields Pt Landing, Mitchell Creek (Boat-in) 1100, Fourth Of July Mtn 3537, Antilon Lake, Echo Valley Ski Area 2620, Washington Butte 4390

Greens Landing, Wapato Lake, Roses Lake, Manson, Manson Bay Park, Old Mill Park, Wapato Point, Minneapolis Beach, Sunnybank, Karma Vineyards

Lake Chelan State Park, Willow Pt Park, Boat Ramp, Mill Bay Casino, Slide Peak 5598, Hollywood Beach, Shrine Beach el 1100, The Narrows

North Cascade Sportsman Club, Chelan Muni Airport 1200, Wells Hatchery, Wells Dam, Azwell 708, Windsor Hill 2662, Cold Springs Basin, Dyer Hill

Boulder Park, Cornell Lake, West Foster Creek Wildlife Area, Deer Mtn 3219, Greater Wenatchee Rod & Gun Club, Lake Chelan Golf Course

COLUMBIA RIVER, DOUGLAS

74

Land Use and Vegetation

Forest
Wetland
Cropland
Grassland
Other
Built-Up Area

Land Ownership (Other public/tribal lands are named)

State Land (blue highlight)
BLM Land (yellow highlight)

Also See Recreation Page 18

LANDSCAPE

Duck Lake
POGUE FLAT
Cherokee
Nichols
Robinson Cyn Rd
Concanully
Wenatchee Valley
DuckLake Rd
Mill
Wanacut Creek
Omak Mountain
Omak Mtn 5749
Lookout
119°20'
Van Brunt Mtn 5169
119°30'
Colville
MOSES MEADOWS
Little Moses Mtn 5963
MACKEY RIDGE
North Star Creek Rd
Stepstone
48°20'

Omak
20
97
French Mem RV Park
Omak Stampede & Suicide Race
Gordon Butte 2845
Hagen Cr Rd
Lyman Lake-Moses Meadow Rd
Harley Rd

Okanogan Valley College
Omak Hatchery
Mill
St Marys Mission
Mission Falls
FRENCH VALLEY
Swanloop Creek
Clark Creek
3785
Colville

Okanogan Co Historical Museum
Okanogan-Omak Lk Rd
Cameron Lk-Omak Lk Rd
Mission Creek
Omak Creek
Disautel el 2510
Omak Creek
Moses Mtn 6674
Lookout
48°20'

Okanogan Airport el 1043
Legion Rd
Okanogan Bingo Casino
Omak Lake-Mission End
Boat Ramp
WEST BASIN
Nimpkish Creek
Indian
Summitt Lake

97
Colville
Cameron Lake
Patterson Lake
Cook Lake
Little Goose Lake
TIMENTWA
Indian
Armstrong Mtn 4587
Lookout
155

140
Salt Hill 2936
Houah Lake
Morris Lake
FLAT
Cameron Lake
Figure Eight Lake
950
Columbia River Rd
Boot Mtn 2842
Smith Condon Creek
Kartar Creek
54
Coyote Creek Rest Area
Armstrong Creek
Coyote Creek
Grant Lake 3598
Great Western Lake
Park Cty Loop

Lawson Lake
McDonald Lake
Reservation
Duley Lake 2411
Rat Lake
Goose Lake
Lookout
Whitmore Mtn 3949
Hopkins Creek
Reservation
Squaw Mtn 3430
Chief Joseph Memorial
Nespelem
48°10'
155
62

Cameron Lake
Greenway Rd
Alkali Lake
Cold Springs Rd
SADDLE HORSE FLAT
Columbia River
Net Pens
Mt Iams
Nespelem Creek
Colville Indian Agency
Confederated Tribes of the Colville Indian Reservation HQ

Blacks Lakes
Bedar Lake
Canyon Rd
STUBBLEFIELD POINT
Rice Creek
RIVER
ALAMEDA FLAT
Strahl Rd
Strahl Rd
Twin Springs Canyon
Black Lake
Strahl Canyon
DOUGLAS
OKANOGAN
Belvedere
155

Delfeld Rd
Wells Rd
RUFUS WOODS LAKE
COLUMBIA
Duley Lake
Trefry
Canyon
RUFUS WOODS LAKE
Trefry Rd
Del Rio Rd
McIntosh Rd
China Creek Rd
Rock Lake
Smith Lake
Sanderson Cr

RUFUS WOODS LAKE
PEARL HILL
Pearl Rd
Murphy Lake
Tag Ear Lake
Nilles Rd
Del Rio
Rattlesnake Lake
Rex Rd
Parks Rd
Smith Lake

Pearl Hill Rd
Coleman Hill Rd
26 NE
Substation
Ragged Butte 2478
Del Rio-Coulee City Rd
Elbow Lake
Nilles
48°00'
1. Coulee Dam Casino
2. National Recreation Area HQ
3. Colville Tribal Museum

Coleman Hill Rd
COLEMAN HILL
N NE
Chalk Hills
Nilles
Buck Lake
Y 5 NE
Crown Point Overlook
DOUGLAS
GRANT
Coulee Dam el 1145

17
Chalk Hills 1862
Mary Jane Hill 2170
East Foster Creek
Tower Rock 2405
174
Rogers Rd
Barker Canyon
Grand Coulee Dam Airport 1590
Grand Coulee el 1640
Visitor Arrival Center
Crescent Bay Boat Launch
Grand Coulee Dam
Electric City el 1655
Lake Roosevelt NRA

21 NE
Bell Butte 2330
20 NE
Leahy Rd North
Leahy
Leahy Cutoff
Cache Butte 1875
Banks Lake Golf Club
Sunbanks Resort
Osborn Bay Lake
Steamboat Rock State Park

Hamilton
Hook Hills 2358
Mayfield Rd
Leahy Cutoff Rd
Barnes Butte 2250
17
FOSTER Creek
COULEE
Boat Ramp
Eagle Rock 1670
Osborne el 1620
Castle Rock 2310
155
Steamboat Rock 2285
Steamboat Rock State Park
Northrup
Long Lake

19 NE
18 NE
17 NE
16 Rd NE
Hawks Cliff
BANKS
LAKE
Wildlife Area 1571
Steamboat Rock
Steamboat Rock State Park
Boat Launch
Devils Punch Bowl
Martin Falls
Martin Falls
119°30'
119°20'
119°10'
119°00'
47
75

© BENCHMARK MAPS

Also See Recreation Page 18

Scale 1:200,000

0   5   10   15 Miles

0   5   10   15   20 Kilometers

LANDSCAPE

48

61

76

MOSES MEADOWS

MACKEY RIDGE

Strawberry Mtn 5855

Little Moses Mtn 5963

Moses Mtn 6774 Lookout

North Star Creek Rd

Gold Lake

Stepstone Creek

Central Peak 4789

West Fork el 2060

Bald Knob 3656

21

Ninemile Cr

21 Mile Creek 1840

Bear Creek

Anderson

Cody Butte 4780 Lookout

Twentyone Mile Creek

Twentythree Mile Creek

South Seventeenmile Mtn 5839

Grizzly M

Armstrong Mtn 4587 Lookout

Coyote Creek Rest Area

155

Armstrong Creek

Grant Lake 2598

Great Western Lake

Squaw Mtn 2430

Johnson Lake

Owhi Lake 2556

Little Owhi Lake

Indian

Cox Lake

Owhi Loop

Cache Creek

13

Cache Creek Rd

Bridge Creek

Bridge Creek Rd

Bridge Creek

Louie Creek

Sélome Mtn 3455

COLVILLE

SANPOIL RIVER

Nespelem River

Chief Joseph Memorial

Nespelem el 1620

13

Colville Indian Agency

Confederated Tribes of the Colville Indian Reservation HQ

Net Pens

Mt Iams

155

Schoolhouse Loop Rd

Buffalo Lake

Little Nespelem

Joe Moses Creek

Reservation

Lime Creek

Empire Creek

Brush Creek

Keller

WATSON RIDGE

Copper Creek

Black Lake

Rock Lake

China Creek Rd

DOUGLAS

OKANOGAN

Five Lakes

Reynolds Resort

Buffalo Lake 2402

Keller Butte 4831 Lookout

Jack Creek

Keller Park

Silver Creek

Rebecca Lake

Belvedere

Rebecca Lake

Buffalo Lake

McGinnis Lake 2375

Mt Tolman 3541

Mt Tolman Complex

John Tom Creek

Whitestone Mtn 4762 Lookout

Parks Rd

Smith Lake

Sanderson Cr

Moses Creek

Seatons Grove

Koontzville

Peter Dan

Manila Creek

Manila Creek Rd

French Johns Lake

Elmer City

155

Crown Point Overlook

Coulee Dam Casino

National Recreation Area HQ

Colville Tribal Museum

Coulee Dam

Visitor Arrival Center

Crescent Bay Boat Launch

Grand Coulee Dam 1289

Mica Mtn 4067

Sugarloaf 2557

Kwel Kwel

Canyon

FRANKLIN D ROOSEVELT

Spring Canyon Boat Launch

Plum Point (Boat-In)

Keller Ferry

Keller Ferry Marina

Goldsmith (Boat-In)

Hanson Harbor Boat Launch

DOUGLAS GRANT

174

Electric City

Sunbanks Resort

Boat Launch

Grand Coulee

1640

174

Osborn Bay Lake

Seaton Canyon

Spring Canyon Rd

Lake Roosevelt National Recreation Area

Mile 10

WAWAWAI BASIN

The River Rue RV Park

Penix Canyon (Boat-In)

Jones Bay

SAND HILLS

Banks Lake Coulee Dam Airport

Grand Banks Lake Golf Club

Osborne el 1620

155

Eagle Rock 1670

Steamboat Rock 2285

Castle Rock 2310

Northrup

Devils Punch Bowl

Martin Hills

Boat Launch

Steamboat Rock State Park

W NE

GRANT

LINCOLN

Long Lake

Menke Rd

Bagdad Rd

Old Coulee

White Rd

Meeker Mtn 2641

Neal Canyon Rd

Broadax Spring

Nesseline

Johnson Rd

21

Hell Gate Canyon

Keller Ferry

Speigle Cyn Rd

Sage Hen Draw

Martin Canyon

Hanson Harbor

Colleton

Stigenwalt Rd

Robertson Rd

Pheas Spri

Cajun Cn

Halverson Cyn

© BENCHMARK MAPS

119°00'

118°50'

118°40'

48°20'

48°10'

48°00'

Land Use and Vegetation

Forest Cropland Other
Wetland Grassland Built-Up Area

Land Ownership (Other public/tribal lands are named)

State Land (blue highlight)
BLM Land (yellow highlight)

LANDSCAPE

Colville Indian Reservation

Lake Roosevelt National Recreation Area

Lake Roosevelt National Rec Area

Spokane Indian Reservation

FRANKLIN D. ROOSEVELT LAKE

STEVENS FERRY

HUCKLEBERRY RANGE

THE SUMMIT RANGE

HUCKLEBERRY MOUNTAIN

RAINY RIDGE

ONION RIDGE

COLVILLE RIDGE

MOUNTAIN RIDGE

NINEMILE FLAT

COLUMBIA RIVER

SPOKANE RIVER

Inchelium el 1560
Gifford
Maud
Hunters el 1580
Cedonia el 1708
Fruitland el 1831
Turk
Rice 1724
Daisy
Impach
Meteor
Kewa
Covada
Wellpinit
Wellpinit Mtn 3413
Spokane Tribal HQ
Columbia
Two Rivers
Ford Spokane
Miles
Springdale-Hunters

Sitdown Mtn 4781
Lynx Mtn 5209
Bitterfoot Mtn 5588
Rocky Point 3580
North Twin Lake
South Twin Lake
Moon Mtn 3888
Stranger Mtn 3047
Monument Butte 2098
Rattlesnake Mtn 2443
Seymour Hill 3897
Middle Mtn 3221
Gold Mtn 4686
Miller Mtn 3115
Mitre Rock
Johnny George 4090
Butcher Mtn 3279
Gold Hill 3677
Quartz Mtn 3563
Bradeen Hill 3677
Deadman Mtn 4815
Colburn Hill 4081
Dumn Mtn 5340
Wellington Peak 4483
Stensgar Mtn 5819
Lane Mtn 4561
Adams Mtn 4686
Cooney Mtn 3520
Empey Mtn 3610
Camas 2160
Blue Mtn 4383
Deer Mtn 3580
Round Mtn 2835
Spokane Mtn 3870
Tower Mtn
Pitney Butte 2631
Lilienthal Mtn 3568
Sterling Point
Seven Bays
Two Rivers Casino
Deer Meadows Golf Course
Spokane Historic Site Visitor Center

Lake Roosevelt National Rec Area

Nicholls Mtn 3484
Granite Mtn 4252
Middle Basin
Arden Hill
Lenz Lake
Erickson
Swiss Valley
Riecker Mtn 2890
Waitts Lake
Fourmile Lake
Mountainview Rd
Cottonwood

© BENCHMARK MAPS

Also See Recreation Page 20

Scale 1:200,000

0   5   10   15 Miles

0   5   10   15   20 Kilometers

LANDSCAPE

63

50

78

© BENCHMARK MAPS

Little Pend Oreille Nat Wildlife Refuge

COLVILLE NATIONAL FOREST

IRON MOUNTAINS

STEVENS

PEND OREILLE

COLVILLE

HUCKLEBERRY MOUNTAIN

COLVILLE VALLEY

Chewelah
el 1671

Addy
el 1636

Bluecreek
el 1610

Valley
el 1700

Kulzer
el 1720

Grays
el 1864

Waitts
el 2000

Springdale
el 2020

Loon Lake
el 2410

Clayton
el 2250

Deer Park
el 2130

Denison
el 1958

Ford

Tumtum

Wellpinit
el 2400

Spokane Indian Reservation

WALKERS PRAIRIE

Camas Valley

WILLIAMS VALLEY

STEVENS

SPOKANE

NATIONAL FOREST

The Butte
2449

Addy Mtn
4885

Dunn Mtn
5340

Deer Mtn
4094

McDonald Mtn
3674

Rocky Butte
3894

Calispell Peak
6855

Saddle Mtn
3645

Dirty Shirt
5798

Tacoma Peak
5015

Boulder Mtn
4668

Wilson Mtn
4528

Johnson Mtn
4509

Goddards Peak
5548

Winchester Peak
3980

Chewelah Mtn
5773

Horseshoe Lake
3064

Quartzite Mtn
3714

Parker Mtn
3461

Roundtop Mtn
3515

Nelson Peak
5102

Boyer Mtn
5277

Granite Mtn
4180

Benson Peak
3925

Bald Mtn
4163

Little Roundtop
3298

Brush Mtn
3216

Jumpoff Joe Mtn
3285

Deer Lake Mtn
3741

Blue Grouse Mtn
3990

Loon Lake Mtn
3427

Fan Lake
1921

Eloika Lake

Round Mtn
2835

Deer Mtn
3580

Scoop Mtn
4004

Negro Mtn
3460

Becks Hill
3355

Saddle Mtn
3575

Dunns Mtn
3575

Mt Godfrey
3410

Happy Hill
2390

Loon Lake
2387

Deer Lake
2478

Deer Lake Resort

Shore Acres Resort

Forshee's Resort

Willow Bay Resort & Marina

Silver Beach Resort

Winona Beach Resort

Jump-Off Lake Resort

Chewelah Golf & CC

Chewelah Trap Club

Spokane Casino

49 Degrees North Ski Area

Chewelah Mtn Nordic Ski Area

Deer Park Airport

Cross Winds Airport

Sand Canyon Airport

Tri County Fairgrounds

Spokane Tribal HQ

Waitts Lake
1946

Fourmile Lake

Browns Lake

Horseshoe Lake

Benson Lake

Jumpoff Joe Lake

Little Coyote Mtn
2964

Lone Mtn
4561

Empey Mtn
3610

Cooney Mtn
3520

Jay Gould Ridge

Cottonwood Creek

Chewelah Creek

Chamokane Creek

Little Chamokane Creek

Deer Creek

395

231

292

11

20

24

Land Use and Vegetation

Forest Cropland Other

Wetland Grassland Built-Up Area

Land Ownership (Other public/tribal lands are named)

State Land (blue highlight)

BLM Land (yellow highlight)

Also See Recreation Page 20

LANDSCAPE

Continues in the Benchmark Idaho Road & Recreation Atlas

KANIKSU

NATIONAL

FOREST

KANIKSU NATIONAL FOREST

COLVILLE

NATIONAL

FOREST

Browns Lake
Browns Lake Historic CCC Cabin
South Baldy 5988
Goose Creek Point 3633
Cooks Mtn 4325
Coats Lake
Mystic Lake
Skookum Peak 5261
No Name Lake
Bead Lake
Bead Lake Peak 4850
Marshall Lake
Marshall Lake Resort
Shearer Lake
Jasper Mtn 3940
Quartz Mtn 4091
Whitetail Butte 3105
Gisborne Mtn 5692
Prater Mtn 4594
Blue Lake 2238
Gold Cup Mtn 4561

Locke
Kalispel Indian Reservation
Gibraltar Rock 3793
Moon Hill 3924
Kings Mtn 4393
Cusick el 2050
Usk el 2055
Ponderay Newsprint Company
Kalispel Indian Res
Westside Calispell
Dalkena el 2045
Furport el 2090
Geophysical Nordic
Wolfred el 2140
Saddle Mtn 3479
Cooks Mtn 3344
Vista Point
Newport
Old American Campground
Newport Ranger Station
Oldtown
Pend Oreille Co. Museum
Priest River
Priest River Municipal Airport 2187
Albeni Falls
Albeni Cove
PEND OREILLE
Thama
Sawyer el 2157
Jewel Lake
Vay el 2184
Hoodoo Mtn 5119
Edgemere el 2176
Hoodoo Lake
Harlem el 2175
Clagstone el 2170
Kelso Lake

Penrith
Moonlight RV Park
Sacheen Lake
Diamond Lake el 2361
Scotia el 2065
Mt Pisgah 3650
Tweedie
Spring Valley
Lake of the Woods 2330
Trask Pond 2260
Chain Lake 1937
Camden
Elk el 1860
Reflection Lake 1838
Blanchard Rd
Blanchard el 2290
Coleman
Blanchard Lake
BONNER
KOOTENAI
Spirit Lake el 2567
Silver Beach el 2460

PEND OREILLE
SPOKANE

Milan 1270
Milan Hill 2677
Laurel
Mount
Spokane
Vista House & Lookout
Mt Spokane 5881
Bald Knob
Mt Spokane Ski Area
Selkirk Lodge
Bear Creek Lodge
Quartz Mtn 5180
Ragged Mtn 4893
Shadow Mtn 4900
Spirit Lake
Paper Company
Inland Empire
Silver Sands Beach
Silver Beach el 2320
Echo Beach
Excelsior Beach
Round Mtn 2456
Twinlow el 2400
Chilco el 2309
Ramsey
Sturgeon
Rathdrum 2005
Timberlands
KANIKSU NF
EIGHTMILE PRAIRIE
North Pole
Corbin Junction

IDAHO

PEND OREILLE
BONNER

ORCHARD BLUFF
Orchard Bluff

© BENCHMARK MAPS

Scale 1:200,000

0　　　　5　　　　10　　　15 Miles

0　　5　　10　　15　　20 Kilometers

52

80

124°40'　　124°30'　　124°20'　　124°10'

47°50'
47°40'
47°30'
47°20'

A B C D E F G H

1 2 3 4 5 6

LANDSCAPE

P A C I F I C

O C E A N

Quillayute Needles National Wildlife Refuge

Copalis National Wildlife Refuge

Olympic

National

Park

Olympic

National

Park

Olympic
National Park

Quillayute Needles
Teahwhit Head
Third Beach
Strawberry Bay
Taylor Point
Giants Graveyard
Strawberry Point
Toleak Point
Rounded Island
Ranger Station (Seasonal)
Alexander Island
Boulder Beach
Hoh Head 300
Jefferson Cove
Oil City
Hoh
Oil City
Oil City Rd
Lower Hoh Rd
Hoh Indian Reservation
Abbey Island
Ruby Beach
Ruby Beach Overlook
South Rock
Beach 6 Overlook
Big Cedar Tree
Destruction Island Lighthouse (Decomission in 2008)
Destruction Island
Beach 4 Overlook
Beach 3
Kalaloch
Kalaloch
Kalaloch Lodge
Kalaloch Information Station
Beach 2
Beach 1 Overlook
Clearwater
South Beach 30
Queets el 30
Queets Trading Post
Tunnel Island
Sea Lion Rock
Hogsback
Little Hogsback
Willoughby Rock
Split Rock
Camp
Cape Elizabeth
Quinault Indian Tribal HQ
Taholah el 17
Point Grenville
Grenville Bay

2932
Undii Rd
Bogachiel River
Dowans Cr Rd
101
Upper Hoh Rd
Willoughby Creek 300
Hard Rain NAT FO
Hard Rain Cafe
Hoh Ox Bow 300
Minnie Peterson 280
Allen Logging Co
HOH
RIVER
Cottonwood 130
Hoh River Resort
Mt Octopus 2486
Olympic Correction Center
Rain Forest Hostel
Braden
Cedar Creek
Nolan Creek
KALALOCH RIDGE
Clearwater
Coppermine Bottom 340
Clearwater River
Clearwater Rd
Hurst Creek
Boulder Creek
Elk Creek
RIVER
Boat Ramp
Olympic National Park
Fisher Rapids
QUEETS
Queets River
Q-1000 W
Q-3000
JEFFERSON
GRAYS HARBOR
101
N Fk Whale Creek
Salmon Creek
RIVER
Whale Creek
Q u i n a u l t
North Fork Raft River
Raft River
4000
Raft River
Red Creek
I n d i a n   R e s e r v a t i o n
7500
7500
7320
Camp Creek
7000
7500
(Limited Public Access)
109
QUINAULT
RIVER
BAKER PRAIRIE
North Fork Moclips
Aloha Mainline

Goodman Creek
Mosquito Creek
Minor Creek
Falls Creek

47°40'
124°30'
124°20'
124°10'

Land Use and Vegetation

- Forest
- Wetland
- Cropland
- Grassland
- Other
- Built-Up Area

Land Ownership (Other public/tribal lands are named)

- State Land (blue highlight)
- BLM Land (yellow highlight)

Olympic

National

Park

Olympic

National

Forest

Quinault

Indian Reservation

(Limited Public Access)

Hoh Rain Forest Visitor Center
Hoh Ranger Station
Olympus Ranger Station (Seasonal)
Stephen Peak 6410
Dodger Point 3760
Ludden Peak 5828
Mt Ferry 6157
Mt Scott 5913
Glacier Meadows Ranger Station (Seasonal)
Nation's Largest Subalpine Fir
West Peak 7965
Mt Mathias 7168
East Peak 7780
Mt Olympus
Blue Glacier
White Glacier
Hoh Glacier
Humes Glacier
Mt Barnes 5993
Mt Dana 6209
Hoh Peak 5572
Mt Tom 7048
Jeffers Glacier
Queets Glacier
Mt Queets 6480
Mt Wilder 5928
Mt Meany 6695
Mt Noyes 6173
Mt Seattle 6246
Lew Divide Ranger Station (Seasonal)
Elwha River
Kimta Peak 5399
Mt Christie 6177
Owl Mtn 3398
Huelsdonk Ridge
South Fork Hoh 550
Boat Ramp
Upper Hoh Rd
Hoh Springs
H-1000
5301
Klootchman Rock 3556
Yahoo Lake 2326
Tshletshy Ridge
Mt Lawson 5401
Muncaster Mtn 5910
National Park's Largest Douglas Fir
Tshletshy Creek
Sams Ridge
Lake Dilly
Round Lake
Stalding Creek
Three Prune Creek
Rustler Creek
Geoduck Creek
Olympic National Forest
Queets Ranger Station (Seasonal)
Queets River Rd
Sams Rapids
Queets
Matheny Ridge
Finley Peak 3419
World's Largest Alaskan Yellow Cedar
North Fork 500
Graves Creek 575
Six Ridge Pass
2180
2170
2160
2140
2190
Hoko Creek
North Fork Quinault
Wynoochee Pass
Sundown Pass
Jefferson
Grays Harbor
Mt Hoquiam 4909
Lake Connie
2270
Higley Peak 2025
Olympic National Park
Quinault Rain Forest Ranger Station (NPS)
Colonel Bob
Burnt Lake
Mt O'Neil 4289
Capitol Peak 5054
Mt Church 4770
Mt Dana
Quinault National Park Largest Western Red Cedar
Gatton Creek 200
Rain Forest Resort
Wooded Peak 3865
Colonel Bob Wilderness
Gibson Peak 4390
Campbell Tree Grove 1035
Three Peaks 4660
2204
2270
Crane Creek Mtn
Lone Mtn 1173
North Shore Rd
South Shore Rd
Lake Quinault
Lake Quinault Lodge
Falls Creek
Willaby Creek
Quinault 1221
Olympic National Forest Pacific RD Office
Quinault Rain Forest & Quinault Lakeshore NRT
Stovepipe Mtn 3610
Moonlight Dome 4156
Wildlife Closure Oct 1–Apr 30
Mt Church 4770
Chapel Peak 3976
Pine Lake
9100
9111
Amanda Park
Bell Mtn 2800
Humptulips Ridge
Wynoochee Lake
Chetwoot 830
Coho
738
Anderson Butte 3370
2372
9406
Neilton el 483
Premier Forest Products
Olympic National Park
Wynoochee Lake Shore
Fitzgerald Peak 2985
Boat Ramp
22
Salsop Work Center (USFS)
2364
2368
Chow Chow Prairie
Quinault River
Boulder Creek
Moclips
2258
2259
040
2280
2208
2204
2206
2281
2294
2281
22
23
23
Grisdale
2370
Quinault National Fish Hatchery
2259
2220
2263
2204
2207
2210
2260
Burnt Hill 1258
Reed Hill 1443
2260
Macafee Hill 655
Promised Land Park
101
Cook Creek
Donkey Creek
West Fork Humptulips
East Fork Humptulips
Cougar Mountain
Olympic Wildlife Area
Wynoochee Mitigation Wildlife Area
Weatherwax Ridge
Canyon
© BENCHMARK MAPS

Scale 1:200,000

0   5   10   15 Miles
0   5   10   15   20 Kilometers

LANDSCAPE

54

CLALLAM
JEFFERSON

Stephen Peak 5760
Dodger Pt
Ludden Peak 5828
Elkhorn Ranger Station (Seasonal)
Windfall Peak 5978
Lake Lillian
Lillian Glacier
Grand Pass
Mt Townsend 6280
Sink Lake Shelter

Nation's Largest Subalpine Fir
Mt Ferry 6157
Olympic
Mt Scott 5913
McCartney Peak 6784
Mt Walkinshaw 7378
Buckhorn Wilderness
Tubal Cain Mine
Camp Handy Shelter

47°50'
Cameron Pass
Mt Cameron 7192
Cedar Lake
Mt Clark 7528
Ranger Station (Seasonal)
Buckhorn Mtn 6956
Big Quilcene

Humes Glacier
National
Lost Peak 6515
Gray Wolf Pass 6485
Mt Deception 7788
Mt Fabrica
Boulder Shelter
Tenmile Shelter

Queets Glacier
Mt Barnes 5993
Mt Dana 6209
Mt Claywood 6836
Claywood Lake
Mt Fromme 6655
Wellesley Peak 6758
Mt Mystery 7631
Little Mystery
Warrior Peak 7310
OLYMPIC

Mt Meany 6695
Mt Wilder 5928
Mt Norton 6319
Hayden Pass 5847
Sentinel Peak 6592
Sentinels Sister 6301
Park
Constance Pass
Mt Constance 7743
Tunnel Creek Shelter

Mt Noyes 6173
Mt Seattle 6246
Crystal Peak 6896
West Peak 7365
Mt Anderson 7321
Diamond Mtn 6824
East Peak 5981
Lake Constance
Dosewallips Ranger Station (Seasonal)
Dosewallips 1600
Tunnel Creek

Low Divide Ranger Station (Seasonal)
Mt Christie 6177
World's Largest Western Hemlock
Anderson Pass
Mt LaCrosse 6417
Mt Elk Lick 6517
NATIONAL
Mt Jupiter 5701

Olympic
Chimney Peak 6911
Enchanted Valley Ranger Station (Seasonal) 2020
Lake LaCrosse
LaCrosse Pass
White Mtn 6249
St Peters Dome 4490
The Duckabush River

47°40'
Mt Lawson 5401
Hart Lake
Mt Steel
Mt Lena 5995
Upper Lena Lake
The Brothers 6866
Brothers
North Rock

Muncaster Mtn 5910
O'Neil Pass
Mt Duckabush 6233
Mt Hopper 6114
Mt Bretherton 5960
Lena Lake (Walk-in)
Wilderness
West Rock 4226
East Rock 4269

National
O'Neil Peak 5758
Hagen Lake
Mt Stone 6612
Scout Lake
Lena Lake
FOREST

Mt Skokomish 6434
Smith Lake
Mildred Lakes
OLYMPIC
Hamma Hamma
Hamma Hamma Cabin (Historic)
Lake Armstrong

Mt Olson 5289
Mt Cruiser 6104
Mt Skokomish 2G
Beaver Pond
NATIONAL
Elk Lake

Park
67
North Fork 500
Graves Creek 575
Mt Gladys 5589
Flapjack Lakes
Mildred Lakes
Mt Pershing
Jefferson Lake
RIDGE
Eldon

Six Ridge Pass
Mt Lincoln 5868
Copper Mtn 5425
Mt Washington 6255
FOREST

Mt Hoquiam 4909
Sundown Pass
Wonder Mountain
Wagonwheel Lake
Staircase Ranger Station
Mt Elinor
Wilderness

47°30'
JEFFERSON
GRAYS HARBOR
Wilderness
Wonder Mtn 4848
Bear Gulch
Mt Rose
Big Creek
Saddle Mtn 1860

2204
Capitol Peak 5054
Harps Shelter
Monarch Tree
Dry Mountain
Lightning Peak 4654
PROSPECT RIDGE
Lake Cushman Park 740

Olympic
Mt Church 4779
Laney
Mt Tebo 4604
Cushman Hill 2394
Dow Mtn 2514
Rest-A-While
Dewatto

Wynoochee Fall
Church Creek Shelter
Le Bar
Lilliwaup
Hoodsport Trail

Wildlife Closure Oct 1–Apr 30
Chapel Peak 3976
Le Bar Horse Camp
Deer Meadows
Glen Ayr Resort

Wynoochee Lake
Chetwoot
Dusk Point
Spider Lake
Wildlife Closure Oct 1–Apr 30
Brown Creek
Oxbow
Lake Cushman Golf Course
Hoodsport
HOOD

Coho
Anderson Butte 1370
Rock Peak 3370
Dennie Ahl Hill 2004
Visitor Info Center
Hood Canal Hatchery

Satsop Work Center (USFS)
NATIONAL
FOREST
Skokomish High Steel Bridge
Potlatch
Hood Canal Recreation Park
Union

Weatherwax Ridge
Skokomish Indian Reservation
Skokomish
Potlatch State Park
Annas Bay
Alderbrook Golf & Yacht Club

47°20'
Reed Hill 1443
South Mtn
Mohrweis
Eells Springs Hatchery
Brockdale
George Adams Salmon Hatchery

© BENCHMARK MAPS
82

Scale 1:200,000

0   5   10   15 Miles

0   5   10   15   20 Kilometers

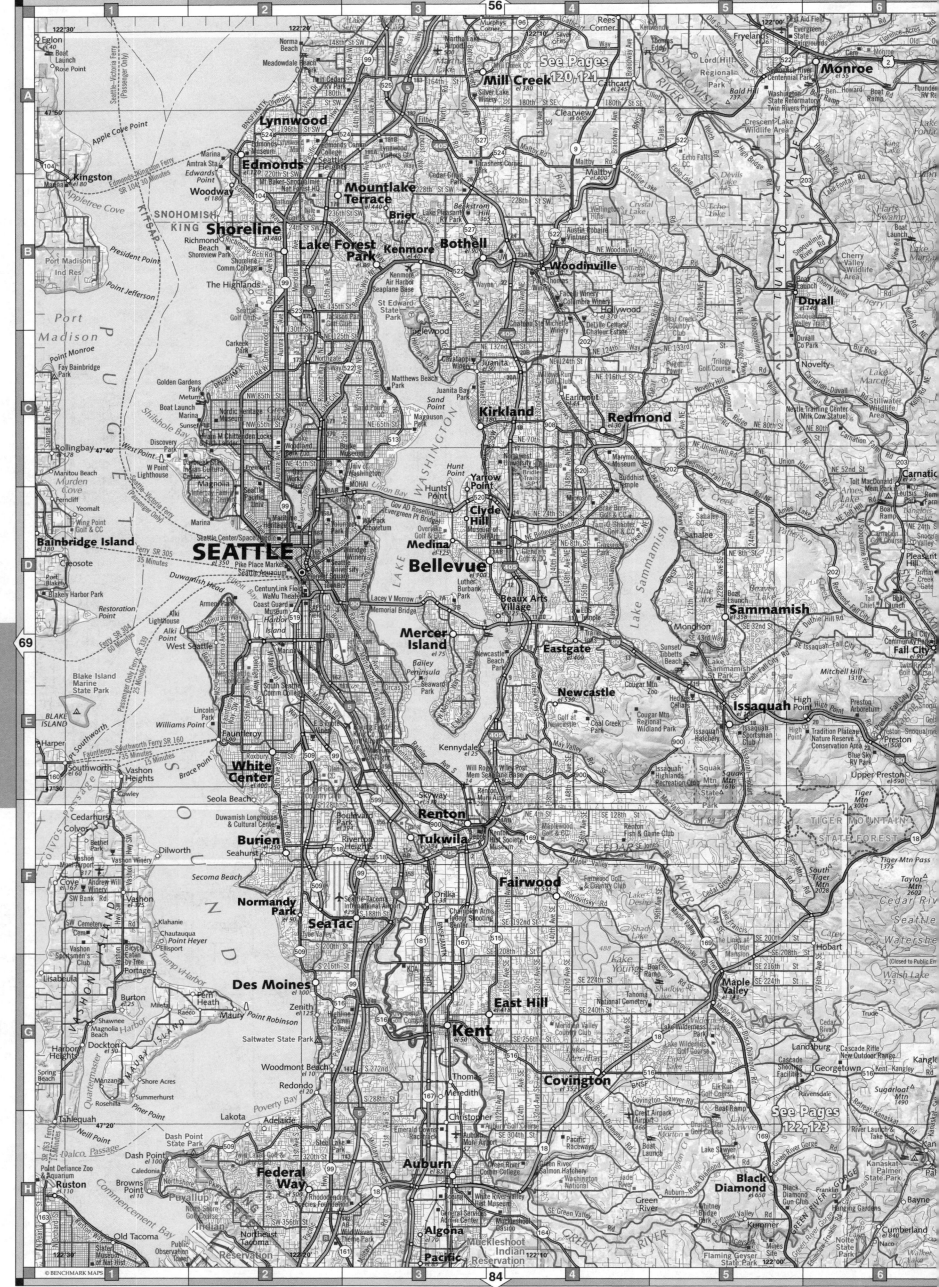

See Pages 120 121

See Pages 122 123

LANDSCAPE

© BENCHMARK MAPS

Also See Recreation Page 14

Land Use and Vegetation

Forest
Wetland
Cropland
Grassland
Other
Built-Up Area

Land Ownership (Other public/tribal lands are named)

State Land (blue highlight)
BLM Land (yellow highlight)

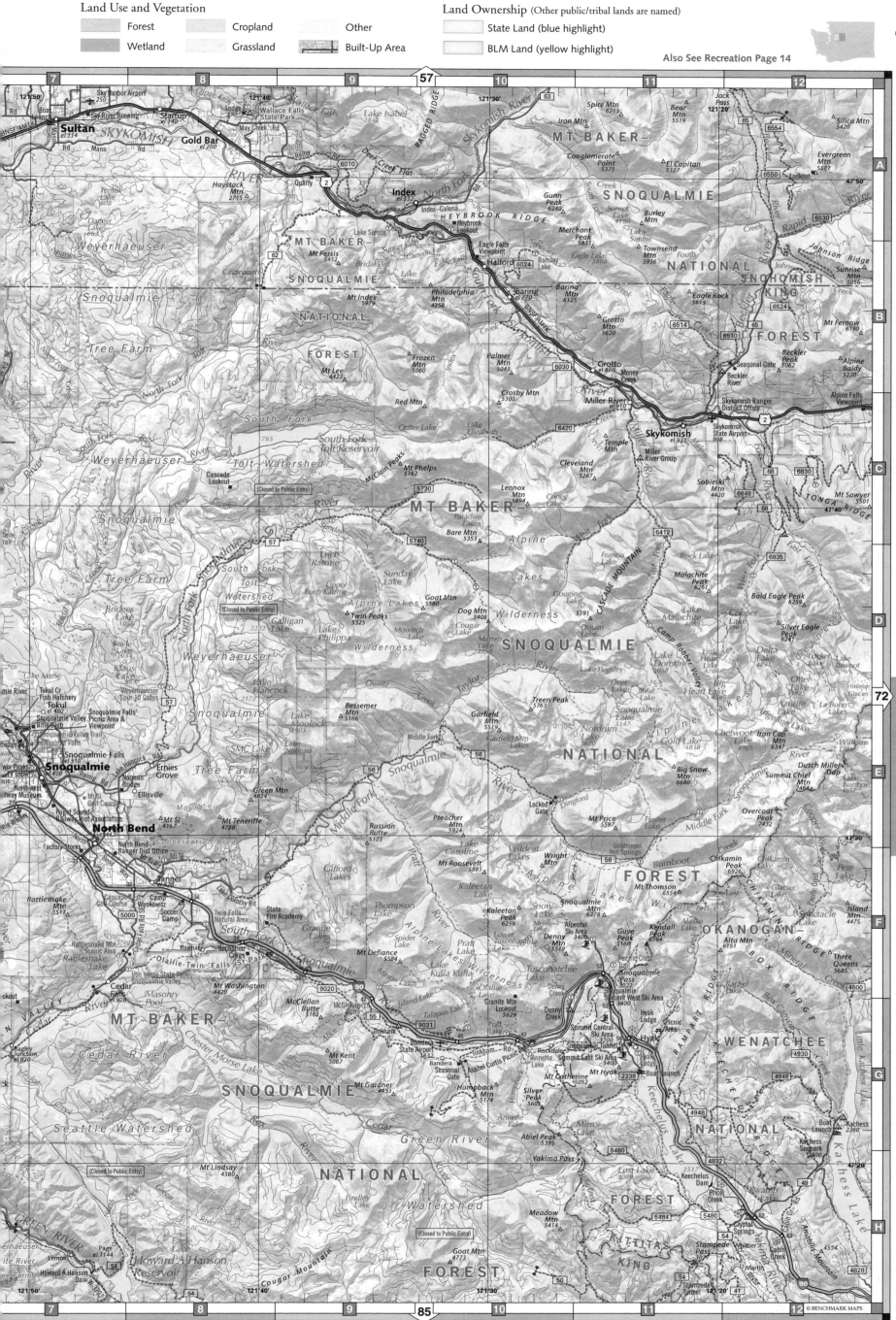

LANDSCAPE

© BENCHMARK MAPS

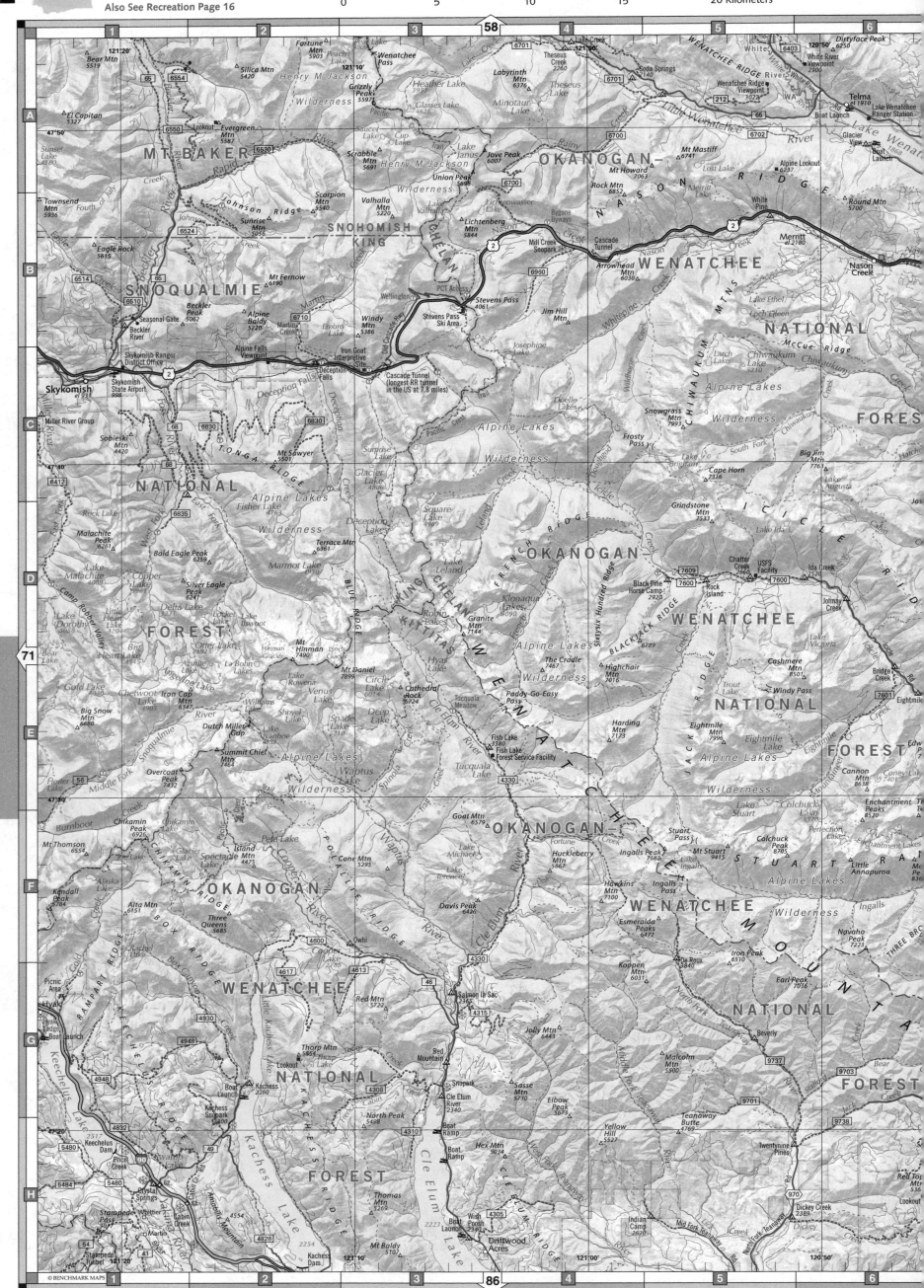

Also See Recreation Page 16

Scale 1:200,000

0   5   10   15 Miles

0   5   10   15   20 Kilometers

LANDSCAPE

71

© BENCHMARK MAPS

Land Use and Vegetation

Forest
Wetland
Cropland
Grassland
Other
Built-Up Area

Land Ownership (Other public/tribal lands are named)

State Land (blue highlight)
BLM Land (yellow highlight)

Also See Recreation Page 16

LANDSCAPE

74

OKANOGAN—WENATCHEE

NATIONAL

FOREST

OKANOGAN—

WENATCHEE

MOUNTAINS

NATIONAL

FOREST

WENATCHEE

Leavenworth el 1180
Peshastin el 1010
Dryden el 977
Cashmere el 795
Monitor el 710
Sunnyslope el 800
Wenatchee el 768
East Wenatchee el 800
Entiat el 800
Orondo el 760
Rock Island el 650
Malaga
Wenatchee Heights
Plain
Chumstick
Ardenvoir el 1280
Wagnersburg
Stayman

ENTIAT VALLEY

COLUMBIA RIVER

LAKE ENTIAT

LAKE CHELAN

DOUGLAS

BADGER MOUNTAIN

CHELAN MOUNTAINS

CHELAN

CASHMERE MOUNTAINS

ENTIAT MOUNTAINS

ROARING RIDGE

MINERS RIDGE

TRONSEN RIDGE

MISSION RIDGE

NANEUM RIDGE

COLOCKUM

1. Wenatchee River Ranger District Office
2. Bavarian Village
3. Waterfront Park
4. Amtrak Station

1. Wenatchee Riverfront Park
2. Amtrak Station
3. North Central Washington Museum

Lake Wenatchee State Park
Lake Chelan State Park
Daroga State Park
Lincoln Rock State Park
Wenatchee Confluence State Park
Squilchuck State Park
Peshastin Pinnacles State Park

Leavenworth Ski Hill
Mission Ridge Ski Area
Entiat Valley Ski Area
Badger Mtn Ski Area

Blewett Pass 4102
Old Blewett Pass 4071
Swauk Pass

© BENCHMARK MAPS

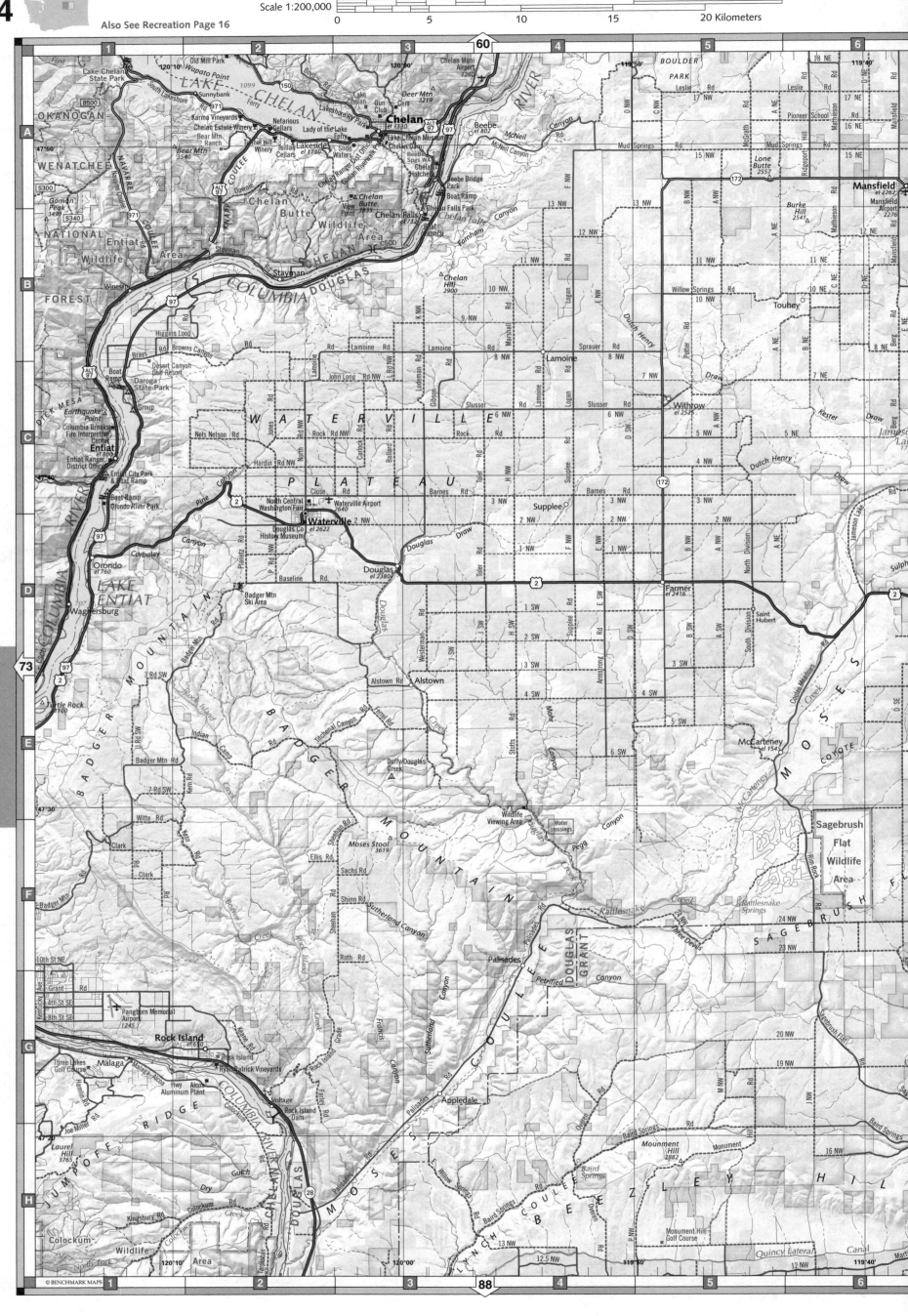

Also See Recreation Page 16

Scale 1:200,000

0   5   10   15 Miles

0   5   10   15   20 Kilometers

LANDSCAPE

OKANOGAN

WENATCHEE

NATIONAL

FOREST

Goman Peak 3499

Dick Mesa

Lake Chelan State Park

Old Mill Park
Wapato Point

LAKE CHELAN

Sunnybank

Karma Vineyards
Chelan Estate Winery
Bear Mtn. Ranch
Tunnel Hill Winery
Tsillan Cellars

Nefarious Cellars
Lady of the Lake Ferry

Chelan

Chelan Museum
Lake Chelan

Deer Mtn 3219

Beebe el 802

McNeil

McNeil Canyon

BOULDER PARK

Leslie   Rd

Leslie   Rd

Pioneer School

Mansfield
el 2262

Mansfield Airport 2276

Burke Hill 2541

Lone Butte 2557

Mud Springs   Rd

Bear Mtn 3540

Chelan Butte 3835

View Point

Chelan Butte Wildlife Area

Stayman

Stayman

Winesap

COLUMBIA DOUGLAS

Chelan Hill 2900

Chelan Falls
Chelan Falls Park
Boat Launch

Beebe Bridge Park
Boat Ramp
Chelan Hatchery

Farnham

Chelan Falls Canyon

13 NW

12 NW

11 NW

10 NW

9 NW

Willow Springs   Rd

Touhey

Higgins Loop   Rd
Browns Canyon   Rd

Desert Canyon Golf Resort

Daroga State Park

Group

Earthquake Point
Columbia Breaks Fire Interpretive Center

Entiat
el 890

Entiat Ranger District Office

Entiat City Park & Boat Ramp

Boat Ramp
Orondo River Park

Brays

Lamoine   Rd

John Long Rd NW

Ludeman   Rd

Gibson

Slusser

Lamoine

8 NW

Lamoine

Logan

Sprauer   Rd

Dutch Henry

Potter   Rd

7 NW

Withrow
el 2525

WATERVILLE

Nels Nelson   Rd
Jones   Rd
Rock Rd NW

Carlock

Ballard

Rock

6 NW

Slusser   Rd

Logan

5 NW

5 NE

Jameson Lake

Oronto
el 760

Corbaley

Hardin   Rd NW

Pine   Canyon

Close   Rd

PLATEAU

Barnes   Rd

Toler   Rd

H   Rd

Supplee   Rd

4 NW

172

Dutch Henry   Draw

4 NW

4 NE

North Central Washington Fair

Waterville Airport 2640

2 NW

Barnes

3 NW

3 NW

Douglas   Draw

Supplee

Douglas   Rd

Planetz   Rd
P   Rd

Waterville
el 2622

Douglas Co History Museum

2 NW

2 NW

1 NW

F NW

E NW

B NW

A NW

A NE

Saint Hubert

Wagnersburg

Badger Mtn Ski Area

Baseline   Rd

Douglas
el 2380

1 SW

1 SW

H SW

Supplee   Rd

D SW

B SW

A SW

Farmer
el 2416

2

LAKE ENTIAT

Turtle Rock
el 700

3 Rd SW

Badger Mtn   Rd

BADGER

Rock Island

2 SW

Westerman   Rd

2 SW

Coulee Meadows Creek

Indian   Camp

Alstown Rd   **Alstown**

Ferrell Rd

Mohn   Rd

3 SW

4 SW

5 SW

6 SW

McCarteney
el 1545

COYOTE

Badger Mtn Rd

7 Rd SW

MOUNTAIN

Titchenal Canyon

Duffy Douglas Creek

Stotts   Rd

Sagebrush Flat Wildlife Area

Witte   Rd

Clark   Rd

Nahl   Rd

Sheaburg Rd

Moses Stool 3619

Ellis   Rd

Wildlife Viewing Area

Water crossings

Pegg   Canyon

Rattlesnake Springs

Clark

Beehler   Creek

Sachs Rd

Shinn Rd

Sutherland Canyon

Sheehan

Rock Island   Creek

Francis   Canyon

Roth   Rd

Palisades

Rattlesnake   Creek

Three Devils

24 NW

23 NW

SAGEBRUSH   FLAT

Badger Mtn   Rd

10th St NE
Grant   Rd
4th St SE
8th St SE

Kentucky Ave   Rd

Pangborn Memorial Airport 1245

Rock Island
el 650

Rock Island

Ryan Patrick Vineyards

Nigone   Rd

Rock Island Grade

DOUGLAS GRANT

COULEE

Petrified   Canyon

20 NW

19 NW

Three Lakes Golf Course

Malaga

Malaga-Alcoa Hwy
Alcoa Aluminum Plant

COLUMBIA

Voltage

Rock Island Dam

Appledale

Palisades

Mounment Hill 2882

Baird Springs

16 NW

Laurel Hill 3765

JUMPOFF RIDGE

Colockum

Wildlife

Area

Kingsbury   Rd

Joe Miller Rd

Dry

Colockum   Creek

North Fork

Colockum   Creek

Tarpiscan   Rd

Faith   Rd

Palisades   Rd

MOSES   COULEE

LYNCH COULEE

Baird Springs

Baird Springs   Rd

Owens   Rd

13 NW

12.5 NW

Monument Hill Golf Course

BEEZLEY HILL

Quincy Lateral   Canal

© BENCHMARK MAPS

73

Land Use and Vegetation

- Forest
- Wetland
- Cropland
- Grassland
- Other
- Built-Up Area

Land Ownership (Other public/tribal lands are named)

- State Land (blue highlight)
- BLM Land (yellow highlight)

LANDSCAPE

Hook Hills 2358 △
Yeager Rock 2307 △
Leahy Cutoff Rd
Barnes Butte 2250 △
Hawks Cliff Rd
Horse Lake
Sims Corner
Sims Corner Reservoir
Hayden Rd
Murphy Rd

Chester Butte Wildlife Area
Long Canyon
Haynes Lake
Stalland Lake 2281
Stalland Lake 2193
St Andrews Rd East
St Andrews 2223
Mold el 2302
Boat Launch

Dormaier Wildlife Area
Burton
Draw
St Andrews Rd South
Pilot Rock 2637 △
Banks
Lakes
Wildlife
Area

Steamboat Rock 2285
Castle Rock 2310
Northrup
Steamboat Rock State Park
Banks
Devils Punch Bowl
Boat Launch
Paynes Gulch

Hanson
Hartline el 1905
Cem

WINTHROW MORAINE (Ice Age Limit of Glacier)
Atkins Lake
Dry Falls Junction
Dry Falls Dam
Coulee City Park
Foxdair
Coulee City el 1559
Odair
Last Stand Rodeo

Viewpoint
Dry Falls Visitor Center
Head Canal Res Powerplant
Castle Lake
Sun Lakes Park Resort
Vic Meyer's Golf Course
Camp Delany ELC
Perch Lake
Deep Lake
Laurent's Sun Village Resort
Coulee Lodge Resort
Park Lake
Sun Lakes—Dry Falls State Park
Sun Lakes Wildlife Area

GRAND COULEE
Blue Lake Resort
Lake Lenore Caves
Pinto Ridge Rd
Trail Lake Coulee
Arbuckle Flats
Summer Falls Powerplant
Dry Coulee
High Hill 2074 △
Dry Coulee Rd

Billy Clapp Lake
Stratford Wildlife Area
Pinto Dam
Brook Lake 1240
Boat Ramp 1336

Little Soap Lake 1079
LOWER GRAND COULEE
Lenore Lake 1074
Stratford
Adco el 1290
Crab Creek
Wilson Creek
Wilson Creek Airport 1440
Krupp (Marlin PO) el 1310
Gun Club

Soap Lake el 1074
Boat Ramp
Lakeview Country Club
Lakeview Park
Round Lake
BNSF/AMTK

Ephrata el 1258
Grant County Museum
WA Dept of Fish & Wildlife North Central WA Regional HQ
Amtrak Station
Ephrata Muni Airport 1271
Willow Lake
Seeps
Gloyd
South Willow Lake
Ephrata Lake
Hatchery Rd
Springs
Wildlife Area
Upland Restoration Wildlife Area

RV Park & Golf
Dodson
Drumheller Rd
Rocky Ford Creek
Black Rock Lake
BLACK ROCK COULEE

© BENCHMARK MAPS

Also See Recreation Page 18

Scale 1:200,000

0 5 10 15 Miles

0 5 10 15 20 Kilometers

62

LANDSCAPE

75

Banks Lake

Castle Rock 2310

Steamboat Rock 228

Boat Launch

Northrup

Steamboat Rock State Park

Martin Falls

Banks Lake Wildlife Area

GRANT LINCOLN

Bagdad Rd

Bagdad Junction

Broadax Spring

Hasseline

White Rd

Cem

Old Coulee

Jack Woods Butte 2819

Douglas Rd

Sorensen

Elliot

Douglas Rd

Broadax Draw

Johnson

Keller

Gelb

Country Lane RV Park

Big Bend Golf

Sage Hen Rd

Stigenwalt Rd

Halverson Car

Robertson Rd

Fraser

Sherman el 2400

Halverson Canyon

Williams Rd

Williams

Wilbur Airport 2175

Wilbur el 2163

Bell RV Park

Creston el 2436

Creston Butte 2816

Govan

Bandy

Haden

Ramsey Rd

Geer Rd

Sherman Draw

Ramsey Rd

Creston South

Hanson

Almira Airfield 1950

Almira el 1911

Wilson Creek

Govan

Crick

Rux

Dreger Rd

Dreger Rd

Hartline el 1905

Cem

Lewis

Bridge

Wilson

O'Brien Rd

Stewart

Wagner Lake 2097

Watson Rd

Watson Rd

Union Valley Rd

Govan Rd

Quirk

Wagner Rd

Schuster Rd

Schuster Rd

Lone Pine

Swanson

Emil Johnson Rd

Monson

Monson Rd

Bergeau Lake 2087

Swanson Schoolhouse

Peha Rd

Peha Rd

Draper Lake 1915

Phillips Lake

Wills Lake

Christensen Rd

Kuchenbuch Rd

Canniwai Creek

Apache Pass

HOLLOW

Highland

Tolonen Rd

Booker Rd

Schmier Rd

Pfeifer Rd

Hull

Kiner Draw

Gibson Rd

Gibson

Thrall

Brown Swell

Eagle Springs Rd

Coffeepot Rd

Coffee Pot

Coffeepot Lake 1814

Rimrock Creek

Reiser Falls

Weisser

Rimrock Rd

Weishaar Rd

Coffeepot Butte 1984

Deer Lake 1738

Kiner Rd

Canniwai

Schlimmer Rd

Delfe

Janke

Lentz Rd

Irby Rd

Goetz Lake 1632

Cem

Coffee Pot

Browns Lake

Duck Lake

Kuch Rd

Schoezman Rd

Sullivan Lake 1546

Numerous Craters

Tavares Lake 1644

Trejbal Back

Tebow

Wilson Creek el 1273

Wilson Creek Airport 1440

CANNIWAI VALLEY

Webley Lake

Little Sullivan Lake

Lakeview Ranch

Neves Lake

Trejbal Back

Duck

Krupp (Marlin PO) el 1310

Burn St

Peterson Manch

Delzar Falls

Pacific Lake 1593

Lakeview

Groh Rd

Gun Club

Marlin

Marlin Rd

Irby Rd

Bobs Lakes

Schott Rd

Kaputa

Peterson Lake

Totusek Rd

Tule Lake

Lakeview Ranch

Loop

Zeiler Rd

Crab

Irby

Old Hwy Loop

Duck Lake

Desert Rd

Coyote Heights

Nemo Rd

BNSF/AMTK

Cem

Odessa el 1544

Odessa Muni Airport 1725

Nemo

Laney Brothers

BLACK ROCK COULEE

Bates Rd

King Ranch

Odessa Historisches Museum

Odessa Golf Club

Sylvan Lake 1599

Hardung

Kissler Rd

Gradel

Fink

Kagle Rd

Batum

Schafer Rd

Star Rd

Cem

Hopp

Heimbigner Rd

Weber Rd

GRANT LINCOLN

Fink Rd

Laurer Rd

Gies Rd

Schoonover Rd

Hardung

CHANNELED SCABLA

© BENCHMARK MAPS

90

Land Use and Vegetation

Forest Cropland Other

Wetland Grassland Built-Up Area

Land Ownership (Other public/tribal lands are named)

State Land (blue highlight)

BLM Land (yellow highlight)

LANDSCAPE

63

91

78

Colville Indian Reservation

Spokane Indian Reservation

Lake Roosevelt

Lake Roosevelt National Recreation Area

FERRY
LINCOLN
STEVENS
LINCOLN

BACHELOR PRAIRIE

BALD RIDGE

Sterling Point Boat-in

Seven Bays

Boat Launch

Lincoln el 490

Creston

Telford

Hawk Creek

Indian Creek

Trinkle Canyon

Larene

Hawk Creek

Swede Flats

Miles-Creston

Reinbold Rd

McCall Grade Rd

Orchard Rd

Teal Hill

Sand Flat Rd

Porcupine Bay

Cayuse Mtn △ 2749

Cayuse Cove Loop

Wilson-Cayuse Mtn

Benjamin Lake

Elijah

Flett

Little Falls Dam

Little Falls

Devils Gap

Long Lake

47°50'

Mathews Lake

Bull Run Rd

Fisher Rd

Spring Creek Canyon

Tamarack Canyon

Farwell Rd

Grange

Spring Cr Grange

Crescen

Bowie

Grays Butte 2510

Euclid Rd

Audubon Lake Wildlife Area

Bisson Rd

PCC

Reardan el 2496

47°40'

Mondovi el 2506

Four Corners

Sunset Hwy

Sunset Highway

Davenport el 2369

Lincoln Co Hist Museum

Lincoln Co Fairgrounds

Davenport Airport el 1416

Rocklyn

Whittaker Lake

Wildlife Area

Wall Lake 2040

Earl

Hanes

Cormana Lake 2033

Duck Lake

Harrington el 2140

Harrington Golf & Country Club

Mohler

Downs

Kramer Farms

Goose Butte

Pioneer Picnic Area

Gravelle

Omans

Denny Station

Hanning Butte 3049

Magnison Butte 2822

Titcheral

Waukon

Sobek

Edwall el 2330

47°30'

Bluestem

BNSF/AMTK

Coleman

Canby

Canby Bridge

Lords Valley

Brown's Lake 2101

Ames Lake

Ringwood Lake

Dixons Ponds

Williams Lake

Croskey

Sprague el 1899

Sprague Lake Resort

Fourth of July

Sprague Lake

47°20'

© BENCHMARK MAPS

US 2

WA 25

WA 28

WA 23

WA 231

WA 254

I-90

US 395

118°20' 118°10' 118°00'

Scale 1:200,000

0   5   10   15 Miles

0   5   10   15   20 Kilometers

LANDSCAPE

77

SPOKANE

Spokane Indian Reservation

Lake Roosevelt NRA

Little Falls

Long Lake

Reardan el 2496

Fairchild AFB

Airway Heights el 2370

Medical Lake el 2420

Four Lakes el 2440

Cheney el 2400

South Cheney

Eastern Washington Univ

Spokane Intl Airport 2372

Nine Mile Falls el 1592

Nine Mile Reservoir

Riverside

Four Mound Prairie

Wild Rose Prairie

Five Mile Prairie

Turnbull National Wildlife Refuge

Turnbull National Wildlife Refuge HQ

Spangle el 2420

Sprague el 1899

Fishtrap el 2272

Tyler el 2295

Edwall el 2330

Gravelle

Amber el 2265

Williams Lake 2052

Silver Lake el 2441

Bald Ridge

Shoemaker Butte 3001

Grays Butte 2510

McDowell Hill 2729

Hanning Butte 3049

Magnison Butte 2822

Fancher Butte 2941

Booth Hill 2949

Wrights Hill 2855

McDowell Lake

Philleo Lake

Chapman Lake 2154

Stubblefield Lake 2332

Badger Lake

Clear Lake el 2341

Willow

Downs Lake

Bonnie Lake

Fourth of July el 2889

Mt Godfrey 3410

Lockhart Hill 2512

Geiger Heights el 2335

Marshall el 2130

Columbia Plateau Trail

Eastern State Hospital

US 2, US 195, US 395, SR 231, SR 902, SR 904, SR 27, SR 291, SR 23

© BENCHMARK MAPS

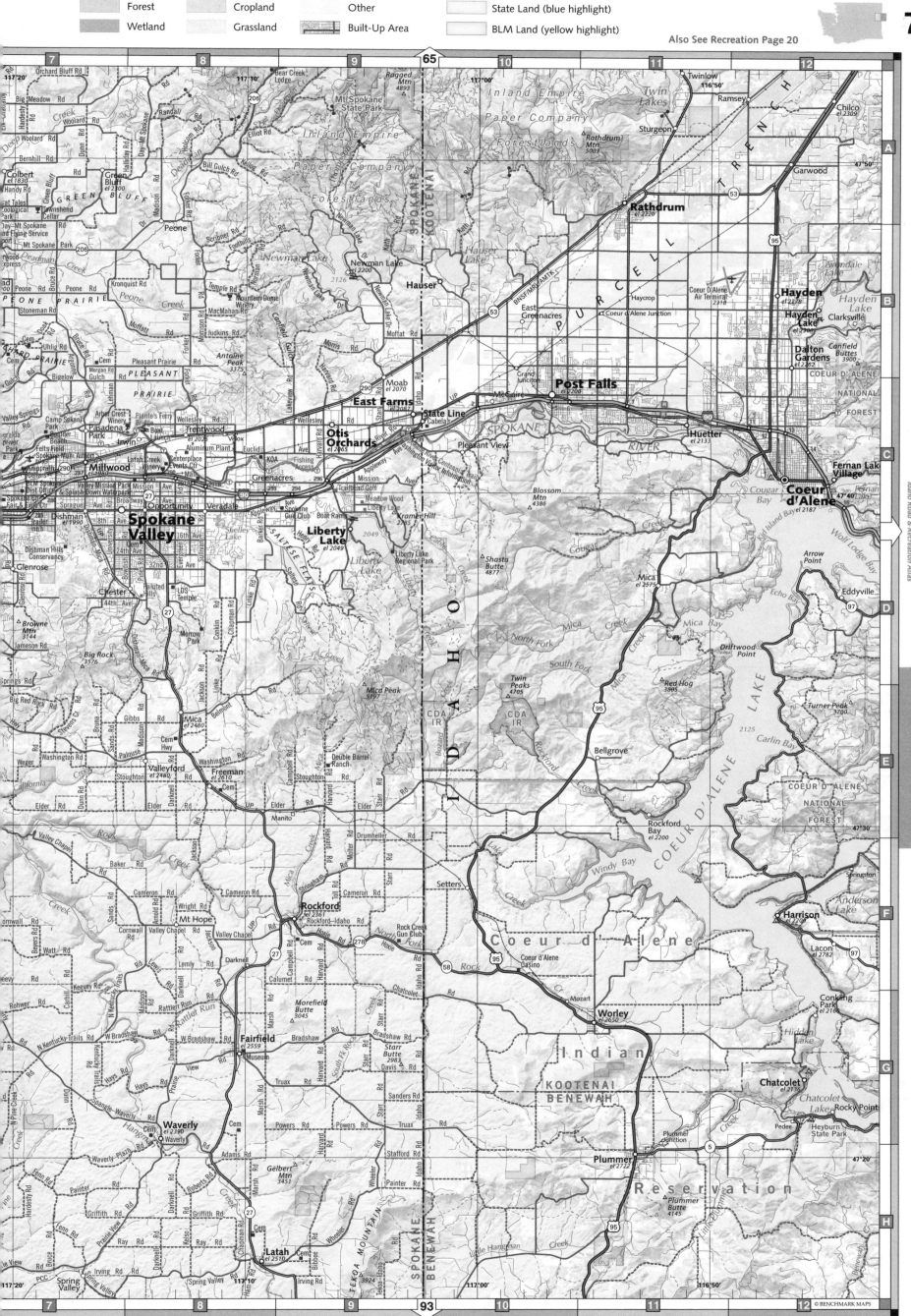

Land Use and Vegetation

Forest   Cropland   Other

Wetland   Grassland   Built-Up Area

Land Ownership (Other public/tribal lands are named)

State Land (blue highlight)

BLM Land (yellow highlight)

Also See Recreation Page 20

Continues in the Benchmark
Idaho Road & Recreation Atlas

LANDSCAPE

Scale 1:200,000

0   5   10   15 Miles

0   5   10   15   20 Kilometers

1   2   3   4   5   6

124°40'   124°30'   124°20'   124°10'

A

B

47°10'

C

D

47°00'

E

F

46°50'

G

H

LANDSCAPE

P A C I F I C

O C E A N

North Beach

State Seashore Conservation Area

Quinault
Baker
Prairie
Indian
Re

109

Moclips
Beach Access
Moclips
el 30
Museum of the
North Beach
Sunset Beach
el 100
Analyde Gap Beach Access
Highland
Heights
NW Fleet Support Center
Pacific Beach
el 50
Pacific Beach
State Park
Aloha
el 60

Ocean Grove

Roosevelt
Beach Access

Iron Springs
Boone

Copalis
Rock

Copalis
State Airport
Griffiths-Priday
Ocean State Park
Driftwood Acres
RV Park
Copalis
Beach

109

Ocean Mist RV Resort
Oceana RV Resort
Blue Pacific RV Park
Beach Access
Ocean City
el 15

Quinault Beach
Resort & Casino
Ho
Co
Ocean City
State Park
Oyhut
Beach Access
115
Oyhu
Duck Lake Wildlife Area
Chance A La Mer Beach Access
Ocean Shores Airport W
Ocean Shores
Pacific Blvd Beach Access
Ocean Lake Way Beach Access

Ocean Shores
el 10
Taurus Beach Access

Marine

North Jetty
Beach Access
Point Brown

Point Che
Westh
State
Westport
State
Grays Ha
(Westport Li

Land Use and Vegetation

Forest
Wetland
Cropland
Grassland
Other
Built-Up Area

Land Ownership (Other public/tribal lands are named)

State Land (blue highlight)
BLM Land (yellow highlight)

Also See Recreation Page 22

LANDSCAPE

Macafee Hill 655
Promised Land Park
Donkey Creek
Humptulips el 137
Humptulips Hatchery
Boat Ramp
McNutt Rd
East Humptulips
W Fk Humptulips
East Fork Humptulips

Weyerhaeuser

Aberdeen Municipal Watershed
Wynoochee
Reed Hill 1443
OWA
Mitigation
Wildlife
Area

Carlisle
Carlisle Lakes
Camp Bethel
Damon Lake
Copalis Crossing el 50
Boat Ramp
Newsom

Hoquiam Gulor Lake Municipal Watershed
Fishing Access
New London
Aberdeen Gardens
Long Swamp Boat Ramp

Weyerhaeuser
Twin
Harbors
Tree
Farm

Wishkah el 140
Nisson
Olympic Wildlife Area
Boat Ramp
Prices Peak 730
Black
Black Cr

North Bay
Grass Creek Wildlife Area
Gray Gables
Humptulips

Cranberry Bogs
Burrows
Goose Island
Sand Island
Point New
Summit
Grays Harbor City el 200
Rapture Bay (Bowerman Basin)
Sandpiper
Moon Island
Bowerman Airport 14

Lake Sylvia State Park
Sylvia Lake
Satsop
Brady
Camp Cr
Black Creek Boat Ramp
Wynoochee Valley

Hoquiam
Hoquiam Plywood
Hoquiam's Castle
Polson Park & Museum
Aberdeen Museum of History
Grays Harbor Visitor Information Center
Aberdeen Seaport Learning Center
Lady Washington (ship)
East Aberdeen
Central Park el 140
Lake Aberdeen Hatchery
Montesano el 66
Chehalis Valley Historical Museum
Monte Elma
Aberdeen el 10
Grays Harbor Paper Mill
Boat Launch
South Aberdeen el 10
Junction City
Cosmopolis
Red Cross
Alder Grove
Ferbrache SWA
South Montesano

Damon Point
Rennie Island
Grays Harbor College
Cooney Mansion
Highland
West Blvd
Devonshire
Friends Landing RV Park
Melbourne el 54

In Westport
1. Harbor Resort
2. Westport Maritime Museum
3. Coho RV Park & Totem Trailer Park
4. Holand Center (RV Park)
5. Hammond's Trailer Park
6. Lighthouse RV Resort

GRAYS HARBOR

South Grays Harbor Wildlife Area
South Arbor Stearns
Bluff
Stafford Creek Corrections Center
Johns River Wildlife Area
Blue Slough
Chehalis

Westport
Westport Airport
Bottle Beach State Park
Markham
Ocosta el 46
Boat Ramp
South Bay
Weyerhaeuser

Artic RV Park
Artic el 105
Weyerhaeuser

Grass Island
Cohassett el 120
Bay City el 36
Elk River Wildlife Area
Twin Harbors Beach State Park
Pacific Motel & Trailer Park
Ocean Gate Resort

NORTH RIVER DIVIDE
Twin Harbors Tree Farm

Western Shores Motel & RV Park
Cranberry Bogs
Heather el 15
Kenanna RV Park
Warrenton Cannery RV Access

Smith Creek North River Wildlife Area
Bishop
A Line
GRAYS HARBOR PACIFIC
Elkhorn Rd
Brooklyn el 188
North River Rd
Pack Sack Peak

North Cove
Cape Shoalwater
Willapa National Wildlife Refuge (Shoalwater Unit)
Shoalwater Indian Reservation
Shoalwater Bay Casino
Dexter by the Sea
Tokeland Hotel
Boat Launch
Tokeland el 15
Toke Point
Sand

WILLAPA BAY
Bruceport Park

Willapa Wetlands Wildlife Area
Smith Creek North River Wildlife Area
Boat Ramp
Butte Creek Picnic Area
Willapa Estuary (Willapa Slough) Wildlife Area
Range Point
Willapa Wetlands (Potter Slough) Wildlife Area
Willapa Harbor Airport
City Park
WILLAPA HILLS

Raymond

WILLAPA Tree Farm

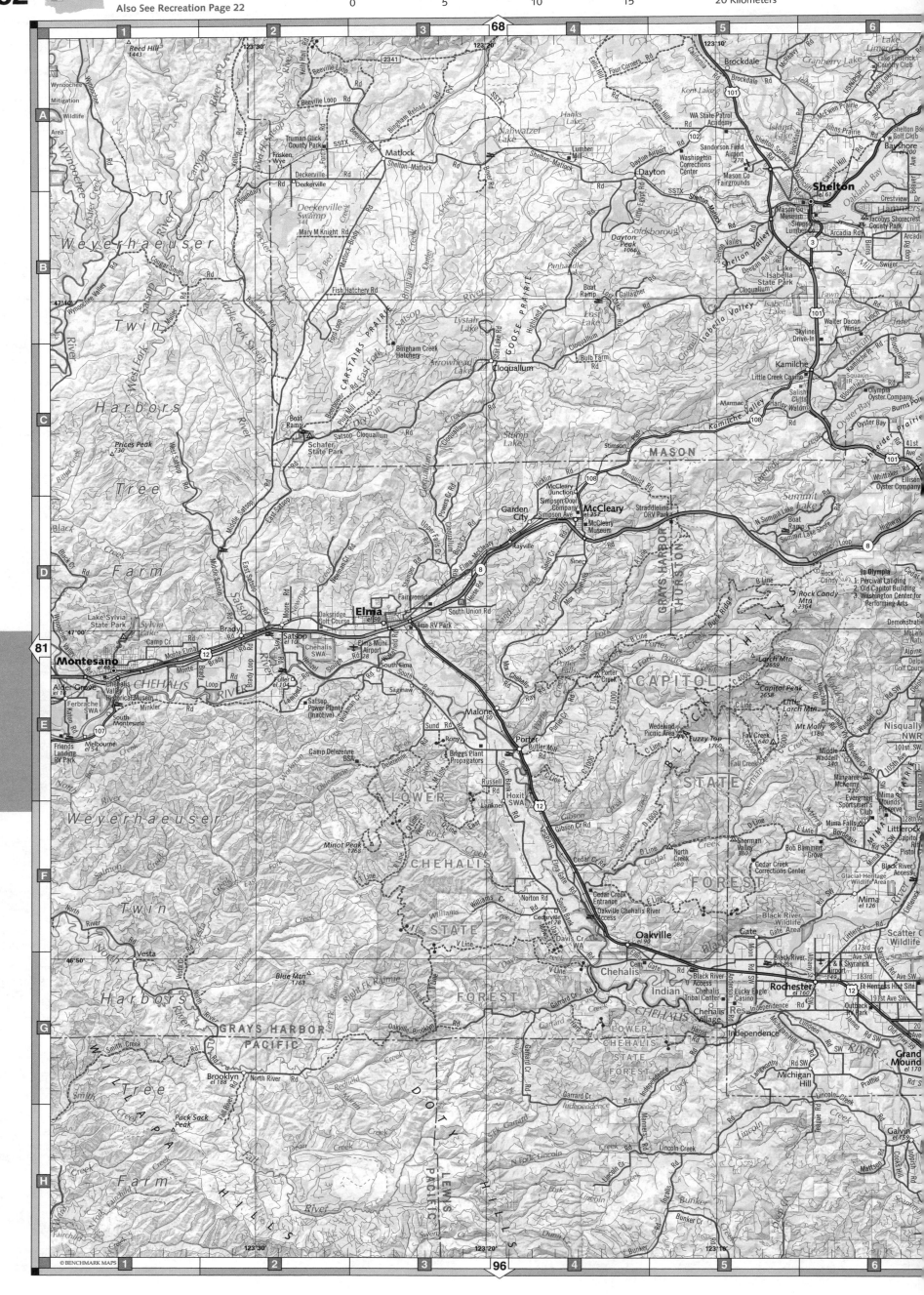

Scale 1:200,000

0   5   10   15 Miles

0   5   10   15   20 Kilometers

LANDSCAPE

© BENCHMARK MAPS

Land Use and Vegetation

- Forest
- Wetland
- Cropland
- Grassland
- Other
- Built-Up Area

Land Ownership (Other public/tribal lands are named)

- State Land (blue highlight)
- BLM Land (yellow highlight)

Also See
Recreation Page 24

LANDSCAPE

See Pages 122–123

In Tacoma
1. Tacoma Art Museum
2. State History Museum
3. Bull's Eye Indoor Range

In Centralia
1. Fort Borst Park & Boat Launch
2. Peppertree West RV Park
3. Veterans Memorial Museum & Downtown Murals
4. Amtrak Station
5. Xylien Shoe Factory
6. Centralia College

TACOMA

Ruston
Fircrest
University Place
Steilacoom
Lakewood
DuPont
Fort Lewis
Olympia
Lacey
Tumwater
Yelm
Rainier
Tenino
Bucoda
Centralia
Midland
Summit
Parkland
McChord AFB
Spanaway
Frederickson
Elk Plain
Fife
Artondale

Joint Base Lewis-McChord

Nisqually Indian Reservation

Nisqually National Wildlife Refuge

Puyallup Indian Reservation

Squaxin Island Indian Reservation

GIFFORD PINCHOT NATIONAL FOREST

© BENCHMARK MAPS

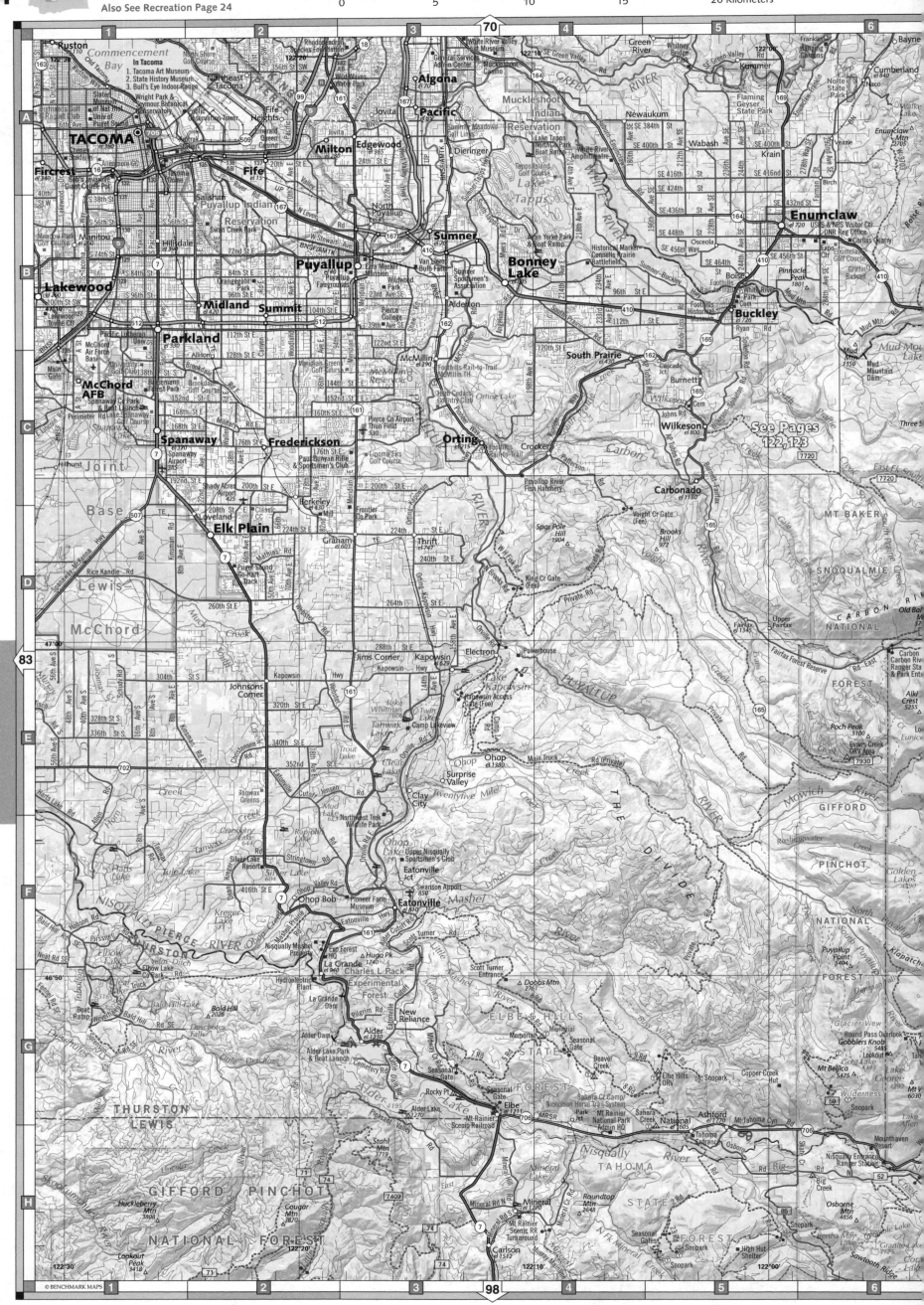

Land Use and Vegetation

- Forest
- Wetland
- Cropland
- Grassland
- Other
- Built-Up Area

Land Ownership (Other public/tribal lands are named)

- State Land (blue highlight)
- BLM Land (yellow highlight)

Also See Recreation Page 26

LANDSCAPE

MT BAKER–SNOQUALMIE NATIONAL FOREST

Howard A Hanson Reservoir
Howard A Hanson Dam
Green River Watershed
Cougar Mountain
Green River
Goat Mtn 4773
Stampede Pass 3072
OKANOGAN
WENATCHEE NATIONAL FOREST
Cabin Mountain
Yakima River WA
Cabin Creek

Rooster Comb Mtn 4105
Humphrey el 1206
(Closed to Public Entry)
Maywood
Nagrom
Lester State Ultralight
Snowshoe Butte 5135
Bearpaw Butte
Sheets Pass
Tacoma Pass

Green River
Kelly Butte 5420
Lookout
Green River Watershed
Blowout Mtn 5750
Cole Butte 5361

Federation Forest State Park
Greenwater
Catherine Montgomery Interpretive Center
MT BAKER
Twin Camp
Colquhoun Peak 5173
Pyramid Peak 5718
Naches Pass

MT BAKER–SNOQUALMIE
NATIONAL FOREST
HUCKLEBERRY MOUNTAIN
Seasonal Gate
Greenwater
Naches Pass
Greenwater Lakes
Pacific Crest Trail
Naches Pass
OKANOGAN
KITTITAS
WENATCHEE
Little Naches River

The Palisades 5300
Skookum Flats
The Dalles
Snopark
PIERCE
SNOQUALMIE
Noble Knob 6011
Lost Lake
Louisiana Saddle
Arch Rock 5903
Norse Peak
Raven Roost
NATIONAL

Frog Mtn 5236
Clearwater Wilderness
Camp Sheppard BSA
Sun Top 5270
Sun Top
Buck Creek Camp
NATIONAL FOREST
Little Ranger Peak
Skookum Flats/Ranger Cr
Noble Nob
Greenwater Lakes
Mutton Mtn
Corral Pass
Louisiana Saddle
Norse Peak
Cougar Valley
Crow Creek Lake
NATIONAL

Clear West Peak 5697
Lonesome Lake
Ranger Creek State Airport
Alta Crystal Resort
Silver Springs
Corral Pass
FOREST

Wallace Peak 5780
Pigeon Peak 4300
Oliver Lake
Lake Eleanor
Slide Mtn 6339
Winter Closure Gate
Snopark
White River
Norse Creek
Fifes Peaks 6793
Hells Crossing
FIFES RIDGE

Chenuis Falls
Insut Creek
Tyee Peak
Redstone Peak 5700
Crescent Lake
Elysian Fields
Old Desolate 6995
Marcus Peak 6962
McNeeley Peak 6786
Glidden Lakes
Closed In Winter
Crystal Mountain Ski Resort 7002
Big Crow Basin
Norse Mtn 6856
Picnic Area
Snopark
Goat Peak 6473
Cougar Flat

Mount Rainier
Mt Fremont 7291
Sunrise Lodge Visitor Center
White River
Crystal Mtn 6800
Gold Hill 6295
Lodgepole
Closed In Winter
OKANOGAN
1800

Fay Peak 6492
PTARMIGAN RIDGE
Russell Cliff
Burroughs Mtn
Goat Island Mtn 7288
White River Ranger Station Entrance
Deadwood Lakes
Mather Memorial Parkway
Rainier Fk American River
WENATCHEE

Liberty Cap 14122
Camp Schurman
Little Tahoma Peak 11138
Fryingpan Glacier
Tamanos Mtn 6790
Barrier Peak 6514
Cayuse Pass 4694
Yakima Peak 6432
Chinook Pass
Naches Peak
Dewey Lake 5112
Big Basin
Bumping Lake Big Trees
Boat Ramp
Bumping Lake 3426

St Andrews Rock 10992
MOUNT RAINIER 14411 (Highest Point in Washington)
Camp Muir
Buell Peak 5933
123

Anvil Rock 9584
Cowlitz Park
Double Peak 6199
Seymour Peak 6391
Swamp Lake
American Lake
WENATCHEE

Pyramid Peak 6937
McClure Rock
Pan Lake
Shriner Peak 5834
Cougar Lake 4015
Mt Aix 7766

Mt Ararat
Copper Mtn
National Park
Paradise Inn
H M Jackson Mem Visitor Ctr
Paradise
Panther Creek
Shriner Lake
Lookout
Crag Mtn 6208
Bismarck Peak 7585

Satulick Mtn 5674
Ricksecker Pt
Reflection Lakes
STEVENS RIDGE
Box Canyon Interpretive Trail
Grove of the Patriarchs
Closed In Winter
PIERCE
LEWIS
Carlton Pass
1808
NATIONAL FOREST

Cougar Rock
Longmire
Longmire Museum & Wilderness Info Center
Kautz Cr View Pt
Carter Falls
Chutla Peak
Pinnacle Peak 6562
Snow Lake
Maple Falls
Stevens Peak 6510
Canyon
Box Canyon Picnic Area
Closed In Winter
Stevens Canyon Entrance
Ohanapecosh
Three Lakes
Carlton Pass
NATIONAL FOREST
Pepr Butte
Rattlesnake Peaks 6583

Wahpenayo Peak 6231
Unicorn Peak 6917
TATOOSH RANGE
Blue Lake
Ohanapecosh Hot Springs
Ranger Station
Ohanapecosh Visitor Center
Frying Pan Mtn
Twin Sisters Lakes
Mosquito Valley
Arnesons Peak 6298

GIFFORD PINCHOT
NATIONAL FOREST
Lookout Mtn 5475
Tatoosh Wilderness
Stevens Cyn Rd
Laurel Hill 4260
Summit Creek
Soda Springs
Jug Lake
Penoyer Lake
Snow Lake
Tumac Mtn 6340
McNeil Peak 6658
Shellrock Peak 6835

GIFFORD PINCHOT NATIONAL FOREST
Palisades
Summit Creek
Pine Lakes
Buesch Lake
Dumbbell Lake
Cramer Lake
Cramer Mtn 5992
Ironstone Mtn 6441

© BENCHMARK MAPS

Scale 1:200,000

0 5 10 15 Miles

0 5 10 15 20 Kilometers

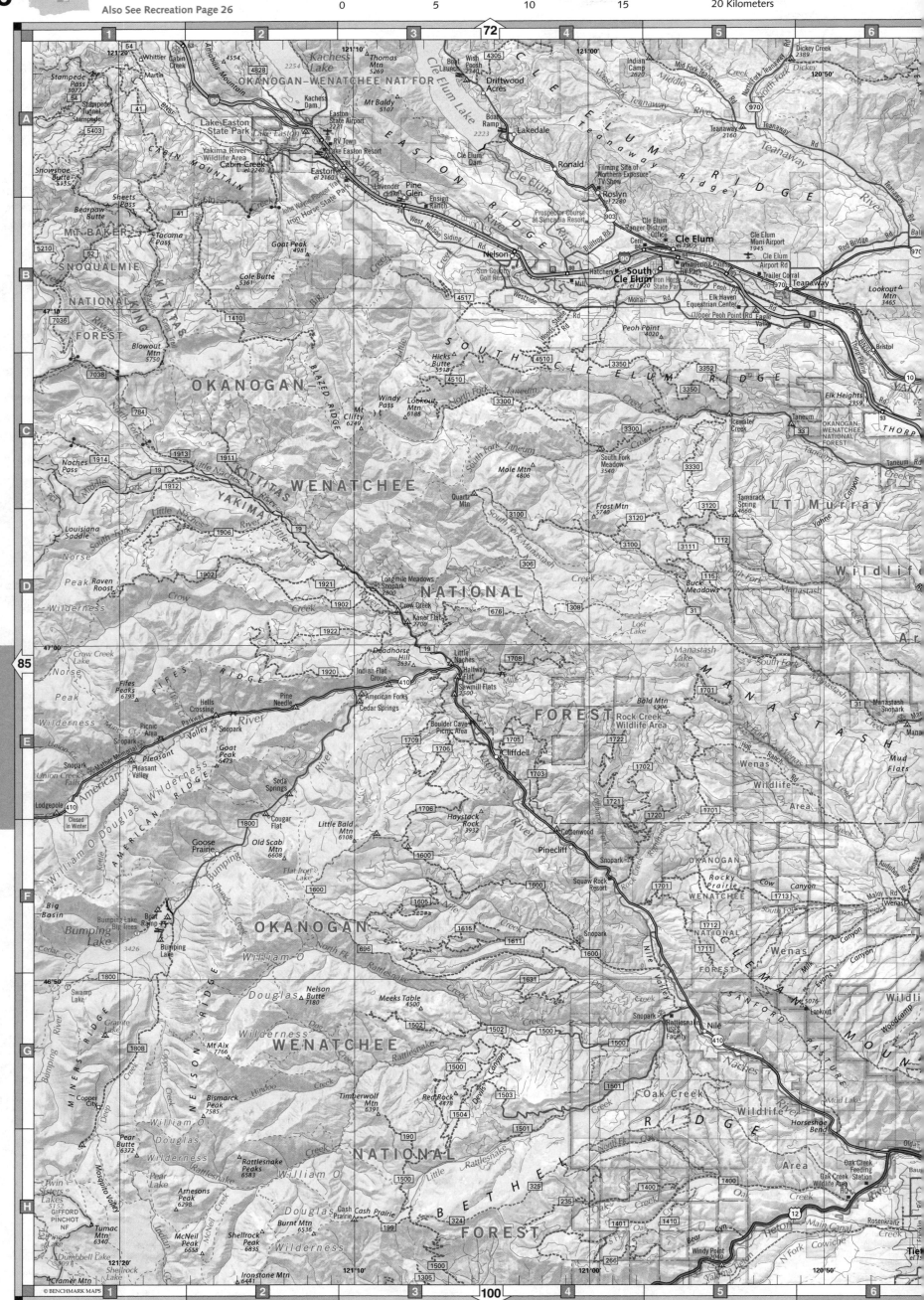

Land Use and Vegetation

- Forest
- Wetland
- Cropland
- Grassland
- Other
- Built-Up Area

Land Ownership (Other public/tribal lands are named)

- State Land (blue highlight)
- BLM Land (yellow highlight)

LANDSCAPE

OKANOGAN-WENATCHEE NATIONAL FOREST

TABLE MOUNTAIN

CHELAN KITTITAS

Colockum Wildlife Area

Colockum Wildlife Area HQ

Mission Ridge Ski Area

Mission Peak 6876

Wenatchee Mtn 6742

Naneum Point

NANEUM RIDGE

JUMPOFF RIDGE

Colockum Pass 5373
Not recommended for passenger cars

Quilomene Wildlife Area

Skookumchuck

Whiskey Dick Mtn 3878

Whiskey Dick Wildlife Area

SCHNEBLY COULEE

KITTITAS VALLEY

Ellensburg

Central Washington University

Bowers Field Airport 1766

WA DNR SE Reg HQ

Kittitas

East Kittitas

Thorp

Liberty

Lion Rock Spring Lookout 6200

Reecer Creek Snopark

Cooke Canyon Hunt Club

BOYLSTON MOUNTAINS

Iron Horse State Park (Permits Required)

Boylston

Ryegrass Pass 2535

Hult Butte 2110

MANASTASH RIDGE

Umtanum Creek Rec Site

Vanderbilt Gap

Manastash Ridge 2672

Viewpoint

BADGER POCKET

BADGER RIDGE

Badger Gap 2381

McDonald Spring

SADDLE MOUNTAINS

Cheviot

Rye

WENAS RIDGE

Wenas Wildlife Area

Wenas Lake

Stagecoach RV Resort

Naches Ranger District Office

Naches

Wymer

Squaw Creek Rec Site

Tendollar Spring

Baldy 3225

Big Pines

Rozah

Roza Rec Site

Boat Ramp

Hillside Siding

Windy Spring

North Umtanum Ridge 2315

South Umtanum Ridge 2265

Selah Butte 3024

YAKIMA FIRING CENTER

KITTITAS
YAKIMA

UMTANUM RIDGE

Pomona

Selah

Pushtay 1845

BURBANK VALLEY

© BENCHMARK MAPS

Scale 1:200,000

| 0 | 5 | 10 | 15 Miles |

| 0 | 5 | 10 | 15 | 20 Kilometers |

LANDSCAPE

© BENCHMARK MAPS

120°10' 120°00' 120°00' 119°50' 119°40'

47°10'

47°00'

46°50'

CHELAN
KITTITAS

DOUGLAS
GRANT

Kingsbury Rd
Colockum Rd
North Fork
South Fork
Colockum Rd
Not recommended for passenger cars
Closed in Winter

Colockum Wildlife Area HQ

Colockum

Tarpiscan Creek
Brewton
Stray Horse Gulch
Tekison

Wildlife
Area

Quilomene
Wildlife
Area

Whiskey Dick Mtn 3878

Whiskey Dick
Wildlife
Area

Skookumchuck
North Fork
Patte Canyon
Hartman Creek
Whiskey Dick Creek

Schnebly Hwy
Vantage
Poison Spring
Ryegrass Pass 2535
Hult Butte 2110
Rock Spring

Ryegrass

Lone Star Spring
ROCKY COULEE
Gingko
Petrified Forest
Vantage Riverstone Resort

RYEGRASS COULEE
State
Park
Ryegrass Mtn 1530

Boylston
Iron Horse State Park (Permits Required)
Cheviot

BOYLSTON MOUNTAINS

Middle Canyon
Johnson
Rye
Foster

SADDLE

MOUNTAINS

McDonald Spring
Doris el 1081
John Wayne Trail Kiosk
Beverly Junction

Yakima

Hanson Creek

Cottonwood Creek
North Fork Squaw
Squaw Creek

Firing Center

KITTITAS
YAKIMA

Alkali Canyon
Corral Canyon
Cow Cyn

COLUMBIA RIVER

West Bar
Cape Horn 2241

Crescent Bar Resort
Crescent Bar
Crescent Bar Resort Golf Course

BABCOCK RIDGE
BABCOCK BENCH

White Heron Cellars
Trinidad
Babcock Ridge Lake Boat Launch
Crater

Quincy Lakes
Ancient Lake
Dusty Lake
Evergreen Reservoir

Wildlife
POTHOLES
Area

The Gorge Amphitheatre
The Gorge Amphitheatre Box Office & Parking
Cave B Estate Winery
Wildhorse

QLWA Sunland Estates
Sunland Rd
Scammon Landing
Frenchman Spring

Vantage
QLWA
Babcock Bench

Boat Ramp
Wild Horses Monument Scenic View

WANAPUM

Wanapum Vista
Wild Horses Monument Scenic View

Vantage Park

137
90
243

Wanapum State Rec Area

Wanapum Dam & Heritage Center

Wanapum Village

Beverly Dunes ORV Site
Merry Lake
Lenice Lake
Jericho

Beverly el 547
Schwana

SENTINEL GAP
SENTINEL BLUFFS
Sentinel Mtn 2410

Levering

Mattawa el 778

GRANT

PRIEST RAPIDS LAKE

Priest Rapids SWA
Fox Estate Winery

Desert Aire Airport 570
Desert Aire

Boat Ramp

WAHLUKE SLOPE

Wahluke Slope Rd

74

102

Quincy Lateral Canal
West Canal

Monument Hill Golf Course
13 NW
12.5 NW
12 NW
11 NW
10.5 NW

Winchester
BNSF/AMTK
Livestock Market
Upland Restoration
Wildlife Area

28
Hospital
Quincy el 1295
9 NW
Quincy Municipal Airport 1268
8 NW
8.5 NW
8.2 NW
283

281
Quincy Valley Golf Course

Stan Collin Lake 1270
Boat Ramps
Quincy Lake
Burke Lake
Boat Ramps
Boat Ramp

Shady Tree RV
N Frontage Rd
151
149
154
Baseline Rd
Baseline Rd

George el 1222

Martha Lake Boat Ramp

Beverly Burke
Feed Lot

Winchester
Wasteway
Wildlife Area

Desert Wildlife Area

N Frontage Rd
S Frontage Rd

FRENCHMAN HILLS

Low Gap
Low Gap Pass
Frenchman Hill

Fishing Access

West Canal

Frenchman Hills Wasteway

26
SAND HOLLOW

Toes Motocross Park

Stillwater Creek Vineyard
Stillwater Creek

Feed Lot

Royal City el 1040
Cash Butte 1065

Columbia National Wildlife Refuge
&
Crab Creek Wildlife Area

SMYRNA

Crab Creek
Lower Crab Creek
Smyrna

SADDLE

Saddle Mtns ORV Area

24
Saddle Mountain Lake

Land Use and Vegetation

Forest
Cropland
Other
Wetland
Grassland
Built-Up Area

Land Ownership (Other public/tribal lands are named)

State Land (blue highlight)
BLM Land (yellow highlight)

© BENCHMARK MAPS

LANDSCAPE

Map labels

Gloyd
Gloyd Seeps Wildlife Area
Black Rock Lake
Artesian Lake 1296
Black Lake 1237
SAND COULEE
ROCKY COULEE
Black Rock Coulee
Rocky Coulee Wasteway
Cem
Ruff
GRANT
ADAMS

RV Park & Golf
Dodson Rd
Empire Rd
Rocky Ford Rd
Old Moses Lake Rd
Drumheller Rd
Stratford Rd
Randolph Rd

GSWA
Boat Ramp
Neppel Rd
Lake Vista Dr
Stonecrest Dr
Moses Lake
Grant County International Airport 1185
Big Bend College
Columbia Basin Habitat Management HQ
Columbia Basin Hatchery
Feed Lot Mitchell
McConihe Rd
Boat Ramp
Connelly Park

Cascade Valley
Cascade Fairgrounds
Cascade Park
Valley Rd
Moses Lake Muni Airport 1200
Weyerhaeuser
Simplot
Cherokee Rd

Moses Lake el 1060
Moses Lake Museum
Nelson
Wheeler
Laing

Mae Valley Rd
Mae
Westlake
Moses Lake CC
Suncrest Resort
Blue Heron Park
Big Sun Resort
Montlake Park
South Campus Golf Course
North Frontage Rd
Atwood
East Low Canal
CBRW

Frontage Rd
Baseline Rd
South Frontage
Baseline E
Baseline SE
Barham
Tiflis
CBRW
Weber Coulee
Lind Coulee

Potholes East Canal Hydroelectric Project
Sand Dunes Rd
Potato Hill
McDonald Willows Trailer Village
Sieler
Upland Restoration
Wildlife Area

Desert
March Lake
Winchester Wildlife
Potholes
POTHOLES RESERVOIR
Grant County Off Road Vehicle Area
Sand Dunes
Wildlife Area
1039
New Warden Airport 1265
West Warden
Warden el 1305
Feed Lot

Frenchman Hills Lakes
Fishing Access
Frenchman Hills Rd
THE POTHOLES
SAND HILLS
Area
Potholes State Park
MarDon Resort
O'Sullivan Dam
O'Sullivan Dam
Soda Lake 998
Seep Lakes
Sage Lakes Area
Sage Hills Golf Club & RV Resort
Windmill Lake
Jackass Mtn 1170

FRENCHMAN HILLS
Upland Restoration Wildlife Area
Potholes Golf Course
Corn Lake
Blue Lake
Chukar Lake
Goose Lakes
Upper Goose Lake
Lower Goose Lake 856
Columbia
National
Wildlife
Pit Lakes
Providence
GRANT
ADAMS

ROYAL SLOPE
Royal City Golf Course
Division Rd
West Canal
Blackbird
Drumheller Channels National Natural Landmark
Royal Lake
Hunter Hill Vineyards
Morgan Lake 821
Herman Lakes
Bad E Dairy
Campbell Lake
Green Giant Fresh Onions
McManamon
Shiner Lake
Deadman Lake
Novara el 1112
Sutton

Refuge
Canoe Launch
Hutchinson Lake
Marsh Unit
Foley
Lee
Foley
Foley
Bruce

MOUNTAINS
Wahatis Peak 2696
Lower Crab Creek
Corfu
Crab Creek
Othello el 1038
Columbia NWR
Lions Park
Cunningham Park
Kiwanis Park
Cunningham
Gillis

BENCH
Wildlife Viewing Area
Saddle Gap
Kuhn Rd
O'Brien Rd
Schaape Rd
Othello Golf Club
Hampton Rd
Othello Muni Airport 1145
Koren
Bench Rd
Hatton
Haynes
Coffman Rd
PARADISE FLATS

HANFORD REACH
Saddle Mountain Unit
WAHLUKE SLOPE
GRANT ADAMS
FRANKLIN ADAMS
Taunton el 848
TSWR
Gillis Rd
Bench Rd
Hatton
Muse
Yeisley

NATIONAL MONUMENT
Wahluke Unit
Hanford Reservation US Dept of Energy Project
Hanford Generating Project
100 D+DR Areas
100 H Area
COLUMBIA RIVER
WHITE BLUFFS
Locke Island
No Public Access
WB-10 Wasteway Wildlife Area
Eagle Lakes
Scooteney Reservoir
Scooteney Reservoir Recreation Area
Boat Ramp
Paradise
Krug Rd
Fox Rd
Coyan

Grid references

7 8 9 75 10 11 12
A B C 90 D E F G H
103
119°30' 119°20' 119°10' 119°00'
47°10' 47°00' 46°50'

Also See Recreation Page 28

Scale 1:200,000

0 ... 5 ... 10 ... 15 Miles
0 ... 5 ... 10 ... 15 ... 20 Kilometers

LANDSCAPE

GRANT
ADAMS
LINCOLN
ADAMS

SAND COULEE
ROCKY COULEE
FARRIER COULEE
BAUER COULEE
LIND COULEE
PROVIDENCE COULEE
CUNNINGHAM COULEE
HATTON COULEE
ALPHA COULEE

Black Rock
Black Rock Lake
Rock Spring
Ruff
Cem
Atwood
East Low Canal
Laing
Tiflis
Barham
Bassett Junction
Ritell
Feed Lot
Upland Restoration Wildlife Area
Warden Hutterian Brethren School
Warden el 1305
New Warden Airport 1263
West Warden
Sage Hills Golf Club
Providence el 1524
Beatrice
Servia
Lind el 1390
Experimental Station
Lind Airport 1491
Lind-Ralston
Sackman
Fode
Phillips
Williams
Presnell
Cunningham el 1190
Bruce
Koren
Othello Muni Airport 1145
Bench
Hampton
Hatton el 1110
Michigan Prairie
Sand Hills
Paradise Flats
Adams Franklin
Eagle Lakes
Scooteney Reservoir
Scooteney Reservoir Recreation Area
Boat Ramp

Roads: Kissler, Graedel, Moody, Fink, Schafer, Davis, Arlt, Johnson, Deal, Klum, Batum, Dyck, Damon, Lobe, Lauer, Gies, Heimbigner, Weber, Hardung, Schoonover, Griffith, Tokio, Seidl, Rehn, Snowden, Neilson, Schoessler, Rosenoff, Weber, Heineman, Koch, Roxboro, Schrag, Gering, Urquhart, Harder, Leisle, Franz, Roloff, Calloway, Hiller, Hoffman, Rowe, Howard, Johnson, Providence, Herman, Sutton, Foley, Lee, Lucy, Booker, Steele, Simenson, Rankin, Lemaster, Billington, Cunningham, Gillis, Haynes, Hatton, Coffman, Yeisley, Rayburn, Fox, Muse, Coyan, Dilling, Paradise, Buehler, Moon, Warehouse, Settler, Krug, Schlomer, Meyers, Myers, Lind, Hoover, Lone Star, Brown, Copp, Struthers, Klaus, Wadsworth, Reader, Ritchards, Watson, Reeves, Lewis, Foulkes, Longmeier, Sievers, Lind-Kahlotus, Lind-Hatton, Lind-Warden, Wahl, Neilson, Jantz, Anderson, Longmeier

Highways: 76, 104, 90, 184, 188, 196, 206, 21, 17, 89, 262, 170, 395, 26, 28

© BENCHMARK MAPS

Land Use and Vegetation

Forest
Wetland
Cropland
Grassland
Other
Built-Up Area

Land Ownership (Other public/tribal lands are named)

State Land (blue highlight)
BLM Land (yellow highlight)

LANDSCAPE

Crab Creek
Goose Butte
LINCOLN / ADAMS
WHITMAN / ADAMS
Sprague el 1899
Sprague Lake Resort
Sprague Lake
Four Seasons Resort
Harper Island
Fishing Access
Sprague Lake Wildlife Area
Keystone
Danekas
Pifer
Palm Lake
Fourth of July Lake 1887
Alkali Lake 1874
Sheep Lake 1924
Crooked Knee Lake 1942
Folsom Lake 1946
Lamont el 1949
Palm Lake 1851
Berry Lake 1884
Swannock
Stoner Lake
Marcellus
Tokio
Carico Hills
Green Lake 1784
Ashby
Rockwell
Columbia Plateau
Twin Lakes 1735
Lugenbeel Lake
Hallin Lake 1760
Cow Lake 1749
Emden
Crane Lake 1709
Sims Lake 1663
Horseshoe Lake
Lakin
Revere
Revere Wildlife Area
Ritzville el 1825
Pru Field Airport 1790
Ritzville Municipal Golf Course
Finnell Lake 1674
Teske
Carlmar
Paxton
Wall Lake 1621
Rock Creek
Harder
McCall
Marengo
Hillcrest
Twelvemile Lake 1540
Tawell Falls
Hergen Lake
Johnson Lake
Lake Sixteen
McELROY COULEE
McElroy Lake
Ralston el 1657
Keller Memorial Park
Calloway
Mud Spring
Ralston–Benge
Thavis
Benge–Ritzville
Columbia Plateau
Benge–Winona
Endicott West
Pizarro
Lind-Ralston
Presnell
Bemis Cemetery
Providence
Benge el 1450
Pheasant Valley Sporting Clays
Sutton
RATTLESNAKE FLAT
Herman
Coyote Butte 1729
Lost Lake 1431
Benge–Washtucna
Mack Creek
ADAMS / WHITMAN
Palouse River
Union Flat
Foley
Ankeny
Negro Lake 1434
Turner Springs
Sutton
Wise
Cunningham
Green Lake
Kennedy Lake 1307
Scharpenberg Hill
La Crosse el 1481
Gillis
Benge–Washtucna COULEE
Staley COULEE
Stark
Gray
Pampa
Willow Creek
COLLIER COULEE
Hampton
Hatton
Washtucna el 1024
ADAMS / FRANKLIN
Hooper Junction
Hooper
Gordon
Old SR 26 Rd
PLRR
Palouse River
Beacon Hill 1880
WASHTUCNA COULEE
Sperry
McAdam
Deep Lake
Little Palouse Falls
Palouse Falls
Wildcat Lake 1122
Thomas Flat
McGregor Lakes
Shreck
Mud Flat

© BENCHMARK MAPS

Scale 1:200,000

15 Miles
20 Kilometers

LANDSCAPE

78

106

91

Sprague el 1899

LINCOLN
WHITMAN
SPOKANE

ADAMS
WHITMAN

Fourth of July Lake 1882

Alkali Lake 1874
Sheep Lake 1924
Crooked Knee 1944
Folsom Lake 1944
Stoner Lake

Lamont el 1949

Berry Lake 1882
Twin Lakes 1735

Rockwell

Reveret
Revere Wildlife Area

Plixton

Wall Lake 1627
Rock Creek

Williams Lake Rd
Columbia Plateau Trail–Martin Road
Martin

Rodna
Downs Lake Resort
Downs Lake 1958
Feustal Lake
Miller Ranch Hunting Preserve
Reed Rd

Martin Rd
Martin

Tule Lake 1725
Alkali Lake 1865

Rock Lake
Boat Ramp
Lavista
Lavista Lake
Gene Webb

Ewan
Rock Creek Falls
Stevens Lake 1723
Duck Lake 1723
Cottonwood
Creek

Pierson
Dodge
Rogers

Lancaster

Cherry Cove Lake 1505

Downing

Palouse River

Towell Falls
Hensen Lake
Lake Sixteen
Johnson Lake

Winona el 1487
Endicott West Rd

Endicott el 1706
Rebel Flat

Pheasant Valley Sporting Clays

Sutton

ADAMS
WHITMAN
Palouse River

Union Flat Creek

La Crosse el 1481
La Crosse Airport

Scharpenberg

Pampa

Jerita el 1568

Beacon Hill 1880
Shreck

THE PALOUSE

SNAKE RIVER
Lake Bryan
Ilia Landing Boat Ramp

Penawawa el 640

Dusty el 1683

Almota

194

Malden el 2140
Rosalia Municipal Airport 2170

Rosa el 22
Ste
Battle State

Pine City el 2040
Kenova

Hole-in-the-Ground

Stepto Battlefield Heritage Area

St John
St John Golf & Country Club
PLRR

Balder
Balder Rd

Stoneham

Thornton el 2291

Huntley Gulch

Cashup
Cashup Flat

Old State Hwy

Thera

Manning

Palouse River

Diamond el 2040
Rebel Flat

Morley

Perkins House

Mockonema el 2130
Palouse Empire Fairgrounds
Whitman Co. Memorial Airport 2171

Co

Wilcox

26

127

Little Alkali

Goose Creek

Summit

127

© BENCHMARK MAPS

26

23

PLEASANT VALLEY

Land Use and Vegetation

- Forest
- Wetland
- Cropland
- Grassland
- Other
- Built-Up Area

Land Ownership (Other public/tribal lands are named)

- State Land (blue highlight)
- BLM Land (yellow highlight)

Also See Recreation Page 30

LANDSCAPE

Continues in the Benchmark
Idaho Road & Recreation Atlas

© BENCHMARK MAPS

Coeur d' Alene

Indian   Reservation

St. Joe National Forest

Benewah   Latah National   Forest

THE   PALOUSE

PALOUSE   RANGE

IDAHO

SPOKANE / WHITMAN

BENEWAH

WHITMAN / LATAH

Major places: Latah, Tekoa, Willard, Tensed, De Smet, Sanders, Benewah, Oaksdale, Farmington, Belmont, Garfield, Elberton, Glenwood, Palouse, Onaway, Potlatch, Harvard, Princeton, Viola, Albion, Pullman, Moscow, Troy, Kitzmiller, Whelan, Shawnee, Parvin, Risbeck

Steptoe Butte State Park, Kamiak Butte County Park / National Natural Landmark, Mary Minerva McCroskey Memorial State Park

Washington State University, University of Idaho

Summits: Steptoe Butte 3612, Granite Butte 2907, Shovel Hill 2930, Stratton Butte 3292, Ladow Butte 3296, Smoot Hill 3022, Kamiak Butte 3651, Ball Butte 3330, Parker Butte 3310, Rocky Point 3737, Basalt Hill 3295, Gold Hill 4661, Moscow Mtn 4983, Tomer Butte 3466, Moses Mtn 4949, Squaw Hump 3060, Mineral Mtn 4128, Mission Mtn 4324, Crane Point 3952, Prospect Peak 4138, Moon Hill 3145, Lolo Pass 3373

Highways: 27, 271, 272, 274, 195, 194, 270, 6, 9, 95, 66, 60, 8, 99, 79, 107

Scale 1:200,000

0   5   10   15 Miles

0   5   10   15   20 Kilometers

80

1   2   3   4   5   6

124°40′   124°30′   124°20′   124°10′

A

46°40′

B

C

46°30′

D

E

46°20′

F

G

46°10′

H

A

124°40′   124°30′   124°20′   124°10′

1   2   3   4   5   6

P A C I F I C

O C E A N

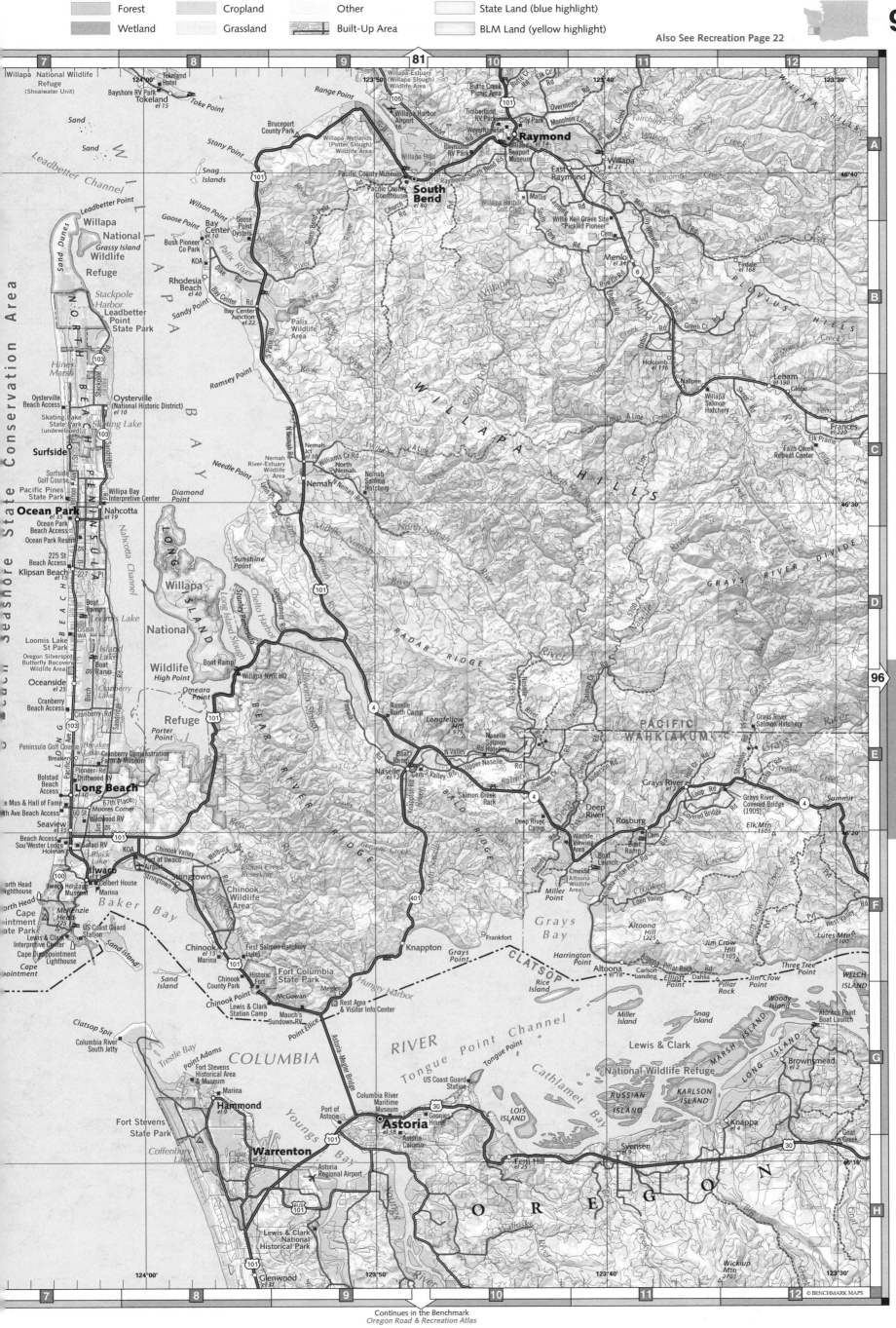

Land Use and Vegetation

Forest   Cropland   Other

Wetland   Grassland   Built-Up Area

Land Ownership (Other public/tribal lands are named)

State Land (blue highlight)

BLM Land (yellow highlight)

LANDSCAPE

Scale 1:200,000

0　　　　　5　　　　　10　　　　　15 Miles

0　　　5　　　10　　　15　　　20 Kilometers

LANDSCAPE

WILLAPA HILLS

PLUVIUS HILLS

DOTY HILLS

Fairchild Cr
Fairchild
Wilson
Whitcomb Creek
Wick Creek
Mill Creek
Mill Wheaton Rd
Menlo
el 34
Firdale el 168
Holcomb el 176
Nallpee
Lebam el 190
Globe
Green Cr Rd
Frances el 220
Willapa Salmon Hatchery
Elk Prairie
Falls Creek Retreat Center
Willapa Falls
Walville Peak 2419
Fall River
Seven Creek
Eight Creek
Elk Cr
Murnen
Chandler Rd
Dryad el 301
Doty el 300
Leudinghaus Rd
Rainbow Falls
Rainbow Falls State Park
Bucks Knob 2395
Bunker
Bunker Creek
Bunker Rd
Ingalls Rd
Meskill
Bunker
Adna
Littell el 790
Brockway
McLaughlin Rd
Claquato
Historic Church
Milburn
Ceres Hill
Ceres el 232
Curtis
Moon Hill Rd
Beaver Cr
Hubbard Rd
Klaber
Crego Rd
el 147
Boistfort
Sam Henry Mtn 1492

Pe Ell el 412
Pe Ell Sportsman's Club
McCormick Rd
Walville
Pluvius
Beam Rd
Pe Ell Ave
Wells Rd
Pe Ell Prairie
Joy Mtn 1780
Stowe Creek

HUCKLEBERRY RIDGE
Crim Creek
Frisk Falls
Bolstfort Peak 3110
Round Knob 2127
Sure Shot Mtn 1704
Little Mtn 1610
Point Hill 740
Wildwood el 352

GRAYS RIVER DIVIDE
LONG RIDGE
East Fork Grays
Kitchell Creek
Thrash Creek
Little Onion 2664
Clinton Knob 2380
Ferrier Peak 2448
Ryderwood el 220
Abernathy Mtn 2620
Stillwater

PACIFIC / WAHKIAKUM
Grays River Salmon Hatchery
Grays River
Grays River Covered Bridge (1905)
Summit
Elk Mtn 1505
Rosburg el 46
Boat Ramp
Covered Bridge
Loop Rd
Eden Valley
Crooked Creek
Altoona Hill 1225
Jim Crow Hill 1105
West Valley
Lutes Mtn 1100
Fairground
Skamokawa Natl Historic District el 26
Skamokawa Vista Park
Redmen Hall River Life Interpretive Center
Boat Ramp
Three Tree Point
Jim Crow Point
Pillar Rock
Carlson Landing
Elliott Point
Dahlia
Skamokawa Pass 1590
Skamokawa Truck Trail
Niger Truck Trail
Standard Creek
Ingalls Rd
Wilson Creek
Crown Point 1815
Alger Creek
Wildlife Viewing Area
Elochoman Hatchery
Bradley Truck Trail
Wisconsin Truck Trail
Incline Truck Trail
Abernathy Truck Trail
East and West Trail

WILDLIFE REFUGE
WELCH ISLAND
Julia Butler Hansen Refuge
Woody Island
Aldrich Point Boat Launch
COLUMBIAN WHITE-TAILED DEER
TENASILLAHE ISLAND
HUNTING ISLANDS
Risk Slough
Steamboat Slough
Refuge HQ
Beaver Cr
Beaver Creek Hatchery
Cathlamet el 53
Wahkiakum Museum
Skyline Golf Course
Greenwood Rd
Cem
Foster Rd
Abernathy Fish Technology Center
Abernathy Cr Wildlife Area
Robertson
Oak Point el 346
Stella el 21
Eufaula

PACIFIC / LEWIS
LEWIS / COWLITZ
WAHKIAKUM / COWLITZ

Miller Island
Snag Island
KARLSON ISLAND
RUSSIAN ISLAND
National
Lewis & Clark
MARSH ISLAND
LONG ISLAND
Brownsmead el 2
Clifton el 15
Bradwood el 8
Knappa
Gnat Creek
WELCH ISLAND
Wahkiakum Ferry
MARV's RV Park
Little Island
Cross Dike Rd
Puget Island
Sunny Sands
Wauna el 16
Brown Island
Flandersville
Cape Horn
Waterford
Eagle Cliffs
Nassa Point
COLUMBIA RIVER
White Island Wildlife Area
Wallace Island
Locoda el 14
Mayger el 19
Quincy el 18
Fisher Island WA
Long Alumi

OREGON
Nicolai Ridge
Wickiup Mtn 2703
Taylorville el 9
Westport
Westport Boat Ramp
Kerry el 20
Marshland el 53
Woodson
Clatskanie el 13
Inglis el 53
County Line Park
Historical Museum
Willow Grove Beach Boat Ramp
Willow Grove
Crims Island
Ocean Beach Hwy
Stella
Oak Pt Rd
Germany Hill
Fall Cr Rd
Coal Cr
Harmony

Minor and 4WD roads shown may be subject to closure or be impassable. Inquire locally for current conditions, closures, and restrictions.

© BENCHMARK MAPS

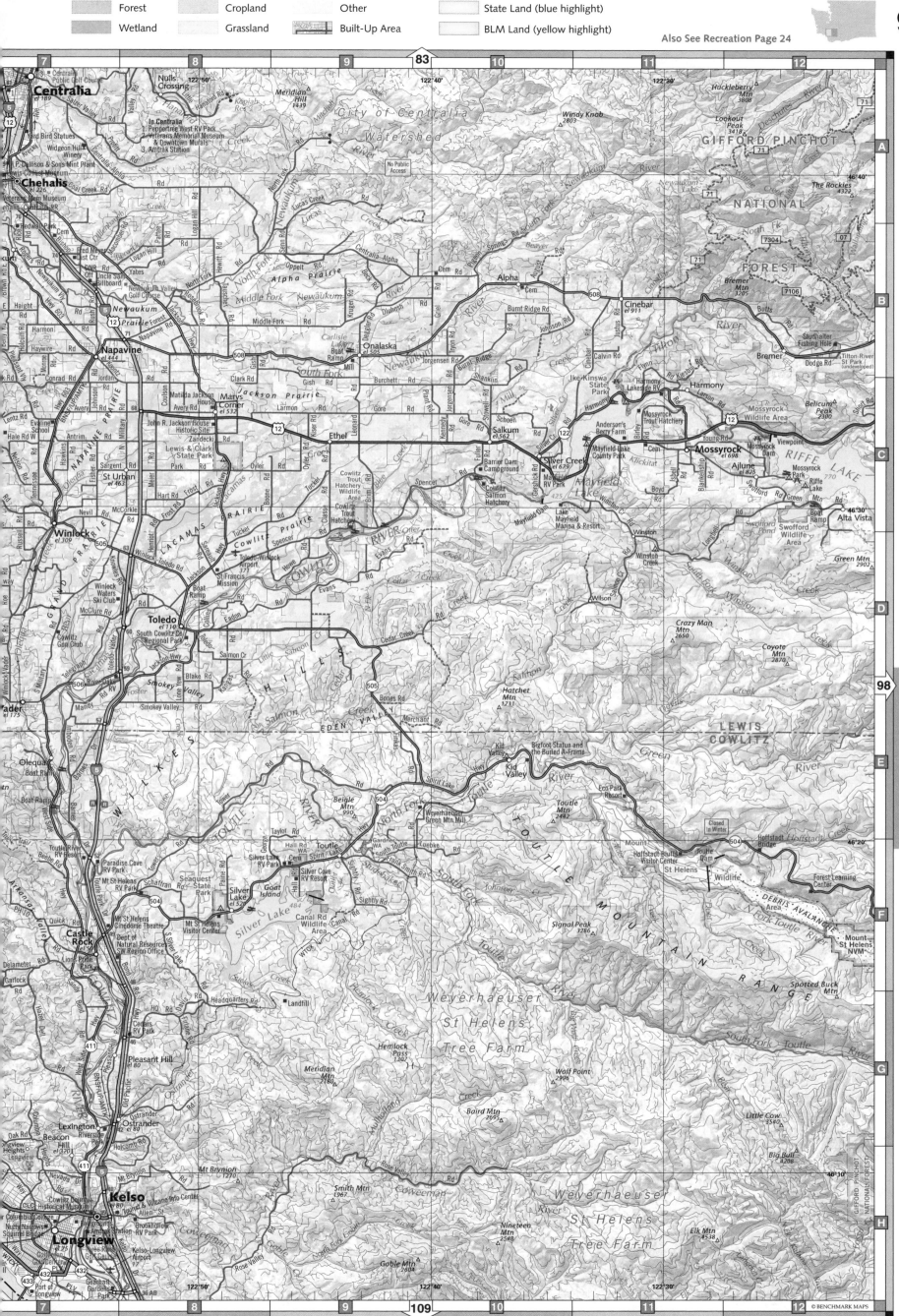

Land Use and Vegetation

Forest Cropland Other

Wetland Grassland Built-Up Area

Land Ownership (Other public/tribal lands are named)

State Land (blue highlight)

BLM Land (yellow highlight)

Also See Recreation Page 24

Scale 1:200,000

0   5   10   15 Miles

0   5   10   15   20 Kilometers

LANDSCAPE

GIFFORD PINCHOT NATIONAL FOREST

Huckleberry Mtn 1808
Lookout Peak 3418
Cougar Mtn 3870
The Rockies 4322
Newaukum Lake
Bremer Mtn 3205
Bergen Mtn 3780
Storm King Mtn 4752
Roundtop Mtn 4648
Mt Rainier Scenic Railroad
Mineral 1770
Carlson 1512
Mineral Lake
TAHOMA STATE FOREST
Osborne Mtn 4856
High Hut Shelter
Snowbowl Hut Shelter
Griffin Mtn 5263

Studhalter Fishing Hole
Bremer
Dodge Rd
Tilton River St Park (undeveloped)
Hapgood Rock
Murray Rd
Johnson Mtn 4330
Lookout
Kiona Peak 4849
Watch Mtn 4805

Mayfield Lake
Mossyrock Trout Hatchery
Mossyrock el 698
Mossyrock Dam
Belicum Peak 2300
Morton el 940
Strom Field Airport 950
Centralia College East
Cottlers Rock 2669
Glenoma el 821
Ironwood Green Hill
Randle
Cowlitz Valley Ranger District Office
Maple Grove Resort
Randle-Kiona Airpark (Pvt)
Maple Grove Spears WA

Ajlune el 825
Mossyrock Park
Riffe Lake
Alta Vista
Swofford Pond
Swofford Wildlife Area
Green Mtn 2902
Peterman Ridge Wildlife Area
Priest Rd
Kosmos Boat Ramp
Kosmos Wildlife Area
Day Use Area & Boat Ramp
Lake Scanewa
Woods Creek Info Station
Bluff Mtn 2620

Winston Creek
Crazy Man Mtn 2650
Coyote Mtn 2870
Winters Mtn 3700
Boat Ramp
Taidnapam Park
Cowlitz Falls Dam
Iron Creek
KRAUS RIDGE
Iron Mtn

RIFFE LAKE

770

GIFFORD PINCHOT NATIONAL FOREST

Tumwater Mtn 5180
Vanson Peak 4948
Vanson Lake 4514
Quartz Creek Big Trees
Strawberry Mtn 5739
Iron Creek Butte 4300
Greenhorn Butte

LEWIS COWLITZ

Green River
Deadmans Lake 4330
Goat Mtn 5487
Black Mtn 5302
Island Lake
Venus Lake
Mt Venus 5607
Green River Horse Camp
Ryan Lake Interpretive Site
Strawberry Mtn overlook
French Butte 5306
Iron Creek Falls
Pinto Rock 5123

COWLITZ SKAMANIA
Tradedollar Lake
Shovel Lake 4565
Mt Whittier 5883
Ghost Lake
Norway Pass 4508
Bismark Mtn 4626
Bear Meadow
Wakepish Snopark
Elk Pass 4080

Hoffstadt Bluffs Visitor Center
Toutle Dam
Hoffstadt Bridge
Forest Lake
Fawn Lake
Panhandle Lake
Coldwater
Mt Margaret 5858
Mt St Helens
St Helens Lake
Meta Lake Interpretive Site
Independence Pass 4075
Cascade Peaks Viewpoint
The Loaf 4540
Badge Pea

Forest Learning Center
Elk Rock 4180
Castle Lake Viewpoint
Elk Rock Viewpoint
Coldwater Ridge Vis Ctr
Coldwater Lake Recreation Area
Birth of a Lake
Hummocks
South Coldwater
Loowit Viewpoint
Johnston Ridge 4314
Johnston Ridge Observatory
Coldwater Lake 4490
Coldwater Peak
Spirit Lake
Harmony
South Creek
Independence Pass
Windy Ridge Viewpoint
Smith Creek Viewpoint
Smith Creek Butte 3780

MOUNT ST HELENS NATIONAL VOLCANIC MONUMENT

DEBRIS AVALANCHE
Wildlife Area
Spotted Buck Mtn
Spud Mtn 4720
Castle Lake
Pumice Plain
Studebaker Ridge
PYROCLASTIC FLOW
National Volcanic Monument
Clearwater Viewpoint
Upper Clear Creek

TOUTLE MOUNTAIN RANGE

Little Cow 3540
Big Bull 4208
Sheep Canyon
Crescent Ridge
The Breach
Lava Dome
East Dome 5280
Pumice Butte 4524
Ape Canyon
Lower Smith Creek
Spencer Butte

GIFFORD PINCHOT NATIONAL FOREST
Goat Mtn 4965
Goat Marsh Research Natural Area
Blue Lake
Blue Lake
Butte Camp Dome 4856
Mt St Helens 8363
June Lake
Lava Canyon
Ape Canyon
Lahar Viewpoint
Breezy Point 5863
Spencer Peak 3841

Elk Mtn 4538
Kalama Horse Camp
Red Rock Pass
Climbers Bivouac
Marble Mtn Snopark
June Lake
Muddy River Viewpoint

Cougar Snopark
Ape Cave
Marble Mtn 4128
Cedar Flat

© BENCHMARK MAPS

Land Use and Vegetation

- Forest
- Wetland
- Cropland
- Grassland
- Other
- Built-Up Area
- Lava

Land Ownership (Other public/tribal lands are named)

- State Land (blue highlight)
- BLM Land (yellow highlight)

Also See Recreation Page 26

GIFFORD PINCHOT

Tatoosh Wilderness

NATIONAL

FOREST

GIFFORD

PINCHOT

NATIONAL

FOREST

GIFFORD PINCHOT

NATIONAL FOREST

OKANOGAN–WENATCHEE NATIONAL FOREST

William O Douglas Wilderness

Goat Rocks Wilderness

Goat Rocks Wilderness

KLICKTON DIVIDE

Yakama Indian Reservation

CASCADE CREST

SKAMANIA YAKIMA LEWIS

BULLGROUSE RIDGE

PINEGRASS RIDGE

PEAVINE RIDGE

Mount Adams Wilderness

Lookout Mtn 5475 5230
Silver Creek Pass
Skate Mtn 4724
Dixon Mtn 5018
Butter Peak
Packwood
Packwood Airport
Skyo Mtn 2420
Cora Rd Bridge
Cascade Peaks Resort
Pompey Peak 5177
Lone Tree Mtn 4620
Twin Sisters 5818
Mission Mtn 5698
Cold Springs Butte 5754
Horseshoe Point 5663
Bishop Mtn 3997
Tongue Mtn 4838
Juniper Peak 5611
Spud Hill 4900
Sunrise Peak 5892
Jumbo Peak 5801
Holdaway Butte 4873
McCoy Peak 5856
Dark Mtn 5238
Table Mtn 4100
Council Bluff 5137
Snagtooth Mtn 5443
Quartz Creek Butte 3719
Steamboat Mtn 5376
Big Mosquito Lake
Tillicum Lake
Squaw Butte 4565
West Twin Butte 4760
East Twin Butte 4700
Cayuse Meadow

Laurel Hill 4260
Fish Ladder Falls
Summit Creek
Seda Springs
Cortright Point
Deer Lake
Dog Lake
White Pass 4500
White Pass Ski Area 4720
Knuppenburg Lake 4100
Hogback Mtn 6789
Shoe Lake
Leech Lake
Round Mtn 5971
Hell Lake
Sand Lake
Cramer Mtn 5992
Cramer Lake 5035
Dancing Lady Lake
Spiral Butte 5920
Penoyer Lake
Pine Lake
Buesch Lake
Dumbbell Lake
Shellrock Lake
Tumac Mtn 6340
McNeil Peak 6658
Shellrock Peak 6835
Ironstone Mtn 6441
Clear Lake
Clear Lake North
Clear Lake South
Indian Creek
Rimrock Lake

Beargrass Butte 5830
Coyote Lake
Lost Lake
Snyder Mtn 5011
Packwood Lake
Chimney Rock 6708
Goat Rocks
Packwood Saddle
Johnson Peak 7487
Angry Mtn 6045
South Point
Heart Lake
Lily Basin
Goat Lake
Elk Pass
Old Snowy Mtn 7930
Ives Peak 7940
McCall Glacier
Packwood Glacier
Gilbert Peak 8201
Meade Glacier
Cispus Pass
Devils Horn 7060
Tieton Peak 7768
Bear Creek Mtn 7336
Tieton Pass
Tieton Meadows
Coyote Rocks 6121

Twin Sisters 5818
Stonewall Ridge
St Michael Lakes
Chambers Lake 4438
Elk Peak 5441
Wobbly Lake 3533
Hamilton Buttes 5756
Blue Lake
Black Rock Pond 3059
Nannie Peak 6140
Walupt Lake Horse Camp
Walupt Lake 3926
Lakeview Mtn 6660
Howard Lake 4891
Jennies Butte 6410
Hussey Meadow
Johns Butte 5910
Fish Lake 4010
LeConte Lake 5792
Gertrude Lake 5736
Petross Sidehill 5836
Spencer Point 6634
Diamond Butte 5792
Butte Meadows
Diamond Lake 5238
McCormick River
Meadow
Caldwell Prairie

Hamilton Buttes
Blue Lake Ridge
Spud Hill
Adams Fork
Green Mtn 5107
Potato Hill 5387
Two Lakes
Holdaway Meadow
Windy Point 4612
Cat Creek
Olallie Lake
Takhlakh Lake 4385
Council Lake
Red Butte 7204
Glaciate Butte 5453
Mulligan Butte 5854
Mt Adams Lake 4499
Goat Butte 7484
Keenes Horse Camp
Horseshoe Lake
Chain of Lakes 4380
Killen Creek
Olallie Lake
Table Mtn
Council Bluff
Mount Adams 12276
Burnt Rock 5376
Pinnacle Glacier
Rusk Glacier
Avalanche Valley
The Castle
Bartlement Ridge
Big Muddy
Little Mt Adams 6821
Ridge of Wonders
Hellroaring
Snowplow Mtn 5087
Bench Lake
Jungle Butte 3956
Bird Lake
Cougar

Steamboat Mtn 5376
Steamboat Lake
Saddle
Quartz Creek
Island Shelter
Twin Falls 2660
Lewis River
Swampy Meadows
Crofton Butte 5272
Morrison Creek Shelter
Morrison Creek Horse Camp
Lower Butte 4870
Eckhart Point
Cold Springs
South Butte 7820
Snipes Mtn 4761

© BENCHMARK MAPS

LANDSCAPE

Scale 1:200,000

0   5   10   15 Miles

0   5   10   15   20 Kilometers

LANDSCAPE

99

OKANOGAN

William O. Douglas Wilderness

Tumac Mtn 6340
Pipe Lake
Dumbell Lake
Gamer Lake
Cramer Lake
McNeil Peak 6658
Shellrock Peak 6835
Burnt Mtn 6536
Ironstone Mtn 6441
Cramer Mtn 5992
Shellrock Douglas
Dancing Lady Lake
Spiral Butte 5940
Sand Ridge
Silver Beach Resort
Westfall Rocks
Rimrock Goose Egg Mtn 4566
Tieton Basin
Hause
River Bend
Wild Rose
Willows
Sentinel Rock
Weddle
Cowiche Mill
Cowiche
Windy Point 3040
Main Canyon
Rosenkranz Creek

121°20'   121°10'   199   235   121°00'   1401   1410   Oak   12   120°50'
1500
1305
1306
1308
1382
1381
1201
1302
1202
570
Jump Off Joe 5670
Lookout
Kloochman Rock 4532
Lost Lake
Sentinel Rock

A

46°40'
Dog Lake 4220
Dog Lake
White Pass 4500
Peak Lake
White Pass Ski Area 4220
Round Mtn 5971
Hell Lake
Boat Ramp
12
Clear
Tieton
Clear Lake Bar Use Area
Clear Lake North
Clear Lake South
Tieton Res
Indian Creek
Masters Resort
Horseshoe Cove
Tieton
The Cove Resort
Boat Ramp
Peninsula 3000
South Flat
Tieton State Airport 3957
South Fork Snopark
South Fork
Mud Flat
1333
1200
1205
1204
1000
1241
1203

B

Goat Rocks Wilderness
Shoe Lake
Tieton
PINEGRASS RIDGE
North Fork
South Fork Tieton
Blue Slide Ridge
Short and Dirty Ridge
Dome Peak 6597
DIVIDE RIDGE
S Fk Cowiche
Ahtanum
Reynolds
Cowiche
Nasty
Pine Mtn 4300
COWICHE MOUNT
Cowiche Basin
3282
1207
1205
1204
1040
770
1040
1000

WENATCHEE

C

46°30'
Section 3 Lakes
Tieton Meadows
Goat Rocks Wilderness
Devils Horn 7060
Bear Creek Mtn 7336
Narrowneck Gap
Darland Mtn 6981
Clover Flats
Eagle Nest Vista
Blue Lake
Green Lake
Multiple Use Area
Snow Cabin
Grey Rock Picnic Area
North Fork
Ahtanum
FOUNDATION RIDGE
Ahtanum Meadows Snopark 5060
Ahtanum Snopark
North Fork Ahtanum
SEDGE RIDGE
Tampico El 2118
Cottonwood Canyon
Ahtanum
Slavin Rd

NATIONAL FOREST

D

46°30'
Conrad Creek
Surprise Lake 2735
Cuque Lake 5346
KLICKTON DIVIDE
Petross Sidehill 5836
Spencer Point 6634
Diamond Lake 5518
Diamond Butte 5797
Butte Meadows
Coyote Rocks 6121
Diamond Fork
Tree Phones
FAIRVIEW RIDGE
Cultus
North Fork
South Fork Ahtanum
RATTLESNAKE RIDGE
Simcoe
Old Maid
South Fork
Simcoe Creek
Poison
Canyon
Rattlesnake Canyon
MEDICINE VALLE
Medicine
Old Maid Rd

Huckleberry Creek
Klickitat

E

Howard Lake 3891
McCormick Meadow
Coldwell Prairie
Jennies Butte 6410
Hussey Meadow
Johns Butte 5910
Fish Lake 4010
Sheep Point 4924
Piscoe Meadow
Piscoe
Yakama
LOST HORSE PLATEAU
W McDonald
Moses Rd
Pine Cone
Fort Simcoe
Agency
Wahtum
Hawk

F

46°20'
Fish Lake
Holdaway Meadow
Windy Point 4612
Clearwater Stream
BULLGROUSE RIDGE
Klickitat River
LINCOLN PLATEAU
Indian
Toppenish
Hunt
Deer Butte 4133
Willy Dick Canyon
Coon Canyon
Canyon
Fort Simcoe Job Corps Center
Fort Simcoe State Park
Woodchoppers Canyon

G

Little Muddy Creek
West Fork Klickitat
Swamp Creek
Mt Adams Lake 4499
Soda Spring
Crawford
Mulligan Butte 5854
Signal Peak 5100
Lookout
PINEGRASS RIDGE
South Fork Toppenish
White Creek
North Fork
Reservation
North Fork Dry
Whiskey Jim Flat
Starvation Flats
Simon Butte 3988
TOPPE

H

Bellroaring Creek
46°10'
Big Muddy
Cunningham Creek
KLICKITAT RIVER
PEAVINE RIDGE
Jungle Butte 3956
Saxton Rock 4401
Cougar
Sixprong Creek
CEDAR VALLEY
Oak Hill 4010
White Pine
McKays Butte 4038
Vessey Springs
Camas Patch
Wall Creek
Middle Fork Dry
South Fork
White

121°20'   121°10'   121°00'   120°50'

© BENCHMARK MAPS

Land Use and Vegetation

- Forest
- Wetland
- Cropland
- Grassland
- Other
- Built-Up Area

Land Ownership (Other public/tribal lands are named)

- State Land (blue highlight)
- BLM Land (yellow highlight)

Also See Recreation Page 26

LANDSCAPE

© BENCHMARK MAPS

Scale 1:200,000

Also See Recreation Page 26

0　　　　5　　　　10　　　　15 Miles
0　　5　　10　　15　　20 Kilometers

88

LANDSCAPE

101

114

UMTANUM

Yakima

Firing Center

YAKIMA RIDGE

RATTLESNAKE

Alkali

Corral Canyon

Cow Canyon

Sourdough Canyon

HOG RANCH BUTTES

Black Rock Spring

Cairn Hope Peak
△3354

Horsethief Point
1414

BLACK ROCK VALLEY

High Top
3021

Zillah Peak
2186

Eagle Peak
2286

Rochpole Cyn

Wineries Below
1. Maison de Padgett Winery
2. Paradisos del Sol

Silver Lake Winery

Portteus Vineyards

Highland

Horizons Edge Winery

Zillah
el 850

Severino Cellars

Teapot Dome Service Station (Est 1922)

Sun Valley Shooting Park

Eaton Hill Winery

Tefft Cellars

Liberty

Granger
el 770

Outlook
el 760

Sunnyside
el 770

Sunnyside Municipal Airport

Washington Hills Cellars

Yakima Valley Hwy

Tappenish

Satus

YAKIMA

Headquarters Boat Launch (Sunnyside)

Giffen Lake

Horseshoe Lake

Yakama

Indian

Reservation

Wildlife Area

Mabton
el 708

Grandview
el 800

Stassen Park

Manchego Real Apricot

Pontin del Roza Winery

SAGEBRUSH

Grandview Butte
1008

Royer Hill
1630

The Gap

Willow Crest Winery

VALLEY

Prosser
el 665

Benton County Historical Museum

Horse Heaven Shooting Range

Buena Vista

Old Inland Empire Hwy

Wine Country

Whitstran
el 675

Wineries in Prosser
1. Hinzerling Vineyards
2. Snoqualmie Vineyards
3. Hogue Cellars
4. Kestrel Vintners
5. Alexandria Nicole Cellars
6. Chinook Winery

HORSE HEAVEN HILLS

MISSOURI FLATS

COLUMBIA RIVER

Priest Rapids Lake

Priest Rapids WA

Boat Ramp

Desert Aire Airport

Desert Aire

Desert Aire Golf Course

Priest Rapids Dam

Moran Slough

RIVER

McCoy Canyon

Hanford Reach National

GRANT

BENTON

B and C Reactors (World's first large scale reactor)

Midway Substation

China Bar

Midway

McGee Ranch

Riverlands Unit

Yakima Barricade

Route 11A

COLD CREEK VALLEY

Summit

Fitzner-Eberhart Arid Lands Ecology Reserve Unit

No Public Access

SNIVELY BASIN

SNIVELY GULCH

HILLS

Thorton Wildlife Area

RIDGE

North Prosser

© BENCHMARK MAPS

Land Use and Vegetation

- Forest
- Wetland
- Cropland
- Grassland
- Other
- Built-Up Area

Land Ownership (Other public/tribal lands are named)

- State Land (blue highlight)
- BLM Land (yellow highlight)

Also See Recreation Page 28

LANDSCAPE

Wahluke

Hanford Generating Project

100 D+DR Areas
100 H Area
100 N Area
100 F Area
No Public Access
Ginger
Bettie
Nancy
Ruth
W+KE
Pierce
Route 1
Route 2 North
Route 4 North

GRANT
FRANKLIN
GRANT / FRANKLIN

Hanford Reach National Monument

Wahluke Unit
Wahluke Ponds

Scenic Overlook
White Bluffs Boat Launch
White Bluffs

Butte
Pearl
GABLE MOUNTAIN △ 1085

Hanford
Reservation

Route 3
200 East Area

US Dept of Energy

Route 4 South
Army Loop Rd

May Junction
Route 2 South
Parking / Boat Ramp
Hanford

Wye Barricade (Main Gate)
Columbia Generating Station
LIGO Observatory
Geneva Junction
White Bluffs Solar Station

Scenic Viewing Area
Route 10
Route 40
Route 4 South
400 Area Fast Flux Test Facilities

Fitzner-Eberhart Arid Lands Ecology Reserve Unit

IOWA FLATS

Rattlesnake Slope Wildlife Area
Rattlesnake Mtn Shooting Facility
No Public Access
The Horn
Horn Rapids County Park
Horn Rapids Dam

YAKIMA RIVER

Wooded Island
Johnson Island
Mesquit Island
Claar Cellars
Ringold Fish Hatchery
Glenwood
300 E Area
Ruby

HORSE HEAVEN HILLS

COLUMBIA RIVER

Hendricks Rd
Eagle Lakes
Scooteney Reservoir
Scooteney Reservoir Recreation Area
Paradise
Krug Rd

WB-10 Wasteway Wildlife Area
Mountain Vista

Bailie Memorial Youth Camp
Bailie Wildlife Area
Windmill Ranch Wildlife Area
Esquatzel Coulee Wildlife Area
Ribbon Lakes
Snakebite Reservoir

Basin City
Basin Hill
Bellflower
West Klamath
East Klamath
Sheffield
Russell
Juniper
Ironwood
Millwood
Nipper WA
Clark Pond Wildlife Area
Clark Pond
Hope Valley WA
Garfield
Hooper
Homestead Corner
Eltopia West
Eltopia
Bellevue
Everett
Jackass Mtn 911 △
Dogwood
Cedar
Sagemoor
West Sagemoor
Birch
Dayton
Alder
Fairfield Dr
Country Mercantile
Preston Wine Cellars
East Vineyard Dr
Beads

Mesa
Mesa Lake Boat Ramp

BUSH / ANTK

ESQUATZEL COULEE

Washington State University Tri-Cities
Leslie Groves Park

West Richland
West Richland Muni Golf Course
Red Mtn Tri-Cities Raceway
Tapteil Winery
Hedges Cellars
Kiona Vineyards
Sandhill Winery

Richland
Wineries in Richland
1. Tagaris Winery
2. Barnard Griffin Winery
3. Bookwalter Winery

Benton City
Chandler Reach Winery
Oakwood Cellars
Buckmaster Cellars
Seth Ryan Winery
Terra Blanca Vintners
Kiona

Chandler Butte 2046
Badger Slope
McBee
Goose Hill 1339
Ganache Vintners
Badger Mtn 1579
Goose Ridge Estate Winery
Candy Mtn 1391

Three Rivers Childrens Museum
Johnson Park
Columbia Point
Sandy Heights RV
Columbia Park

Factory Outlets & Childrens Mus
Broadmoor Ave
TRAC Center
Gesa Stadium
Tri-Cities Airport
Burden Blvd
Belcomb & Moe Winery
Amtrak Station / Washington State Historical Society Museum

Pasco
West Pasco
Kennewick

Bateman Island View
Yakima River Delta Wildlife Area
Wright's Desert Gold RV
Bateman Island
Chiawana Park

West Highlands
Vista
Clover Island Yacht Club
Columbia Park Golf Course
Tri-Cities RV

Burbank
Burbank Heights
McNary ELC
Sacajawea St Park
Two Rivers Park
McNary NWR

SNAKE RIVER

WALLULA

Meadow Springs Country Club
Badger 677
Reata Rd
Sundowns Race Track
County Fair & Rodeo Grounds
Kennewick Arboretum

In Kennewick
1. Columbia Center
2. Tri-Cities Coliseum

Canyon Lakes Golf Course

Nine Canyon Wind Project
Jump Off Joe 2200 △
The Butte 1140 △
Hover Rd
Lechert Rd
Finley

Also See Recreation Page 28

Scale 1:200,000

0 5 10 15 Miles

0 5 10 15 20 Kilometers

103

90

116

Connell el 840

Kahlotus el 901

Mesa

Pasco

Kennewick

Burbank

McNary

Eltopia el 2067

Sheffler

Eureka el 1061

Scooteney Reservoir
Scooteney Reservoir Recreation Area
Boat Ramp

Eagle Lakes

Ribbon Lakes

Bailie Wildlife Area

Snakebite Reservoir

Windmill Ranch Wildlife Area

Esquatzel Coulee Wildlife Area

Clark Pond Wildlife Area

Hope Valley WA

Jackass Mtn 911

Juniper Dunes

Sand Dunes

Restricted Access

Wilderness

Rice Hill 1364

Emma Lake

Dalton Lake

Fishhook Park

Gordon Brothers Winery

Levey Landing Park

Charbonneau Park

Ice Harbor Lock & Dam

Snake River Vineyards

Preston Wine Cellars East Vineyard

Country Mercantile

Tri-Cities Airport

Columbia Basin College

Amtrak Station/ Washington State Historical Society Museum

Franklin

Sacajawea State Park

Two Rivers Park

McNary ELC & Refuge HQ

Visitor Center

Nine Canyon Wind Project

Jump Off Joe 2200

The Butte 1140

Badger Island

Lower Monumental Dam

Windust Park

Lower Monumental State Rec Area 813

Devils Canyon

Lake Kahlotus 865

WASHTUCNA COULEE

OLD MAID COULEE

DUNNIGAN COULEE

RYE GRASS FLAT

RYE GRASS COULEE

SNAKE RIVER

WALLA WALLA RIVER

LAKE SACAJAWEA

LAKE WALLULA

FRANKLIN

BENTON

WALLULA

EUREKA

FLAT

Rattlesnake

Coyote Ridge Prison

Sulphur Lake 690

Sulphur Rd

Five Corners

Attalia

Wildlife Refuge

National

Welland

Adkins

Herrold Hatch el 1041

Walkley

Humorist

Le Grow

Slater

© BENCHMARK MAPS

Land Use and Vegetation

Forest Cropland Other
Wetland Grassland Built-Up Area

Land Ownership (Other public/tribal lands are named)

State Land (blue highlight)
BLM Land (yellow highlight)

Also See Recreation Page 28

91

117

COULEE

FRANKLIN

SNAKE RIVER

WALLA WALLA

WHITMAN

COLUMBIA

GARFIELD

LAKE BRYAN

New York Island

Ridpath

Beacon Hill 1880

Hay el 1093

Big Alkali Creek

Alkali Flat

McAdam
Sperry
260
118°20'
118°10'
118°00'
116°00'
46°40'

Palouse Falls
Palouse Falls State Park

Deep Lake
Winn Lake
Sims Spring
Marmes Rock Shelter

Little Goose Dam
Visitor Center
Little Goose Lock & Dam
Road closed across dam
Boat Ramp
Little Goose Lock And Dam
Airport

Ayer Boat Basin
Ayer
Ayer Junction
Lyons Ferry Park & Marina

Riparia Goose Dam
Texas Rapids Rec Area Boat Launch
Little Goose Dam

Skookum
West Basin
Magallon Ranch
Casey

CSP
261

Powers
Starbuck el 645

Tucannon River

Chard
Jackson
12
Delaney
Miller Gulch
Dry Hollow
Emerson
Turner el 2175
Whetstone el 2060
Ronan

261

Fletcher
Davidson
Clyde el 1226
Reser
Pickard
Badger
Smith Springs
Hollow

SKYROCKET HILLS
COLVILLE
SPRINGS
TOUCHET VALLEY

Alto el 1900
Balch
Mead
Relief Creek
Petticord
Brambali
Messner
Poulsen

Whetstone
McKay
Shea
Fountain Springs
Lower Whetstone

Prescott el 1055
124
Bolles
Menoken
Millrace

Dayton el 1613
Patit Creek Cellars
RR Depot & Museum
Touchet Valley Golf Course
Cameron Court RV Park
City Park

Lewis & Clark Trail State Park
Huntsville el 1355
Baileysburg

Waitsburg el 1260
Bruce Memorial Museum
Fairgrounds
Coppei Creek
Whiskey Creek

Hogeye
Dustin Hollow
Payne
Warren Rd

Mountain Home Park el 2151
Cahill Mtn 3705

NORTH FORK TOUCHET RIVER
SOUTH FORK TOUCHET RIVER

Berryman
125
Hadley Spring
Ennis
Paddock

WALLA WALLA COLUMBIA

Minnick el 1914
Robinette Mtn 3997
3475

Valley Grove
Russell
Bergevin Springs
Dixie el 1547
Sapphire Mountain Cellars
Eastman
Gilliam

NEW BLUE MOUNTAIN
UMATILLA NATIONAL FOREST

Chase Mtn 5642
6437
5206

118°20'
118°10'
118°00'
46°30'
46°20'
46°10'

106

© BENCHMARK MAPS

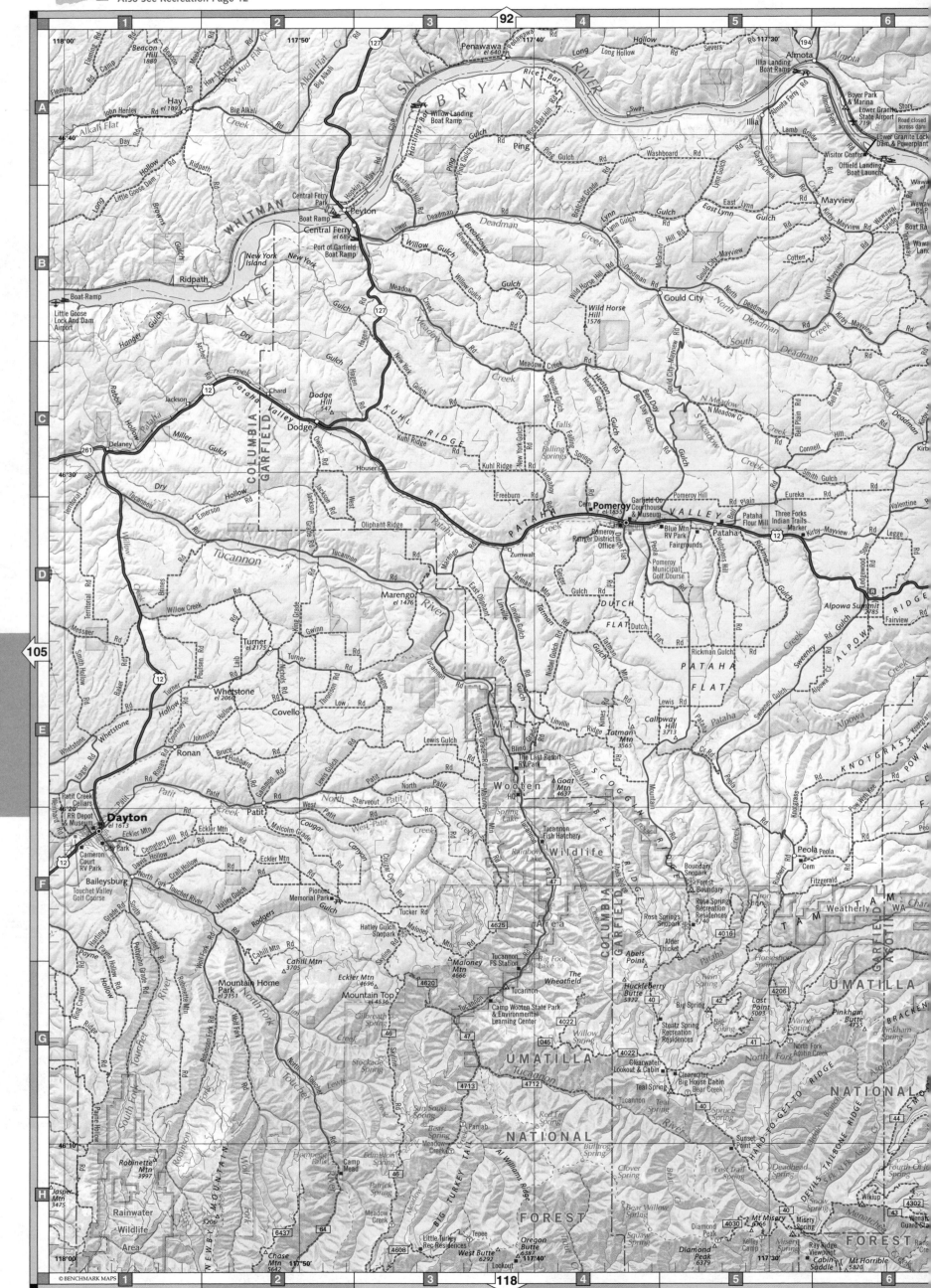

Also See Recreation Page 12

Scale 1:200,000

0   5   10   15 Miles
0   5   10   15   20 Kilometers

LANDSCAPE

© BENCHMARK MAPS

Land Use and Vegetation

- Forest
- Wetland
- Cropland
- Grassland
- Other
- Built-Up Area

Land Ownership (Other public/tribal lands are named)

- State Land (blue highlight)
- BLM Land (yellow highlight)

Also See Recreation Page 14

In Clarkston/Lewiston
1. Hells Canyon Resort Marina
2. Gateway Golf Center
3. Granite Lake RV Park
4. Greenbelt Boat Ramp
5. Lewis & Clark Interpretive Center
6. Clearwater Landing Interpretive Center

Continues in the Benchmark Idaho Road & Recreation Atlas

LANDSCAPE

Clarkston Lewiston Colton Uniontown Genesee Asotin Anatone Lapwai Spalding

IDAHO WASHINGTON WHITMAN LATAH NEZ PERCE GARFIELD ASOTIN

Snake River Clearwater River Palouse River Lower Granite Lake

Nez Perce Indian Reservation

© BENCHMARK MAPS

Scale 1:200,000

| 0 | 5 | 10 | 15 Miles |

| 0 | 5 | 10 | 15 | 20 Kilometers |

Continues in the Benchmark
Oregon Road & Recreation Atlas

96

Westport
el 20

Kerry
el 20

Woodson
el 14

Columbia River

Marshland
el 53

Clatskanie
el 13

Inglis
el 132

Alston
el 414

30

Wickiup
Mtn
2703

Nicolai Mtn
3020

Clatskanie
Mtn

47

Elk Mtn
2754

N. Klaskanine R.

46°00'

Birkenfeld
el 560

Mist
el 600

RIVER

47

Fishhawk
Lake

Fish
Ponds

202

Jewell
el 580

Big Eddy

Oak Ranch

Baker Point
3875

Fishhawk Falls

Green
Mtn
2493

Keasey
el 800

Vernonia
el 621

26

Elsie
el 430

45°50'

Rock Creek

47

Braun
el 711

COLUMBIA
WASHINGTON

Tater Hill
2033

Sunset
Rest Area

CLATSOP
TILLAMOOK

Hoffman
Hill
1138

Tophill
el 1003

Belfort

Timber
el 975

Scofield
el 639

Belding
el 920

Cochran
el 780

Strassel
el 990

Buxton
el 325

Round
Top
2986

45°40'

Rogers Peak
3680

Manning
el 235

Gales
Creek

Glenwood
el 480

Kings Mtn
3225

Elk Creek Hwy

Banks
el 245

6

Roy
el 187

Cedar
Butte
2907

Gales
Creek
el 287

47

Wilson River

6

Verboort
el 185

Scheffli
el 179

Keening

Gales
Peak
1801

Forest
Grove
el 211

Corneliu
el 179

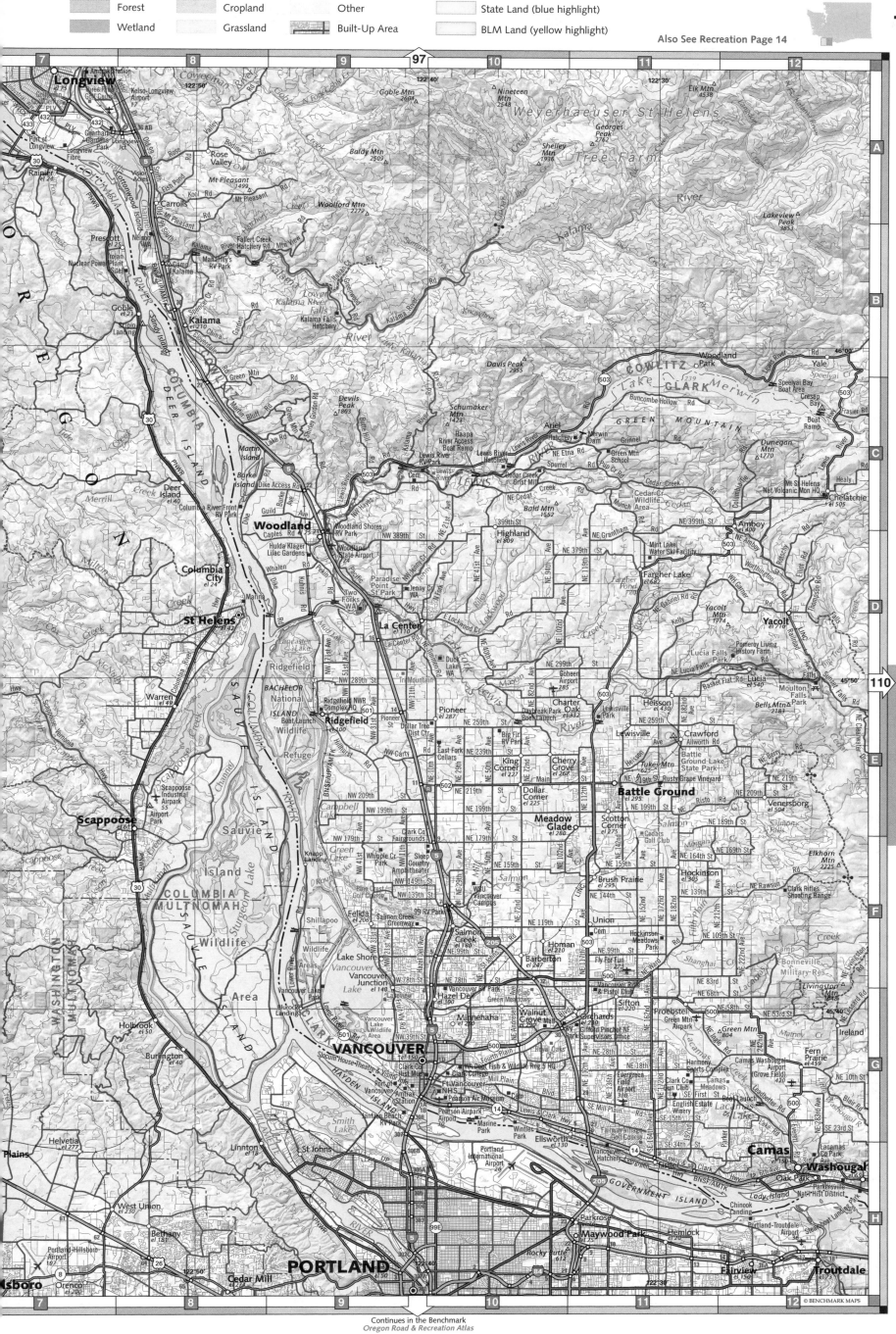

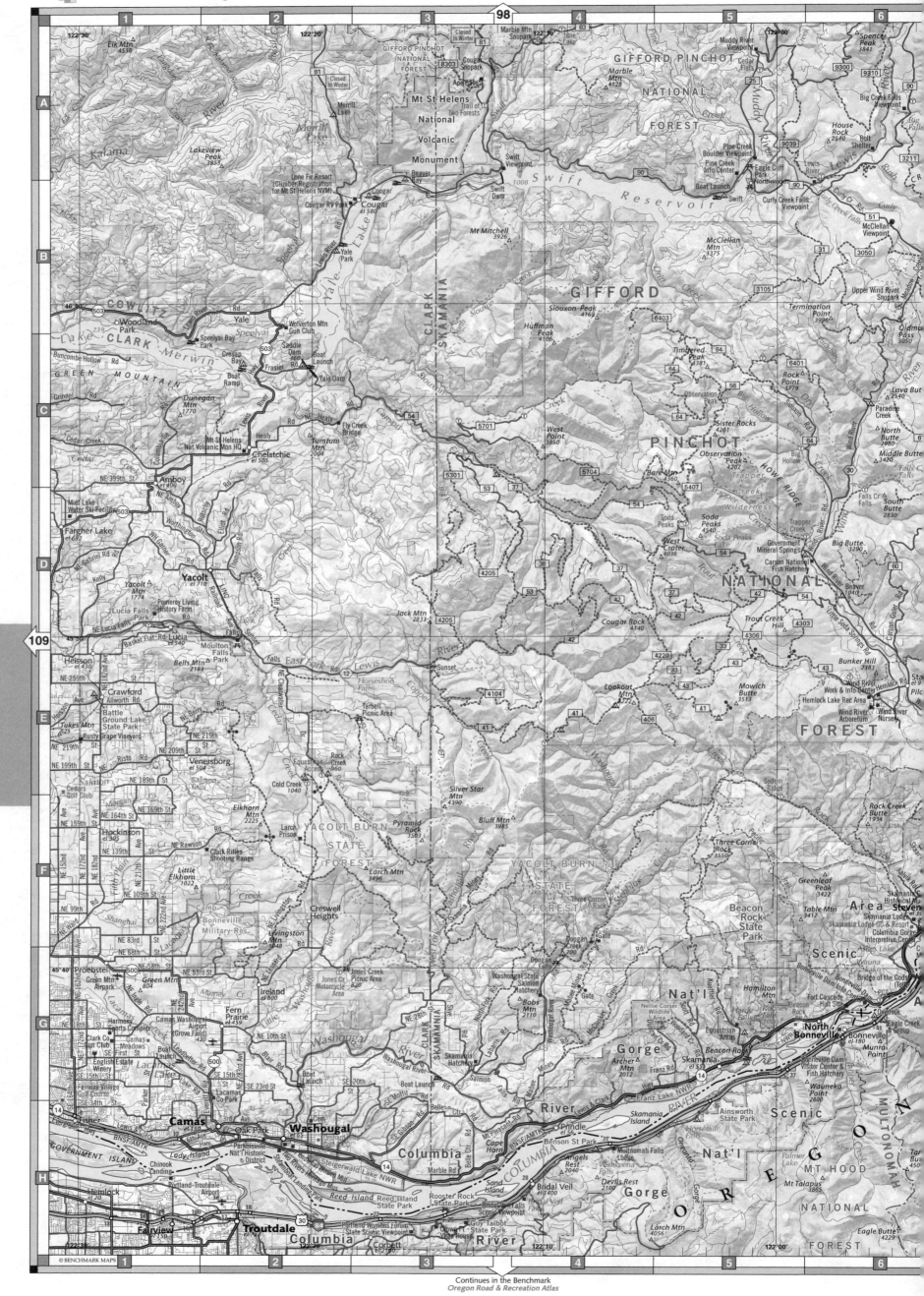

Scale 1:200,000

0   5   10   15 Miles

0   5   10   15   20 Kilometers

109

LANDSCAPE

98

Continues in the Benchmark
Oregon Road & Recreation Atlas

© BENCHMARK MAPS

Land Use and Vegetation

- Forest
- Wetland
- Cropland
- Grassland
- Other
- Built-Up Area
- Lava

Land Ownership (Other public/tribal lands are named)

- State Land (blue highlight)
- BLM Land (yellow highlight)

Also See Recreation Page 26

Also See Recreation Page 26

LANDSCAPE

GIFFORD PINCHOT NATIONAL FOREST

YAKIMA KLICKITAT

Yakama Indian Reservation

CASCADE RANGE

Indian Heaven Wilderness

Trout Lake

Conboy Lake National Wildlife Refuge

CAMAS PRAIRIE

THE PLATEAU

BIG LAVA BED

MONTE CRISTO RANGE

KLICKITAT

SKAMANIA

White Salmon

Bingen

Husum

Underwood

COLUMBIA RIVER GORGE

Hood River

National Scenic Area

OREGON

MOUNT HOOD NATIONAL FOREST

HOOD RIVER VALLEY

Columbia River Gorge

Mosier

Rowena

Carson

Home Valley

Wyeth

WASCO

Chenoweth

Selected labels and elevations:

Squaw Butte 4565, Twin Butte 4710, West Twin Butte, East Twin Butte 4700, Saddle, Tillicum, Steamboat Lake, Cayuse Mdw, Lone Butte 4780, Sawtooth Mtn 5353, Berry Fields, Surprise Lakes Indian Camp, Cold Spring Indian Camp, Meadow Creek Indian Camp 4140, Bird Mtn 5706, Little Goose, Smoky Creek, Deadhorse Meadow, Placid Lake, Chenamus Lake, Lemei Rock 5925, Lake Wapiki, East Crater, Gifford Peak 5368, Lake Sebago, Berry Mtn 4987, Forlorn Lakes, Paterson Butte 3900, Petersons Prairie 2981, Ice Cave Picnic Area, Atkisson Snopark, Red Mtn 4968, Goose Lake, The Wart 3700, Crest Horse Camp 3480, Little Huckleberry Mtn 4781, Oklahoma, Mann Butte 3980, Trail Peak 3980, Monte Cristo 4171, Monte Carlo 4020, Timberhead Mtn 3632, Guler Mtn 4260, Big Huckleberry Mtn 4202, Grassy Knoll 3649, Goat Point 2361, Moss Creek, Triangle Pass 1611, Shingle Mtn 2196, Nestor Peak 3088, Little Baldy Peak 2924, Big Cedars County Park, Baldy Peak 2529, Wind River Cellars, BZ Corner 717, Gilmer 1490, Bill Moore Rd, Snowden 2330, Sleepy Hollow, Appleton 2308, Weigle Hill 2540, Willard, Little White Salmon National Fish Hatchery, Hauk Butte 2900, Cook Hill 3044, Augspurger Mtn 3184, Mill A, Dog Mtn 2948, Carson 520, Boat Ramp, Home Valley Waterfront Park, Wind Mtn 1903, Bald Mtn 1653, Bates, Laws Corner, Underwood Mtn 2728, Buck Mtn 1330, Burdoin Mtn, Lyle 140, Doug's Beach State Park, Mayer State Park, Fisher Hill Bridge, Klickitat, Centerville Hwy, Dillacort Wildlife Area, Columbia River Gorge National Scenic Area HQ, Mt Hood Railroad, Hood River Marina, Inn Beach, Bad Seed Cider House, Syncline Wine Cellars, Mt Elise Vineyards, Bridge RV Park, Rockford, Hood River Airport, Oak Grove 1032, Van Horn 800, Summit 737, Odell 730, Mt Defiance 4959, Kingsley Res, North Lake, Rainy Lake, Wahtum Lake, Chinidere Mtn 4673, Tomlike Mtn 4549, Indian Mtn 4900, Green Point, Dee 1600, Trout Creek 1120, Middle Mtn, Booth Hill 1998, Bald Butte 3775, Mt Hood National Forest, Wahtum Lake

Roads/highways: 99, 14, 30, 35, 141, 142, 281, 41

© BENCHMARK MAPS

Also See Recreation Page 26

Scale 1:200,000

0 5 10 15 Miles
0 5 10 15 20 Kilometers

111

LANDSCAPE

YAKAMA INDIAN RESERVATION

Oak Hill 4010
Klose Butte 2871
Sheep Butte 4422
Hagerty Butte 3603
Stagman Butte 5166
Twin Buttes 2887
Tadpole Lake

Island Camp
Bird Creek
Red Butte 3121
Castle Rock 5656
Potato Butte 5178
Kaiser Butte 4165
Indian Rock 5823

YAKIMA KLICKITAT

Glenwood-Goldendale Rd
Glenwood el 1895
Klickitat Fish Hatchery
Klickitat River Viewpoint
Grayback Mtn 3266
White Pine Buttes 3196
Conboy Lake National Wildlife Refuge
Laurel el 1884
BZ Corner-Glenwood
Dead Canyon
Boat Ramp Leidl
Soda Springs
Black Butte 3053
Myrtle Park Butte 2281
Jackknife Butte 2942
Pothole Lake
Pine Forest Rd
Gunn Butte 2195
Orchard

THE PLATEAU
Wahkiacus Heights
Panakanic
Gregory Spring
Woodruff Mill el 1937
Klickitat Wildlife Area
Calvert
Blockhouse Butte 1970
Blockhouse el 1590
Goldendale Fish Hatchery
Goldendale Airport
Klickitat County Fairgrounds
Goldendale Observatory State Park
Snowden el 2330
Bill Moore Rd
Fisher Hill
Wahkiacus el 440
Horseshoe
HORSESHOE BEND
Little Klickitat River
142
Goldendale el 1633
Sleepy Hollow
Klickitat-Appleton Rd
Klickitat el 443
Appleton el 2308
Wildlife Springs Canyon
Pitt Hang Gliding Area
Wheeler
Lorena Butte 2255
Hoctor

Acme
Pitt el 383
Mineral
HIGH PRAIRIE
High Prairie
Wahkiacus-High Prairie Rd
SWALE CANYON
Centerville Hwy Scenic Viewpoint
Davies Pass
Centerville el 1605
KLICKITAT

Columbia
River
Dillacort
Dillacort Wildlife Area
Fisher
Fisher Hill Bridge
Fisher Hill Wildlife Area
Stacker Butte 3220
Swale Creek Wildlife Area
Rattlesnake
Loops Road Overlook
Maryhill Loops Rd

Rowland Lake Boat Ramp
Incline Winery
Memaloose State Park
Lyle el 140
Doug's Beach State Park
Columbia Hills State Park
Haystack Butte 2936
Maryhill State Park
Stonehenge Memorial
Maryhill Museum of Art
Maryhill Winery
Biggs

Mosier el 112
Historic Columbia River Hwy
Mayer State Park
Rowena
ROWENA GAP
COLUMBIA NATIONAL SCENIC AREA
Dalles Mtn Ranch
Wishram Heights
Lewis & Clark Hwy
Biggs Pt
Peach Beach RV Park

Columbia
River
Gorge
Chenoweth el 440
Crates Pt 2020
The Columbia Gorge Discovery Center Wasco Co Hist Museum
Murdock el 332
Marshal's Winery
Cascade Cliffs Winery Lewis & Clark
Horsethief Lake Boat Launch
Wishram
Celilo Park
Miller Island
SHERMAN
Deschutes River State Recreation Area

OREGON
Chenoweth el 440
Google Data Ctr
Dallesport el 220
Columbia Hills RV Park
The Dalles Muni Airport
The Dalles Lock & Dam
The Dalles Visitor Ctr & Fish Ladder
Riverfront Park
Signal Hill 968
WASCO Scenic Area
Fairbanks el 478
Celilo Village
Heritage Landing Boat Launch
Moody

The Dalles el 92
Fort Dalles Museum
Lewis and Clark Memorial
Nat
Petersburg el 578
DESCHUTES RIVER

Continues in the Benchmark
Oregon Road & Recreation Atlas

© BENCHMARK MAPS

Land Use and Vegetation

- Forest
- Wetland
- Cropland
- Grassland
- Other
- Built-Up Area

Land Ownership (Other public/tribal lands are named)

- State Land (blue highlight)
- BLM Land (yellow highlight)

Also See Recreation Page 26

Yakama Indian Reservation

HORSE HEAVEN HILLS

BICKLETON RIDGE

YAKIMA
KLICKITAT

Bluelight 2700

Highbridge Spring

Devils Pocket

Lone Pine Butte 4721

Satus Pass 3107

Brooks Spring

Bean Spring

Box Springs

Pine Creek

Cemetery Rd

Bickleton el 3020

Bluebird Inn

Goldendale

Rodeo Grounds

Cleveland

Honey-Do-Ache'rs RV Park

Pine Springs Resort

Brooks Memorial State Park

Ranger Station & ELC Group

St. John's Monastery & Bakery

Box Canyon Rd

Tumwater Butte 2758

Three Creeks Resort

Woodland

Badger Gulch Rd

Holter Rd

Hillcrest Airport 2390

Bickleton

Old Mtn Highway

Andersen Flat

Pleasant Valley

Badger Gulch

Rogers Rd

Saxton Bane

Luna Butte 2244

Oak Flat

OAK FLAT

No 4 Rd

Fenton

Luna

Bigby Rd

Hoctor

Hoctor Rd

MUNSON PRAIRIE

HARRISON RIDGE

Quartz Creek

Rock Creek

Squaw Creek

Glass Canyon

Historic Dot Schoolhouse

Gadeberg Rd

Brannon Rd

Schrantz Rd

Big Horn

Van Nostern Rd

Hooker Rd

Duree Rd

Coleman Rd

Crider Vly

Stegeman Rd

Matsen Rd

Ferguson Rd

Gander Rd

Mabton

Nelson Rd

Timber Rd

Middle Rd

Naught Rd

Dot Rd

Six Prong

Whitmore Rd

WOOD GULCH

Roosevelt Grade

Roosevelt Regional Landfill

Sixprong Creek

SAND RIDGE

Van Horn Rd

Crider Valley

Stegeman Canyon

Alder Creek

Pine Creek

Newell Rd

Chapman

Chamberlain

Goodnoe Rd

Goodnoe Hills el 1288

Goodnoe Station

Sand Spring Cyn

Boat Launch

Rock Creek

Lewis & Clark Highway

Sundale Rd

Old Hwy 8

Old Lady Canyon

THE BURN

North Roosevelt

West Roosevelt

Roosevelt Park Boat Launch

Arlington Municipal Airport 890

Port of Arlington Marina

Snell Park

Arlington el 285

Sundale Park

Sundale

Boat Launch

Columbia River Highway

Blalock

KLICKITAT
GILLIAM

LAKE UMATILLA

BNSF/AMTK

UP

Boat Ramp

John Day Lock & Dam

LePage Park

Helm

GILLIAM

SHERMAN

Warm Springs

Ind Res

JOHN DAY

OREGON

Biglow Canyon

Emigrant Canyon

Emigrant Springs

Scott Canyon

Bidlow Canyon

Turner Butte 1271

Diamond Butte 1172

Old Oregon Trail Monument

Weatherford Historical Monument

Wasco el 1270

Klondike el 1549

Sherman

GRASS VALLEY CANYON

JOHN DAY RIVER

Rock Creek

Scott Canyon

Alkali Canyon

Jones Canyon

Continues in the Benchmark Oregon Road & Recreation Atlas

© BENCHMARK MAPS

LANDSCAPE

Scale 1:200,000

0   5   10   15 Miles

0   5   10   15   20 Kilometers

102

LANDSCAPE

Yakama Indian Reservation

HORSE HEAVEN HILLS

MISSOURI FLATS

Summit

Wendling Rd

Glade

Peebles Rd

Township

Sellards

Bert James

Davis

Glade Creek

Coyote Canyon

Alderdale Rd

YAKIMA
KLICKITAT

BENTON

McKinley Springs

Young

Lincoln

Farnum

Bluelight
2700

Sand Ridge

Tule

Prong

McKinley Springs Rd

Coyote Canyon

Gander Rd

Matsen

Ferguson

Ferguson Rd

Alderdale Rd

McKinley Springs

Moore

Horrigan

Stegeman

Van Horn Rd

McKinley Springs Winery

DEAD

Crider Vly

Coleman Rd

SAND RIDGE

Alder Spring

Willow

Sand Ridge Canyon

Doug

Tule Canyon

Peterson Rd

CANYON

Glade

Crider Valley

Stegeman

Canyon

Peterson

Stegeman Rd

Alder Creek

Whitmore

Sixprong

Alder Creek

Hereford Rd

Phinny Hill
795

Mercer Ranch

PATERS

Viewpoint

Sand Island

Refuge

Middle Rd

Six Prong

Hale Rd

Sanova Rd

Alderdale

Quarry Butte
695

Canoe Ridge Vineyard

CANOE RIDGE

14

Wildlife

Big Horn Canyon

Six Prong

Sixprong

Golgotha Butte
1051

Crow Butte Park

Crow Butte

Umatilla

National

Boat Ramp

Boardman Park & Marina

Power Plant

Port of Morrow

WOOD GULCH

Pine Creek

ALDER RIDGE

Alderdale

Boat Launch

Alderdale Park

LAKE

Boardman

RV Park

113

45°50'

Roosevelt Grade

Roosevelt Regional Landfill

Pine Creek Boat Launch

McCredie

Highway

Quesnel Park

151

Lewis & Clark

Columbia River

Boardman Airstrip
390

No Public Access to Boardman Bombing Range

BNSF/AMTK

KLICKITAT
GILLIAM

COLUMBIA RIVER

North Roosevelt

West Roosevelt

Roosevelt Park Boat Launch

Port of Arlington Marina

14

I-84

30

OREGON

147

Willow Creek

74

B o a r d m a n

B o m b i n g

R a n g e

Arlington Municipal Airport
890

Dalreed Butte
765

Snell Park

137

Arlington
el 285

James Canyon

19

Alkali Canyon

Willow Creek

Heppner

GILLIAM
MORROW

PG&E Boardman Coal Power Plant

Well Spring

45°40'

Weatherford Historical Monument

UP

EIGHTMILE

Fourmile

Fourmile Oregon Trail Interpretive Site

Cecil
el 700

Ella Butte
1610

Juniper

McDav Spring

Taylor Spring

Rock Creek

19

JOHN DAY

Morgan
el 900

Juniper Canyon

Strawb

© BENCHMARK MAPS

Continues in the Benchmark
Oregon Road & Recreation Atlas

Land Use and Vegetation

- Forest
- Wetland
- Cropland
- Grassland
- Other
- Built-Up Area

Land Ownership (Other public/tribal lands are named)

- State Land (blue highlight)
- BLM Land (yellow highlight)

Also See Recreation Page 28

LANDSCAPE

LAKE WALLULA

Horse Haven Hills

The Butte 1140

Jump Off Joe 2200

Johnson Butte 2043

Nine Canyon Wind Project

Lower Blair

Les Blair Rd

Tomar

McNary

McNary National Wildlife Refuge

OREGON

COLUMBIA RIVER

Umatilla NWR

Umatilla Fish Hatchery

Irrigon el 292

Umatilla el 290

McNary Lock & Dam

Pacific Salmon Visitor Ctr

McNary Beach

Sillusi Butte 927

Plymouth el 289

Plymouth Park

Power City

Power City Wildlife Area

Bensel

Umatilla Butte 869

Hat Rock State Park

McNary Yacht Club

Warehouse Beach Rec Area

Cold Springs NWR

Cold Springs Reservoir

No Public Access to Umatilla Ordnance Depot

Umatilla Ordnance Depot

Hermiston Butte

Hermiston

Hermiston Municipal Airport 637

Despain Gulch

Ordnance el 581

Westland el 540

Hinkle el 605

Stanfield el 590

Echo el 638

Emigrant Buttes 753

Echo Meadows Oregon Trail Interpretive Site

Ward Butte 933

Finley Buttes 993

Nolin

Rieth

Service Springs

Service Buttes 1685

Carpenter Butte 1542

MORROW / UMATILLA

BENTON

RIDGE

Columbia Crest

Continues in the Benchmark Oregon Road & Recreation Atlas

© BENCHMARK MAPS

Also See Recreation Page 28

Scale 1:200,000

0　　　　5　　　　10　　　　15 Miles

0　　5　　10　　15　　20 Kilometers

104

LANDSCAPE

OREGON

WASHINGTON

WALLULA / BENTON

WALLA WALLA

WALLA WALLA / UMATILLA

BENTON / UMATILLA

Nine Canyon Wind Project
Jump Off Joe 2200
The Butte 1140
Lower Blair
McNary
Dodd Rd
Dodd Rd
Attalia
National Boise Paper Mill
Fort Walla Walla Monument
Wallula el 400
Nine Mile Ranch
Riek Rd
Piert Rd
Meals Rd
Hover Rd
Hover Park
Albright Rd
Finley
Kirk
Mills Rd
Beck Rd
Boat Ramp
Madame Dorion Memorial Park
Mullins Harbor
N Shore
Pierce's Green Valley RV Park
Walla Walla
Nine Mile Rd
Ninemile
Touchet River
Woodward Canyon Winery
L'Ecole No 41
Lowden
BLMR
Wallula Junction
Yellepit
Twin Sisters 600
Clover Hill 1130
Walla Walla Yacht Club
Port Kelley
Hatch Grade
Hatch Grade Rd
Byrnes Rd
Cummins Rd
Touchet N
McDole Rd
McDonald Bridge Wildlife Area
Detour Monument
Frenchtown
Touchet el 443
Sand Pit Rd
Barney Rd
Gardena Rd
Mud
Blalock
Les Blair Rd
Spring Gulch
Blalock Ranch
WALLA WALLA UMATILLA
Gardena
Riggs Rd
Stateline Rd
Frog Hollow
Waterbrook Winery
Feedlot
Tomar
McNary
46°00'
Mottinger
National
BENTON UMATILLA
Switzler
BNSFAMTK
COLUMBIA
RIVER
730
Wildlife
Juniper
Canyon
North Fork Juniper
South Fork Juniper
Vansycle
Canyon
Refuge
Warehouse Beach Rec Area
Cold Springs
Pendleton-Cold Springs
Hwy
Canyon
37
Holdman el 1007
Middle Fork
South Fork
North Fork
Cold Springs
Cold Springs
Canyon
Helix el 1754
Greasewood
Cold Springs Reservoir
45°50'
115
Despain
Gulch
Cold Springs
Hwy
Canyon
37
Canyon
Athena-Holdman Hwy
334
UP
335
Missouri
Gulch
Gulch
Stage
Haven-Helix
Adams el 1513
334
Spring Hollow
Stage
Gulch
37
Hwy
Wildhorse Creek
11
193
84
30
395
198
199
202
Eastern Oregon Regional Airport
Pendleton-Cold Springs
Oregon-Washington
Umatilla
Umatilla
Mission el 1215
Cayuse el 1461
Rieth Rd
Nolin
45°40'
Mud Spring
Speare
Canyon
Canyon
Barnhart
Rieth Rd
Rieth
Umatilla
River
Umatilla National Forest HQ
Pendleton el 1068
207
219
218
210
213
84
30
216
Wildhorse Casino
Tamastslikt Cultural Institute
Indian
Reservation
Patawa
Creek
Pendleton-John Day
Birch
Canyon
Alkali
Canyon
Coombs
Canyon
McKay Creek
McKay Creek
National
Wildlife
Refuge
McKay Rd
George
Canyon
Spring Hollow
Cabbage Hill 3568
Emigrant Hill 3835
224
North Fork
Bell Cow
Dead
UP
395
119°00'
118°50'
118°40'

© BENCHMARK MAPS

Continues in the Benchmark
Oregon Road & Recreation Atlas

Land Use and Vegetation

- Forest
- Wetland
- Cropland
- Grassland
- Other
- Built-Up Area

Land Ownership (Other public/tribal lands are named)

- State Land (blue highlight)
- BLM Land (yellow highlight)

In Walla Walla
A. Four Seasons RV Resort
B. Army Corps of Engineers
   Walla Walla District Office
C. Carnegie Art Center
D. Walla Walla RD Office
E. Fort Walla Walla Park & Museum

Wineries Above
1. Three Rivers Winery
2. Reininger Winery
3. Bergevin Lane Vineyards
4. K Vintners
5. Walla Walla Vintners
6. Leonetti Cellar
7. Beresan Winery
8. Dusted Valley Vintners
9. Basel Cellars Estate Winery
10. Isenhower Cellars
11. Rulo
12. Northstar Winery
13. Va Piano Vineyards
14. Pepper Bridge
15. Glen Fiona
16. Gifford Hirlinger
17. Saviah Cellars
18. Zerba Cellars

Walla Walla el 1000
College Place
Milton-Freewater el 1033
Weston el 1838
Kooskooskie el 1190
Gibbon el 1754
Thorn Hollow el 1623
Tollgate el 4292
Lookingglass el 2360
Palmer Junction
Elgin el 2716
Duncan el 2370
Emigrant Springs State Park

Washington State Penitentiary
Walla Walla Regional Airport el 1205
Walla Walla Community College
Whitman College
Bennington Lake
Veterans Memorial

OREGON
UMATILLA NATIONAL FOREST
WALLOWA-WHITMAN NATIONAL FOREST
BLUE MOUNTAINS
UMATILLA INDIAN Res
HORSESHOE RIDGE
NATIONAL FOREST

Wenaha-Tucannon Wilderness
North Fork Umatilla Wilderness
Rainwater Wildlife Area

Griffin Peak 5682
Deadman Peak 5873
Green Peak 5156
Squaw Peak 5976
Chase Mtn 5642
Lookout Table Rock 6250
Squaw Spring
Bald Mtn 4080
Grouse Mtn 4121
Graves Butte 3540
Black Mtn 5440
Huckleberry Mtn 5137
Thimbleberry Mtn 5565
Huckleberry Mtn
Buck Mtn 4561
Blalock Mtn 4595
Linton Mtn 2944
Saddle Mtn 3331
Pikes Peak 3858
Klicker Mtn 3860
Lewis Peak 4888
Chase Mtn 5206

Mill Creek Watershed
Walla Walla Watershed
Umatilla Watershed
Peterson Ridge
Green Ridge
Biscuit Ridge
Blacksnake Ridge
Rodgers Ridge
Goodman Ridge
The Shimmiehorn
Ruckel Ridge

North Fork Walla Walla River
South Fork Walla Walla River
North Fork Umatilla River
Umatilla River
South Fork Wenaha River
Grande Ronde River
Touchet River

Harris County Park
Jubilee Lake 4696
Target Meadows
Tollgate Visitor Center
Spout Springs Ski Area
Bingham Springs el 2161
Umatilla Forks
Timothy Springs
Timothy USFS Station
Mottet
Bone Spring
Woodward
Woodland

Blue Mtn Ski Area 4040
Scenic Viewpoint
Indian
Kiwanis Camp

Continues in the Benchmark
Oregon Road & Recreation Atlas

© BENCHMARK MAPS

Scale 1:200,000

0   5   10   15 Miles
0   5   10   15   20 Kilometers

106

LANDSCAPE

117

BLUE MOUNTAIN

UMATILLA NATIONAL FOREST

COLUMBIA GARFIELD

ASOTIN

WALLOWA

OREGON

Rainwater Wildlife Area

Lewis Peak 4888
Griffin Peak 5682
Deadman Peak 5873
Green Peak 5156
Lookout Table Rock 6250
Squaw Peak 5976
Indian

NEWBY MOUNTAIN 5206
Chase Mtn 5642
Bluewood Ski Area 6040
Scenic Viewpoint
Cold Spring
Sawtooth

Touchet Snopark
Godman Guard Station
Sugarloaf 4697
Elwell Spring
Stavawhile Spring
Berry Spring
Slick Ear

Meadow Creek
West Butte 6387
Oregon Butte 6292 Lookout
Danger Point
Big Turkey Tail
Little Turkey Recreation Residences
Twin Buttes 5674
Twin Springs

Bear Wallow Spring
Squaw Spring
Diamond Peak
Mt Misery 6366
Misery Spring
Kelley Camp
Diamond Peak 6379
Bald Butte 5479
Halsey Butte 5395
Weller Butte 5540

Snow Spring
Wikiup
Misery Spring
Wenatchee Guard Station
Cabin Spring
Mt Horrible 5820
Saddle Butte 5980
Saddle Spring
Grouse Flat Rd
Bucker Spring
Not maintained in winter

Wenaha-Tucannon Wilderness
Lodgepole Spring
Crooked Creek
Three Forks
Kessler Mill Rd
GROUSE FLAT
Grouse el 2860
Bartlett

Mill Creek Watershed
Paradise Ridge

UMATILLA WALLOWA
COLUMBIA WALLOWA WALLOWA

Wenaha-Tucannon Wilderness

Squaw Spring
Skyline
Bone Spring
Timothy Springs
Motet
Timothy USFS Station
Jubilee Lake

Wenaha River
South Fork Wenaha
Elk Flats
Big Hole Viewpoint
ELK FLAT
Cross Canyon
Cross

Wenaha
Hoodoo Lookout 4219
Long Meadows USFS Station

Wenaha River
Dry Gulch
Troy el 1607
Wenaha Wildlife Area Headquarters
Grand Ronde Lodge

Mud Creek
Puwatka Ridge
Promise el 3500

WALLOWA UNION

NATIONAL FOREST

Jarboe Meadow
Fry Meadow USFS Station

GRANDE RONDE RIVER

Lookout Mtn 5229

UNION WALLOWA

Lookingglass
Palmer Junction
Kimmell el 2355
Howard Butte 4314
Howard Meadow
Maxville el 4059
Akers Butte 4448

WALLOWA WHITMAN NATIONAL FOREST

WASHBOARD RIDGE
POWWATKA
KUHN

GRANDE RONDE RIVER
Rysdam Canyon

Minam State Recreation Area
Raft Launch Site
Minam el 2637

CRICKET FLAT
Minam Hill 3865

82

Elgin el 2716
204

Wallowa River
Deer Creek
Water Canyon
Whisky Creek
DIAMOND PRAIRIE
Wallowa el 2948
South Fork

© BENCHMARK MAPS

Land Use and Vegetation

Forest Cropland Other
Wetland Grassland Built-Up Area

Land Ownership (Other public/tribal lands are named)

State Land (blue highlight)
BLM Land (yellow highlight)

Also See Recreation Page 30

LANDSCAPE

Continues in the Benchmark
Idaho Road & Recreation Atlas

Grid columns: 7, 8, 9, 107, 10, 11, 12
Grid rows: A, B, C, D, E, F, G, H

OREGON · **IDAHO** · **WALLOWA** · **NEZ PERCE** · **ASOTIN**

Big Butte 5010, West Mtn, Anatone Butte 4884, Anatone el 3570, Montgomery, Rattlesnake Summit 3965, Wohelo Lodge Environmental Learning Center (ELC), Puffer Butte Lodge (ELC), Puffer Butte 4500, Fields Spring State Park, McLoughlin Oasis, Broggan's Oasis, Boat Ramp, Shumaker, Black Butte 4134, Joseph Chief

Hells Canyon Resort, Heller Bar, Heller Bar Boat Ramp, No Key RV Park, Captain Lewis Rapids, Limekiln Rapids, Rogersburg, Wild Goose Rapids, Shovel Creek Rapids, McDuff Rapids, Zaza

Mt Wilson 4919, Not maintained in winter, Cache Creek Ranch, Hells Canyon, Downey Saddle, Frog Pond Butte, Cold Spring, Frenchy Rapids, Mile 185, Mile 180, Mile 175, Mile 170, Mile 165, Mile 190, Mile 195

Paradise el 4115, Flora el 4333, Cem, Table Mtn 4968, Joseph Canyon Viewpoint, Bear Spring, Baldwin Spring, Coyote, Yew Wood Spring, Dougherty, Red Hill 5028, WALLOWA–WHITMAN NATIONAL FOREST, STARVATION RIDGE, Vigne, Deadhorse Butte, Imnaha Rapids, Cactus Mtn, Buckhorn Spring, Buckhorn, Buckhorn Overlook, National, Recreation

Greenwood Butte 4652, Roberts Butte 4605, Zumwalt School Site, Elk Mtn 5120, Imnaha, Area, WALLOWA WHITMAN NATIONAL FOREST

GRANDE RONDE RIVER, Shumaker Wildlife Area, Wildlife Area, SNAKE RIVER, SALMON RIVER, CRAIG MOUNTAIN, WAPSHILLA RIDGE, COLD SPRING RIDGE, HELLS CANYON, JOSEPH CREEK, IDAHO CO, NEZ PERCE

Rds: 3, 129, 201, 285, 206, 46, 4680, 4304, 060, 121

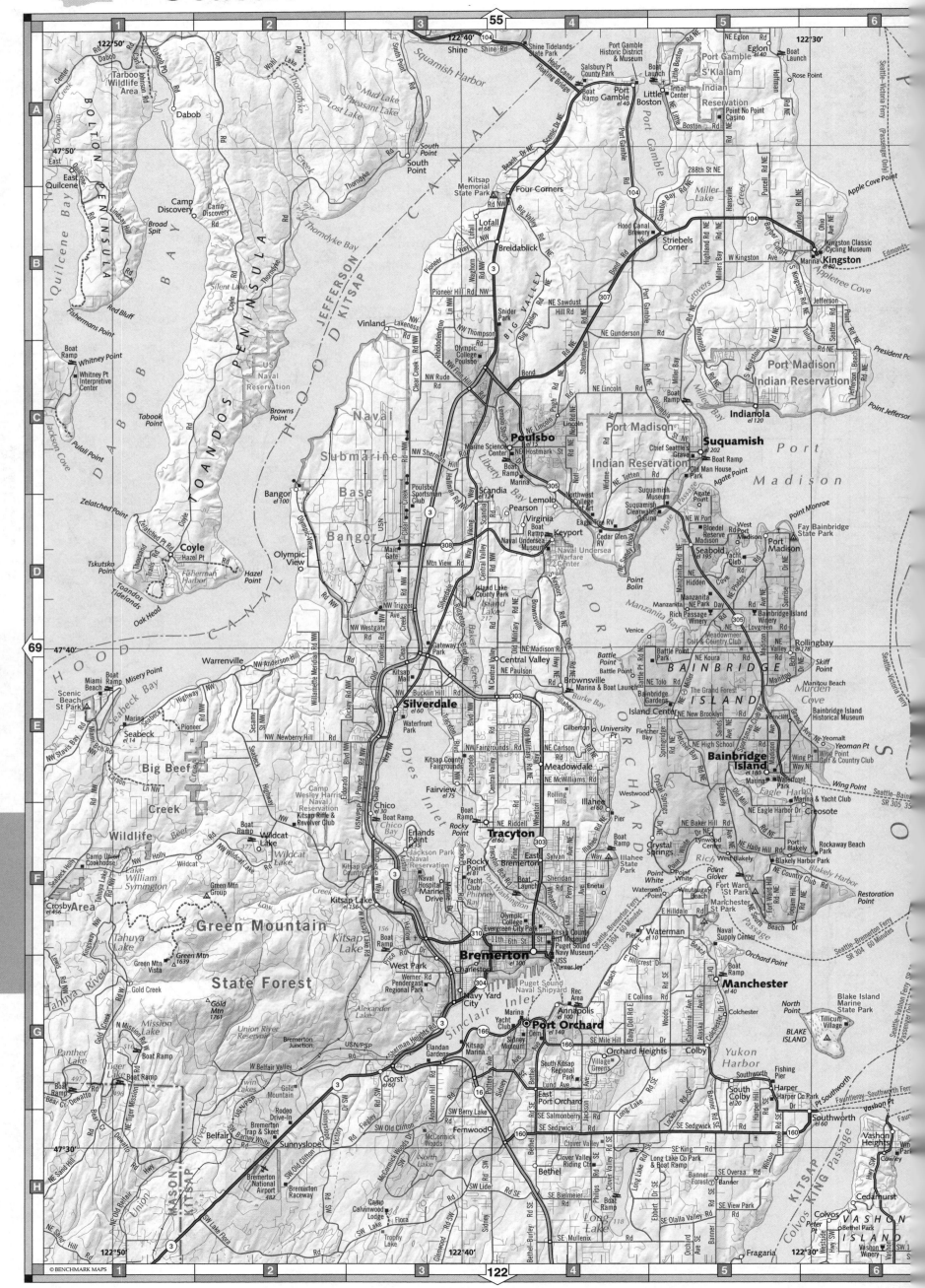

Scale 1:133,000

0   5   10 Miles

0   5   10   15 Kilometers

Edmonds

Lynnwood

Mountlake Terrace

Brier

Mill Creek

Woodway

Shoreline

Lake Forest Park

Kenmore

Bothell

Woodinville

Hollywood

Inglewood

Kirkland

Redmond

SEATTLE

Hunts Point

Yarrow Point

Medina

Clyde Hill

Bellevue

In Bellevue
1. Bellevue Square Mall
2. Rosalie Whyel Museum of Doll Art
3. Art Museum

Beaux Arts Village

Mercer Island

Eastgate

Sammamish

West Seattle

Newcastle

Issaquah

White Center

Kennydale

Burien

Tukwila

Renton

LAKE WASHINGTON

Lake Sammamish

Cougar Mountain Regional Wildland Park

Squak Mtn State Park

SNOHOMISH
KING

© BENCHMARK MAPS

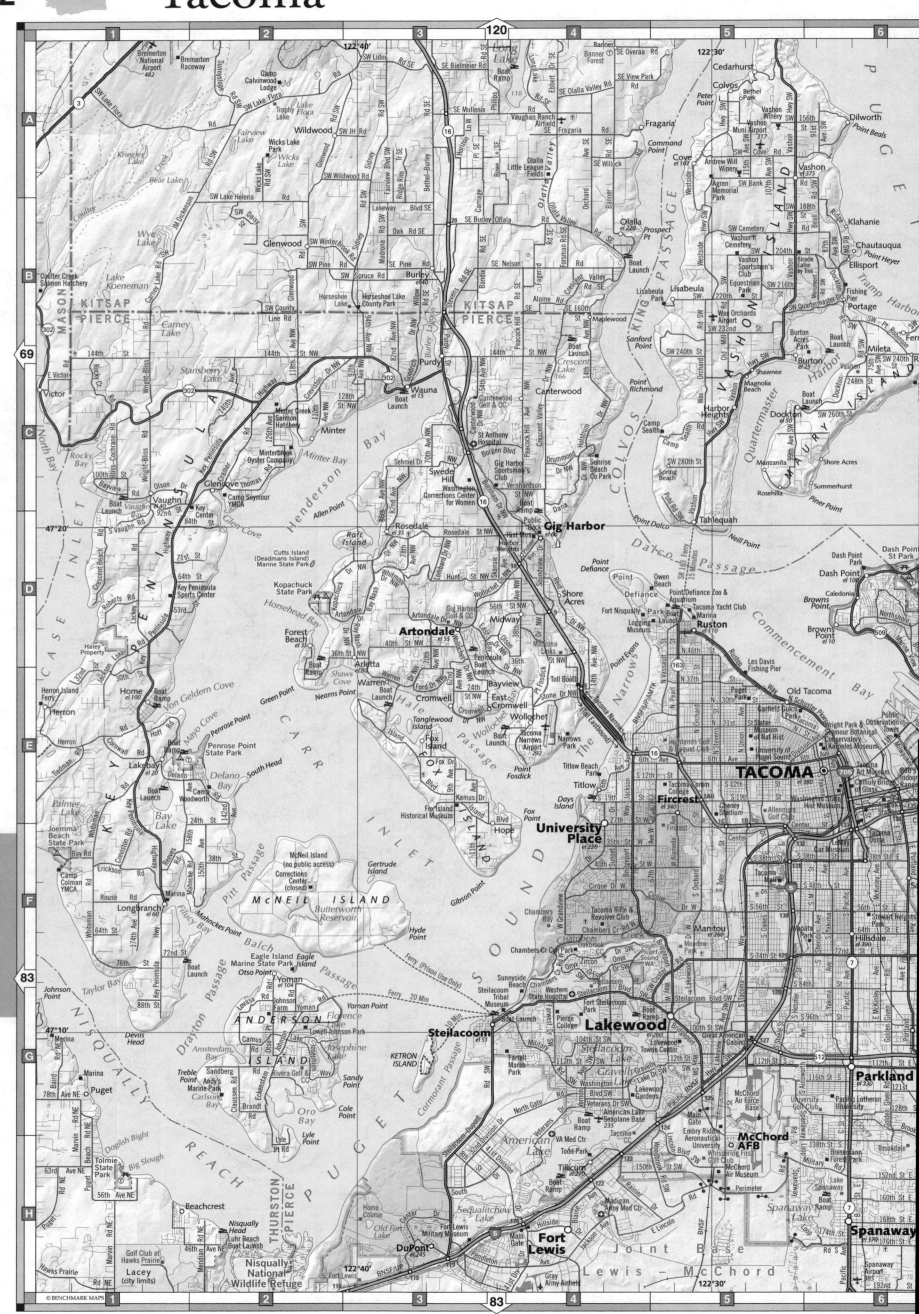

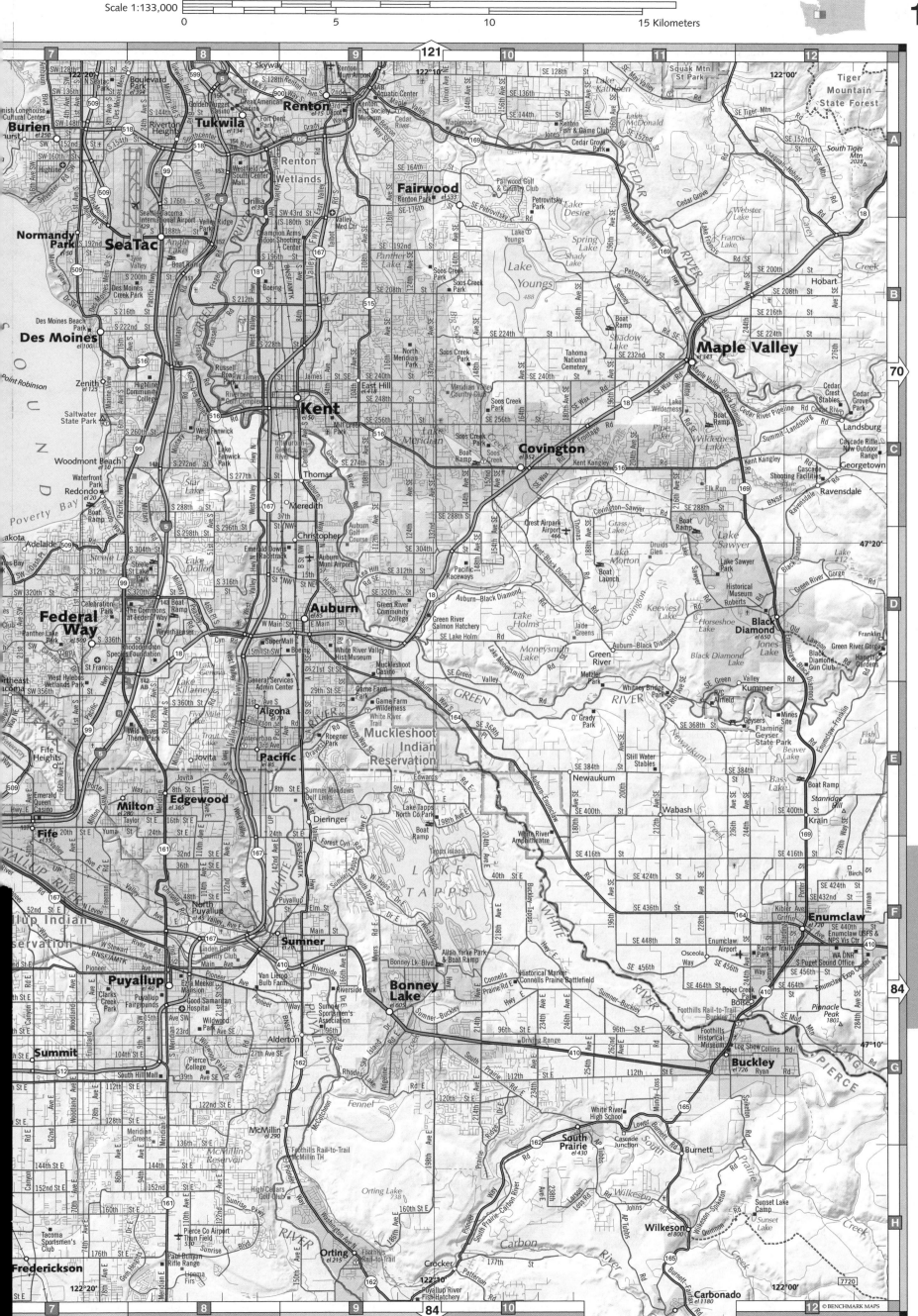

TACOMA

Scale 1:133,000

0   5   10 Miles
0   5   10   15 Kilometers

© BENCHMARK MAPS

NATIONAL PARKS, MONUMENTS, RECREATION AREAS, and FORESTS

STATE PARKS

WILDERNESS and WILDLIFE AREAS